Emeril Lagasse Power Air Fryer 360 Cookbook

1000 Foolproof, Healthy and Everyday Recipes
For the Power Airfryer 360 to Air Fry, Bake,
Rotisserie, Dehydrate, Roast, and Slow Cook

Maria B. Betances

Table of Contents

iv ▪ Table of Contents

Forewords

Welcome to the enticing and mouthwatering world of Emeril Lagasse Power Air Fryer recipes. Are you observing for a vigorous and healthy alternative to deep fried foods! 'Air fryer cooking' is a popular and healthy cooking method to relish your most beloved fried recipes; since you get low fat and low calorie food from an Emeril Lagasse Power Air Fryer, compared to deep fried items. An air fryer is a small, turbo-powered convection oven for your kitchen counter, which heats up much faster than an oven. It's faster because you don't have to preheat it like micro wave. By using it, will help to save you hundreds of calories; easy to use, extremely safe, and amazingly resourceful. Thus air fryer is a convenient counter top appliance for a small family.

You can explore collection air fryer recipes from various categories here. This edition is uniquely envisioned to help you prepare varieties of delicious air fryer recipes. You can cook anything from chicken fingers and nuggets, Vegetables fry, Onion rings and French fries, Cheese sticks, Fish and Pizza, Doughnuts with low-fat cooking style and extra-crispy results. So shall we start the crispy and crunchy air fryer culinary journey!

Benefits of Emeril Lagasse Power Air Fryer Cooking

Healthy option for frying food	Unlike the deep-fried foods loaded with lots of calories and unhealthy oils, an air fryer uses 70 to 80 percent less oil. So it is a healthy cooking method for your heart and overall health.
It can save both time and space	The device requires very less space to occupy so it will fit to the smallest kitchen as well and you can cook variety of air fryer recipes within a couple of minutes.
It is very flexible and safe to operate.	Since the air fryer has 4 separate parts i.e drawer, mesh basket, rack and the shell, you can use in very flexible ways. Some Air fryer models furthermore have preset buttons for the most general dishes. Air fryers are safer than conventional methods of deep frying since it is self-contained, there's no chance of burning your face, hands, or arms with splattered oil while cooking.
It is very easy to clean	Air fryer parts have nonstick coating, which will resist the residue and are dishwasher safe so it would be very easy to clean after cooking. Even your house will not be filled with smell after cooking as the air fryer does it work within the air fryer.
Use Frozen Foods can be cooked well	You can cook frozen foods like French fries, onion rings and chicken wings in an air fryer perfectly.
It's versatile appliance	Using an air fryer you can do anything from grilling, roasting to baking of poultry, meat or veggies. It will provide delicious crunchy outside and juicy inside food within a short time since an air fryer circulates heat and air 360 degrees all around the food so it's perfect for cooking fries, veggies, and other once-frozen treats.
Suitable for a small family	It is an ideal choice for couples and small families. Even though you can't overcrowd the cooking basket, which means you can cook food in multiple batches. So this appliance is enough to cook for a family of 3-5 members.

Chapter 1 Breakfasts

Cinnamon Rolls

Prep time: 10 minutes | Cook time: 9 minutes | Serves 8

1 pound (454 g) frozen bread dough, thawed
¼ cup butter, melted
¾ cup brown sugar
1½ tablespoons ground cinnamon
Cream Cheese Glaze:
4 ounces (113 g) cream cheese, softened
2 tablespoons butter, softened
1¼ cups powdered sugar
½ teaspoon vanilla extract

1. Let the bread dough come to room temperature on the counter. On a lightly floured surface, roll the dough into a 13-inch by 11-inch rectangle. Position the rectangle so the 13-inch side is facing you. Brush the melted butter all over the dough, leaving a 1-inch border uncovered along the edge farthest away from you.
2. Combine the brown sugar and cinnamon in a small bowl. Sprinkle the mixture evenly over the buttered dough, keeping the 1-inch border uncovered. Roll the dough into a log, starting with the edge closest to you. Roll the dough tightly, rolling evenly, and push out any air pockets. When you get to the uncovered edge of the dough, press the dough onto the roll to seal it together.
3. Cut the log into 8 pieces, slicing slowly with a sawing motion so you don't flatten the dough. Turn the slices on their sides and cover with a clean kitchen towel. Let the rolls sit in the warmest part of the kitchen for 1½ to 2 hours to rise.
4. To make the glaze, place the cream cheese and butter in a microwave-safe bowl. Soften the mixture in the microwave for 30 seconds at a time until it is easy to stir. Gradually add the powdered sugar and stir to combine. Add the vanilla extract and whisk until smooth. Set aside.
5. Transfer 4 of the rolls to the air fryer basket. Cook at the corresponding preset mode or Air Fry at 350°F (177°C) for 9 minutes. Repeat with the remaining 4 rolls.
6. Let the rolls cool for two minutes before glazing. Spread large dollops of cream cheese glaze on top of the warm cinnamon rolls, allowing some glaze to drip down the side of the rolls. Serve warm.

Bacon and Broccoli Brioche Bread Pudding

Prep time: 15 minutes | Cook time: 48 minutes | Serves 2 to 4

½ pound (227 g) thick cut bacon, cut into ¼-inch pieces
3 cups brioche bread, cut into ½-inch cubes
2 tablespoons butter, melted
3 eggs
1 cup milk
½ teaspoon salt
Freshly ground black pepper, to taste
1 cup frozen broccoli florets, thawed and chopped
1½ cups grated Swiss cheese

1. Cook the bacon at the corresponding preset mode or Air Fry at 400°F (204°C) for 8 minutes until crispy. Remove the bacon and set it aside on a paper towel.
2. Cook the brioche bread cubes at the corresponding preset mode or Air Fry for 2 more minutes to dry and toast lightly.
3. Butter a cake pan. Combine all the remaining ingredients in a large bowl and toss well. Transfer the mixture to the buttered nonstick round cake pan, cover with aluminum foil and refrigerate the bread pudding overnight, or for at least 8 hours.
4. Remove the cake pan from the refrigerator an hour before you plan to bake and let it sit on the countertop to come to room temperature.
5. Detach the rotating blade of the air fryer basket. Transfer the covered cake pan to the basket of the air fryer, lowering the pan into the basket. Fold the ends of the aluminum foil over the top of the pan before returning the basket to the air fryer.
6. Cook at the corresponding preset mode or Bake at 330°F (166°C) for 20 minutes. Remove the foil and air fry for an additional 20 minutes. If the top browns a little too much before the custard has set, simply return the foil to the pan. The bread pudding has cooked through when a skewer inserted into the center comes out clean.
7. Serve warm.

Grit and Ham Fritters

Prep time: 15 minutes | Cook time: 20 minutes | Serves 6 to 8

4 cups water
1 cup quick-cooking grits
¼ teaspoon salt
2 tablespoons butter
2 cups grated Cheddar cheese, divided
1 cup finely diced ham
1 tablespoon chopped chives
Salt and freshly ground black pepper, to taste
1 egg, beaten
2 cups panko bread crumbs
Cooking spray

1. Bring the water to a boil in a saucepan. Whisk in the grits and ¼ teaspoon of salt, and cook for 7 minutes until the grits are soft. Remove the pan from the heat and stir in the butter and 1 cup of the grated Cheddar cheese. Transfer the grits to a bowl and let them cool for 10 to 15 minutes.
2. Stir the ham, chives and the rest of the cheese into the grits and season with salt and pepper to taste. Add the beaten egg and refrigerate the mixture for 30 minutes.
3. Put the panko bread crumbs in a shallow dish. Measure out ¼-cup portions of the grits mixture and shape them into patties. Coat all sides of the patties with the panko bread crumbs, patting them with the hands so the crumbs adhere to the patties. You should have about 16 patties. Spritz both sides of the patties with cooking spray.
4. Detach the rotating blade of the air fryer basket. In batches of 5 or 6, cook the fritters at the corresponding preset mode or Air Fry at 400ºF (204ºC) for 8 minutes. Using a flat spatula, flip the fritters over and air fry for another 4 minutes.
5. Serve hot.

Apple and Walnut Muffins

Prep time: 15 minutes | Cook time: 10 minutes | Makes 8 muffins

1 cup flour
⅓ cup sugar
1 teaspoon baking powder
¼ teaspoon baking soda
¼ teaspoon salt
1 teaspoon cinnamon
¼ teaspoon ginger
¼ teaspoon nutmeg
1 egg
2 tablespoons pancake syrup, plus 2 teaspoons
2 tablespoons melted butter, plus 2 teaspoons
¾ cup unsweetened applesauce
½ teaspoon vanilla extract
¼ cup chopped walnuts
¼ cup diced apple

1. In a large bowl, stir together the flour, sugar, baking powder, baking soda, salt, cinnamon, ginger, and nutmeg.
2. In a small bowl, beat egg until frothy. Add syrup, butter, applesauce, and vanilla and mix well.
3. Pour egg mixture into dry ingredients and stir just until moistened.
4. Gently stir in nuts and diced apple.
5. Divide batter among 8 parchment paper-lined muffin cups.
6. Detach the rotating blade of the air fryer basket. Put 4 muffin cups in air fryer basket and cook at the corresponding preset mode or Bake at 330ºF (166ºC) for 10 minutes.
7. Repeat with remaining 4 muffins or until toothpick inserted in center comes out clean.
8. Serve warm.

Ham and Corn Muffins

Prep time: 10 minutes | Cook time: 6 minutes | Makes 8 muffins

¾ cup yellow cornmeal
¼ cup flour
1½ teaspoons baking powder
¼ teaspoon salt
1 egg, beaten
2 tablespoons canola oil
½ cup milk
½ cup shredded sharp Cheddar cheese
½ cup diced ham

1. In a medium bowl, stir together the cornmeal, flour, baking powder, and salt.
2. Add the egg, oil, and milk to dry ingredients and mix well.
3. Stir in shredded cheese and diced ham.
4. Divide batter among 8 parchment paper-lined muffin cups.
5. Detach the rotating blade of the air fryer basket. Put 4 filled muffin cups in air fryer basket and Cook at the corresponding preset mode or Bake at 390ºF (199ºC) for 5 minutes.
6. Reduce temperature to 330ºF (166ºC) and bake for 1 minute or until a toothpick inserted in center of the muffin comes out clean.
7. Repeat steps 6 and 7 to bake remaining muffins.
8. Serve warm.

Nut and Seed Muffins

Prep time: 15 minutes | Cook time: 10 minutes | Makes 8 muffins

½ cup whole-wheat flour, plus 2 tablespoons
¼ cup oat bran
2 tablespoons flaxseed meal
¼ cup brown sugar
½ teaspoon baking soda
½ teaspoon baking powder
¼ teaspoon salt
½ teaspoon cinnamon
½ cup buttermilk
2 tablespoons melted butter
1 egg
½ teaspoon pure vanilla extract
½ cup grated carrots
¼ cup chopped pecans
¼ cup chopped walnuts
1 tablespoon pumpkin seeds
1 tablespoon sunflower seeds
Cooking spray

Special Equipment:
16 foil muffin cups, paper liners removed

1. In a large bowl, stir together the flour, bran, flaxseed meal, sugar, baking soda, baking powder, salt, and cinnamon.
2. In a medium bowl, beat together the buttermilk, butter, egg, and vanilla. Pour into flour mixture and stir just until dry ingredients moisten. Do not beat.
3. Gently stir in carrots, nuts, and seeds.
4. Double up the foil cups so you have 8 total and spritz with cooking spray.
5. Detach the rotating blade of the air fryer basket. Put 4 foil cups in air fryer basket and divide half the batter among them.
6. Cook at the corresponding preset mode or Bake at 330°F (166°C) for 10 minutes or until a toothpick inserted in center comes out clean.
7. Repeat step 7 to bake remaining 4 muffins.
8. Serve warm.

Orange-Glazed Walnut and Cranberry Rolls

Prep time: 15 minutes | Cook time: 8 minutes | Makes 8 rolls

3 ounces (85 g) cream cheese
1 tablespoon sour cream or plain yogurt
2 teaspoons sugar
¼ teaspoon pure vanilla extract
¼ teaspoon orange extract
1 can (8 count) organic crescent roll dough
¼ cup chopped walnuts
¼ cup dried cranberries
¼ cup shredded, sweetened coconut
Butter-flavored cooking spray

Orange Glaze:
½ cup powdered sugar
1 tablespoon orange juice
¼ teaspoon orange extract
Dash of salt

1. Cut a circular piece of parchment paper slightly smaller than the bottom of the air fryer basket. Set aside.
2. In a small bowl, combine the cream cheese, sour cream or yogurt, sugar, and vanilla and orange extracts. Stir until smooth.
3. Separate crescent roll dough into 8 triangles and divide cream cheese mixture among them. Starting at wide end, spread cheese mixture to within 1 inch of point.
4. Sprinkle nuts and cranberries evenly over cheese mixture.
5. Starting at wide end, roll up triangles, then sprinkle with coconut, pressing in lightly to make it stick. Spray tops of rolls with butter-flavored cooking spray.
6. Detach the rotating blade of the air fryer basket. Put parchment paper in air fryer basket, and place 4 rolls on top, spaced evenly.
7. Cook at the corresponding preset mode or Air Fry at 300°F (149°C) for 8 minutes, until rolls are golden brown and cooked through. Flip the rolls halfway through.
8. Repeat steps 7 and 8 to air fry remaining 4 rolls. You should be able to use the same piece of parchment paper twice.
9. In a small bowl, stir together ingredients for glaze and drizzle over warm rolls. Serve warm.

Avocado and Cheddar Quesadillas with Salsa

Prep time: 10 minutes | Cook time: 11 minutes | Serves 4

4 eggs
2 tablespoons skim milk
Salt and ground black pepper, to taste
Cooking spray
4 flour tortillas
4 tablespoons salsa
2 ounces (57 g) Cheddar cheese, grated
½ small avocado, peeled and thinly sliced

1. Beat together the eggs, milk, salt, and pepper.
2. Spray a nonstick round baking pan lightly with cooking spray and add egg mixture. Detach the rotating blade of the air fryer basket. Arrange the baking pan in the air fryer.
3. Cook at the corresponding preset mode or Bake at 270°F (132°C) for 8 minutes, stirring every 1 to 2 minutes, until eggs are scrambled to the liking. Remove and set aside.
4. Spray one side of each tortilla with cooking spray. Flip over.
5. Divide eggs, salsa, cheese, and avocado among the tortillas, covering only half of each tortilla.
6. Fold each tortilla in half and press down lightly. Increase the temperature of the air fryer to 390°F (199°C).
7. Put 2 tortillas in air fryer basket and air fry for 3 minutes or until cheese melts and outside feels slightly crispy. Repeat with remaining two tortillas.
8. Cut each cooked tortilla into halves. Serve warm.

Banana Bread

Prep time: 10 minutes | Cook time: 22 minutes | Makes 3 loaves

3 ripe bananas, mashed
1 cup sugar
1 large egg
4 tablespoons (½ stick) unsalted butter, melted
1½ cups all-purpose flour
1 teaspoon baking soda
1 teaspoon salt

1. Coat the insides of 3 mini loaf pans with cooking spray.
2. In a large mixing bowl, mix the bananas and sugar.
3. In a separate large mixing bowl, combine the egg, butter, flour, baking soda, and salt and mix well.
4. Add the banana mixture to the egg and flour mixture. Mix well.
5. Divide the batter evenly among the prepared pans.
6. Detach the rotating blade of the air fryer basket. Set the mini loaf pans into the air fryer basket.
7. Cook at the corresponding preset mode or Bake at 310°F (154°C) for 22 minutes. Insert a toothpick into the center of each loaf; if it comes out clean, they are done.
8. When the loaves are cooked through, remove the pans from the air fryer basket. Turn out the loaves onto a wire rack to cool.
9. Serve warm.

Egg in a Hole

Prep time: 5 minutes | Cook time: 5 minutes | Serves 1

1 slice bread
1 teaspoon butter, softened
1 egg
Salt and pepper, to taste
1 tablespoon shredded Cheddar cheese
2 teaspoons diced ham

1. On a flat work surface, cut a hole in the center of the bread slice with a 2½-inch-diameter biscuit cutter.
2. Spread the butter evenly on each side of the bread slice and transfer to the baking dish.
3. Crack the egg into the hole and season as desired with salt and pepper. Scatter the shredded cheese and diced ham on top.
4. Detach the rotating blade of the air fryer basket. Arrange the bread slice in the air fryer.
5. Cook at the corresponding preset mode or Air Fry at 330°F (166°C) for 5 minutes until the bread is lightly browned and the egg is cooked to the preference.
6. Remove from the basket and serve hot.

Spinach and Bacon Rolls

Prep time: 5 minutes | Cook time: 8 to 9 minutes | Serves 4

4 flour tortillas (6- or 7-inch size)
4 slices Swiss cheese
1 cup baby spinach leaves
4 slices turkey bacon

Special Equipment:
4 toothpicks, soak in water for at
    least 30 minutes

1. On a clean work surface, top each tortilla with one slice of cheese and ¼ cup of spinach, then tightly roll them up.
2. Wrap each tortilla with a strip of turkey bacon and secure with a toothpick.
3. Detach the rotating blade of the air fryer basket. Arrange the rolls in the air fryer basket, leaving space between each roll.
4. Cook at the corresponding preset mode or Air Fry at 390°F (199°C) for 4 minutes. Flip the rolls with tongs and rearrange them for more even cooking. Air fry for another 4 to 5 minutes until the bacon is crisp.
5. Rest for 5 minutes and remove the toothpicks before serving.

Bacon and Cheese Sandwiches

Prep time: 5 minutes | Cook time: 8 minutes | Serves 4

4 English muffins, split
8 slices Canadian bacon
4 slices cheese
Cooking spray

1. Make the sandwiches: Top each of 4 muffin halves with 2 slices of Canadian bacon, 1 slice of cheese, and finish with the remaining muffin half.
2. Detach the rotating blade of the air fryer basket. Put the sandwiches in the air fryer basket and spritz the tops with cooking spray.
3. Cook at the corresponding preset mode or Air Fry at 370°F (188°C) for 4 minutes. Flip the sandwiches and bake for another 4 minutes.
4. Divide the sandwiches among four plates and serve warm.

Ham and Cheddar Sandwiches

Prep time: 5 minutes | Cook time: 8 minutes | Serves 2

1 teaspoon butter, softened
4 slices bread
4 slices smoked country ham
4 slices Cheddar cheese
4 thick slices tomato

1. Spoon ½ teaspoon of butter onto one side of 2 slices of bread and spread it all over.
2. Assemble the sandwiches: Top each of 2 slices of unbuttered bread with 2 slices of ham, 2 slices of cheese, and 2 slices of tomato. Place the remaining 2 slices of bread on top, butter-side up.
3. Detach the rotating blade of the air fryer basket. Arrange the sandwiches in the air fryer basket, buttered side down.
4. Cook at the corresponding preset mode or Air Fry at 370°F (188°C) for 8 minutes until the sandwiches are golden brown on both sides and the cheese has melted, flipping the sandwiches halfway through.
5. Allow to cool for 5 minutes before slicing to serve.

Baked Eggs with Cheddar

Prep time: 5 minutes | Cook time: 6 minutes | Serves 2

2 large eggs
2 tablespoons half-and-half
2 teaspoons shredded Cheddar
    cheese
Salt and freshly ground black pepper,
    to taste
Cooking spray

1. Spritz 2 ramekins lightly with cooking spray. Crack an egg into each ramekin.
2. Top each egg with 1 tablespoon of half-and-half and 1 teaspoon of Cheddar cheese. Sprinkle with salt and black pepper. Stir the egg mixture with a fork until well combined.
3. Detach the rotating blade of the air fryer basket. Place the ramekins in the air fryer basket and cook at the corresponding preset mode or Bake at 330°F (166°C) for 6 minutes until set. Check for doneness and cook for 1 minute as needed.
4. Allow to cool for 5 minutes in the basket before removing and serving.

Maple Bacon Knots

Prep time: 5 minutes | Cook time: 7 to 8 minutes | Serves 6

1 pound (454 g) maple smoked center-cut bacon
¼ cup maple syrup
¼ cup brown sugar
Coarsely cracked black peppercorns, to taste

1. On a clean work surface, tie each bacon strip in a loose knot.
2. Stir together the maple syrup and brown sugar in a bowl. Generously brush this mixture over the bacon knots.
3. Working in batches, arrange the bacon knots in the air fryer basket. Sprinkle with the coarsely cracked black peppercorns.
4. Cook at the corresponding preset mode or Air Fry at 390ºF (199ºC) for 5 minutes. Flip the bacon knots and continue cooking for 2 to 3 minutes more, or until the bacon is crisp.
5. Remove from the basket to a paper towel-lined plate. Repeat with the remaining bacon knots.
6. Let the bacon knots cool for a few minutes and serve warm.

Potato with Peppers

Prep time: 10 minutes | Cook time: 35 minutes | Serves 4

1 pound (454 g) red potatoes, cut into ½-inch dices
1 large red bell pepper, cut into ½-inch dices
1 large green bell pepper, cut into ½-inch dices
1 medium onion, cut into ½-inch dices
1½ tablespoons extra-virgin olive oil
1¼ teaspoons kosher salt
¾ teaspoon sweet paprika
¾ teaspoon garlic powder
Freshly ground black pepper, to taste

1. Mix together the potatoes, bell peppers, onion, oil, salt, paprika, garlic powder, and black pepper in a large mixing and toss to coat.
2. Transfer the potato mixture to the air fry basket.
3. Select Air Fry, Super Convection, set temperature to 350ºF (180ºC) and set time to 35 minutes. Select Start/Stop to begin preheating.
4. Once preheated, place the air fry basket on the air fry position. Stir the potato mixture three times during cooking.
5. When done, the potatoes should be nicely browned.
6. Remove from the oven to a plate and serve warm.

Chili Brown Rice Cheese Quiches

Prep time: 10 minutes | Cook time: 14 minutes | Serves 6

4 ounces (113 g) diced green chilies
3 cups cooked brown rice
1 cup shredded reduced-fat Cheddar cheese, divided
½ cup egg whites
⅓ cup fat-free milk
¼ cup diced pimiento
½ teaspoon cumin
1 small eggplant, cubed
1 bunch fresh cilantro, finely chopped
Cooking spray

1. Spritz a 12-cup muffin pan with cooking spray.
2. In a large bowl, stir together all the ingredients, except for ½ cup of the cheese.
3. Scoop the mixture evenly into the muffin cups and sprinkle the remaining ½ cup of the cheese on top.
4. Select Bake, Super Convection, set temperature to 400ºF (205ºC) and set time to 14 minutes. Select Start/Stop to begin preheating.
5. Once the unit has preheated, place the pan on the bake position.
6. When cooking is complete, remove the pan and check the quiches. They should be set.
7. Carefully transfer the quiches to a platter and serve immediately.

Egg and Avocado Cheese Burrito

Prep time: 10 minutes | Cook time: 4 minutes | Serves 4

4 low-sodium whole-wheat flour tortillas
Filling:
1 hard-boiled egg, chopped
2 hard-boiled egg whites, chopped
1 ripe avocado, peeled, pitted, and chopped
1 red bell pepper, chopped
1 (1.2-ounce / 34-g) slice low-sodium, low-fat American cheese, torn into pieces
3 tablespoons low-sodium salsa, plus additional for serving (optional)

Special Equipment:
4 toothpicks (optional), soaked in water for at least 30 minutes

1. Make the filling: Combine the egg, egg whites, avocado, red bell pepper, cheese, and salsa in a medium bowl and stir until blended.
2. Assemble the burritos: Arrange the tortillas on a clean work surface and place ¼ of the prepared filling in the middle of each tortilla, leaving about 1½-inch on each end unfilled. Fold in the opposite sides of each tortilla and roll up. Secure with toothpicks through the center, if needed.
3. Transfer the burritos to the air fry basket.
4. Select Air Fry, Super Convection, set temperature to 390°F (199°C) and set time to 4 minutes. Select Start/Stop to begin preheating.
5. Once the oven has preheated, place the air fry basket on the air fry position.
6. When cooking is complete, the burritos should be crisp and golden brown.
7. Allow to cool for 5 minutes and serve with salsa, if desired.

Banana and Chocolate Bread

Prep time: 10 minutes | Cook time: 30 minutes | Serves 4

¼ cup cocoa powder
6 tablespoons plus 2 teaspoons all-purpose flour, divided
½ teaspoon kosher salt
¼ teaspoon baking soda
1½ ripe bananas
1 large egg, whisked
¼ cup vegetable oil
½ cup sugar
3 tablespoons buttermilk or plain yogurt (not Greek)
½ teaspoon vanilla extract
6 tablespoons chopped white chocolate
6 tablespoons chopped walnuts

1. Mix together the cocoa powder, 6 tablespoons of the flour, salt, and baking soda in a medium bowl.
2. Mash the bananas with a fork in another medium bowl until smooth. Fold in the egg, oil, sugar, buttermilk, and vanilla, and whisk until thoroughly combined. Add the wet mixture to the dry mixture and stir until well incorporated.
3. Combine the white chocolate, walnuts, and the remaining 2 tablespoons of flour in a third bowl and toss to coat. Add this mixture to the batter and stir until well incorporated. Pour the batter into a baking pan and smooth the top with a spatula.
4. Select Bake, Super Convection, set temperature to 310°F (154°C) and set time to 30 minutes. Select Start/Stop to begin preheating.
5. Once the oven has preheated, place the pan on the bake position.
6. When done, a toothpick inserted into the center of the bread should come out clean.
7. Remove from the oven and allow to cool on a wire rack for 10 minutes before serving.

Chicken Sausages with Apple

Prep time: 15 minutes | Cook time: 10 minutes | Makes 8 patties

1 Granny Smith apple, peeled and finely chopped
2 tablespoons apple juice
2 garlic cloves, minced
1 egg white
⅓ cup minced onion
3 tablespoons ground almonds
⅛ teaspoon freshly ground black pepper
1 pound (454 g) ground chicken breast

1. Combine all the ingredients except the chicken in a medium mixing bowl and stir well.
2. Add the chicken breast to the apple mixture and mix with your hands until well incorporated.
3. Divide the mixture into 8 equal portions and shape into patties. Arrange the patties in the air fry basket.
4. Select Air Fry, Super Convection, set temperature to 330°F (166°C) and set time to 10 minutes. Select Start/Stop to begin preheating.
5. Once the oven has preheated, place the air fry basket on the air fry position.
6. When done, a meat thermometer inserted in the center of the chicken should reach at least 165°F (74°C).
7. Remove from the oven to a plate. Let the chicken cool for 5 minutes and serve warm.

Blueberry Cheese Quesadilla

Prep time: 5 minutes | Cook time: 4 minutes | Serves 2

¼ cup nonfat Ricotta cheese
¼ cup plain nonfat Greek yogurt
2 tablespoons finely ground flaxseeds
1 tablespoon granulated stevia
½ teaspoon cinnamon
¼ teaspoon vanilla extract
2 (8-inch) low-carb whole-wheat tortillas
½ cup fresh blueberries, divided

1. Line the sheet pan with the aluminum foil.
2. In a small bowl, whisk together the Ricotta cheese, yogurt, flaxseeds, stevia, cinnamon and vanilla.
3. Place the tortillas on the sheet pan. Spread half of the yogurt mixture on each tortilla, almost to the edges. Top each tortilla with ¼ cup of blueberries. Fold the tortillas in half.
4. Select Bake, Super Convection, set temperature to 400ºF (205ºC) and set time to 4 minutes. Select Start/Stop to begin preheating.
5. Once the unit has preheated, place the pan on the bake position.
6. When cooking is complete, remove the pan from the oven. Serve immediately.

Canadian Bacon Muffin Sandwiches

Prep time: 5 minutes | Cook time: 8 minutes | Serves 4

4 English muffins, split
8 slices Canadian bacon
4 slices cheese
Cooking spray

5. Make the sandwiches: Top each of 4 muffin halves with 2 slices of Canadian bacon, 1 slice of cheese, and finish with the remaining muffin half.
6. Put the sandwiches in the air fryer basket and spritz the tops with cooking spray.
7. Select Bake, Super Convection, set temperature to 370ºF (188ºC), and set time to 8 minutes. Select Start/Stop to begin preheating.
8. Once preheated, place the basket on the bake position. Flip the sandwiches halfway through the cooking time.
9. When cooking is complete, remove the basket from the oven. Divide the sandwiches among four plates and serve warm.

Cornmeal Pancake

Prep time: 10 minutes | Cook time: 6 minutes | Serves 4

1½ cups yellow cornmeal
½ cup all-purpose flour
2 tablespoons sugar
1 teaspoon salt
1 teaspoon baking powder
1 cup whole or 2% milk
1 large egg, lightly beaten
1 tablespoon butter, melted
Cooking spray

1. Line the air fryer basket with parchment paper.
2. Stir together the cornmeal, flour, sugar, salt, and baking powder in a large bowl. Mix in the milk, egg, and melted butter and whisk to combine.
3. Drop tablespoonfuls of the batter onto the parchment paper for each pancake. Spray the pancakes with cooking spray.
4. Select Bake, Super Convection, set temperature to 350ºF (180ºC) and set time to 6 minutes. Select Start/Stop to begin preheating.
5. Once the oven has preheated, place the basket on the bake position. Flip the pancakes and spray with cooking spray again halfway through the cooking time.
6. When cooking is complete, remove the pancakes from the oven to a plate.
7. Cool for 5 minutes and serve immediately.

Avocado and Egg with Cheese

Prep time: 5 minutes | Cook time: 9 minutes | Serves 2

1 large avocado, halved and pitted

2 large eggs

2 tomato slices, divided

½ cup nonfat Cottage cheese, divided

½ teaspoon fresh cilantro, for garnish

1. Line the sheet pan with the aluminium foil.
2. Slice a thin piece from the bottom of each avocado half so they sit flat. Remove a small amount from each avocado half to make a bigger hole to hold the egg.
3. Arrange the avocado halves on the pan, hollow-side up. Break 1 egg into each half. Top each half with 1 tomato slice and ¼ cup of the Cottage cheese.
4. Select Bake, Super Convection, set temperature to 425°F (220°C) and set time to 9 minutes. Select Start/Stop to begin preheating.
5. Once the unit has preheated, place the pan on the bake position.
6. When cooking is complete, remove the pan from the oven. Garnish with the fresh cilantro and serve.

Cheese Egg Florentine with Spinach

Prep time: 10 minutes | Cook time: 15 minutes | Serves 4

3 cups frozen spinach, thawed and drained

2 tablespoons heavy cream

¼ teaspoon kosher salt

⅛ teaspoon freshly ground black pepper

4 ounces (113 g) Ricotta cheese

2 garlic cloves, minced

½ cup panko bread crumbs

3 tablespoons grated Parmesan cheese

2 teaspoons unsalted butter, melted

4 large eggs

1. In a medium bowl, whisk together the spinach, heavy cream, salt, pepper, Ricotta cheese and garlic.
2. In a small bowl, whisk together the bread crumbs, Parmesan cheese and butter. Set aside.
3. Spoon the spinach mixture on the sheet pan and form four even circles.
4. Select Roast, Super Convection, set temperature to 375°F (190°C) and set time to 15 minutes. Select Start/Stop to begin preheating.
5. Once the unit has preheated, place the pan on the roast position.
6. After 8 minutes, remove the pan from the oven. The spinach should be bubbling. With the back of a large spoon, make indentations in the spinach for the eggs. Crack the eggs into the indentations and sprinkle the panko mixture over the surface of the eggs. Return the pan to the oven to continue cooking.
7. When cooking is complete, remove the pan from the oven. Serve hot.

Brown Sugar Butter Rolls

Prep time: 5 minutes | Cook time: 25 minutes | Makes 18 rolls

⅓ cup light brown sugar

2 teaspoons cinnamon

1 (9-by-9-inch) frozen puff pastry sheet, thawed

All-purpose flour, for dusting

6 teaspoons unsalted butter, melted, divided

1. In a small bowl, stir together the brown sugar and cinnamon.
2. On a clean work surface, lightly dust with the flour and lay the puff pastry sheet. Using a rolling pin, press the folds together and roll the dough out in one direction so that it measures about 9 by 11 inches. Cut it in half to form two squat rectangles of about 5½ by 9 inches.
3. Brush 2 teaspoons of the butter over each pastry half. Sprinkle with 2 tablespoons of the cinnamon sugar. Pat it down lightly with the palm of your hand to help it adhere to the butter.
4. Starting with the 9-inch side of one rectangle. Using your hands, carefully roll the dough into a cylinder. Repeat with the other rectangle. To make slicing easier, refrigerate the rolls for 10 to 20 minutes.
5. Using a sharp knife, slice each roll into nine 1-inch pieces. Transfer the rolls to the center of the sheet pan. They should be very close to each other, but not quite touching. Drizzle the remaining 2 teaspoons of the butter over the rolls and sprinkle with the remaining cinnamon sugar.
6. Select Bake, Super Convection, set temperature to 350°F (180°C) and set time to 25 minutes. Select Start/Stop to begin preheating.
7. Once the unit has preheated, place the pan on the bake position.
8. When cooking is complete, remove the pan and check the rolls. They should be puffed up and golden brown.
9. Let the rolls rest for 5 minutes and transfer them to a wire rack to cool completely. Serve.

Carrot and Banana Muffins

Prep time: 10 minutes | Cook time: 20 minutes | Serves 12

1½ cups whole-wheat flour
1 cup grated carrot
1 cup mashed banana
½ cup bran
½ cup low-fat buttermilk
2 tablespoons agave nectar
2 teaspoons baking powder
1 teaspoon vanilla
1 teaspoon baking soda
½ teaspoon nutmeg
Pinch cloves
2 egg whites

1. Line a muffin pan with 12 paper liners.
2. In a large bowl, stir together all the ingredients. Mix well, but do not over beat.
3. Scoop the mixture into the muffin cups.
4. Select Bake, Super Convection, set temperature to 400°F (205°C) and set time to 20 minutes. Select Start/Stop to begin preheating.
5. Once the unit has preheated, place the pan on the bake position.
6. When cooking is complete, remove the pan and let rest for 5 minutes.
7. Serve warm or at room temperature.

Kale Cheese Eggs

Prep time: 5 minutes | Cook time: 11 minutes | Serves 2

1 cup roughly chopped kale leaves, stems and center ribs removed
¼ cup grated pecorino cheese
¼ cup olive oil
1 garlic clove, peeled
3 tablespoons whole almonds
Kosher salt and freshly ground black pepper, to taste
4 large eggs
2 tablespoons heavy cream
3 tablespoons chopped pitted mixed olives

1. Place the kale, pecorino, olive oil, garlic, almonds, salt, and pepper in a small blender and blitz until well incorporated.
2. One at a time, crack the eggs in a baking pan. Drizzle the kale pesto on top of the egg whites. Top the yolks with the cream and swirl together the yolks and the pesto.
3. Select Bake, Super Convection, set temperature to 300°F (150°C) and set time to 11 minutes. Select Start/Stop to begin preheating.
4. Once preheated, place the pan on the bake position.
5. When cooked, the top should begin to brown and the eggs should be set.
6. Allow the eggs to cool for 5 minutes. Scatter the olives on top and serve warm.

Artichoke Mushroom Cheese Frittata

Prep time: 10 minutes | Cook time: 15 minutes | Serves 6

8 eggs
½ teaspoon kosher salt
¼ cup whole milk
¾ cup shredded Mozzarella cheese, divided
2 tablespoons unsalted butter, melted
1 cup coarsely chopped artichoke hearts
¼ cup chopped onion
½ cup mushrooms
¼ cup grated Parmesan cheese
¼ teaspoon freshly ground black pepper

1. In a medium bowl, whisk together the eggs and salt. Let rest for a minute or two, then pour in the milk and whisk again. Stir in ½ cup of the Mozzarella cheese.
2. Grease the sheet pan with the butter. Stir in the artichoke hearts and onion and toss to coat with the butter.
3. Select Roast, Super Convection, set temperature to 375°F (190°C) and set time to 12 minutes. Select Start/Stop to begin preheating.
4. Once the unit has preheated, place the pan on the roast position.
5. After 5 minutes, remove the pan. Spread the mushrooms over the vegetables. Pour the egg mixture on top. Stir gently just to distribute the vegetables evenly. Return the pan to the oven and continue cooking for 5 to 7 minutes, or until the edges are set. The center will still be quite liquid.
6. Select Broil, Super Convection, set temperature to Low and set time to 3 minutes. Place the pan on the broil position.
7. After 1 minute, remove the pan and sprinkle the remaining ¼ cup of the Mozzarella and Parmesan cheese over the frittata. Return the pan to the oven and continue cooking for 2 minutes.
8. When cooking is complete, the cheese should be melted with the top completely set but not browned. Sprinkle the black pepper on top and serve.

Banana and Oat Bread Pudding

Prep time: 10 minutes | Cook time: 18 minutes | Serves 4

2 medium ripe bananas, mashed
½ cup low-fat milk
2 tablespoons maple syrup
2 tablespoons peanut butter
1 teaspoon vanilla extract
1 teaspoon ground cinnamon
2 slices whole-grain bread, torn into bite-sized pieces
¼ cup quick oats
Cooking spray

1. Spritz the sheet pan with cooking spray.
2. In a large bowl, combine the bananas, milk, maple syrup, peanut butter, vanilla extract and cinnamon. Use an immersion blender to mix until well combined.
3. Stir in the bread pieces to coat well. Add the oats and stir until everything is combined.
4. Transfer the mixture to the sheet pan. Cover with the aluminum foil.
5. Select Air Fry, Super Convection, set temperature to 375ºF (190ºC) and set time to 18 minutes. Select Start/Stop to begin preheating.
6. Once the unit has preheated, place the pan on the air fry position.
7. After 10 minutes, remove the foil and continue to cook for 8 minutes.
8. Serve immediately.

Fast Coffee Donuts

Prep time: 5 minutes | Cook time: 6 minutes | Serves 6

¼ cup sugar
½ teaspoon salt
1 cup flour
1 teaspoon baking powder
¼ cup coffee
1 tablespoon aquafaba
1 tablespoon sunflower oil

1. In a large bowl, combine the sugar, salt, flour, and baking powder.
2. Add the coffee, aquafaba, and sunflower oil and mix until a dough is formed. Leave the dough to rest in and the refrigerator.
3. Preheat the air fryer oven to 400ºF (204ºC).
4. Remove the dough from the fridge and divide up, kneading each section into a doughnut. Put the doughnuts in the air fryer basket.
5. Place the air fryer basket onto the baking pan, select Air Fry, Super Convection, and set time to 6 minutes.
6. Serve immediately.

Fried Cheese Grits

Prep time: 10 minutes | Cook time: 11 minutes | Serves 4

⅔ cup instant grits
1 teaspoon salt
1 teaspoon freshly ground black pepper
¾ cup whole or 2% milk
3 ounces (85 g) cream cheese, at room temperature
1 large egg, beaten
1 tablespoon butter, melted
1 cup shredded mild Cheddar cheese
Cooking spray

1. Mix the grits, salt, and black pepper in a large bowl. Add the milk, cream cheese, beaten egg, and melted butter and whisk to combine. Fold in the Cheddar cheese and stir well.
2. Spray a baking pan with cooking spray. Spread the grits mixture into the baking pan.
3. Select Air Fry, Super Convection, set temperature to 400ºF (205ºC) and set time to 11 minutes. Select Start/Stop to begin preheating.
4. Once preheated, place the pan on the air fry position. Stir the mixture halfway through the cooking time.
5. When done, a knife inserted in the center should come out clean.
6. Rest for 5 minutes and serve warm.

Breakfast Tater Tot Casserole

Prep time: 5 minutes | Cook time: 17 to 18 minutes | Serves 4

4 eggs
1 cup milk
Salt and pepper, to taste
12 ounces (340 g) ground chicken
  sausage
1 pound (454 g) frozen tater tots,
  thawed
¾ cup grated Cheddar cheese
Cooking spray

1. Whisk together the eggs and milk in a medium bowl. Season with salt and pepper to taste and stir until mixed. Set aside.
2. Place a skillet over medium-high heat and spritz with cooking spray. Place the ground sausage in the skillet and break it into smaller pieces with a spatula or spoon. Cook for 3 to 4 minutes until the sausage Start/Stops to brown, stirring occasionally. Remove from heat and set aside.
3. Coat a baking pan with cooking spray. Arrange the tater tots in the baking pan.
4. Select Bake, Super Convection, set temperature to 400ºF (205ºC) and set time to 14 minutes. Select Start/Stop to begin preheating.
5. Once preheated, place the pan on the bake position.
6. After 6 minutes, remove the pan from the oven. Stir the tater tots and add the egg mixture and cooked sausage. Return the pan to the oven and continue cooking.
7. After another 6 minutes, remove the pan from the oven. Scatter the cheese on top of the tater tots. Return the pan to the oven and continue to cook for 2 minutes more.
8. When done, the cheese should be bubbly and melted.
9. Let the mixture cool for 5 minutes and serve warm.

Crustless Broccoli Quiche

Prep time: 5 minutes | Cook time: 10 minutes | Serves 4

1 cup broccoli florets
¾ cup chopped roasted red peppers
1¼ cups grated Fontina cheese
6 eggs
¾ cup heavy cream
½ teaspoon salt
Freshly ground black pepper, to taste
Cooking spray

1. Spritz a baking pan with cooking spray
2. Add the broccoli florets and roasted red peppers to the pan and scatter the grated Fontina cheese on top.
3. In a bowl, beat together the eggs and heavy cream. Sprinkle with salt and pepper. Pour the egg mixture over the top of the cheese. Wrap the pan in foil.
4. Select Air Fry, Super Convection, set temperature to 325ºF (163ºC) and set time to 10 minutes. Select Start/Stop to begin preheating.
5. Once preheated, place the pan on the air fry position.
6. After 8 minutes, remove the pan from the oven. Remove the foil. Return the pan to the oven and continue to cook another 2 minutes.
7. When cooked, the quiche should be golden brown.
8. Rest for 5 minutes before cutting into wedges and serve warm.

Bacon and Egg Bread Cups

Prep time: 10 minutes | Cook time: 10 minutes | Serves 4

4 (3-by-4-inch) crusty rolls
4 thin slices Gouda or Swiss cheese
  mini wedges
5 eggs
2 tablespoons heavy cream
3 strips precooked bacon, chopped
½ teaspoon dried thyme
Pinch salt
Freshly ground black pepper, to taste

1. On a clean work surface, cut the tops off the rolls. Using your fingers, remove the insides of the rolls to make bread cups, leaving a ½-inch shell. Place a slice of cheese onto each roll bottom.
2. Whisk together the eggs and heavy cream in a medium bowl until well combined. Fold in the bacon, thyme, salt, and pepper and stir well.
3. Scrape the egg mixture into the prepared bread cups. Arrange the bread cups in the air fryer basket.
4. Select Bake, Super Convection, set temperature to 330ºF (166ºC) and set time to 10 minutes. Select Start/Stop to begin preheating.
5. Once preheated, place the basket on the bake position.
6. When cooked, the eggs should be cooked to your preference.
7. Serve warm.

Eggs in Bell Pepper Rings

Prep time: 5 minutes | Cook time: 7 minutes | Serves 4

1 large red, yellow, or orange bell pepper, cut into four ¾-inch rings
4 eggs
Salt and freshly ground black pepper, to taste
2 teaspoons salsa
Cooking spray

1. Coat a baking pan lightly with cooking spray.
2. Put 4 bell pepper rings in the prepared baking pan. Crack one egg into each bell pepper ring and sprinkle with salt and pepper. Top each egg with ½ teaspoon of salsa.
3. Select Air Fry, Super Convection, set temperature to 350°F (180°C) and set time to 7 minutes. Select Start/Stop to begin preheating.
4. Once preheated, place the pan on the air fry position.
5. When done, the eggs should be cooked to your desired doneness.
6. Remove the rings from the pan to a plate and serve warm.

Tomato-Corn Frittata with Avocado Dressing

Prep time: 10 minutes | Cook time: 20 minutes | Serves 2 or 3

½ cup cherry tomatoes, halved
Kosher salt and freshly ground black pepper, to taste
6 large eggs, lightly beaten
½ cup fresh corn kernels
¼ cup milk
1 tablespoon finely chopped fresh dill
½ cup shredded Monterey Jack cheese
Avocado Dressing:
1 ripe avocado, pitted and peeled
2 tablespoons fresh lime juice
¼ cup olive oil
1 scallion, finely chopped
8 fresh basil leaves, finely chopped

1. Put the tomato halves in a colander and lightly season with salt. Set aside for 10 minutes to drain well. Pour the tomatoes into a large bowl and fold in the eggs, corn, milk, and dill. Sprinkle with salt and pepper and stir until mixed.
2. Pour the egg mixture into a baking pan.
3. Select Bake, Super Convection, set temperature to 300°F (150°C) and set time to 15 minutes. Select Start/Stop to begin preheating.
4. Once the oven has preheated, place the pan on the bake position.
5. When done, remove the pan from the oven. Scatter the cheese on top.
6. Select Bake, Super Convection, set temperature to 315°F (157°C) and set time to 5 minutes. Return the pan to the oven.
7. Meanwhile, make the avocado dressing: Mash the avocado with the lime juice in a medium bowl until smooth. Mix in the olive oil, scallion, and basil and stir until well incorporated.
8. When cooking is complete, the frittata will be puffy and set. Let the frittata cool for 5 minutes and serve alongside the avocado dressing.

Sausage and Cheese Quiche

Prep time: 5 minutes | Cook time: 25 minutes | Serves 4

12 large eggs
1 cup heavy cream
Salt and black pepper, to taste
12 ounces (340 g) sugar-free breakfast sausage
2 cups shredded Cheddar cheese
Cooking spray

1. Coat a casserole dish with cooking spray.
2. Beat together the eggs, heavy cream, salt and pepper in a large bowl until creamy. Stir in the breakfast sausage and Cheddar cheese.
3. Pour the sausage mixture into the prepared casserole dish.
4. Select Bake, Super Convection, set temperature to 375°F (190°C) and set time to 25 minutes. Select Start/Stop to begin preheating.
5. Once the oven has preheated, place the dish on the bake position.
6. When done, the top of the quiche should be golden brown and the eggs will be set.
7. Remove from the oven and let sit for 5 to 10 minutes before serving.

Breakfast Chimichangas

Prep time: 5 minutes | Cook time: 10 minutes | Serves 2

2 large (10- to 12-inch) flour tortillas
½ cup canned refried beans
4 large scrambled eggs (whole, cooked)
4 corn tortilla chips, crushed
½ cup grated Pepper Jack cheese
12 pickled jalapeño slices
1 tablespoon vegetable oil

1. Preheat the air fryer to 350°F (177°C).
2. Arrange the tortillas on a work surface and divide the refried beans between them, spreading them in a rough rectangle in the center of the tortillas. Top the beans with the scrambled eggs, crushed chips, Pepper Jack, and finish with jalapeño slices. Fold one side over the fillings, then fold in each short side and roll up the rest of the way like a burrito.
3. Brush the outside of the burritos with the vegetable oil, then transfer to the air fryer basket, seam-side down.
4. Select Air Fry, Super Convection, and set time to 10 minutes, or until the tortillas are browned and crisp and the filling is warmed through.
5. Remove from the basket and serve on a plate.

Veggie Frittata

Prep time: 10 minutes | Cook time: 12 minutes | Serves 4

½ cup chopped red bell pepper
⅓ cup grated carrot
⅓ cup minced onion
1 teaspoon olive oil
1 egg
6 egg whites
⅓ cup 2% milk
1 tablespoon shredded Parmesan cheese

1. Mix together the red bell pepper, carrot, onion, and olive oil in a baking pan and stir to combine.
2. Select Bake, Super Convection, set temperature to 350°F (180°C) and set time to 12 minutes. Select Start/Stop to begin preheating.
3. Once preheated, place the pan on the bake position.
4. After 3 minutes, remove the pan from the oven. Stir the vegetables. Return the pan to the oven and continue cooking.
5. Meantime, whisk together the egg, egg whites, and milk in a medium bowl until creamy.
6. After 3 minutes, remove the pan from the oven. Pour the egg mixture over the top and scatter with the Parmesan cheese. Return the pan to the oven and continue cooking for additional 6 minutes.
7. When cooking is complete, the eggs will be set and the top will be golden around the edges.
8. Allow the frittata to cool for 5 minutes before slicing and serving.

Brown Rice Porridge

with Dates

Prep time: 5 minutes | Cook time: 23 minutes | Serves 1 or 2

½ cup cooked brown rice
1 cup canned coconut milk
¼ cup unsweetened shredded coconut
¼ cup packed dark brown sugar
4 large Medjool dates, pitted and roughly chopped
½ teaspoon kosher salt
¼ teaspoon ground cardamom
Heavy cream, for serving (optional)

1. Place all the ingredients except the heavy cream in a baking pan and stir until blended.
2. Select Bake. Set temperature to 375°F (190°C) and set time to 23 minutes. Press Start to begin preheating.
3. Once the oven has preheated, place the pan into the oven. Stir the porridge halfway through the cooking time.
4. When cooked, the porridge will be thick and creamy.
5. Remove from the oven and ladle the porridge into bowls.
6. Serve hot with a drizzle of the cream, if desired.

Vanilla Blueberry Cobbler

Prep time: 5 minutes | Cook time: 15 minutes | Serves 4

¾ teaspoon baking powder
⅓ cup whole-wheat pastry flour
Dash sea salt
⅓ cup unsweetened nondairy milk
2 tablespoons maple syrup
½ teaspoon vanilla
Cooking spray
½ cup blueberries
¼ cup granola
Nondairy yogurt, for topping (optional)

1. Spritz a baking pan with cooking spray.
2. Mix together the baking powder, flour, and salt in a medium bowl. Add the milk, maple syrup, and vanilla and whisk to combine.
3. Scrape the mixture into the prepared pan. Scatter the blueberries and granola on top.
4. Select Bake. Set temperature to 347ºF (175ºC) and set time to 15 minutes. Press Start to begin preheating.
5. Once preheated, place the pan into the oven.
6. When done, the top should begin to brown and a knife inserted in the center should come out clean.
7. Let the cobbler cool for 5 minutes and serve with a drizzle of nondairy yogurt.

Asparagus Strata with Havarti Cheese

Prep time: 10 minutes | Cook time: 17 minutes | Serves 4

6 asparagus spears, cut into 2-inch pieces
1 tablespoon water
2 slices whole-wheat bread, cut into ½-inch cubes
4 eggs
3 tablespoons whole milk
2 tablespoons chopped flat-leaf parsley
½ cup grated Havarti or Swiss cheese
Pinch salt
Freshly ground black pepper, to taste
Cooking spray

1. Add the asparagus spears and 1 tablespoon of water in a baking pan.
2. Select Bake. Set temperature to 330ºF (166ºC) and set time to 4 minutes. Press Start to begin preheating.
3. Once preheated, place the pan into the oven.
4. When cooking is complete, the asparagus spears will be crisp-tender.
5. Remove the asparagus from the pan and drain on paper towels.
6. Spritz the pan with cooking spray. Place the bread and asparagus in the pan.
7. Whisk together the eggs and milk in a medium mixing bowl until creamy. Fold in the parsley, cheese, salt, and pepper and stir to combine. Pour this mixture into the baking pan.
8. Select Bake and set time to 13 minutes. Place the pan back to the oven. When done, the eggs will be set and the top will be lightly browned.
9. Let cool for 5 minutes before slicing and serving.

Garlic Potatoes with Peppers and Onions

Prep time: 10 minutes | Cook time: 35 minutes | Serves 4

1 pound (454 g) red potatoes, cut into ½-inch dices
1 large red bell pepper, cut into ½-inch dices
1 large green bell pepper, cut into ½-inch dices
1 medium onion, cut into ½-inch dices
1½ tablespoons extra-virgin olive oil
1¼ teaspoons kosher salt
¾ teaspoon sweet paprika
¾ teaspoon garlic powder
Freshly ground black pepper, to taste

1. Mix together the potatoes, bell peppers, onion, oil, salt, paprika, garlic powder, and black pepper in a large mixing and toss to coat.
2. Transfer the potato mixture to the perforated pan.
3. Select Air Fry. Set temperature to 350ºF (180ºC) and set time to 35 minutes. Press Start to begin preheating.
4. Once preheated, place the pan into the oven. Stir the potato mixture three times during cooking.
5. When done, the potatoes should be nicely browned.
6. Remove from the oven to a plate and serve warm.

Brown Rice Quiches with Pimiento

Prep time: 10 minutes | Cook time: 14 minutes | Serves 6

4 ounces (113 g) diced green chilies
3 cups cooked brown rice
1 cup shredded reduced-fat Cheddar cheese, divided
½ cup egg whites
⅓ cup fat-free milk
¼ cup diced pimiento
½ teaspoon cumin
1 small eggplant, cubed
1 bunch fresh cilantro, finely chopped
Cooking spray

1. Spritz a 12-cup muffin pan with cooking spray.
2. In a large bowl, stir together all the ingredients, except for ½ cup of the cheese.
3. Scoop the mixture evenly into the muffin cups and sprinkle the remaining ½ cup of the cheese on top.
4. Select Bake. Set temperature to 400ºF (205ºC) and set time to 14 minutes. Press Start to begin preheating.
5. Once the unit has preheated, place the pan into the oven.
6. When cooking is complete, remove the pan and check the quiches. They should be set.
7. Carefully transfer the quiches to a platter and serve immediately.

Avocado and Egg Burrito

Prep time: 10 minutes | Cook time: 4 minutes | Serves 4

4 low-sodium whole-wheat flour tortillas
Filling:
1 hard-boiled egg, chopped
2 hard-boiled egg whites, chopped
1 ripe avocado, peeled, pitted, and chopped
1 red bell pepper, chopped
1 (1.2-ounce / 34-g) slice low-sodium, low-fat American cheese, torn into pieces
3 tablespoons low-sodium salsa, plus additional for serving (optional)

Special Equipment:
4 toothpicks (optional) soaked in water for at least 30 minutes

1. Make the filling: Combine the egg, egg whites, avocado, red bell pepper, cheese, and salsa in a medium bowl and stir until blended.
2. Assemble the burritos: Arrange the tortillas on a clean work surface and place ¼ of the prepared filling in the middle of each tortilla, leaving about 1½-inch on each end unfilled. Fold in the opposite sides of each tortilla and roll up. Secure with toothpicks through the center, if needed.
3. Transfer the burritos to the perforated pan.
4. Select Air Fry. Set temperature to 390ºF (199ºC) and set time to 4 minutes. Press Start to begin preheating.
5. Once the oven has preheated, place the pan into the oven.
6. When cooking is complete, the burritos should be crisp and golden brown.
7. Allow to cool for 5 minutes and serve with salsa, if desired.

Banana Chocolate Bread with Walnuts

Prep time: 10 minutes | Cook time: 30 minutes | Serves 4

¼ cup cocoa powder
6 tablespoons plus 2 teaspoons all-purpose flour, divided
½ teaspoon kosher salt
¼ teaspoon baking soda
1½ ripe bananas
1 large egg, whisked
¼ cup vegetable oil
½ cup sugar
3 tablespoons buttermilk or plain yogurt (not Greek)
½ teaspoon vanilla extract
6 tablespoons chopped white chocolate
6 tablespoons chopped walnuts

1. Mix together the cocoa powder, 6 tablespoons of the flour, salt, and baking soda in a medium bowl.
2. Mash the bananas with a fork in another medium bowl until smooth. Fold in the egg, oil, sugar, buttermilk, and vanilla, and whisk until thoroughly combined. Add the wet mixture to the dry mixture and stir until well incorporated.
3. Combine the white chocolate, walnuts, and the remaining 2 tablespoons of flour in a third bowl and toss to coat. Add this mixture to the batter and stir until well incorporated. Pour the batter into a baking pan and smooth the top with a spatula.
4. Select Bake. Set temperature to 310ºF (154ºC) and set time to 30 minutes. Press Start to begin preheating.
5. Once the oven has preheated, place the pan into the oven.
6. When done, a toothpick inserted into the center of the bread should come out clean.
7. Remove from the oven and allow to cool on a wire rack for 10 minutes before serving.

Baked Eggs with Kale Pesto

Prep time: 5 minutes | Cook time: 11 minutes | Serves 2

1 cup roughly chopped kale leaves, stems and center ribs removed
¼ cup grated pecorino cheese
¼ cup olive oil
1 garlic clove, peeled
3 tablespoons whole almonds
Kosher salt and freshly ground black pepper, to taste
4 large eggs
2 tablespoons heavy cream
3 tablespoons chopped pitted mixed olives

1. Place the kale, pecorino, olive oil, garlic, almonds, salt, and pepper in a small blender and blitz until well incorporated.
2. One at a time, crack the eggs in a baking pan. Drizzle the kale pesto on top of the egg whites. Top the yolks with the cream and swirl together the yolks and the pesto.
3. Select Bake. Set temperature to 300ºF (150ºC) and set time to 11 minutes. Press Start to begin preheating.
4. Once preheated, place the pan into the oven.
5. When cooked, the top should begin to brown and the eggs should be set.
6. Allow the eggs to cool for 5 minutes. Scatter the olives on top and serve warm.

Chicken Breakfast Sausages

Prep time: 15 minutes | Cook time: 10 minutes | Makes 8 patties

1 Granny Smith apple, peeled and finely chopped
2 tablespoons apple juice
2 garlic cloves, minced
1 egg white
⅓ cup minced onion
3 tablespoons ground almonds
⅛ teaspoon freshly ground black pepper
1 pound (454 g) ground chicken breast

1. Combine all the ingredients except the chicken in a medium mixing bowl and stir well.
2. Add the chicken breast to the apple mixture and mix with your hands until well incorporated.
3. Divide the mixture into 8 equal portions and shape into patties. Arrange the patties in the perforated pan.
4. Select Air Fry. Set temperature to 330ºF (166ºC) and set time to 10 minutes. Press Start to begin preheating.
5. Once the oven has preheated, place the pan into the oven.
6. When done, a meat thermometer inserted in the center of the chicken should reach at least 165ºF (74ºC).
7. Remove from the oven to a plate. Let the chicken cool for 5 minutes and serve warm.

Blueberries Quesadillas

Prep time: 5 minutes | Cook time: 4 minutes | Serves 2

¼ cup nonfat Ricotta cheese
¼ cup plain nonfat Greek yogurt
2 tablespoons finely ground flaxseeds
1 tablespoon granulated stevia
½ teaspoon cinnamon
¼ teaspoon vanilla extract
2 (8-inch) low-carb whole-wheat tortillas
½ cup fresh blueberries, divided

1. Line the sheet pan with the aluminum foil.
2. In a small bowl, whisk together the Ricotta cheese, yogurt, flaxseeds, stevia, cinnamon and vanilla.
3. Place the tortillas on the sheet pan. Spread half of the yogurt mixture on each tortilla, almost to the edges. Top each tortilla with ¼ cup of blueberries. Fold the tortillas in half.
4. Select Bake. Set temperature to 400ºF (205ºC) and set time to 4 minutes. Press Start to begin preheating.
5. Once the unit has preheated, place the pan into the oven.
6. When cooking is complete, remove the pan from the oven. Serve immediately.

Beef Roast with Carrot

Chapter 2 Meats

Mushroom and Beef Patties Rolls

Prep time: 5 minutes | Cook time: 15 minutes | Serves 4

1 pound (454 g) ground chuck
2 garlic cloves, minced
1 small onion, chopped
1 cup chopped mushrooms
1 teaspoon cayenne pepper
Sea salt and ground black pepper, to taste
4 brioche rolls

1. Start by preheating the air fryer to 380°F (193°C).
2. Mix the ground chuck, garlic, onion, mushrooms, cayenne pepper, salt, and black pepper until everything is well combined. Form the mixture into four patties.
3. Arrange the patties in the crisper tray.
4. Place the crisper tray in the corresponding position in the air fryer. Select Air Fry and cook the patties for about 15 minutes or until cooked through; make sure to turn them over halfway through the cooking time.
5. Serve the patties on the prepared brioche rolls and enjoy!

Pork Cheese Sandwich

Prep time: 10 minutes | Cook time: 55 minutes | Serves 4

1½ pounds (680 g) pork butt
1 teaspoon stone-ground mustard
½ teaspoon ground cumin
2 cloves garlic, crushed
Kosher salt and freshly ground black pepper, to taste
½ teaspoon ground allspice
2 tablespoons fresh pineapple juice
2 ounces (57 g) Swiss cheese, sliced
16 ounces (454 g) Cuban bread loaf, sliced

1. Start by preheating the air fryer to 360°F (182°C).
2. Toss all ingredients , except for the cheese and bread, in a lightly greased crisper tray.
3. Place the crisper tray in the corresponding position in the air fryer. Select Air Fry and cook the pork butt for 55 minutes, turning it over halfway through the cooking time.
4. Using two forks, shred the pork; assemble the sandwiches with cheese and bread. Serve warm and enjoy!

Basil Pork Butt

Prep time: 5 minutes | Cook time: 55 minutes | Serves 4

1½ pounds (680 g) pork butt
1 teaspoon olive oil
1 teaspoon dried rosemary
1 teaspoon dried thyme
1 teaspoon dried oregano
1 teaspoon dried basil
1 teaspoon cayenne pepper
Sea salt and ground black pepper, to taste

1. Start by preheating the air fryer to 360°F (182°C).
2. Toss all ingredients in a lightly greased crisper tray.
3. Place the crisper tray in the corresponding position in the air fryer. Select Air Fry and cook the pork for 55 minutes, turning it over halfway through the cooking time.
4. Serve warm and enjoy!

Air Fried Sausage with Ginger

Prep time: 5 minutes | Cook time: 15 minutes | Serves 4

1 pound (454 g) Frankfurter sausage
¼ cup ginger ale
2 tablespoons liquid honey
Red pepper flakes, to taste

1. Start by preheating the air fryer to 370°F (188°C).
2. Place all ingredients in a lightly greased crisper tray.
3. Place the crisper tray in the corresponding position in the air fryer. Select Air Fry and cook the sausage for approximately 15 minutes, tossing crisper tray halfway through the cooking time.
4. Bon appétit!

Pork Patties with Teriyaki Sauce

Prep time: 10 minutes | Cook time: 15 minutes | Serves 4

1 pound (454 g) ground pork
Kosher salt and ground black pepper, to taste
1 tablespoon chopped fresh parsley
1 tablespoon chopped fresh coriander
1 teaspoon sliced habanero pepper
1 tablespoon teriyaki sauce
1 small onion, chopped
1 clove garlic, minced
4 brioche hamburger buns, lightly toasted

1. Start by preheating the air fryer to 380°F (193°C).
2. In a mixing bowl, thoroughly combine the pork, spices, habanero pepper, teriyaki sauce, onion, and garlic. Then, roll the mixture into four patties.
3. Arrange the patties in the crisper tray.
4. Place the crisper tray in the corresponding position in the air fryer. Select Air Fry and cook the pork patties for about 15 minutes or until cooked through; make sure to turn them over halfway through the cooking time.
5. Serve the patties with the brioche hamburger buns. Enjoy!

Pork Ribs with Tomato Sauce

Prep time: 5 minutes | Cook time: 35 minutes | Serves 4

1 tablespoon sesame oil
1½ pounds (680 g) back ribs
½ cup tomato sauce
1 tablespoon soy sauce
2 tablespoons agave syrup
2 tablespoons rice wine

1. Start by preheating the air fryer to 350°F (180°C).
2. Toss all ingredients in a lightly greased crisper tray.
3. Place the crisper tray in the corresponding position in the air fryer. Select Air Fry and cook the pork ribs for 35 minutes, turning them over halfway through the cooking time.
4. Bon appétit!

Pork Rolls with Fish Sauce

Prep time: 5 minutes | Cook time: 55 minutes | Serves 4

1 pound (454 g) pork shoulder
1 tablespoon olive oil
2 cloves garlic, minced
1 teaspoon cayenne pepper
1 tablespoon chopped fresh sage
1 tablespoon chopped fresh thyme
1 tablespoon brown sugar
2 tablespoons fish sauce
Kosher salt and freshly ground pepper, to taste
8 dinner rolls

1. Start by preheating the air fryer to 360°F (182°C).
2. Toss all ingredients, except for the dinner rolls, in a lightly greased crisper tray.
3. Place the crisper tray in the corresponding position in the air fryer. Select Air Fry and cook the pork for 55 minutes, turning it over halfway through the cooking time.
4. Serve on dinner rolls and enjoy!

Bacon Squash and Eggplant Kebabs

Prep time: 15 minutes | Cook time: 10 minutes | Serves 3

1 tablespoon freshly squeezed lemon juice
1 teaspoon peeled and finely grated fresh ginger
1 tablespoon maple syrup
½ pound (227 g) bacon
½ pound (227 g) squash, diced
½ pound (227 g) eggplant, diced
1 large onion, cut into wedges

1. Start by preheating the air fryer to 400ºF (205ºC).
2. Toss all ingredients in a mixing bowl until well coated on all sides.
3. Thread the ingredients onto skewers and place them in the crisper tray.
4. Place the crisper tray in the corresponding position in the air fryer. Select Air Fry and cook the skewers for approximately 10 minutes, turning them over halfway through the cooking time.
5. Serve warm with sauce on the side, if desired. Bon appétit!

Pork Gyros

Prep time: 5 minutes | Cook time: 55 minutes | Serves 4

1 pound (454 g) pork shoulder
1 teaspoon smoked paprika
½ teaspoon onion powder
1 teaspoon garlic powder
½ teaspoon ground cumin
½ teaspoon ground bay leaf
Sea salt and ground black pepper, to taste
4 pitta bread, warmed

1. Start by preheating the air fryer to 360ºF (182ºC).
2. Toss the pork on all sides, top and bottom, with the spices. Place the pork in a lightly greased crisper tray.
3. Place the crisper tray in the corresponding position in the air fryer. Select Air Fry and cook the pork for 55 minutes, turning it over halfway through the cooking time.
4. Shred the pork with two forks and serve on warmed pitta bread and some extra toppings of choice. Enjoy!

Fennel and Pork Souvlaki

Prep time: 15 minutes | Cook time: 15 minutes | Serves 4

1 tablespoon olive oil
½ teaspoon sweet paprika
1 pound (454 g) pork tenderloin, cubed
1 small lemon, freshly juiced
1 eggplant, diced
2 bell peppers, diced
½ pound (227 g) fennel, diced

1. Start by preheating the air fryer to 400ºF (205ºC).
2. Toss all ingredients in a mixing bowl until well coated on all sides.
3. Thread the ingredients onto skewers and place them in the crisper tray.
4. Place the crisper tray in the corresponding position in the air fryer. Select Air Fry and cook the skewers for approximately 15 minutes, turning them over halfway through the cooking time.
5. Bon appétit!

Pork with Shaoxing Wine

Prep time: 10 minutes | Cook time: 15 minutes | Serves 4

1½ pounds (680 g) pork loin porterhouse, cut into 4 slices
1½ tablespoons sesame oil
½ teaspoon five-spice powder
2 garlic cloves, crushed
1 tablespoon soy sauce
1 tablespoon hoisin sauce
2 tablespoons Shaoxing wine

1. Start by preheating the air fryer to 400ºF (205ºC).
2. Place all ingredients in a lightly greased crisper tray.
3. Place the crisper tray in the corresponding position in the air fryer. Select Air Fry and cook the pork loin chops for 15 minutes, turning them over halfway through the cooking time.
4. Bon appétit!

Spareribs with Sriracha Sauce

Prep time: 5 minutes | Cook time: 35 minutes | Serves 5

2 pounds (907 g) spareribs
¼ cup Sriracha sauce
1 teaspoon paprika
Sea salt and ground black pepper,
   to taste

1. Start by preheating the air fryer to 350ºF (180ºC).
2. Toss all ingredients in a lightly greased crisper tray.
3. Place the crisper tray in the corresponding position in the air fryer. Select Air Fry and cook the pork ribs for 35 minutes, turning them over halfway through the cooking time.
4. Bon appétit!

Sirloin Chops with Cheese

Prep time: 5 minutes | Cook time: 15 minutes | Serves 3

1 pound (454 g) sirloin chops
1 egg
2 tablespoons butter, at room
   temperature
Sea salt and ground black pepper,
   to taste
3 tablespoons grated Pecorino
   cheese
½ cup bread crumbs
1 teaspoon paprika
1 teaspoon garlic powder

1. Start by preheating the air fryer to 400ºF (205ºC).
2. Pat the pork sirloin chops dry with kitchen towels.
3. In a shallow bowl, whisk the egg until pale and frothy.
4. In another shallow bowl, thoroughly combine the remaining ingredients. Dip the pork chops into the egg, then the cheese and crumb mixture.
5. Place the pork sirloin chops in a lightly oiled crisper tray.
6. Place the crisper tray in the corresponding position in the air fryer. Select Air Fry and cook the pork sirloin chops for 15 minutes, turning them over halfway through the cooking time.
7. Bon appétit!

Pork Loin Roast

Prep time: 5 minutes | Cook time: 55 minutes | Serves 4

1½ pounds (680 g) pork loin roast
2 tablespoons butter, melted
Sea salt and ground black pepper, to
   taste
1 teaspoon cayenne pepper
1 teaspoon crushed garlic
1 teaspoon dried rosemary

1. Start by preheating the air fryer to 360ºF (182ºC).
2. Toss all ingredients in a lightly greased crisper tray.
3. Place the crisper tray in the corresponding position in the air fryer. Select Air Fry and cook the pork for 55 minutes, turning it over halfway through the cooking time.
4. Serve warm and enjoy!

Rosemary Pork Belly

Prep time: 5 minutes | Cook time: 45 minutes | Serves 5

1 pound (454 g) pork belly
1 tablespoon tomato sauce
2 tablespoons rice vinegar
1 teaspoon dried thyme
1 teaspoon dried rosemary

1. Start by preheating the air fryer to 320ºF (160ºC).
2. Toss all ingredients in a lightly greased baking pan.
3. Place the baking pan in the corresponding position in the air fryer. Select Bake and cook the pork belly for 20 minutes. Now, turn it over and continue cooking for a further 25 minutes.
4. Serve warm and enjoy!

Herbed Beef

Prep time: 5 minutes | Cook time: 22 minutes | Serves 6

1 teaspoon dried dill
1 teaspoon dried thyme
1 teaspoon garlic powder
2 pounds (907 g) beef steak
3 tablespoons butter

1. Preheat the air fryer oven to 360°F (182°C).
2. Combine the dill, thyme, and garlic powder in a small bowl, and massage into the steak. Place the steak in the air fryer basket.
3. Place the air fryer basket onto the baking pan and slide into Rack Position 2, select Air Fry and set time to 20 minutes.
4. Remove from the oven, shred, and return to the oven. Add the butter and air fry the shredded steak for a further 2 minutes at 365°F (185°C). Make sure the beef is coated in the butter before serving.

Beef and Zucchini

Prep time: 5 minutes | Cook time: 12 minutes | Serves 4

1½ pounds (680 g) ground beef
1 pound (454 g) chopped zucchini
2 tablespoons extra-virgin olive oil
1 teaspoon dried oregano
1 teaspoon dried basil
1 teaspoon dried rosemary
2 tablespoons fresh chives, chopped

1. In a large bowl, combine all the ingredients, except for the chives, until well blended.
2. Place the beef and zucchini mixture in the baking pan.
3. Select Bake, Super Convection, set temperature to 400°F (205°C) and set time to 12 minutes. Press Start/Stop to begin preheating.
4. Once preheated, place the pan on the bake position.
5. When cooking is complete, the beef should be browned and the zucchini should be tender.
6. Divide the beef and zucchini mixture among four serving dishes. Top with fresh chives and serve hot.

Panko Calf's Liver Strips

Prep time: 15 minutes | Cook time: 5 minutes | Serves 4

1 pound (454 g) sliced calf's liver, cut into ½-inch wide strips
2 eggs
2 tablespoons milk
½ cup whole wheat flour
2 cups panko bread crumbs
Salt and ground black pepper, to taste
Cooking spray

1. Spritz the air fry basket with cooking spray.
2. Rub the calf's liver strips with salt and ground black pepper on a clean work surface.
3. Whisk the eggs with milk in a large bowl. Pour the flour in a shallow dish. Pour the panko on a separate shallow dish.
4. Dunk the liver strips in the flour, then in the egg mixture. Shake the excess off and roll the strips over the panko to coat well.
5. Arrange the liver strips in the basket and spritz with cooking spray.
6. Select Air Fry, Super Convection. Set temperature to 390°F (199°C) and set time to 5 minutes. Press Start/Stop to begin preheating.
7. Once preheated, place the basket on the air fry position. Flip the strips halfway through.
8. When cooking is complete, the strips should be browned.
9. Serve immediately.

Steaks with Snap Pea Salad

Prep time: 15 minutes | Cook time: 15 minutes | Serves 4

1 (1½-pound / 680-g) boneless top sirloin steak, trimmed and halved crosswise
1½ teaspoons chili powder
1½ teaspoons ground cumin
¾ teaspoon ground coriander
⅛ teaspoon cayenne pepper
⅛ teaspoon ground cinnamon
1¼ teaspoons plus ⅛ teaspoon salt, divided
½ teaspoon plus ⅛ teaspoon ground black pepper, divided
1 teaspoon plus 1½ tablespoons extra-virgin olive oil, divided
3 tablespoons mayonnaise
1½ tablespoons white wine vinegar
1 tablespoon minced fresh dill
1 small garlic clove, minced
8 ounces (227 g) sugar snap peas, strings removed and cut in half on bias
½ English cucumber, halved lengthwise and sliced thin
2 radishes, trimmed, halved and sliced thin
2 cups baby arugula

1. In a bowl, mix chili powder, cumin, coriander, cayenne pepper, cinnamon, 1¼ teaspoons salt and ½ teaspoon pepper until well combined.
2. Add the steaks to another bowl and pat dry with paper towels. Brush with 1 teaspoon oil and transfer to the bowl of spice mixture. Roll over to coat thoroughly.
3. Arrange the coated steaks in the air fry basket, spaced evenly apart.
4. Select Air Fry, Super Convection. Set temperature to 400ºF (205ºC) and set time to 15 minutes. Press Start/Stop to begin preheating.
5. Once preheated, place the basket on the air fry position. Flip the steak halfway through to ensure even cooking.
6. When cooking is complete, an instant-read thermometer inserted in the thickest part of the meat should register at least 145ºF (63ºC).
7. Transfer the steaks to a clean work surface and wrap with aluminum foil. Let stand while preparing salad.
8. Make the salad: In a large bowl, stir together 1½ tablespoons olive oil, mayonnaise, vinegar, dill, garlic, ⅛ teaspoon salt, and ⅛ teaspoon pepper. Add snap peas, cucumber, radishes and arugula. Toss to blend well.
9. Slice the steaks and serve with the salad.

Beef Loin with Thyme and Parsley

Prep time: 5 minutes | Cook time: 15 minutes | Serves 4

1 tablespoon butter, melted
¼ dried thyme
1 teaspoon garlic salt
¼ teaspoon dried parsley
1 pound (454 g) beef loin

1. Preheat the air fryer oven to 400ºF (204ºC).
2. In a bowl, combine the melted butter, thyme, garlic salt, and parsley.
3. Cut the beef loin into slices and generously apply the seasoned butter using a brush. Transfer to the air fryer basket.
4. Place the air fryer basket onto the baking pan and slide into Rack Position 2, select Air Fry and set time to 15 minutes.
5. Serve hot.

Beef Lahmacun with Mint

Prep time: 20 minutes | Cook time: 10 minutes | Serves 4

4 (6-inch) flour tortillas

For the Meat Topping:
4 ounces (113 g) ground lamb or 85% lean ground beef
¼ cup finely chopped green bell pepper
¼ cup chopped fresh parsley
1 small plum tomato, deseeded and chopped
2 tablespoons chopped yellow onion
1 garlic clove, minced
2 teaspoons tomato paste
¼ teaspoon sweet paprika
¼ teaspoon ground cumin
⅛ to ¼ teaspoon red pepper flakes
⅛ teaspoon ground allspice
⅛ teaspoon kosher salt
⅛ teaspoon black pepper

For Serving:
¼ cup chopped fresh mint
1 teaspoon extra-virgin olive oil
1 lemon, cut into wedges

1. Combine all the ingredients for the meat topping in a medium bowl until well mixed.
2. Lay the tortillas on a clean work surface. Spoon the meat mixture on the tortillas and spread all over.
3. Place the tortillas in the air fry basket.
4. Select Air Fry, Super Convection. Set temperature to 400ºF (205ºC) and set time to 10 minutes. Press Start/Stop to begin preheating.
5. Once preheated, place the basket on the air fry position.
6. When cooking is complete, the edge of the tortilla should be golden and the meat should be lightly browned.
7. Transfer them to a serving dish. Top with chopped fresh mint and drizzle with olive oil. Squeeze the lemon wedges on top and serve.

Beef Meatballs with Lime

Prep time: 5 minutes | Cook time: 15 minutes | Serves 4

1 pound (454 g) ground beef
1 tablespoon sesame oil
2 teaspoons chopped lemongrass
1 teaspoon red Thai curry paste
1 teaspoon Thai seasoning blend
Juice and zest of ½ lime
Cooking spray

1. Spritz the air fry basket with cooking spray.
2. In a medium bowl, combine all the ingredients until well blended.
3. Shape the meat mixture into 24 meatballs and arrange them in the basket.
4. Select Air Fry, Super Convection. Set temperature to 380ºF (193ºC) and set time to 15 minutes. Press Start/Stop to begin preheating.
5. Once preheated, place the basket on the air fry position. Flip the meatballs halfway through.
6. When cooking is complete, the meatballs should be browned.
7. Transfer the meatballs to plates. Let cool for 5 minutes before serving.

Veal Loin with Rosemary

Prep time: 1 hour 10 minutes | Cook time: 12 minutes | Makes 3 veal chops

1½ teaspoons crushed fennel seeds
1 tablespoon minced fresh rosemary leaves
1 tablespoon minced garlic
1½ teaspoons lemon zest
1½ teaspoons salt
½ teaspoon red pepper flakes
2 tablespoons olive oil
3 (10-ounce / 284-g) bone-in veal loin, about ½ inch thick

1. Combine all the ingredients, except for the veal loin, in a large bowl. Stir to mix well.
2. Dunk the loin in the mixture and press to submerge. Wrap the bowl in plastic and refrigerate for at least an hour to marinate.
3. Arrange the veal loin in the air fry basket.
4. Select Air Fry, Super Convection. Set temperature to 400ºF (205ºC) and set time to 12 minutes. Press Start/Stop to begin preheating.
5. Once preheated, place the basket on the air fry position. Flip the veal halfway through.
6. When cooking is complete, the internal temperature of the veal should reach at least 145ºF (63ºC) for medium rare.
7. Serve immediately.

Air Fried Venison

Prep time: 10 minutes | Cook time: 10 minutes | Serves 4

2 eggs
¼ cup milk
1 cup whole wheat flour
½ teaspoon salt
¼ teaspoon ground black pepper
1 pound (454 g) venison backstrap, sliced
Cooking spray

1. Spritz the air fry basket with cooking spray.
2. Whisk the eggs with milk in a large bowl. Combine the flour with salt and ground black pepper in a shallow dish.
3. Dredge the venison in the flour first, then into the egg mixture. Shake the excess off and roll the venison back over the flour to coat well.
4. Arrange the venison in the pan and spritz with cooking spray.
5. Select Air Fry, Super Convection. Set temperature to 360ºF (182ºC) and set time to 10 minutes. Press Start/Stop to begin preheating.
6. Once preheated, place the basket on the air fry position. Flip the venison halfway through.
7. When cooking is complete, the internal temperature of the venison should reach at least 145ºF (63ºC) for medium rare.
8. Serve immediately.

Beef Tenderloin with Cheese

Prep time: 10 minutes | Cook time: 10 minutes | Serves 4

1½ pounds (680 g) beef tenderloin, pounded to ¼ inch thick
3 teaspoons sea salt
1 teaspoon ground black pepper
2 ounces (57 g) creamy goat cheese
½ cup crumbled feta cheese
¼ cup finely chopped onions
2 cloves garlic, minced
Cooking spray

1. Spritz the air fry basket with cooking spray.
2. Unfold the beef tenderloin on a clean work surface. Rub the salt and pepper all over the beef tenderloin to season.
3. Make the filling for the stuffed beef tenderloins: Combine the goat cheese, feta, onions, and garlic in a medium bowl. Stir until well blended.
4. Spoon the mixture in the center of the tenderloin. Roll the tenderloin up tightly like rolling a burrito and use some kitchen twine to tie the tenderloin.
5. Arrange the tenderloin in the air fry basket.
6. Select Air Fry, Super Convection. Set temperature to 400°F (205°C) and set time to 10 minutes. Press Start/Stop to begin preheating.
7. Once preheated, place the basket on the air fry position. Flip the tenderloin halfway through.
8. When cooking is complete, the instant-read thermometer inserted in the center of the tenderloin should register 135°F (57°C) for medium-rare.
9. Transfer to a platter and serve immediately.

Lamb Rack with Pistachio

Prep time: 10 minutes | Cook time: 20 minutes | Serves 2

½ cup finely chopped pistachios
1 teaspoon chopped fresh rosemary
3 tablespoons panko bread crumbs
2 teaspoons chopped fresh oregano
1 tablespoon olive oil
Salt and freshly ground black pepper, to taste
1 lamb rack, bones fat trimmed and frenched
1 tablespoon Dijon mustard

1. Put the pistachios, rosemary, bread crumbs, oregano, olive oil, salt, and black pepper in a food processor. Pulse to combine until smooth.
2. Rub the lamb rack with salt and black pepper on a clean work surface, then place it in the air fry basket.
3. Select Air Fry, Super Convection. Set temperature to 380°F (193°C) and set time to 12 minutes. Press Start/Stop to begin preheating.
4. Once preheated, place the basket on the air fry position. Flip the lamb halfway through.
5. When cooking is complete, the lamb should be lightly browned.
6. Transfer the lamb on a plate and brush with Dijon mustard on the fat side, then sprinkle with the pistachios mixture over the lamb rack to coat well.
7. Put the lamb rack back to the oven and air fry for 8 more minutes or until the internal temperature of the rack reaches at least 145°F (63°C).
8. Remove the lamb rack from the oven with tongs and allow to cool for 5 minutes before slicing to serve.

Lamb Loin Chops with Cream Sauce

Prep time: 10 minutes | Cook time: 13 minutes | Serves 4

For the Lamb:
4 lamb loin chops
2 tablespoons vegetable oil
1 clove garlic, minced
½ teaspoon kosher salt
½ teaspoon black pepper

For the Horseradish Cream Sauce:
1 to 1½ tablespoons prepared horseradish
1 tablespoon Dijon mustard
½ cup mayonnaise
2 teaspoons sugar
Cooking spray

1. Spritz the air fry basket with cooking spray.
2. Place the lamb chops on a plate. Rub with the oil and sprinkle with the garlic, salt and black pepper. Let sit to marinate for 30 minutes at room temperature.
3. Make the horseradish cream sauce: Mix the horseradish, mustard, mayonnaise, and sugar in a bowl until well combined. Set half of the sauce aside until ready to serve.
4. Arrange the marinated chops in the air fry basket.
5. Select Air Fry, Super Convection. Set temperature to 325°F (163°C) and set time to 10 minutes. Press Start/Stop to begin preheating.
6. Once preheated, place the basket on the air fry position. Flip the lamb chops halfway through.
7. When cooking is complete, the lamb should be lightly browned.
8. Transfer the chops from the oven to the bowl of the horseradish sauce. Roll to coat well.
9. Put the coated chops back in the air fry basket on the air fry position. Select Air Fry, Super Convection. Set the temperature to 400°F (205°C) and the time to 3 minutes.
10. When cooking is complete, the internal temperature should reach 145°F (63°C) on a meat thermometer (for medium-rare). Flip the lamb halfway through.
11. Serve hot with the horseradish cream sauce.

BBQ Pork Steaks

Prep time: 5 minutes | Cook time: 15 minutes | Serves 4

4 pork steaks
1 tablespoon Cajun seasoning
2 tablespoons BBQ sauce
1 tablespoon vinegar
1 teaspoon soy sauce
½ cup brown sugar
½ cup ketchup

1. Preheat the air fryer oven to 290°F (143°C).
2. Sprinkle pork steaks with Cajun seasoning.
3. Combine remaining ingredients and brush onto steaks. Add coated steaks to the air fryer basket.
4. Place the air fryer basket onto the baking pan and slide into Rack Position 2, select Air Fry and set time to 15 minutes, until just browned.
5. Serve immediately.

Golden Wasabi Spam

Prep time: 5 minutes | Cook time: 12 minutes | Serves 3

⅔ cup all-purpose flour
2 large eggs
1½ tablespoons wasabi paste
2 cups panko bread crumbs
6 ½-inch-thick spam slices
Cooking spray

1. Spritz the air fry basket with cooking spray.
2. Pour the flour in a shallow plate. Whisk the eggs with wasabi in a large bowl. Pour the panko in a separate shallow plate.
3. Dredge the spam slices in the flour first, then dunk in the egg mixture, and then roll the spam over the panko to coat well. Shake the excess off.
4. Arrange the spam slices in the basket and spritz with cooking spray.
5. Select Air Fry, Super Convection. Set temperature to 400°F (205°C) and set time to 12 minutes. Press Start/Stop to begin preheating.
6. Once preheated, place the basket on the air fry position. Flip the spam slices halfway through.
7. When cooking is complete, the spam slices should be golden and crispy.
8. Serve immediately.

Pork Chops with Apple

Prep time: 15 minutes | Cook time: 19 minutes | Serves 4

1 sliced apple
1 small onion, sliced
2 tablespoons apple cider vinegar, divided
½ teaspoon thyme
½ teaspoon rosemary
¼ teaspoon brown sugar
3 tablespoons olive oil, divided
¼ teaspoon smoked paprika
4 pork chops
Salt and ground black pepper, to taste

1. Combine the apple slices, onion, 1 tablespoon of vinegar, thyme, rosemary, brown sugar, and 2 tablespoons of olive oil in a baking pan. Stir to mix well.
2. Select Bake, Super Convection, set temperature to 350°F (180°C) and set time to 4 minutes. Press Start/Stop to begin preheating.
3. Once preheated, place the pan on the bake position. Stir the mixture halfway through.
4. Meanwhile, combine the remaining vinegar and olive oil, and paprika in a large bowl. Sprinkle with salt and ground black pepper. Stir to mix well. Dredge the pork in the mixture and toss to coat well. Place the pork in the air fry basket.
5. When cooking is complete, remove the baking pan from the oven and place in the air fry basket.
6. Select Air Fry, Super Convection and set time to 10 minutes. Place the basket on the air fry position. Flip the pork chops halfway through.
7. When cooking is complete, the pork should be lightly browned.
8. Remove the pork from the oven and baste with baked apple mixture on both sides. Put the pork back to the oven and air fry for an additional 5 minutes. Flip halfway through.
9. Serve immediately.

Pork Tenderloin with Mustard

Prep time: 5 minutes | Cook time: 10 minutes | Serves 6

2 large egg whites
1½ tablespoons Dijon mustard
2 cups crushed pretzel crumbs
1½ pounds (680 g) pork tenderloin, cut into ¼-pound (113-g) sections
Cooking spray

1. Spritz the air fry basket with cooking spray.
2. Whisk the egg whites with Dijon mustard in a bowl until bubbly. Pour the pretzel crumbs in a separate bowl.
3. Dredge the pork tenderloin in the egg white mixture and press to coat. Shake the excess off and roll the tenderloin over the pretzel crumbs.
4. Arrange the well-coated pork tenderloin in the basket and spritz with cooking spray.
5. Select Air Fry, Super Convection. Set temperature to 350°F (180°C) and set time to 10 minutes. Press Start/Stop to begin preheating.
6. Once preheated, place the basket on the air fry position.
7. After 5 minutes, remove the basket from the oven. Flip the pork. Return the basket to the oven and continue cooking.
8. When cooking is complete, the pork should be golden brown and crispy.
9. Serve immediately.

Asparagus and Prosciutto Tart

Prep time: 10 minutes | Cook time: 25 minutes | Serves 4

All-purpose flour, for dusting
1 sheet (½ package) frozen puff pastry, thawed
½ cup grated Parmesan cheese
1 pound (454 g) (or more) asparagus, trimmed
8 ounces (227 g) thinly sliced prosciutto, sliced into ribbons about ½-inch wide
2 teaspoons aged balsamic vinegar

1. On a lightly floured cutting board, unwrap and unfold the puff pastry and roll it lightly with a rolling pin so as to press the folds together. Place it on the sheet pan.
2. Roll about ½ inch of the pastry edges up to form a ridge around the perimeter. Crimp the corners together to create a solid rim around the pastry. Using a fork, pierce the bottom of the pastry all over. Scatter the cheese over the bottom of the pastry.
3. Arrange the asparagus spears on top of the cheese in a single layer with 4 or 5 spears pointing one way, the next few pointing the opposite direction. You may need to trim them so they fit within the border of the pastry shell. Lay the prosciutto on top more or less evenly.
4. Select Bake, Super Convection, set temperature to 375°F (190°C), and set time to 25 minutes. Select Start/Stop to begin preheating.
5. Once the unit has preheated, place the pan on the bake position.
6. After about 15 minutes, check the tart, rotating the pan if the crust is not browning evenly and continue cooking until the pastry is golden brown and the edges of the prosciutto pieces are browned.
7. Remove the pan from the oven. Allow to cool for 5 minutes before slicing.
8. Drizzle with the balsamic vinegar just before serving.

Lamb Chops with Paprika

Prep time: 5 minutes | Cook time: 25 minutes | Serves 4

1 cup all purpose flour
2 teaspoons dried sage leaves
2 teaspoons garlic powder
1 tablespoon mild paprika
1 tablespoon salt
4 (6-ounce / 170-g) bone-in lamb shoulder chops, fat trimmed
Cooking spray

1. Spritz the air fry basket with cooking spray.
2. Combine the flour, sage leaves, garlic powder, paprika, and salt in a large bowl. Stir to mix well. Dunk in the lamb chops and toss to coat well.
3. Arrange the lamb chops in the basket and spritz with cooking spray.
4. Select Air Fry, Super Convection. Set temperature to 375°F (190°C) and set time to 25 minutes. Press Start/Stop to begin preheating.
5. Once preheated, place the basket on the air fry position. Flip the chops halfway through.
6. When cooking is complete, the chops should be golden brown and reaches your desired doneness.
7. Serve immediately.

Pork Char Siu with Honey

Prep time: 8 hours 10 minutes | Cook time: 15 minutes | Serves 4

¼ cup honey
1 teaspoon Chinese five-spice powder
1 tablespoon Shaoxing wine (rice cooking wine)
1 tablespoon hoisin sauce
2 teaspoons minced garlic
2 teaspoons minced fresh ginger
2 tablespoons soy sauce
1 tablespoon sugar
1 pound (454 g) fatty pork shoulder, cut into long, 1-inch-thick pieces
Cooking spray

1. Combine all the ingredients, except for the pork should, in a microwave-safe bowl. Stir to mix well. Microwave until the honey has dissolved. Stir periodically.
2. Pierce the pork pieces generously with a fork, then put the pork in a large bowl. Pour in half of the honey mixture. Set the remaining sauce aside until ready to serve.
3. Press the pork pieces into the mixture to coat and wrap the bowl in plastic and refrigerate to marinate for at least 8 hours.
4. Spritz the air fry basket with cooking spray.
5. Discard the marinade and transfer the pork pieces in the air fry basket.
6. Select Air Fry, Super Convection. Set temperature to 400ºF (205ºC) and set time to 15 minutes. Press Start/Stop to begin preheating.
7. Once preheated, place the basket on the air fry position. Flip the pork halfway through.
8. When cooking is complete, the pork should be well browned.
9. Meanwhile, microwave the remaining marinade on high for a minute or until it has a thick consistency. Stir periodically.
10. Remove the pork from the oven and allow to cool for 10 minutes before serving with the thickened marinade.

Tangy Pork Carnitas

Prep time: 1 hour 10 minutes | Cook time: 25 minutes | Serves 6

2½ pounds (1.1 kg) boneless country-style pork ribs, cut into 2-inch pieces
3 tablespoons olive brine
1 tablespoon minced fresh oregano leaves
⅓ cup orange juice
1 teaspoon ground cumin
1 tablespoon minced garlic
1 teaspoon salt
1 teaspoon ground black pepper
Cooking spray

1. Combine all the ingredients in a large bowl. Toss to coat the pork ribs well. Wrap the bowl in plastic and refrigerate for at least an hour to marinate.
2. Spritz the air fry basket with cooking spray.
3. Arrange the marinated pork ribs in the basket and spritz with cooking spray.
4. Select Air Fry, Super Convection. Set temperature to 400ºF (205ºC) and set time to 25 minutes. Press Start/Stop to begin preheating.
5. Once preheated, place the basket on the air fry position. Flip the ribs halfway through.
6. When cooking is complete, the ribs should be well browned.
7. Serve immediately.

Pork Schnitzel

Prep time: 5 minutes | Cook time: 14 minutes | Serves 2

½ cup pork rinds
½ tablespoon fresh parsley
½ teaspoon fennel seed
½ teaspoon mustard
⅓ tablespoon cider vinegar
1 teaspoon garlic salt
⅓ teaspoon ground black pepper
2 eggs
2 pork schnitzel, halved
Cooking spray

1. Spritz the air fry basket with cooking spray.
2. Put the pork rinds, parsley, fennel seeds, and mustard in a food processor. Pour in the vinegar and sprinkle with salt and ground black pepper. Pulse until well combined and smooth.
3. Pour the pork rind mixture in a large bowl. Whisk the eggs in a separate bowl.
4. Dunk the pork schnitzel in the whisked eggs, then dunk in the pork rind mixture to coat well. Shake the excess off.
5. Arrange the schnitzel in the basket and spritz with cooking spray.
6. Select Air Fry, Super Convection. Set temperature to 350ºF (180ºC) and set time to 14 minutes. Press Start/Stop to begin preheating.
7. Once preheated, place the basket on the air fry position.
8. After 7 minutes, remove the basket from the oven. Flip the schnitzel. Return the basket to the oven and continue cooking.
9. When cooking is complete, the schnitzel should be golden and crispy.
10. Serve immediately.

Italian Sausages and Red Grapes

Prep time: 10 minutes | Cook time: 20 minutes | Serves 6

2 pounds (905 g) seedless red grapes
3 shallots, sliced
2 teaspoons fresh thyme
2 tablespoons olive oil
½ teaspoon kosher salt
Freshly ground black pepper, to taste
6 links (about 1½ pounds / 680 g) hot Italian sausage
3 tablespoons balsamic vinegar

1. Place the grapes in a large bowl. Add the shallots, thyme, olive oil, salt, and pepper. Gently toss. Place the grapes in a baking pan. Arrange the sausage links evenly in the pan.
2. Select Roast, Super Convection, set temperature to 375ºF (190ºC), and set time to 20 minutes. Press Start/Stop to begin preheating.
3. Once preheated, place the pan on the roast position.
4. After 10 minutes, remove the pan. Turn over the sausages and sprinkle the vinegar over the sausages and grapes. Gently toss the grapes and move them to one side of the pan. Return the pan to the oven and continue cooking.
5. When cooking is complete, the grapes should be very soft and the sausages browned. Serve immediately.

Easy Beef Schnitzel

Prep time: 5 minutes | Cook time: 12 minutes | Serves 1

½ cup friendly bread crumbs
2 tablespoons olive oil
Pepper and salt, to taste
1 egg, beaten
1 thin beef schnitzel

1. Preheat the air fryer oven to 350ºF (177ºC).
2. In a shallow dish, combine the bread crumbs, oil, pepper, and salt.
3. In a second shallow dish, place the beaten egg.
4. Dredge the schnitzel in the egg before rolling it in the bread crumbs.
5. Put the coated schnitzel in the air fryer basket. Place the air fryer basket onto the baking pan and slide into Rack Position 2, select Air Fry and set time to 12 minutes. Flip the schnitzel halfway through.
6. Serve immediately.

Calf's Liver Golden Strips

Prep time: 15 minutes | Cook time: 4 to 5 minutes | Serves 4

1 pound (454 g) sliced calf's liver, cut into about ½-inch-wide strips
Salt and ground black pepper, to taste
2 eggs
2 tablespoons milk
½ cup whole wheat flour
1½ cups panko bread crumbs
⅓ cup plain bread crumbs
½ teaspoon salt
¼ teaspoon ground black pepper
Cooking spray

1. Sprinkle the liver strips with salt and pepper.
2. Beat together the egg and milk in a bowl. Place wheat flour in a shallow dish. In a second shallow dish, mix panko, plain bread crumbs, ½ teaspoon salt, and ¼ teaspoon pepper.
3. Dip liver strips in flour, egg wash, and then bread crumbs, pressing in coating slightly to make crumbs stick.
4. Spritz the air fry basket with cooking spray. Place strips in a single layer in the air fry basket.
5. Select Air Fry, Super Convection. Set the temperature to 400ºF (205ºC) and set the time to 4 minutes. Press Start/Stop to begin preheating.
6. Once preheated, place the basket on the air fry position.
7. After 2 minutes, remove the basket from the oven. Flip the strips with tongs. Return the basket to the oven and continue cooking.
8. When cooking is complete, the liver strips should be crispy and golden.
9. Serve immediately.

Pork Chop Stir Fry

Prep time: 10 minutes | Cook time: 20 minutes | Serves 4

1 tablespoon olive oil
¼ teaspoon ground black pepper
½ teaspoon salt
1 egg white
4 (4-ounce / 113-g) pork chops
¾ cup almond flour
2 sliced jalapeño peppers
2 sliced scallions
2 tablespoons olive oil
¼ teaspoon ground white pepper
1 teaspoon sea salt

1. Coat the air fryer basket with olive oil.
2. Whisk black pepper, salt, and egg white together until foamy.
3. Cut pork chops into pieces, leaving just a bit on bones. Pat dry.
4. Add pieces of pork to egg white mixture, coating well. Let sit for marinade 20 minutes.
5. Preheat the air fryer oven to 360°F (182°C).
6. Put marinated chops into a large bowl and add almond flour. Dredge and shake off excess and put into the air fryer basket.
7. Place the air fryer basket onto the baking pan and slide into Rack Position 2, select Air Fry and set time to 12 minutes.
8. Increase the temperature to 400°F (205°C) and air fry for another 6 minutes, until pork chops are nice and crisp.
9. Meanwhile, remove jalapeño seeds and chop up. Chop scallions and mix with jalapeño pieces.
10. Heat a skillet with olive oil. Stir-fry the white pepper, salt, scallions, and jalapeños 60 seconds. Then add fried pork pieces to skills and toss with scallion mixture. Stir-fry for 1 to 2 minutes until well coated and hot.
11. Serve immediately.

Simple Pulled Pork

Prep time: 5 minutes | Cook time: 24 minutes | Serves 1

2 tablespoons barbecue dry rub
1 pound (454 g) pork tenderloin
⅓ cup heavy cream
1 teaspoon butter, melted

1. Preheat the air fryer oven to 370°F (188°C).
2. Massage the dry rub into the tenderloin, coating it well. Transfer to the air fryer basket.
3. Place the air fryer basket onto the baking pan and slide into Rack Position 2, select Air Fry and set time to 20 minutes.
4. When done, shred with two forks. Toss with the heavy cream and butter.
5. Return to the oven and air fry for a further 4 minutes.
6. Serve warm.

Spicy Pork Lettuce Wraps

Prep time: 10 minutes | Cook time: 12 minutes | Serves 4

1 (1-pound / 454-g) medium pork tenderloin, silver skin and external fat trimmed
⅔ cup soy sauce, divided
1 teaspoon cornstarch
1 medium jalapeño, deseeded and minced
1 can diced water chestnuts
½ large red bell pepper, deseeded and chopped
2 scallions, chopped, white and green parts separated
1 head butter lettuce
½ cup roasted, chopped almonds
¼ cup coarsely chopped cilantro

1. Cut the tenderloin into ¼-inch slices and place them on a baking pan. Baste with about 3 tablespoons of soy sauce. Stir the cornstarch into the remaining sauce and set aside.
2. Select Roast, Super Convection, set temperature to 375°F (190°C), and set time to 12 minutes. Press Start/Stop to begin preheating.
3. Once preheated, place the pan on the roast position.
4. After 5 minutes, remove the pan from the oven. Place the pork slices on a cutting board. Place the jalapeño, water chestnuts, red pepper, and the white parts of the scallions on the baking pan and pour the remaining sauce over. Stir to coat the vegetables with the sauce. Return the pan to the oven and continue cooking.
5. While the vegetables cook, chop the pork into small pieces. Separate the lettuce leaves, discarding any tough outer leaves and setting aside the small inner leaves for another use. You'll want 12 to 18 leaves, depending on size and your appetites.
6. After 5 minutes, remove the pan from the oven. Add the pork to the vegetables, stirring to combine. Return the pan to the oven and continue cooking for the remaining 2 minutes until the pork is warmed back up and the sauce has reduced slightly.
7. When cooking is complete, remove the pan from the oven. Place the pork and vegetables in a medium serving bowl and stir in half the green parts of the scallions. To serve, spoon some pork and vegetables into each of the lettuce leaves. Top with the remaining scallion greens and garnish with the nuts and cilantro.

Easy Pork Chop Roast

Prep time: 5 minutes | Cook time: 20 minutes | Serves 2

2 (10-ounce / 284-g) bone-in, center cut pork chops, 1-inch thick
2 teaspoons Worcestershire sauce
Salt and ground black pepper, to taste
Cooking spray

1. Rub the Worcestershire sauce on both sides of pork chops.
2. Season with salt and pepper to taste.
3. Spritz the air fry basket with cooking spray and place the chops in the air fry basket side by side.
4. Select Roast, Super Convection. Set the temperature to 350ºF (180ºC) and set the time to 20 minutes. Press Start/Stop to begin preheating.
5. Once preheated, place the basket on the roast position.
6. After 10 minutes, remove the basket from the oven. Flip the pork chops with tongs. Return the basket to the oven and continue cooking.
7. When cooking is complete, the pork should be well browned on both sides.
8. Let rest for 5 minutes before serving.

Worcestershire Ribeye Steaks

Prep time: 35 minutes | Cook time: 10 to 12 minutes | Serves 2 to 4

2 (8-ounce / 227-g) boneless ribeye steaks
4 teaspoons Worcestershire sauce
½ teaspoon garlic powder
Salt and ground black pepper, to taste
4 teaspoons olive oil

1. Brush the steaks with Worcestershire sauce on both sides. Sprinkle with garlic powder and coarsely ground black pepper. Drizzle the steaks with olive oil. Allow steaks to marinate for 30 minutes.
2. Transfer the steaks in the air fry basket.
3. Select Roast, Super Convection. Set the temperature to 400ºF (205ºC) and set time to 4 minutes. Press Start/Stop to begin preheating.
4. Once preheated, place the basket on the roast position.
5. After 2 minutes, remove the basket from the oven. Flip the steaks. Return the basket to the oven and continue cooking.
6. When cooking is complete, the steaks should be well browned.
7. Remove the steaks from the air fry basket and let sit for 5 minutes. Salt and serve.

Sriracha Beef and Broccoli

Prep time: 10 minutes | Cook time: 15 minutes | Serves 4

12 ounces (340 g) broccoli, cut into florets (about 4 cups)
1 pound (454 g) flat iron steak, cut into thin strips
½ teaspoon kosher salt
¾ cup soy sauce
1 teaspoon Sriracha sauce
3 tablespoons freshly squeezed orange juice
1 teaspoon cornstarch
1 medium onion, thinly sliced

1. Line a baking pan with aluminum foil. Place the broccoli on top and sprinkle with 3 tablespoons of water. Seal the broccoli in the foil in a single layer.
2. Select Roast, Super Convection, set temperature to 375ºF (190ºC), and set time to 6 minutes. Press Start/Stop to begin preheating.
3. Once preheated, place the pan on the roast position.
4. While the broccoli steams, sprinkle the steak with the salt. In a small bowl, whisk together the soy sauce, Sriracha, orange juice, and cornstarch. Place the onion and beef in a large bowl.
5. When cooking is complete, remove the pan from the oven. Open the packet of broccoli and use tongs to transfer the broccoli to the bowl with the beef and onion, discarding the foil and remaining water. Pour the sauce over the beef and vegetables and toss to coat. Place the mixture in the baking pan.
6. Select Roast, Super Convection, set temperature to 375ºF (190ºC), and set time to 9 minutes. Press Start/Stop to begin preheating.
7. Once preheated, place the pan on the roast position.
8. After about 4 minutes, remove the pan from the oven and gently toss the ingredients. Return the pan to oven and continue cooking.
9. When cooking is complete, the sauce should be thickened, the vegetables tender, and the beef barely pink in the center. Serve warm.

Sirloin Steak and Pepper Fajitas

Prep time: 10 minutes | Cook time: 15 minutes | Serves 4

8 (6-inch) flour tortillas
1 pound (454 g) top sirloin steak, sliced ¼-inch thick
1 red bell pepper, deseeded and sliced ½-inch thick
1 green bell pepper, deseeded and sliced ½-inch thick
1 jalapeño, deseeded and sliced thin
1 medium onion, sliced ½-inch thick
2 tablespoons vegetable oil
2 tablespoons Mexican seasoning
1 teaspoon kosher salt
2 tablespoons salsa
1 small avocado, sliced

1. Line a baking pan with aluminum foil. Place the tortillas on the foil in two stacks and wrap in the foil.
2. Select Roast, Super Convection, set temperature to 325°F (163°C), and set time to 6 minutes. Press Start/Stop to begin preheating.
3. Once preheated, place the pan on the roast position. After 3 minutes, remove the pan from the oven and flip the packet of tortillas over. Return the pan to the oven and continue cooking.
4. While the tortillas warm, place the steak, bell peppers, jalapeño, and onion in a large bowl and drizzle the oil over. Sprinkle with the Mexican seasoning and salt, and toss to coat.
5. When cooking is complete, remove the pan from the oven and place the packet of tortillas on top of the oven to keep warm. Place the beef and peppers mixture on the baking pan, spreading out into a single layer as much as possible.
6. Select Roast, Super Convection, set temperature to 375°F (190°C), and set time to 9 minutes. Press Start/Stop to begin preheating.
7. Once preheated, place the pan on the roast position.
8. After about 5 minutes, remove the pan from the oven and stir the ingredients. Return the pan to the oven and continue cooking.
9. When cooking is complete, the vegetables will be soft and browned in places, and the beef will be browned on the outside and barely pink inside. Remove the pan from the oven. Unwrap the tortillas and spoon the fajita mixture into the tortillas. Serve with salsa and avocado slices.

Ravioli with Beef-Marinara Sauce

Prep time: 10 minutes | Cook time: 10 minutes | Serves 4

1 (20-ounce / 567-g) package frozen cheese ravioli
1 teaspoon kosher salt
1¼ cups water
6 ounces (170 g) cooked ground beef
2½ cups Marinara sauce
¼ cup grated Parmesan cheese, for garnish

1. Place the ravioli in an even layer on a baking pan. Stir the salt into the water until dissolved and pour it over the ravioli.
2. Select Bake, Super Convection, set temperature to 450°F (235°C), and set time to 10 minutes. Press Start/Stop to begin preheating.
3. Once preheated, place the pan on the bake position.
4. While the ravioli is cooking, mix the ground beef into the marinara sauce in a medium bowl.
5. After 6 minutes, remove the pan from the oven. Blot off any remaining water, or drain the ravioli and return them to the pan. Pour the meat sauce over the ravioli. Return the pan to the oven and continue cooking.
6. When cooking is complete, remove the pan from the oven. The ravioli should be tender and sauce heated through. Gently stir the ingredients. Serve the ravioli with the Parmesan cheese, if desired.

Gold Cutlets with Aloha Salsa

Prep time: 20 minutes | Cook time: 7 minutes | Serves 4

2 eggs
2 tablespoons milk
¼ cup all-purpose flour
¼ cup panko bread crumbs
4 teaspoons sesame seeds
1 pound (454 g) boneless, thin pork cutlets (½-inch thick)
¼ cup cornstarch
Salt and ground lemon pepper, to taste
Cooking spray

Aloha Salsa:
1 cup fresh pineapple, chopped in small pieces
¼ cup red bell pepper, chopped
½ teaspoon ground cinnamon
1 teaspoon soy sauce
¼ cup red onion, finely chopped
⅛ teaspoon crushed red pepper
⅛ teaspoon ground black pepper

1. In a medium bowl, stir together all ingredients for salsa. Cover and refrigerate while cooking the pork.
2. Beat together eggs and milk in a large bowl. In another bowl, mix the flour, panko, and sesame seeds. Pour the cornstarch in a shallow dish.
3. Sprinkle pork cutlets with lemon pepper and salt. Dip pork cutlets in cornstarch, egg mixture, and then panko coating. Spritz both sides with cooking spray.
4. Select Air Fry, Super Convection. Set the temperature to 400ºF (205ºC) and set the time to 7 minutes. Press Start/Stop to begin preheating.
5. Once preheated, place the pan into the oven.
6. After 3 minutes, remove the pan from the oven. Flip the cutlets with tongs. Return the pan to the oven and continue cooking.
7. When cooking is complete, the pork should be crispy and golden brown on both sides.
8. Serve the fried cutlets with the Aloha salsa on the side.

Dijon Pork Tenderloin

Prep time: 15 minutes | Cook time: 15 minutes | Serves 4

3 tablespoons Dijon mustard
3 tablespoons honey
1 teaspoon dried rosemary
1 tablespoon olive oil
1 pound (454 g) pork tenderloin, rinsed and drained
Salt and freshly ground black pepper, to taste

1. In a small bowl, combine the Dijon mustard, honey, and rosemary. Stir to combine.
2. Rub the pork tenderloin with salt and pepper on all sides on a clean work surface.
3. Heat the olive oil in an oven-safe skillet over high heat. Sear the pork loin on all sides in the skillet for 6 minutes or until golden brown. Flip the pork halfway through.
4. Remove from the heat and spread honey-mustard mixture evenly to coat the pork loin. Transfer the pork to a sheet pan.
5. Select Bake, Super Convection, set temperature to 425ºF (220ºC) and set time to 15 minutes. Press Start/Stop to begin preheating.
6. Once preheated, place the pan on the bake position.
7. When cooking is complete, an instant-read thermometer inserted in the pork should register at least 145ºF (63ºC).
8. Remove from the oven and allow to rest for 3 minutes. Slice the pork into ½-inch slices and serve.

Citrus Pork Loin Roast

Prep time: 10 minutes | Cook time: 45 minutes | Serves 8

1 tablespoon lime juice
1 tablespoon orange marmalade
1 teaspoon coarse brown mustard
1 teaspoon curry powder
1 teaspoon dried lemongrass
2 pound (907 g) boneless pork loin roast
Salt and ground black pepper, to taste
Cooking spray

1. Preheat the air fryer oven to 360ºF (182ºC).
2. Mix the lime juice, marmalade, mustard, curry powder, and lemongrass.
3. Rub mixture all over the surface of the pork loin. Season with salt and pepper.
4. Spray the air fryer basket with cooking spray and place pork roast diagonally in the basket.
5. Place the air fryer basket onto the baking pan and slide into Rack Position 2, select Air Fry and set time to 45 minutes, or until the internal temperature reaches at least 145ºF (63ºC).
6. Wrap roast in foil and let rest for 10 minutes before slicing and serving.

Hearty Mushroom and Sausage Calzones

Prep time: 10 minutes | Cook time: 24 minutes | Serves 4

2 links Italian sausages (about ½ pound / 227 g)
1 pound (454 g) pizza dough, thawed
3 tablespoons olive oil, divided
¼ cup Marinara sauce
½ cup roasted mushrooms
1 cup shredded Mozzarella cheese

1. Place the sausages in a baking pan.
2. Select Roast, Super Convection, set temperature to 375°F (190°C), and set time to 12 minutes. Press Start/Stop to begin preheating.
3. Once preheated, place the pan on the roast position.
4. After 6 minutes, remove the pan from the oven and turn over the sausages. Return the pan to the oven and continue cooking.
5. While the sausages cook, divide the pizza dough into 4 equal pieces. One at a time, place a piece of dough onto a square of parchment paper 9 inches in diameter. Brush the dough on both sides with ¾ teaspoon of olive oil, then top the dough with another piece of parchment. Press the dough into a 7-inch circle. Remove the top piece of parchment and set aside. Repeat with the remaining pieces of dough.
6. When cooking is complete, remove the pan from the oven. Place the sausages on a cutting board. Let them cool for several minutes, then slice into ¼-inch rounds and cut each round into 4 pieces.
7. One at a time, spread a tablespoon of marinara sauce over half of a dough circle, leaving a ½-inch border at the edges. Cover with a quarter of the sausage pieces and add a quarter of the mushrooms. Sprinkle with ¼ cup of cheese. Pull the other side of the dough over the filling and pinch the edges together to seal. Transfer from the parchment to the baking pan. Repeat with the other rounds of dough, sauce, sausage, mushrooms, and cheese.
8. Brush the tops of the calzones with 1 tablespoon of olive oil.
9. Select Roast, Super Convection, set temperature to 450°F (235°C), and set time to 12 minutes. Press Start/Stop to begin preheating.
10. Once preheated, place the pan on the roast position.
11. After 6 minutes, remove the pan from the oven. The calzones should be golden brown. Turn over the calzones and brush the tops with the remaining olive oil. Return the pan to the oven and continue cooking.
12. When cooking is complete, the crust should be a deep golden brown on both sides. Remove the pan from the oven. The center should be molten; let cool for several minutes before serving.

Chapter 3 Poultry

Chicken Salad with Cucumber

Prep time: 10 minutes | Cook time: 12 minutes | Serves 4

1 pound (454 g) chicken breasts, boneless, skinless
1 red onion, thinly sliced
1 bell pepper, sliced
4 Kalamata olives, pitted and minced
1 small Greek cucumber, grated and squeezed
4 tablespoons Greek yogurt
4 tablespoons mayonnaise
1 tablespoon fresh lemon juice
Coarse sea salt and red pepper flakes, to taste

1. Start by preheating the air fryer to 380ºF (193ºC).
2. Pat the chicken dry with paper towels. Place the chicken breasts in a lightly oiled crisper tray.
3. Place the crisper tray in the corresponding position in the air fryer. Select Roast and cook the chicken for 12 minutes, turning them over halfway through the cooking time.
4. Chop the chicken breasts and transfer it to a salad bowl; add in the remaining ingredients and toss to combine well.
5. Serve chilled.

Spinach and Cheese Stuffed Chicken

Prep time: 10 minutes | Cook time: 20 minutes | Serves 4

1 pound (454 g) chicken breasts, skinless, boneless, and cut into pieces
2 tablespoons chopped olives
1 garlic clove, minced
2 cups spinach, torn into pieces
2 ounces (57 g) feta cheese
Sea salt and ground black pepper, to taste
2 tablespoons olive oil

1. Start by preheating the air fryer to 400ºF (205ºC).
2. Flatten the chicken breasts with a mallet.
3. Stuff each piece of chicken with olives, garlic, spinach, and cheese. Roll them up and secure with toothpicks.
4. Sprinkle the chicken with the salt, black pepper, and olive oil.
5. Place the stuffed chicken breasts in the crisper tray. Place the crisper tray in the corresponding position in the air fryer. Select Air Fry and cook the chicken for about 20 minutes, turning them over halfway through the cooking time.
6. Bon appétit!

Golden Breaded Chicken Nuggets

Prep time: 5 minutes | Cook time: 12 minutes | Serves 4

1 egg, whisked
¼ cup all-purpose flour
1 cup seasoned bread crumbs
1 tablespoon olive oil
Sea salt and ground black pepper, to taste
1½ pounds (680 g) chicken breasts, cut into small pieces

1. Start by preheating the air fryer to 380ºF (193ºC).
2. Mix the egg and flour in a shallow bowl. In a separate bowl, whisk the bread crumbs, olive oil, salt, and black pepper.
3. Dip the chicken breasts into the egg mixture. Then, roll the chicken breasts over the bread crumb mixture.
4. Arrange the chicken breasts in the crisper tray.
5. Place the crisper tray in the corresponding position in the air fryer. Select Air Fry and cook the chicken for 12 minutes, turning them over halfway through the cooking time.
6. Bon appétit!

Pomegranate-Glazed Chicken with Couscous Salad

Prep time: 15 minutes | Cook time: 20 minutes | Serves 4

3 tablespoons plus 2 teaspoons
    pomegranate molasses
½ teaspoon ground cinnamon
1 teaspoon minced fresh thyme
Salt and ground black pepper, to taste
2 (12-ounce / 340-g) bone-in split chicken
    breasts, trimmed
¼ cup chicken broth
¼ cup water
½ cup couscous
1 tablespoon minced fresh parsley
2 ounces (57 g) cherry tomatoes,
    quartered
1 scallion, white part minced, green part
    sliced thin on bias
1 tablespoon extra-virgin olive oil
1 ounce (28 g) feta cheese, crumbled
Cooking spray

1. Spritz the air fry basket with cooking spray.
2. Combine 3 tablespoons of pomegranate molasses, cinnamon, thyme, and ⅛ teaspoon of salt in a small bowl. Stir to mix well. Set aside.
3. Place the chicken breasts in the air fry basket, skin side down, and spritz with cooking spray. Sprinkle with salt and ground black pepper.
4. Select Air Fry, Set temperature to 350°F (180°C) and set time to 20 minutes. Press Start/Stop to begin preheating.
5. Once preheated, place the basket on the air fry position. Flip the chicken and brush with pomegranate molasses mixture halfway through.
6. Meanwhile, pour the broth and water in a pot and bring to a boil over medium-high heat. Add the couscous and sprinkle with salt. Cover and simmer for 7 minutes or until the liquid is almost absorbed.
7. Combine the remaining ingredients, except for the cheese, with cooked couscous in a large bowl. Toss to mix well. Scatter with the feta cheese.
8. When cooking is complete, remove the chicken from the oven and allow to cool for 10 minutes. Serve with vegetable and couscous salad.

Ginger Chicken Thighs

Prep time: 10 minutes | Cook time: 10 minutes | Serves 4

¼ cup julienned peeled fresh ginger
2 tablespoons vegetable oil
1 tablespoon honey
1 tablespoon soy sauce
1 tablespoon ketchup
1 teaspoon garam masala
1 teaspoon ground turmeric
¼ teaspoon kosher salt
½ teaspoon cayenne pepper
Vegetable oil spray
1 pound (454 g) boneless, skinless
    chicken thighs, cut crosswise into
    thirds
¼ cup chopped fresh cilantro, for garnish

1. In a small bowl, combine the ginger, oil, honey, soy sauce, ketchup, garam masala, turmeric, salt, and cayenne. Whisk until well combined. Place the chicken in a resealable plastic bag and pour the marinade over. Seal the bag and massage to cover all of the chicken with the marinade. Marinate at room temperature for 30 minutes or in the refrigerator for up to 24 hours.
2. Preheat the air fryer oven to 350°F (177°C).
3. Spray a baking pan with vegetable oil spray and add the chicken and as much of the marinade and julienned ginger as possible.
4. Slide the baking pan into Rack Position 1, select Convection Bake and set time to 10 minutes. Use a meat thermometer to ensure the chicken has reached an internal temperature of 165°F (74°C).
5. To serve, garnish with cilantro.

Bacon and Cheese Stuffed Chicken

Prep time: 5 minutes | Cook time: 20 minutes | Serves 4

1 pound (454 g) chicken breasts
4 tablespoons goat cheese
4 tablespoons bacon
1 tablespoon olive oil
½ teaspoon garlic powder
1 teaspoon dried basil
1 teaspoon dried oregano
1 teaspoon dried parsley flakes

1. Start by preheating the air fryer to 400°F (205°C).
2. Flatten the chicken breasts with a mallet.
3. Stuff each piece of chicken with cheese and bacon. Roll them up and secure with toothpicks.
4. Then, sprinkle the chicken with olive oil, garlic powder, basil, oregano, and parsley.
5. Place the stuffed chicken breasts in the crisper tray. Place the crisper tray in the corresponding position in the air fryer. Select Air Fry and cook the chicken for about 20 minutes, turning them over halfway through the cooking time.
6. Bon appétit!

Panko Chicken with Olives

Prep time: 10 minutes | Cook time: 12 minutes | Serves 4

1 pound (454 g) chicken fillets, boneless, skinless
2 eggs, whisked
1 teaspoon dried basil
½ teaspoon dried rosemary
½ teaspoon dried oregano
½ teaspoon crushed red pepper flakes
½ cup seasoned bread crumbs
2 ounces (57 g) Kalamata olives, pitted and sliced

1. Start by preheating the air fryer to 380°F (193°C).
2. Pat the chicken dry with paper towels.
3. In a shallow bowl, thoroughly combine the eggs and spices. Place the bread crumbs in a separate shallow bowl.
4. Dip the chicken fillets into the egg mixture. Then, roll the chicken fillets over the bread crumbs. Arrange the chicken fillets in the crisper tray.
5. Place the crisper tray in the corresponding position in the air fryer. Select Air Fry and cook the chicken fillets for 12 minutes, turning them over halfway through the cooking time.
6. Serve with Kalamata olives and enjoy!

Tempero Baiano Brazilian Chicken

Prep time: 5 minutes | Cook time: 25 minutes | Serves 4

1 teaspoon cumin seeds
1 teaspoon dried oregano
1 teaspoon dried parsley
1 teaspoon ground turmeric
½ teaspoon coriander seeds
1 teaspoon kosher salt
½ teaspoon black peppercorns
½ teaspoon cayenne pepper
¼ cup fresh lime juice
2 tablespoons olive oil
1½ pounds (680 g) chicken drumsticks

1. In a clean coffee grinder or spice mill, combine the cumin, oregano, parsley, turmeric, coriander seeds, salt, peppercorns, and cayenne. Process until finely ground.
2. In a small bowl, combine the ground spices with the lime juice and oil. Place the chicken in a resealable plastic bag. Add the marinade, seal, and massage until the chicken is well coated. Marinate at room temperature for 30 minutes or in the refrigerator for up to 24 hours.
3. Preheat the air fryer oven to 400°F (204°C).
4. Place the drumsticks skin-side up in the air fryer basket.
5. Place the air fryer basket onto the baking pan and slide into Rack Position 2, select Air Fry and set time to 25 minutes. Flip the drumsticks halfway through the cooking time. Use a meat thermometer to ensure that the chicken has reached an internal temperature of 165°F (74°C). Serve immediately.

Israeli Chicken Schnitzel

Prep time: 5 minutes | Cook time: 10 minutes | Serves 4

2 large boneless, skinless chicken breasts, each weighing about 1 pound (454 g)
1 cup all-purpose flour
2 teaspoons garlic powder
2 teaspoons kosher salt
1 teaspoon black pepper
1 teaspoon paprika
2 eggs beaten with 2 tablespoons water
2 cups panko bread crumbs
Vegetable oil spray
Lemon juice, for serving

1. Preheat the air fryer oven to 375°F (191°C).
2. Place 1 chicken breast between 2 pieces of plastic wrap. Use a mallet or a rolling pin to pound the chicken until it is ¼ inch thick. Set aside. Repeat with the second breast. Whisk together the flour, garlic powder, salt, pepper, and paprika on a large plate. Place the panko in a separate shallow bowl or pie plate.
3. Dredge 1 chicken breast in the flour, shaking off any excess, then dip it in the egg mixture. Dredge the chicken breast in the panko, making sure to coat it completely. Shake off any excess panko. Place the battered chicken breast on a plate. Repeat with the second chicken breast.
4. Spray the air fryer basket with oil spray. Put the battered chicken breasts in the basket and spray the top with oil spray.
5. Place the air fryer basket onto the baking pan and slide into Rack Position 2, select Air Fry and set time to 5 minutes.
6. Flip the chicken and spray with oil spray. Air fry until the second side is browned and crispy and the internal temperature reaches 165°F (74°C).
7. Serve hot with lemon juice.

Buttery Turkey Breasts

Prep time: 5 minutes | Cook time: 1 hour | Serves 5

2 pounds (907 g) turkey breasts, rib bones trimmed
4 tablespoons butter, melted
1 teaspoon Sriracha sauce
1 tablespoon chopped fresh cilantro
1 tablespoon chopped fresh parsley
1 tablespoon chopped fresh thyme
Kosher salt and freshly ground black pepper, to taste

1. Start by preheating the air fryer to 350ºF (180ºC).
2. Pat the turkey breasts dry with paper towels. Toss the turkey breasts with the remaining ingredients. Place the turkey breasts in the crisper tray.
3. Place the crisper tray in the corresponding position in the air fryer. Select Roast and cook the turkey breasts for 1 hour, turning them over every 20 minutes.
4. Bon appétit!

Honey Rosemary Chicken

Prep time: 10 minutes | Cook time: 20 minutes | Serves 4

¼ cup balsamic vinegar
¼ cup honey
2 tablespoons olive oil
1 tablespoon dried rosemary leaves
1 teaspoon salt
½ teaspoon freshly ground black pepper
2 whole boneless, skinless chicken breasts
    (about 1 pound / 454 g each), halved
Cooking spray

1. In a large resealable bag, combine the vinegar, honey, olive oil, rosemary, salt, and pepper. Add the chicken pieces, seal the bag, and refrigerate to marinate for at least 2 hours.
2. Preheat the air fryer oven to 325ºF (163ºC). Line a baking pan with parchment paper.
3. Remove the chicken from the marinade and place it on the parchment. Spritz with cooking spray.
4. Slide the baking pan into Rack Position 1, select Convection Bake and set time to 20 minutes, flipping the chicken and spraying it with cooking spray halfway through, or until the internal temperature reaches 165ºF (74ºC) and the chicken is no longer pink inside.
5. Let sit for 5 minutes before serving.

Duck with Miso Paste

Prep time: 5 minutes | Cook time: 30 minutes | Serves 5

2 pounds (907 g) duck breasts
1 tablespoon butter, melted
2 tablespoons pomegranate molasses
2 tablespoons miso paste
1 teaspoon minced garlic
1 teaspoon peeled and minced ginger
1 teaspoon five-spice powder

1. Start by preheating the air fryer to 330ºF (166ºC).
2. Pat the duck breasts dry with paper towels. Toss the duck breasts with the remaining ingredients. Place the duck breasts in the baking pan.
3. Place the baking pan in the corresponding position in the air fryer. Select Bake and cook the duck breasts for 15 minutes, turning them over halfway through the cooking time.
4. Increase the temperature to 350ºF (180ºC) and continue to cook for about 15 minutes or until cooked through.
5. Let it rest for 10 minutes before carving and serving. Bon appétit!

Chicken Fillets with Cheese

Prep time: 5 minutes | Cook time: 12 minutes | Serves 4

1½ pounds (680 g) chicken fillets
2 tablespoons olive oil
1 teaspoon smoked paprika
1 teaspoon Italian seasoning mix
Sea salt and ground black pepper, to taste
½ cup grated Pecorino Romano cheese

1. Start by preheating the air fryer to 380ºF (193ºC).
2. Pat the chicken fillets dry with paper towels. Toss the chicken fillets with the olive oil and spices. Place the chicken fillets in the crisper tray.
3. Place the crisper tray in the corresponding position in the air fryer. Select Air Fry and cook the chicken fillets for 12 minutes, turning them over halfway through the cooking time.
4. Top the chicken fillets with grated cheese and serve warm. Bon appétit!

Baked Turkey Cheese Taquitos

Prep time: 5 minutes | Cook time: 24 minutes | Serves 6

1 pound (454 g) turkey breasts, boneless and skinless
Kosher salt and freshly ground black pepper, to taste
1 clove garlic, minced
1 habanero pepper, minced
4 ounces (113 g) Mexican cheese blend, shredded
6 small corn tortillas
½ cup salsa

1. Start by preheating the air fryer to 380°F (193°C).
2. Pat the turkey breasts dry with kitchen towels. Toss the turkey breasts with the salt and black pepper. Arrange the turkey breasts in the crisper tray.
3. Place the crisper tray in the corresponding position in the air fryer. Select Air Fry and cook the turkey breasts for 18 minutes, turning them over halfway through the cooking time.
4. Place the shredded chicken, garlic, habanero pepper, and cheese on one end of each tortilla. Roll them up tightly and transfer them to a lightly oiled baking pan.
5. Reduce the temperature to 360°F (182°C). Place the baking pan in the corresponding position in the air fryer. Select Bake and cook the taquitos for 6 minutes. Serve the taquitos with salsa and enjoy!

Chicken Cheese Tortilla

Prep time: 8 minutes | Cook time: 12 minutes | Serves 4

1 egg, whisked
½ cup grated Parmesan cheese
½ cup crushed tortilla chips
½ teaspoon onion powder
½ teaspoon garlic powder
1 teaspoon red chili powder
1½ pounds (680 g) chicken breasts, boneless, skinless, cut into strips

1. Start by preheating the air fryer to 380°F (193°C).
2. Whisk the egg in a shallow bowl. In a separate bowl, whisk the Parmesan cheese, tortilla chips, onion powder, garlic powder, and red chili powder.
3. Dip the chicken pieces into the egg mixture. Then, roll the chicken pieces over the bread crumb mixture. Place the chicken in the crisper tray.
4. Place the crisper tray in the corresponding position in the air fryer. Select Air Fry and cook the chicken for 12 minutes, turning them over halfway through the cooking time.
5. Bon appétit!

Tandoori Drumsticks

Prep time: 10 minutes | Cook time: 14 minutes | Serves 4

8 (4- to 5-ounce / 113- to 142-g) skinless bone-in chicken drumsticks
½ cup plain full-fat or low-fat yogurt
¼ cup buttermilk
2 teaspoons minced garlic
2 teaspoons minced fresh ginger
2 teaspoons ground cinnamon
2 teaspoons ground coriander
2 teaspoons mild paprika
1 teaspoon salt
1 teaspoon Tabasco hot red pepper sauce

1. In a large bowl, stir together all the ingredients except for chicken drumsticks until well combined. Add the chicken drumsticks to the bowl and toss until well coated. Cover in plastic and set in the refrigerator to marinate for 1 hour, tossing once.
2. Arrange the marinated drumsticks in the air fry basket, leaving enough space between them.
3. Select Air Fry, Super Convection. Set temperature to 375°F (190°C) and set time to 14 minutes. Press Start/Stop to begin preheating.
4. Once preheated, place the basket on the air fry position. Flip the drumsticks once halfway through to ensure even cooking.
5. When cooking is complete, the internal temperature of the chicken drumsticks should reach 160°F (71°C) on a meat thermometer.
6. Transfer the drumsticks to plates. Rest for 5 minutes before serving.

Tangy Chicken Breast with Cilantro

Prep time: 10 minutes | Cook time: 10 minutes | Serves 4

4 (4-ounce / 113-g) boneless, skinless chicken breasts
½ cup chopped fresh cilantro
Juice of 1 lime
Chicken seasoning or rub, to taste
Salt and ground black pepper, to taste
Cooking spray

1. Put the chicken breasts in the large bowl, then add the cilantro, lime juice, chicken seasoning, salt, and black pepper. Toss to coat well.
2. Wrap the bowl in plastic and refrigerate to marinate for at least 30 minutes.
3. Spritz the air fry basket with cooking spray.
4. Remove the marinated chicken breasts from the bowl and place in the air fry basket. Spritz with cooking spray.
5. Select Air Fry, Super Convection. Set temperature to 400ºF (205ºC) and set time to 10 minutes. Press Start/Stop to begin preheating.
6. Once preheated, place the basket on the air fry position. Flip the breasts halfway through.
7. When cooking is complete, the internal temperature of the chicken should reach at least 165ºF (74ºC).
8. Serve immediately.

Chicken Goulash

Prep time: 5 minutes | Cook time: 17 minutes | Serves 2

2 red bell peppers, chopped
1 pound (454 g) ground chicken
2 medium tomatoes, diced
½ cup chicken broth
Salt and ground black pepper, to taste
Cooking spray

1. Spritz a baking pan with cooking spray.
2. Set the bell pepper in the baking pan.
3. Select Broil, Super Convection, set temperature to 365ºF (185ºC) and set time to 5 minutes. Press Start/Stop to begin preheating.
4. Once preheated, place the pan on the broil position. Stir the bell pepper halfway through.
5. When broiling is complete, the bell pepper should be tender.
6. Add the ground chicken and diced tomatoes in the baking pan and stir to mix well.
7. Set the time of oven to 12 minutes. Press Start/Stop. Stir the mixture and mix in the chicken broth, salt and ground black pepper halfway through.
8. When cooking is complete, the chicken should be well browned.
9. Serve immediately.

Air Fried Naked Chicken Tenders

Prep time: 5 minutes | Cook time: 7 minutes | Serves 4

Seasoning:
1 teaspoon kosher salt
½ teaspoon garlic powder
½ teaspoon onion powder
½ teaspoon chili powder
¼ teaspoon sweet paprika
¼ teaspoon freshly ground black pepper
Chicken:
8 chicken breast tenders (1 pound / 454 g total)
2 tablespoons mayonnaise

1. Preheat the air fryer oven to 375ºF (191ºC).
2. For the seasoning: In a small bowl, combine the salt, garlic powder, onion powder, chili powder, paprika, and pepper.
3. For the chicken: Place the chicken in a medium bowl and add the mayonnaise. Mix well to coat all over, then sprinkle with the seasoning mix.
4. Arrange a single layer of the chicken in the air fryer basket.
5. Place the air fryer basket onto the baking pan and slide into Rack Position 2, select Air Fry and set time to 7 minutes. Flip the chicken halfway through the cooking time, or until cooked through in the center.
6. Serve immediately.

Blackened Chicken Breasts

Prep time: 10 minutes | Cook time: 20 minutes | Serves 4

1 large egg, beaten
¾ cup Blackened seasoning
2 whole boneless, skinless chicken breasts (about 1 pound / 454 g each), halved
Cooking spray

1. Preheat the air fryer oven to 360°F (182°C). Line the air fryer basket with parchment paper.
2. Place the beaten egg in one shallow bowl and the Blackened seasoning in another shallow bowl.
3. One at a time, dip the chicken pieces in the beaten egg and the Blackened seasoning, coating thoroughly.
4. Place the chicken pieces on the parchment and spritz with cooking spray.
5. Place the air fryer basket onto the baking pan and slide into Rack Position 2, select Air Fry and set time to 20 minutes. Flip the chicken and spritz it with cooking spray halfway through, or until the internal temperature reaches 165°F (74°C) and the chicken is no longer pink inside.
6. Let sit for 5 minutes before serving.

Japanese Skewered Chicken (Yakitori)

Prep time: 10 minutes | Cook time: 15 minutes | Serves 4

½ cup mirin
¼ cup dry white wine
½ cup soy sauce
1 tablespoon light brown sugar
1½ pounds (680 g) boneless, skinless chicken thighs, cut into 1½-inch pieces, fat trimmed
4 medium scallions, trimmed, cut into 1½-inch pieces
Cooking spray

Special Equipment:
4 (4-inch) bamboo skewers, soaked in water for at least 30 minutes

1. Combine the mirin, dry white wine, soy sauce, and brown sugar in a saucepan. Bring to a boil over medium heat. Keep stirring.
2. Boil for another 2 minutes or until it has a thick consistency. Turn off the heat.
3. Spritz the air fry basket with cooking spray.
4. Run the bamboo skewers through the chicken pieces and scallions alternatively.
5. Arrange the skewers in the air fry basket, then brush with mirin mixture on both sides. Spritz with cooking spray.
6. Select Air Fry, Super Convection. Set temperature to 400°F (205°C) and set time to 10 minutes. Press Start/Stop to begin preheating.
7. Once preheated, place the basket on the air fry position. Flip the skewers halfway through.
8. When cooking is complete, the chicken and scallions should be glossy.
9. Serve immediately.

Baked Garlicky Whole Chicken

Prep time: 10 minutes | Cook time: 1 hour | Serves 2 to 4

½ cup melted butter
3 tablespoons garlic, minced
Salt, to taste
1 teaspoon ground black pepper
1 (1-pound / 454-g) whole chicken

1. Combine the butter with garlic, salt, and ground black pepper in a small bowl.
2. Brush the butter mixture over the whole chicken, then place the chicken in the air fry basket, skin side down.
3. Select Bake, Super Convection, set temperature to 350°F (180°C) and set time to 60 minutes. Press Start/Stop to begin preheating.
4. Once preheated, place the basket on the bake position. Flip the chicken halfway through.
5. When cooking is complete, an instant-read thermometer inserted in the thickest part of the chicken should register at least 165°F (74°C).
6. Remove the chicken from the oven and allow to cool for 15 minutes before serving.

Air-Fried Chicken Wings

Prep time: 10 minutes | Cook time: 15 minutes | Serves 4

1 tablespoon olive oil
8 whole chicken wings
Chicken seasoning or rub, to taste
1 teaspoon garlic powder
Freshly ground black pepper, to taste

1. Grease the air fry basket with olive oil.
2. On a clean work surface, rub the chicken wings with chicken seasoning and rub, garlic powder, and ground black pepper.
3. Arrange the well-coated chicken wings in the air fry basket.
4. Select Air Fry, Super Convection. Set temperature to 400°F (205°C) and set time to 15 minutes. Press Start/Stop to begin preheating.
5. Once preheated, place the basket on the air fry position. Flip the chicken wings halfway through.
6. When cooking is complete, the internal temperature of the chicken wings should reach at least 165°F (74°C).
7. Remove the chicken wings from the oven. Serve immediately.

Spanish Chicken and Sweet Pepper

Prep time: 10 minutes | Cook time: 20 minutes | Serves 2

1¼ pounds (567 g) assorted small chicken parts, breasts cut into halves
¼ teaspoon salt
¼ teaspoon ground black pepper
2 teaspoons olive oil
½ pound (227 g) mini sweet peppers
¼ cup light mayonnaise
¼ teaspoon smoked paprika
½ clove garlic, crushed
Baguette, for serving
Cooking spray

1. Spritz the air fry basket with cooking spray.
2. Toss the chicken with salt, ground black pepper, and olive oil in a large bowl.
3. Arrange the sweet peppers and chicken in the air fry basket.
4. Select Air Fry, Super Convection. Set temperature to 375°F (190°C) and set time to 20 minutes. Press Start/Stop to begin preheating.
5. Once preheated, place the basket on the air fry position. Flip the chicken and transfer the peppers on a plate halfway through.
6. When cooking is complete, the chicken should be well browned.
7. Meanwhile, combine the mayo, paprika, and garlic in a small bowl. Stir to mix well.
8. Assemble the baguette with chicken and sweet pepper, then spread with mayo mixture and serve.

Dill Chicken Strips

Prep time: 15 minutes | Cook time: 10 minutes | Serves 4

2 whole boneless, skinless chicken breasts, halved lengthwise
1 cup Italian dressing
3 cups finely crushed potato chips
1 tablespoon dried dill weed
1 tablespoon garlic powder
1 large egg, beaten
Cooking spray

1. In a large resealable bag, combine the chicken and Italian dressing. Seal the bag and refrigerate to marinate at least 1 hour.
2. In a shallow dish, stir together the potato chips, dill, and garlic powder. Place the beaten egg in a second shallow dish.
3. Remove the chicken from the marinade. Roll the chicken pieces in the egg and the potato chip mixture, coating thoroughly.
4. Preheat the air fryer oven to 325°F (163°C). Line the air fryer basket with parchment paper.
5. Place the coated chicken on the parchment and spritz with cooking spray.
6. Place the air fryer basket onto the baking pan and slide into Rack Position 2, select Air Fry and set time to 10 minutes, flipping the chicken and spritzing it with cooking spray halfway through, or until the outsides are crispy and the insides are no longer pink. Serve immediately.

Sweet-Sour Chicken Nuggets

Prep time: 10 minutes | Cook time: 15 minutes | Serves 4

1 cup cornstarch
Chicken seasoning or rub, to taste
Salt and ground black pepper, to taste
2 eggs
2 (4-ounce/ 113-g) boneless, skinless chicken breasts, cut into 1-inch pieces
1½ cups sweet-and-sour sauce
Cooking spray

1. Spritz the air fry basket with cooking spray.
2. Combine the cornstarch, chicken seasoning, salt, and pepper in a large bowl. Stir to mix well. Whisk the eggs in a separate bowl.
3. Dredge the chicken pieces in the bowl of cornstarch mixture first, then in the bowl of whisked eggs, and then in the cornstarch mixture again.
4. Arrange the well-coated chicken pieces in the air fry basket. Spritz with cooking spray.
5. Select Air Fry, Super Convection. Set temperature to 360ºF (182ºC) and set time to 15 minutes. Press Start/Stop to begin preheating.
6. Once preheated, place the basket on the air fry position. Flip the chicken halfway through.
7. When cooking is complete, the chicken should be golden brown and crispy.
8. Transfer the chicken pieces on a large serving plate, then baste with sweet-and-sour sauce before serving.

Teriyaki Chicken with Lemony Snow Peas

Prep time: 20 minutes | Cook time: 34 minutes | Serves 4

¼ cup chicken broth
½ teaspoon grated fresh ginger
⅛ teaspoon red pepper flakes
1½ tablespoons soy sauce
4 (5-ounce / 142-g) bone-in chicken thighs, trimmed
1 tablespoon mirin
½ teaspoon cornstarch
1 tablespoon sugar
6 ounces (170 g) snow peas, strings removed
⅛ teaspoon lemon zest
1 garlic clove, minced
¼ teaspoon salt
Ground black pepper, to taste
½ teaspoon lemon juice

1. Combine the broth, ginger, pepper flakes, and soy sauce in a large bowl. Stir to mix well.
2. Pierce 10 to 15 holes into the chicken skin. Put the chicken in the broth mixture and toss to coat well. Let sit for 10 minutes to marinate.
3. Transfer the marinated chicken on a plate and pat dry with paper towels.
4. Scoop 2 tablespoons of marinade in a microwave-safe bowl and combine with mirin, cornstarch and sugar. Stir to mix well. Microwave for 1 minute or until frothy and has a thick consistency. Set aside.
5. Arrange the chicken in the air fry basket, skin side up.
6. Select Air Fry, Super Convection. Set temperature to 400ºF (205ºC) and set time to 25 minutes. Press Start/Stop to begin preheating.
7. Once preheated, place the basket on the air fry position. Flip the chicken halfway through.
8. When cooking is complete, brush the chicken skin with marinade mixture. Air fry the chicken for 5 more minutes or until glazed.
9. Remove the chicken from the oven. Allow the chicken to cool for 10 minutes.
10. Meanwhile, combine the snow peas, lemon zest, garlic, salt, and ground black pepper in a small bowl. Toss to coat well.
11. Transfer the snow peas in the air fry basket.
12. Select Air Fry, Super Convection. Set temperature to 400ºF (205ºC) and set time to 3 minutes. Place the basket on the air fry position.
13. When cooking is complete, the peas should be soft.
14. Remove the peas from the oven and toss with lemon juice.
15. Serve the chicken with lemony snow peas.

Chinese Spiced Turkey Thighs

Prep time: 10 minutes | Cook time: 25 minutes | Serves 6

2 pounds (907 g) turkey thighs
1 teaspoon Chinese five-spice powder
¼ teaspoon Sichuan pepper
1 teaspoon pink Himalayan salt
1 tablespoon Chinese rice vinegar
1 tablespoon mustard
1 tablespoon chili sauce
2 tablespoons soy sauce
Cooking spray

1. Spritz the air fry basket with cooking spray.
2. Rub the turkey thighs with five-spice powder, Sichuan pepper, and salt on a clean work surface.
3. Put the turkey thighs in the air fry basket and spritz with cooking spray.
4. Select Air Fry, Super Convection. Set temperature to 360ºF (182ºC) and set time to 22 minutes. Press Start/Stop to begin preheating.
5. Once preheated, place the basket on the air fry position. Flip the thighs at least three times during the cooking.
6. When cooking is complete, the thighs should be well browned.
7. Meanwhile, heat the remaining ingredients in a saucepan over medium-high heat. Cook for 3 minutes or until the sauce is thickened and reduces to two thirds.
8. Transfer the thighs onto a plate and baste with sauce before serving.

Herby Turkey with Dijon Sauce

Prep time: 10 minutes | Cook time: 30 minutes | Serves 4

1 teaspoon chopped fresh sage
1 teaspoon chopped fresh tarragon
1 teaspoon chopped fresh thyme leaves
1 teaspoon chopped fresh rosemary leaves
1½ teaspoons sea salt
1 teaspoon ground black pepper
1 (2-pound / 907-g) turkey breast
3 tablespoons Dijon mustard
3 tablespoons butter, melted
Cooking spray

1. Spritz the air fry basket with cooking spray.
2. Combine the herbs, salt, and black pepper in a small bowl. Stir to mix well. Set aside.
3. Combine the Dijon mustard and butter in a separate bowl. Stir to mix well.
4. Rub the turkey with the herb mixture on a clean work surface, then brush the turkey with Dijon mixture.
5. Arrange the turkey in the air fry basket.
6. Select Air Fry, Super Convection. Set temperature to 390ºF (199ºC) and set time to 30 minutes. Press Start/Stop to begin preheating.
7. Once preheated, place the basket on the air fry position. Flip the turkey breast halfway through.
8. When cooking is complete, an instant-read thermometer inserted in the thickest part of the turkey breast should reach at least 165ºF (74ºC).
9. Transfer the cooked turkey breast on a large plate and slice to serve.

Lettuce Turkey and Mushroom Taco

Prep time: 20 minutes | Cook time: 15 minutes | Serves 6

Sauce:
2 tablespoons tamari
2 tablespoons tomato sauce
1 tablespoon lime juice
¼ teaspoon peeled and grated fresh ginger
1 clove garlic, smashed to a paste
½ cup chicken broth
⅓ cup sugar
2 tablespoons toasted sesame oil
Cooking spray

Meatballs:
2 pounds (907 g) ground turkey
¾ cup finely chopped button mushrooms
2 large eggs, beaten
1½ teaspoons tamari
¼ cup finely chopped green onions, plus more for garnish
2 teaspoons peeled and grated fresh ginger
1 clove garlic, smashed
2 teaspoons toasted sesame oil
2 tablespoons sugar
For Serving:
Lettuce leaves, for serving
Sliced red chiles, for garnish (optional)
Toasted sesame seeds, for garnish (optional)

1. Spritz the air fry basket with cooking spray.
2. Combine the ingredients for the sauce in a small bowl. Stir to mix well. Set aside.
3. Combine the ingredients for the meatballs in a large bowl. Stir to mix well, then shape the mixture in twelve 1½-inch meatballs.
4. Arrange the meatballs in the air fry basket, then baste with the sauce.
5. Select Air Fry, Super Convection. Set temperature to 350ºF (180ºC) and set time to 15 minutes. Press Start/Stop to begin preheating.
6. Once preheated, place the basket on the air fry position. Flip the balls halfway through.
7. When cooking is complete, the meatballs should be golden brown.
8. Unfold the lettuce leaves on a large serving plate, then transfer the cooked meatballs on the leaves. Spread the red chiles and sesame seeds over the balls, then serve.

Maple-Mustard Turkey Breast

Prep time: 15 minutes | Cook time: 30 minutes | Serves 6

½ teaspoon dried rosemary
2 minced garlic cloves
2 teaspoons salt
1 teaspoon ground black pepper
¼ cup olive oil
2½ pounds (1.1 kg) turkey breast
¼ cup pure maple syrup
1 tablespoon stone-ground brown mustard
1 tablespoon melted vegan butter

1. Combine the rosemary, garlic, salt, ground black pepper, and olive oil in a large bowl. Stir to mix well.
2. Dunk the turkey breast in the mixture and wrap the bowl in plastic. Refrigerate for 2 hours to marinate.
3. Remove the bowl from the refrigerator and let sit for half an hour before cooking.
4. Spritz the air fry basket with cooking spray.
5. Remove the turkey from the marinade and place in the air fry basket.
6. Select Air Fry, Super Convection. Set temperature to 400ºF (205ºC) and set time to 20 minutes. Press Start/Stop to begin preheating.
7. Once preheated, place the basket on the air fry position. Flip the breast halfway through.
8. When cooking is complete, the breast should be well browned.
9. Meanwhile, combine the remaining ingredients in a small bowl. Stir to mix well.
10. Pour half of the butter mixture over the turkey breast in the oven and air fry for 10 more minutes. Flip the breast and pour the remaining half of butter mixture over halfway through.
11. Transfer the turkey on a plate and slice to serve.

Cherry Sauce-Glazed Duck

Prep time: 10 minutes | Cook time: 32 minutes | Serves 12

1 whole duck (about 5 pounds / 2.3 kg in total), split in half, back and rib bones removed, fat trimmed
1 teaspoon olive oil
Salt and freshly ground black pepper, to taste
Cherry Sauce:
1 tablespoon butter
1 shallot, minced
½ cup sherry
1 cup chicken stock
1 teaspoon white wine vinegar
¾ cup cherry preserves
1 teaspoon fresh thyme leaves
Salt and freshly ground black pepper, to taste

1. On a clean work surface, rub the duck with olive oil, then sprinkle with salt and ground black pepper to season.
2. Place the duck in the air fry basket, breast side up.
3. Select Air Fry, Super Convection. Set temperature to 400ºF (205ºC) and set time to 25 minutes. Press Start/Stop to begin preheating.
4. Once preheated, place the basket on the air fry position. Flip the ducks halfway through the cooking time.
5. Meanwhile, make the cherry sauce: Heat the butter in a skillet over medium-high heat or until melted.
6. Add the shallot and sauté for 5 minutes or until lightly browned.
7. Add the sherry and simmer for 6 minutes or until it reduces in half.
8. Add the chicken stick, white wine vinegar, and cherry preserves. Stir to combine well. Simmer for 6 more minutes or until thickened.
9. Fold in the thyme leaves and sprinkle with salt and ground black pepper. Stir to mix well.
10. When the cooking of the duck is complete, glaze the duck with a quarter of the cherry sauce, then air fry for another 4 minutes.
11. Flip the duck and glaze with another quarter of the cherry sauce. Air fry for an additional 3 minutes.
12. Transfer the duck on a large plate and serve with remaining cherry sauce.

Roasted Chicken and Sausage with Peppers

Prep time: 10 minutes | Cook time: 27 minutes | Serves 4

4 bone-in, skin-on chicken thighs (about 1½ pounds / 680 g)
1½ teaspoon kosher salt, divided
1 link sweet Italian sausage (about 4 ounces / 113 g), whole
8 ounces (227 g) miniature bell peppers, halved and deseeded
1 small onion, thinly sliced
2 garlic cloves, minced
1 tablespoon olive oil
4 hot pickled cherry peppers, deseeded and quartered, along with 2 tablespoons pickling liquid from the jar
¼ cup chicken stock
Cooking spray

1. Salt the chicken thighs on both sides with 1 teaspoon of kosher salt. Spritz a baking pan with cooking spray and place the thighs skin-side down on the pan. Add the sausage.
2. Select Roast, Super Convection, set temperature to 375ºF (190ºC), and set time to 27 minutes. Press Start/Stop to begin preheating.
3. Once preheated, place the pan on the roast position.
4. While the chicken and sausage cook, place the bell peppers, onion, and garlic in a large bowl. Sprinkle with the remaining kosher salt and add the olive oil. Toss to coat.
5. After 10 minutes, remove the pan from the oven and flip the chicken thighs and sausage. Add the pepper mixture to the pan. Return the pan to the oven and continue cooking.
6. After another 10 minutes, remove the pan from the oven and add the pickled peppers, pickling liquid, and stock. Stir the pickled peppers into the peppers and onion. Return the pan to the oven and continue cooking.
7. When cooking is complete, the peppers and onion should be soft and the chicken should read 165ºF (74ºC) on a meat thermometer. Remove the pan from the oven. Slice the sausage into thin pieces and stir it into the pepper mixture. Spoon the peppers over four plates. Top with a chicken thigh.

Strawberry Puréed-Glazed Turkey Breast

Prep time: 5 minutes | Cook time: 37 minutes | Serves 2

2 pounds (907 g) turkey breast
1 tablespoon olive oil
Salt and ground black pepper, to taste
1 cup fresh strawberries

1. Rub the turkey bread with olive oil on a clean work surface, then sprinkle with salt and ground black pepper.
2. Transfer the turkey in the air fry basket and spritz with cooking spray.
3. Select Air Fry, Super Convection. Set temperature to 375ºF (190ºC) and set time to 30 minutes. Press Start/Stop to begin preheating.
4. Once preheated, place the basket on the air fry position. Flip the turkey breast halfway through.
5. Meanwhile, put the strawberries in a food processor and pulse until smooth.
6. When cooking is complete, spread the puréed strawberries over the turkey and fry for 7 more minutes.
7. Serve immediately.

Coconut Chicken Meatballs

Prep time: 10 minutes | Cook time: 14 minutes | Serves 4

1 pound (454 g) ground chicken
2 scallions, finely chopped
1 cup chopped fresh cilantro leaves
¼ cup unsweetened shredded coconut
1 tablespoon hoisin sauce
1 tablespoon soy sauce
2 teaspoons sriracha or other hot sauce
1 teaspoon toasted sesame oil
½ teaspoon kosher salt
1 teaspoon black pepper

1. Preheat the air fryer oven to 350ºF (177ºC).
2. In a large bowl, gently mix the chicken, scallions, cilantro, coconut, hoisin, soy sauce, sriracha, sesame oil, salt, and pepper until thoroughly combined (the mixture will be wet and sticky).
3. Place a sheet of parchment paper in the air fryer basket. Using a small scoop or teaspoon, drop rounds of the mixture in a single layer onto the parchment paper.
4. Place the air fryer basket onto the baking pan and slide into Rack Position 2, select Air Fry and set time to 10 minutes, flipping the meatballs halfway through the cooking time.
5. Increase the temperature to 400ºF (204ºC) and air fry for 4 minutes more to brown the outsides of the meatballs. Use a meat thermometer to ensure the meatballs have reached an internal temperature of 165ºF (74ºC).
6. Transfer the meatballs to a serving platter. Repeat with any remaining chicken mixture. Serve warm.

Air-Fried Duck Leg

Prep time: 5 minutes | Cook time: 45 minutes | Serves 4

4 (½-pound / 227-g) skin-on duck leg quarters
2 medium garlic cloves, minced
½ teaspoon salt
½ teaspoon ground black pepper

1. Spritz the air fry basket with cooking spray.
2. On a clean work surface, rub the duck leg quarters with garlic, salt, and black pepper.
3. Arrange the leg quarters in the air fry basket and spritz with cooking spray.
4. Select Air Fry, Super Convection. Set temperature to 300°F (150°C) and set time to 30 minutes. Press Start/Stop to begin preheating.
5. Once preheated, place the basket on the air fry position.
6. After 30 minutes, remove the basket from the oven. Flip the leg quarters. Increase temperature to 375°F (190°C) and set time to 15 minutes. Return the basket to the oven and continue cooking.
7. When cooking is complete, the leg quarters should be well browned and crispy.
8. Remove the duck leg quarters from the oven and allow to cool for 10 minutes before serving.

Orange-Balsamic Glazed Duck Breasts

Prep time: 5 minutes | Cook time: 13 minutes | Serves 4

4 (6-ounce / 170-g) skin-on duck breasts
1 teaspoon salt
¼ cup orange marmalade
1 tablespoon white balsamic vinegar
¾ teaspoon ground black pepper

1. Cut 10 slits into the skin of the duck breasts, then sprinkle with salt on both sides.
2. Place the breasts in the air fry basket, skin side up.
3. Select Air Fry, Super Convection. Set temperature to 400°F (205°C) and set time to 10 minutes. Press Start/Stop to begin preheating.
4. Once preheated, place the basket on the air fry position.
5. Meanwhile, combine the remaining ingredients in a small bowl. Stir to mix well.
6. When cooking is complete, brush the duck skin with the marmalade mixture. Flip the breast and air fry for 3 more minutes or until the skin is crispy and the breast is well browned.
7. Serve immediately.

Fried Thai Hens with Vegetable Salad

Prep time: 15 minutes | Cook time: 25 minutes | Serves 6

2 (1¼-pound / 567-g) Cornish game hens, giblets discarded
1 tablespoon fish sauce
6 tablespoons chopped fresh cilantro
2 teaspoons lime zest
1 teaspoon ground coriander
2 garlic cloves, minced
2 tablespoons packed light brown sugar
2 teaspoons vegetable oil
Salt and ground black pepper, to taste
1 English cucumber, halved lengthwise and sliced thin
1 Thai chile, stemmed, deseeded, and minced
2 tablespoons chopped dry-roasted peanuts
1 small shallot, sliced thinly
1 tablespoon lime juice
Lime wedges, for serving
Cooking spray

1. Arrange a game hen on a clean work surface, remove the backbone with kitchen shears, then pound the hen breast to flat. Cut the breast in half. Repeat with the remaining game hen.
2. Loose the breast and thigh skin with your fingers, then pat the game hens dry and pierce about 10 holes into the fat deposits of the hens. Tuck the wings under the hens.
3. Combine 2 teaspoons of fish sauce, ¼ cup of cilantro, lime zest, coriander, garlic, 4 teaspoons of sugar, 1 teaspoon of vegetable oil, ½ teaspoon of salt, and ⅛ teaspoon of ground black pepper in a small bowl. Stir to mix well.
4. Rub the fish sauce mixture under the breast and thigh skin of the game hens, then let sit for 10 minutes to marinate.
5. Spritz the air fry basket with cooking spray.
6. Arrange the marinated game hens in the basket, skin side down.
7. Select Air Fry, Super Convection. Set temperature to 400°F (205°C) and set time to 25 minutes. Press Start/Stop to begin preheating.
8. Once preheated, place the basket on the air fry position. Flip the game hens halfway through the cooking time.
9. When cooking is complete, the hen skin should be golden brown and the internal temperature of the hens should read at least 165°F (74°C).
10. Meanwhile, combine all the remaining ingredients, except for the lime wedges, in a large bowl and sprinkle with salt and black pepper. Toss to mix well.
11. Transfer the fried hens on a large plate, then sit the salad aside and squeeze the lime wedges over before serving.

Turkey Scotch Eggs

Prep time: 15 minutes | Cook time: 12 minutes | Serves 4

1 egg
1 cup panko bread crumbs
½ teaspoon rosemary
1 pound (454 g) ground turkey
4 hard-boiled eggs, peeled
Salt and ground black pepper, to taste
Cooking spray

1. Spritz the air fry basket with cooking spray.
2. Whisk the egg with salt in a bowl. Combine the bread crumbs with rosemary in a shallow dish.
3. Stir the ground turkey with salt and ground black pepper in a separate large bowl, then divide the ground turkey into four portions.
4. Wrap each hard-boiled egg with a portion of ground turkey. Dredge in the whisked egg, then roll over the bread crumb mixture.
5. Place the wrapped eggs in the air fry basket and spritz with cooking spray.
6. Select Air Fry, Super Convection. Set temperature to 400°F (205°C) and set time to 12 minutes. Press Start/Stop to begin preheating.
7. Once preheated, place the basket on the air fry position. Flip the eggs halfway through.
8. When cooking is complete, the scotch eggs should be golden brown and crunchy.
9. Serve immediately.

Bacon-Wrapped Balsamic Turkey with Carrots

Prep time: 10 minutes | Cook time: 25 minutes | Serves 4

2 (12-ounce / 340-g) turkey tenderloins
1 teaspoon kosher salt, divided
6 slices bacon
3 tablespoons balsamic vinegar
2 tablespoons honey
1 tablespoon Dijon mustard
½ teaspoon dried thyme
6 large carrots, peeled and cut into ¼-inch rounds
1 tablespoon olive oil

1. Sprinkle the turkey with ¾ teaspoon of the salt. Wrap each tenderloin with 3 strips of bacon, securing the bacon with toothpicks. Place the turkey in a baking pan.
2. In a small bowl, mix the balsamic vinegar, honey, mustard, and thyme.
3. Place the carrots in a medium bowl and drizzle with the oil. Add 1 tablespoon of the balsamic mixture and ¼ teaspoon of kosher salt and toss to coat. Place these on the pan around the turkey tenderloins. Baste the tenderloins with about one-half of the remaining balsamic mixture.
4. Select Roast, Super Convection, set temperature to 375°F (190°C), and set time to 25 minutes. Press Start/Stop to begin preheating.
5. Once preheated, place the pan on the roast position.
6. After 13 minutes, remove the pan from the oven. Gently stir the carrots. Flip the tenderloins and baste with the remaining balsamic mixture. Return the pan to the oven and continue cooking.
7. When cooking is complete, the carrots should tender and the center of the tenderloins should register 165°F (74°C) on a meat thermometer. Remove the pan from the oven. Slice the turkey and serve with the carrots.

Chicken Shawarma

Prep time: 10 minutes | Cook time: 18 minutes | Serves 4

1½ pounds (680 g) boneless, skinless chicken thighs
1¼ teaspoon kosher salt, divided
2 tablespoons plus 1 teaspoon olive oil, divided
⅔ cup plus 2 tablespoons plain Greek yogurt, divided
2 tablespoons freshly squeezed lemon juice (about 1 medium lemon)
4 garlic cloves, minced, divided

1 tablespoon Shawarma Seasoning
4 pita breads, cut in half
2 cups cherry tomatoes
½ small cucumber, peeled, deseeded, and chopped
1 tablespoon chopped fresh parsley

1. Sprinkle the chicken thighs on both sides with 1 teaspoon of kosher salt. Place in a resealable plastic bag and set aside while you make the marinade.
2. In a small bowl, mix 2 tablespoons of olive oil, 2 tablespoons of yogurt, the lemon juice, 3 garlic cloves, and Shawarma Seasoning until thoroughly combined. Pour the marinade over the chicken. Seal the bag, squeezing out as much air as possible. And massage the chicken to coat it with the sauce. Set aside.
3. Wrap 2 pita breads each in two pieces of aluminum foil and place on a baking pan.
4. Select Bake, Super Convection, set temperature to 300ºF (150ºC), and set time to 6 minutes. Press Start/Stop to begin preheating.
5. Once the oven has preheated, place the pan on the bake position. After 3 minutes, remove the pan from the oven and turn over the foil packets. Return the pan to the oven and continue cooking. When cooking is complete, remove the pan from the oven and place the foil-wrapped pitas on the top of the oven to keep warm.
6. Remove the chicken from the marinade, letting the excess drip off into the bag. Place them on the baking pan. Arrange the tomatoes around the sides of the chicken. Discard the marinade.
7. Select Broil, Super Convection, set temperature to High, and set time to 12 minutes. Press Start/Stop to begin preheating.
8. Once preheated, place the pan on the broil position.
9. After 6 minutes, remove the pan from the oven and turn over the chicken. Return the pan to the oven and continue cooking.
10. Wrap the cucumber in a paper towel to remove as much moisture as possible. Place them in a small bowl. Add the remaining yogurt, kosher salt, olive oil, garlic clove, and parsley. Whisk until combined.
11. When cooking is complete, the chicken should be browned, crisp along its edges, and sizzling. Remove the pan from the oven and place the chicken on a cutting board. Cut each thigh into several pieces. Unwrap the pitas. Spread a tablespoon of sauce into a pita half. Add some chicken and add 2 roasted tomatoes. Serve

Cheesy Marinara Chicken Breasts

Prep time: 30 minutes | Cook time: 1 hour | Serves 2

1 large egg
¼ cup almond meal
2 (6-ounce / 170-g) boneless, skinless chicken breast halves
1 (8-ounce / 227-g) jar marinara sauce, divided
4 tablespoons shredded Mozzarella cheese, divided
4 tablespoons grated Parmesan cheese, divided
4 tablespoons chopped fresh basil, divided
Salt and freshly ground black pepper, to taste
Cooking spray

1. Spritz the air fry basket with cooking spray.
2. In a shallow bowl, beat the egg.
3. In a separate shallow bowl, place the almond meal.
4. Dip 1 chicken breast half into the egg, then into the almond meal to coat. Place the coated chicken in the air fry basket. Repeat with the remaining 1 chicken breast half.
5. Select Bake, Super Convection, set temperature to 350ºF (180ºC) and set time to 40 minutes. Press Start/Stop to begin preheating.
6. Once preheated, place the basket on the bake position.
7. After 20 minutes, remove the basket from the oven and flip the chicken. Return the basket to oven and continue cooking.
8. When cooking is complete, the chicken should no longer pink and the juices run clear.
9. In a baking pan, pour half of marinara sauce.
10. Place the cooked chicken in the sauce. Cover with the remaining marinara.
11. Sprinkle 2 tablespoons of Mozzarella cheese and 2 tablespoons of soy Parmesan cheese on each chicken breast. Top each with 2 tablespoons of basil.
12. Place the baking pan back in the oven and set the baking time to 20 minutes. Flip the chicken halfway through the cooking time.
13. When cooking is complete, an instant-read thermometer inserted into the center of the chicken should read at least 165ºF (74ºC).
14. Remove the pan from oven and divide between 2 plates. Season with salt and pepper and serve.

Chicken Thighs with Radish Slaw

Prep time: 10 minutes | Cook time: 27 minutes | Serves 4

4 bone-in, skin-on chicken thighs
1½ teaspoon kosher salt, divided
1 tablespoon smoked paprika
½ teaspoon granulated garlic
½ teaspoon dried oregano
¼ teaspoon freshly ground black pepper
3 cups shredded cabbage
½ small red onion, thinly sliced
4 large radishes, julienned
3 tablespoons red wine vinegar
2 tablespoons olive oil
Cooking spray

1. Salt the chicken thighs on both sides with 1 teaspoon of kosher salt. In a small bowl, combine the paprika, garlic, oregano, and black pepper. Sprinkle half this mixture over the skin sides of the thighs. Spritz a baking pan with cooking spray and place the thighs skin-side down on the pan. Sprinkle the remaining spice mixture over the other sides of the chicken pieces.
2. Select Roast, Super Convection, set temperature to 375°F (190°C), and set time to 27 minutes. Press Start/Stop to begin preheating.
3. Once preheated, place the pan on the roast position.
4. After 10 minutes, remove the pan from the oven and turn over the chicken thighs. Return the pan to the oven and continue cooking.
5. While the chicken cooks, place the cabbage, onion, and radishes in a large bowl. Sprinkle with the remaining kosher salt, vinegar, and olive oil. Toss to coat.
6. After another 9 to 10 minutes, remove the pan from the oven and place the chicken thighs on a cutting board. Place the cabbage mixture in the pan and toss with the chicken fat and spices.
7. Spread the cabbage in an even layer on the pan and place the chicken on it, skin-side up. Place the pan on the roast position and continue cooking. Roast, Super Convection for another 7 to 8 minutes.
8. When cooking is complete, the cabbage is just becoming tender. Remove the pan from the oven. Taste and adjust the seasoning if necessary. Serve.

Chicken with Potatoes and Corn

Prep time: 10 minutes | Cook time: 25 minutes | Serves 4

4 bone-in, skin-on chicken thighs
2 teaspoons kosher salt, divided
1 cup Bisquick baking mix
½ cup butter, melted, divided
1 pound (454 g) small red potatoes, quartered
3 ears corn, shucked and cut into rounds 1- to 1½-inches thick
⅓ cup heavy whipping cream
½ teaspoon freshly ground black pepper

1. Sprinkle the chicken on all sides with 1 teaspoon of kosher salt. Place the baking mix in a shallow dish. Brush the thighs on all sides with ¼ cup of butter, then dredge them in the baking mix, coating them all on sides. Place the chicken in the center of a baking pan.
2. Place the potatoes in a large bowl with 2 tablespoons of butter and toss to coat. Place them on one side of the chicken on the pan.
3. Place the corn in a medium bowl and drizzle with the remaining butter. Sprinkle with ¼ teaspoon of kosher salt and toss to coat. Place on the pan on the other side of the chicken.
4. Select Roast, Super Convection, set temperature to 375°F (190°C), and set time to 25 minutes. Press Start/Stop to begin preheating.
5. Once preheated, place the pan on the roast position.
6. After 20 minutes, remove the pan from the oven and transfer the potatoes back to the bowl. Return the pan to oven and continue cooking.
7. As the chicken continues cooking, add the cream, black pepper, and remaining kosher salt to the potatoes. Lightly mash the potatoes with a potato masher.
8. When cooking is complete, the corn should be tender and the chicken cooked through, reading 165°F (74°C) on a meat thermometer. Remove the pan from the oven and serve the chicken with the smashed potatoes and corn on the side.

Pineapple Chicken

Prep time: 10 minutes | Cook time: 10 minutes | Serves 6

1½ pounds (680 g) boneless, skinless chicken breasts, cut into 1-inch chunks
¾ cup soy sauce
2 tablespoons ketchup
2 tablespoons brown sugar
2 tablespoons rice vinegar
1 red bell pepper, cut into 1-inch chunks
1 green bell pepper, cut into 1-inch chunks
6 scallions, cut into 1-inch pieces
1 cup (¾-inch chunks) fresh pineapple, rinsed and drained
Cooking spray

1. Place the chicken in a large bowl. Add the soy sauce, ketchup, brown sugar, vinegar, red and green peppers, and scallions. Toss to coat.
2. Spritz a baking pan with cooking spray and place the chicken and vegetables on the pan.
3. Select Roast, Super Convection, set temperature to 375°F (190°C), and set time to 10 minutes. Press Start/Stop to begin preheating.
4. Once preheated, place the pan on the roast position.
5. After 6 minutes, remove the pan from the oven. Add the pineapple chunks to the pan and stir. Return the pan to the oven and continue cooking.
6. When cooking is complete, remove the pan from the oven. Serve with steamed rice, if desired.

Gnocchi with Chicken and Spinach

Prep time: 10 minutes | Cook time: 13 minutes | Serves 4

1 (1-pound / 454-g) package shelf-stable gnocchi
1¼ cups chicken stock
½ teaspoon kosher salt
1 pound (454 g) chicken breast, cut into 1-inch chunks
1 cup heavy whipping cream
2 tablespoons sun-dried tomato purée
1 garlic clove, minced
1 cup frozen spinach, thawed and drained
1 cup grated Parmesan cheese

1. Place the gnocchi in an even layer on a baking pan. Pour the chicken stock over the gnocchi.
2. Select Bake, Super Convection, set temperature to 450°F (235°C), and set time to 7 minutes. Press Start/Stop to begin preheating.
3. Once preheated, place the pan on the bake position.
4. While the gnocchi are cooking, sprinkle the salt over the chicken pieces. In a small bowl, mix the cream, tomato purée, and garlic.
5. When cooking is complete, blot off any remaining stock, or drain the gnocchi and return it to the pan. Top the gnocchi with the spinach and chicken. Pour the cream mixture over the ingredients in the pan.
6. Select Roast, Super Convection, set temperature to 400°F (205°C), and set time to 6 minutes. Press Start/Stop to begin preheating.
7. Once preheated, place the pan on the roast position.
8. After 4 minutes, remove the pan from the oven and gently stir the ingredients. Return the pan to the oven and continue cooking.
9. When cooking is complete, the gnocchi should be tender and the chicken should be cooked through. Remove the pan from the oven. Stir in the Parmesan cheese until it's melted and serve.

Peach and Cherry Chicken

Prep time: 8 minutes | Cook time: 15 minutes | Serves 4

⅓ cup peach preserves
1 teaspoon ground rosemary
½ teaspoon black pepper
½ teaspoon salt
½ teaspoon marjoram
1 teaspoon light olive oil
1 pound (454 g) boneless chicken breasts, cut in 1½-inch chunks
1 (10-ounce / 284-g) package frozen dark cherries, thawed and drained
Cooking spray

2. In a medium bowl, mix peach preserves, rosemary, pepper, salt, marjoram, and olive oil.
3. Stir in chicken chunks and toss to coat well with the preserve mixture.
4. Spritz the air fry basket with cooking spray and lay chicken chunks in the air fry basket.
5. Select Bake, Super Convection. Set the temperature to 400°F (205°C) and set the time to 15 minutes. Press Start/Stop to begin preheating.
6. Once preheated, place the basket on the bake position.
7. After 7 minutes, remove the basket from the oven. Flip the chicken chunks. Return the basket to the oven and continue cooking.
8. When cooking is complete, the chicken should no longer pink and the juices should run clear.
9. Scatter the cherries over and cook for an additional minute to heat cherries.
10. Serve immediately.

Turkey and Carrot Meatloaves

Prep time: 6 minutes | Cook time: 24 minutes | Serves 4

¼ cup grated carrot
2 garlic cloves, minced
2 tablespoons ground almonds
⅓ cup minced onion
2 teaspoons olive oil
1 teaspoon dried marjoram
1 egg white
¾ pound (340 g) ground turkey breast

1. In a medium bowl, stir together the carrot, garlic, almonds, onion, olive oil, marjoram, and egg white.
2. Add the ground turkey. Mix until combined.
3. Double 16 foil muffin cup liners to make 8 cups. Divide the turkey mixture evenly among the liners.
4. Select Bake, Super Convection, set temperature to 400°F (205°C) and set time to 24 minutes. Press Start/Stop to begin preheating.
5. Once preheated, place the muffin cups on the bake position.
6. When cooking is complete, the meatloaves should reach an internal temperature of 165°F (74°C) on a meat thermometer.
7. Serve immediately.

Golden Chicken Fries

Prep time: 20 minutes | Cook time: 6 minutes | Serves 4 to 6

1 pound (454 g) chicken tenders, cut into about ½-inch-wide strips
Salt, to taste
¼ cup all-purpose flour
2 eggs
¾ cup panko bread crumbs
¾ cup crushed organic nacho cheese tortilla chips
Cooking spray

Seasonings:
½ teaspoon garlic powder
1 tablespoon chili powder
½ teaspoon onion powder
1 teaspoon ground cumin

1. Stir together all seasonings in a small bowl and set aside.
2. Sprinkle the chicken with salt. Place strips in a large bowl and sprinkle with 1 tablespoon of the seasoning mix. Stir well to distribute seasonings.
3. Add flour to chicken and stir well to coat all sides.
4. Beat eggs in a separate bowl.
5. In a shallow dish, combine the panko, crushed chips, and the remaining 2 teaspoons of seasoning mix.
6. Dip chicken strips in eggs, then roll in crumbs. Mist with oil or cooking spray. Arrange the chicken strips in a single layer in the air fry basket.
7. Select Air Fry, Super Convection. Set the temperature to 400°F (205°C) and set the time to 6 minutes. Press Start/Stop to begin preheating.
8. Once preheated, place the basket on the air fry position.
9. After 4 minutes, remove the basket from the oven. Flip the strips with tongs. Return the basket to the oven and continue cooking.
10. When cooking is complete, the chicken should be crispy and its juices should be run clear.
11. Allow to cool under room temperature before serving.

Ritzy Chicken Roast

Prep time: 15 minutes | Cook time: 1 hour | Serves 6

1 teaspoon Italian seasoning
½ teaspoon garlic powder
½ teaspoon paprika
1 teaspoon salt
½ teaspoon freshly ground black pepper
½ teaspoon onion powder
2 tablespoons olive oil
1 (3-pound / 1.4-kg) whole chicken, giblets removed, pat dry
Cooking spray

1. Spritz the air fry basket with cooking spray.
2. In a small bowl, mix the Italian seasoning, garlic powder, paprika, salt, pepper, and onion powder.
3. Brush the chicken with the olive oil and rub it with the seasoning mixture.
4. Tie the chicken legs with butcher's twine. Place the chicken in the air fry basket, breast side down.
5. Select Air Fry, Super Convection. Set the temperature to 350°F (180°C) and set the time to an hour. Press Start/Stop to begin preheating.
6. Once preheated, place the basket on the air fry position.
7. After 30 minutes, remove the basket from the oven. Flip the chicken over and baste it with any drippings collected in the bottom drawer of the oven. Return the basket to the oven and continue cooking.
8. When cooking is complete, a thermometer inserted into the thickest part of the thigh should reach at least 165°F (74°C).
9. Let the chicken rest for 10 minutes before carving and serving.

Super Lemon Chicken

Prep time: 5 minutes | Cook time: 35 minutes | Serves 6

3 (8-ounce / 227-g) boneless, skinless chicken breasts, halved, rinsed
1 cup dried bread crumbs
¼ cup olive oil
¼ cup chicken broth
Zest of 1 lemon
3 medium garlic cloves, minced
½ cup fresh lemon juice
½ cup water
¼ cup minced fresh oregano
1 medium lemon, cut into wedges
¼ cup minced fresh parsley, divided
Cooking spray

1. Pour the bread crumbs in a shadow dish, then roll the chicken breasts in the bread crumbs to coat.
2. Spritz a skillet with cooking spray, and brown the coated chicken breasts over medium heat about 3 minutes on each side. Transfer the browned chicken to a baking pan.
3. In a small bowl, combine the remaining ingredients, except the lemon and parsley. Pour the sauce over the chicken.
4. Select Bake, Super Convection. Set the temperature to 325°F (163°C) and set the time to 30 minutes. Press Start/Stop to begin preheating.
5. Once preheated, place the pan on the bake position.
6. After 15 minutes, remove the pan from the oven. Flip the breasts. Return the pan to the oven and continue cooking.
7. When cooking is complete, the chicken should no longer pink.
8. Transfer to a serving platter, and spoon the sauce over the chicken. Garnish with the lemon and parsley.

Sweet-and-Sour Chicken Breasts

Prep time: 15 minutes | Cook time: 15 minutes | Serves 4

1 cup cornstarch
Chicken seasoning or rub, to taste
Salt and ground black pepper, to taste
2 eggs
2 (4-ounce/ 113-g) boneless, skinless chicken breasts, cut into 1-inch pieces
1½ cups sweet-and-sour sauce
Cooking spray

1. Spritz the perforated pan with cooking spray.
2. Combine the cornstarch, chicken seasoning, salt, and pepper in a large bowl. Stir to mix well. Whisk the eggs in a separate bowl.
3. Dredge the chicken pieces in the bowl of cornstarch mixture first, then in the bowl of whisked eggs, and then in the cornstarch mixture again.
4. Arrange the well-coated chicken pieces in the perforated pan. Spritz with cooking spray.
5. Select Air Fry. Set temperature to 360°F (182°C) and set time to 15 minutes. Press Start to begin preheating.
6. Once preheated, place the pan into the oven. Flip the chicken halfway through.
7. When cooking is complete, the chicken should be golden brown and crispy.
8. Transfer the chicken pieces on a large serving plate, then baste with sweet-and-sour sauce before serving.

Teriyaki Chicken Thighs

Prep time: 30 minutes | Cook time: 34 minutes | Serves 4

¼ cup chicken broth
½ teaspoon grated fresh ginger
⅛ teaspoon red pepper flakes
1½ tablespoons soy sauce
4 (5-ounce / 142-g) bone-in chicken thighs, trimmed
1 tablespoon mirin
½ teaspoon cornstarch
1 tablespoon sugar

6 ounces (170 g) snow peas, strings removed
⅛ teaspoon lemon zest
1 garlic clove, minced
¼ teaspoon salt
Ground black pepper, to taste
½ teaspoon lemon juice

1. Combine the broth, ginger, pepper flakes, and soy sauce in a large bowl. Stir to mix well.
2. Pierce 10 to 15 holes into the chicken skin. Put the chicken in the broth mixture and toss to coat well. Let sit for 10 minutes to marinate.
3. Transfer the marinated chicken on a plate and pat dry with paper towels.
4. Scoop 2 tablespoons of marinade in a microwave-safe bowl and combine with mirin, cornstarch and sugar. Stir to mix well. Microwave for 1 minute or until frothy and has a thick consistency. Set aside.
5. Arrange the chicken in the perforated pan, skin side up.
6. Select Air Fry. Set temperature to 400°F (205°C) and set time to 25 minutes. Press Start to begin preheating.
7. Once preheated, place the pan into the oven. Flip the chicken halfway through.
8. When cooking is complete, brush the chicken skin with marinade mixture. Air fry the chicken for 5 more minutes or until glazed.
9. Remove the chicken from the oven. Allow the chicken to cool for 10 minutes.
10. Meanwhile, combine the snow peas, lemon zest, garlic, salt, and ground black pepper in a small bowl. Toss to coat well.
11. Transfer the snow peas in the perforated pan.
12. Select Air Fry. Set temperature to 400°F (205°C) and set time to 3 minutes. Place the pan into the oven.
13. When cooking is complete, the peas should be soft.
14. Remove the peas from the oven and toss with lemon juice.
15. Serve the chicken with lemony snow peas.

Five-Spice Turkey Thighs

Prep time: 10 minutes | Cook time: 25 minutes | Serves 6

2 pounds (907 g) turkey thighs
1 teaspoon Chinese five-spice powder
¼ teaspoon Sichuan pepper
1 teaspoon pink Himalayan salt
1 tablespoon Chinese rice vinegar
1 tablespoon mustard
1 tablespoon chili sauce
2 tablespoons soy sauce
Cooking spray

1. Spritz the perforated pan with cooking spray.
2. Rub the turkey thighs with five-spice powder, Sichuan pepper, and salt on a clean work surface.
3. Put the turkey thighs in the perforated pan and spritz with cooking spray.
4. Select Air Fry. Set temperature to 360°F (182°C) and set time to 22 minutes. Press Start to begin preheating.
5. Once preheated, place the pan into the oven. Flip the thighs at least three times during the cooking.
6. When cooking is complete, the thighs should be well browned.
7. Meanwhile, heat the remaining ingredients in a saucepan over medium-high heat. Cook for 3 minutes or until the sauce is thickened and reduces to two thirds.
8. Transfer the thighs onto a plate and baste with sauce before serving.

Dijon Turkey Breast with Sage

Prep time: 5 minutes | Cook time: 30 minutes | Serves 4

1 teaspoon chopped fresh sage
1 teaspoon chopped fresh tarragon
1 teaspoon chopped fresh thyme leaves
1 teaspoon chopped fresh rosemary leaves
1½ teaspoons sea salt
1 teaspoon ground black pepper
1 (2-pound / 907-g) turkey breast
3 tablespoons Dijon mustard
3 tablespoons butter, melted
Cooking spray

1. Spritz the perforated pan with cooking spray.
2. Combine the herbs, salt, and black pepper in a small bowl. Stir to mix well. Set aside.
3. Combine the Dijon mustard and butter in a separate bowl. Stir to mix well.
4. Rub the turkey with the herb mixture on a clean work surface, then brush the turkey with Dijon mixture.
5. Arrange the turkey in the perforated pan.
6. Select Air Fry. Set temperature to 390°F (199°C) and set time to 30 minutes. Press Start to begin preheating.
7. Once preheated, place the pan into the oven. Flip the turkey breast halfway through.
8. When cooking is complete, an instant-read thermometer inserted in the thickest part of the turkey breast should reach at least 165°F (74°C).
9. Transfer the cooked turkey breast on a large plate and slice to serve.

Chicken and Ham Rochambeau

Prep time: 25 minutes | Cook time: 30 minutes | Serves 4

1 tablespoon melted butter
¼ cup all-purpose flour
4 chicken tenders, cut in half crosswise
4 slices ham, ¼-inch thick, large enough to cover an English muffin
2 English muffins, split in halves
Salt and ground black pepper, to taste
Cooking spray
Mushroom Sauce:
2 tablespoons butter
½ cup chopped mushrooms
½ cup chopped green onions
2 tablespoons flour
1 cup chicken broth
1½ teaspoons Worcestershire sauce
¼ teaspoon garlic powder

1. Put the butter in a baking pan. Combine the flour, salt, and ground black pepper in a shallow dish. Roll the chicken tenders over to coat well.
2. Arrange the chicken in the baking pan and flip to coat with the melted butter.
3. Select Broil. Set temperature to 390°F (199°C) and set time to 10 minutes. Press Start to begin preheating.
4. Once preheated, place the pan into the oven. Flip the tenders halfway through.
5. When cooking is complete, the juices of chicken tenders should run clear.
6. Meanwhile, make the mushroom sauce: melt 2 tablespoons of butter in a saucepan over medium-high heat.
7. Add the mushrooms and onions to the saucepan and sauté for 3 minutes or until the onions are translucent.
8. Gently mix in the flour, broth, Worcestershire sauce, and garlic powder until smooth.
9. Reduce the heat to low and simmer for 5 minutes or until it has a thick consistency. Set the sauce aside until ready to serve.
10. When broiling is complete, remove the baking pan from the oven and set the ham slices into the perforated pan.
11. Select Air Fry. Set time to 5 minutes. Flip the ham slices halfway through.
12. When cooking is complete, the ham slices should be heated through.
13. Remove the ham slices from the oven and set in the English muffin halves and warm for 1 minute.
14. Arrange each ham slice on top of each muffin half, then place each chicken tender over the ham slice.
15. Transfer to the oven and set time to 2 minutes on Air Fry.
16. Serve with the sauce on top.

Breaded Chicken Fingers

Prep time: 20 minutes | Cook time: 10 minutes | Makes 12 chicken fingers

½ cup all-purpose flour
2 cups panko bread crumbs
2 tablespoons canola oil
1 large egg
3 boneless and skinless chicken breasts, each cut into 4 strips
Kosher salt and freshly ground black pepper, to taste
Cooking spray

1. Spritz the perforated pan with cooking spray.
2. Pour the flour in a large bowl. Combine the panko and canola oil on a shallow dish. Whisk the egg in a separate bowl.
3. Rub the chicken strips with salt and ground black pepper on a clean work surface, then dip the chicken in the bowl of flour. Shake the excess off and dunk the chicken strips in the bowl of whisked egg, then roll the strips over the panko to coat well.
4. Arrange the strips in the perforated pan.
5. Select Air Fry. Set temperature to 360°F (182°C) and set time to 10 minutes. Press Start to begin preheating.
6. Once preheated, place the pan into the oven. Flip the strips halfway through.
7. When cooking is complete, the strips should be crunchy and lightly browned.
8. Serve immediately.

Breaded Chicken Livers

Prep time: 10 minutes | Cook time: 10 minutes | Serves 4

2 eggs
2 tablespoons water
¾ cup flour
2 cups panko bread crumbs
1 teaspoon salt
½ teaspoon ground black pepper
20 ounces (567 g) chicken livers
Cooking spray

1. Spritz the perforated pan with cooking spray.
2. Whisk the eggs with water in a large bowl. Pour the flour in a separate bowl. Pour the panko on a shallow dish and sprinkle with salt and pepper.
3. Dredge the chicken livers in the flour. Shake the excess off, then dunk the livers in the whisked eggs, and then roll the livers over the panko to coat well.
4. Arrange the livers in the perforated pan and spritz with cooking spray.
5. Select Air Fry. Set temperature to 390ºF (199ºC) and set time to 10 minutes. Press Start to begin preheating.
6. Once preheated, place the pan into the oven. Flip the livers halfway through.
7. When cooking is complete, the livers should be golden and crispy.
8. Serve immediately.

Breaded Chicken Tenders with Thyme

Prep time: 15 minutes | Cook time: 5 minutes | Serves 4

½ cup all-purpose flour
1 teaspoon marjoram
½ teaspoon thyme
1 teaspoon dried parsley flakes
½ teaspoon salt
1 egg
1 teaspoon lemon juice
1 teaspoon water
1 cup bread crumbs
4 chicken tenders, pounded thin, cut in half lengthwise
Cooking spray

1. Spritz the perforated pan with cooking spray.
2. Combine the flour, marjoram, thyme, parsley, and salt in a shallow dish. Stir to mix well.
3. Whisk the egg with lemon juice and water in a large bowl. Pour the bread crumbs in a separate shallow dish.
4. Roll the chicken halves in the flour mixture first, then in the egg mixture, and then roll over the bread crumbs to coat well. Shake the excess off.
5. Arrange the chicken halves in the perforated pan and spritz with cooking spray on both sides.
6. Select Air Fry. Set temperature to 390ºF (199ºC) and set time to 5 minutes. Press Start to begin preheating.
7. Once preheated, place the pan into the oven. Flip the halves halfway through.
8. When cooking is complete, the chicken halves should be golden brown and crispy.
9. Serve immediately.

Barbecue Chicken with Coleslaw

Prep time: 15 minutes | Cook time: 10 minutes | Makes 4 tostadas

Coleslaw:
¼ cup sour cream
¼ small green cabbage, finely chopped
½ tablespoon white vinegar
½ teaspoon garlic powder
½ teaspoon salt
¼ teaspoon ground black pepper
Tostadas:
2 cups pulled rotisserie chicken
½ cup barbecue sauce
4 corn tortillas
½ cup shredded Mozzarella cheese
Cooking spray

Make the Coleslaw:
1. Combine the ingredients for the coleslaw in a large bowl. Toss to mix well.
2. Refrigerate until ready to serve.

Make the Tostadas:
1. Spritz the perforated pan with cooking spray.
2. Toss the chicken with barbecue sauce in a separate large bowl to combine well. Set aside.
3. Place one tortilla in the perforated pan and spritz with cooking spray.
4. Select Air Fry. Set temperature to 370ºF (188ºC) and set time to 10 minutes. Press Start to begin preheating.
5. Once preheated, place the pan into the oven. Flip the tortilla and spread the barbecue chicken and cheese over halfway through.
6. When cooking is complete, the tortilla should be browned and the cheese should be melted.
7. Serve the tostadas with coleslaw on top.

Mustard Chicken Thighs in Waffles

Prep time: 1 hour 20 minutes | Cook time: 20 minutes | Serves 4

For the Chicken:
4 chicken thighs, skin on
1 cup low-fat buttermilk
½ cup all-purpose flour
½ teaspoon garlic powder
½ teaspoon mustard powder
1 teaspoon kosher salt
½ teaspoon freshly ground black pepper
¼ cup honey, for serving
Cooking spray

For the Waffles:
½ cup all-purpose flour
½ cup whole wheat pastry flour
1 large egg, beaten
1 cup low-fat buttermilk
1 teaspoon baking powder
2 tablespoons canola oil
½ teaspoon kosher salt
1 tablespoon granulated sugar

1. Combine the chicken thighs with buttermilk in a large bowl. Wrap the bowl in plastic and refrigerate to marinate for at least an hour.
2. Spritz the perforated pan with cooking spray.
3. Combine the flour, mustard powder, garlic powder, salt, and black pepper in a shallow dish. Stir to mix well.
4. Remove the thighs from the buttermilk and pat dry with paper towels. Sit the bowl of buttermilk aside.
5. Dip the thighs in the flour mixture first, then into the buttermilk, and then into the flour mixture. Shake the excess off.
6. Arrange the thighs in the perforated pan and spritz with cooking spray.
7. Select Air Fry. Set temperature to 360°F (182°C) and set time to 20 minutes. Press Start to begin preheating.
8. Once preheated, place the pan into the oven. Flip the thighs halfway through.
9. When cooking is complete, an instant-read thermometer inserted in the thickest part of the chicken thighs should register at least 165°F (74°C).
10. Meanwhile, make the waffles: combine the ingredients for the waffles in a large bowl. Stir to mix well, then arrange the mixture in a waffle iron and cook until a golden and fragrant waffle forms.
11. Remove the waffles from the waffle iron and slice into 4 pieces. Remove the chicken thighs from the oven and allow to cool for 5 minutes.
12. Arrange each chicken thigh on each waffle piece and drizzle with 1 tablespoon of honey. Serve warm.

Gochujang Chicken Wings

Prep time: 10 minutes | Cook time: 25 minutes | Serves 4

Wings:
2 pounds (907 g) chicken wings
1 teaspoon salt
1 teaspoon ground black pepper

Sauce:
2 tablespoons gochujang
1 tablespoon mayonnaise
1 tablespoon minced ginger
1 tablespoon minced garlic
1 teaspoon agave nectar
2 packets Splenda
1 tablespoon sesame oil

For Garnish:
2 teaspoons sesame seeds
¼ cup chopped green onions

2. Line a baking pan with aluminum foil, then arrange the rack on the pan.
3. On a clean work surface, rub the chicken wings with salt and ground black pepper, then arrange the seasoned wings on the rack.
4. Select Air Fry. Set temperature to 400°F (205°C) and set time to 20 minutes. Press Start to begin preheating.
5. Once preheated, place the pan into the oven. Flip the wings halfway through.
6. When cooking is complete, the wings should be well browned.
7. Meanwhile, combine the ingredients for the sauce in a small bowl. Stir to mix well. Reserve half of the sauce in a separate bowl until ready to serve.
8. Remove the air fried chicken wings from the oven and toss with remaining half of the sauce to coat well.
9. Place the wings back to the oven. Select Air Fry. Set time to 5 minutes.
10. When cooking is complete, the internal temperature of the wings should reach at least 165°F (74°C).
11. Remove the wings from the oven and place on a large plate. Sprinkle with sesame seeds and green onions. Serve with reserved sauce.

Chili Chicken Skin with Dill

Prep time: 5 minutes | Cook time: 6 minutes | Serves 4

1 pound (454 g) chicken skin, cut into slices
1 teaspoon melted butter
½ teaspoon crushed chili flakes
1 teaspoon dried dill
Salt and ground black pepper, to taste

1. Combine all the ingredients in a large bowl. Toss to coat the chicken skin well.
2. Transfer the skin in the perforated pan.
3. Select Air Fry. Set temperature to 360ºF (182ºC) and set time to 6 minutes. Press Start to begin preheating.
4. Once preheated, place the pan into the oven. Stir the skin halfway through.
5. When cooking is complete, the skin should be crispy.
6. Serve immediately.

Chicken Drumsticks with Cajun Seasoning

Prep time: 5 minutes | Cook time: 18 minutes | Serves 5

1 tablespoon olive oil
10 chicken drumsticks
1½ tablespoons Cajun seasoning
Salt and ground black pepper, to taste

1. Grease the perforated pan with olive oil.
2. On a clean work surface, rub the chicken drumsticks with Cajun seasoning, salt, and ground black pepper.
3. Arrange the seasoned chicken drumsticks in the perforated pan.
4. Select Air Fry. Set temperature to 390ºF (199ºC) and set time to 18 minutes. Press Start to begin preheating.
5. Once preheated, place the pan into the oven. Flip the drumsticks halfway through.
6. When cooking is complete, the drumsticks should be lightly browned.
7. Remove the chicken drumsticks from the oven. Serve immediately.

Ginger Chicken Bites in Sherry

Prep time: 15 minutes | Cook time: 15 minutes | Serves 4

½ cup pineapple juice
2 tablespoons apple cider vinegar
½ tablespoon minced ginger
½ cup ketchup
2 garlic cloves, minced
½ cup brown sugar
2 tablespoons sherry
½ cup soy sauce
4 chicken breasts, cubed
Cooking spray

1. Combine the pineapple juice, cider vinegar, ginger, ketchup, garlic, and sugar in a saucepan. Stir to mix well. Heat over low heat for 5 minutes or until thickened. Fold in the sherry and soy sauce.
2. Dunk the chicken cubes in the mixture. Press to submerge. Wrap the bowl in plastic and refrigerate to marinate for at least an hour.
3. Spritz the perforated pan with cooking spray.
4. Remove the chicken cubes from the marinade. Shake the excess off and put in the perforated pan. Spritz with cooking spray.
5. Select Air Fry. Set temperature to 360ºF (182ºC) and set time to 15 minutes. Press Start to begin preheating.
6. Once preheated, place the pan into the oven. Flip the chicken cubes at least three times during the air frying.
7. When cooking is complete, the chicken cubes should be glazed and well browned.
8. Serve immediately.

Honey-Ginger Chicken Breasts

Prep time: 5 minutes | Cook time: 10 minutes | Serves 4

4 (4-ounce / 113-g) boneless, skinless chicken breasts
Chicken seasoning or rub, to taste
Salt and ground black pepper, to taste
¼ cup honey
2 tablespoons soy sauce
2 teaspoons grated fresh ginger
2 garlic cloves, minced
Cooking spray

1. Spritz the perforated pan with cooking spray.
2. Rub the chicken breasts with chicken seasoning, salt, and black pepper on a clean work surface.
3. Arrange the chicken breasts in the perforated pan and spritz with cooking spray.
4. Select Air Fry. Set temperature to 400°F (205°C) and set time to 10 minutes. Press Start to begin preheating.
5. Once preheated, place the pan into the oven. Flip the chicken breasts halfway through.
6. When cooking is complete, the internal temperature of the thickest part of the chicken should reach at least 165°F (74°C).
7. Meanwhile, combine the honey, soy sauce, ginger, and garlic in a saucepan and heat over medium-high heat for 3 minutes or until thickened. Stir constantly.
8. Remove the chicken from the oven and serve with the honey glaze.

Parmesan Chicken Cutlets

Prep time: 15 minutes | Cook time: 15 minutes | Serves 4

2 tablespoons panko bread crumbs
¼ cup grated Parmesan cheese
⅛ tablespoon paprika
½ tablespoon garlic powder
2 large eggs
4 chicken cutlets
1 tablespoon parsley
Salt and ground black pepper, to taste
Cooking spray

1. Spritz the perforated pan with cooking spray.
2. Combine the bread crumbs, Parmesan, paprika, garlic powder, salt, and ground black pepper in a large bowl. Stir to mix well. Beat the eggs in a separate bowl.
3. Dredge the chicken cutlets in the beaten eggs, then roll over the bread crumbs mixture to coat well. Shake the excess off.
4. Transfer the chicken cutlets in the perforated pan and spritz with cooking spray.
5. Select Air Fry. Set temperature to 400°F (205°C) and set time to 15 minutes. Press Start to begin preheating.
6. Once preheated, place the pan into the oven. Flip the cutlets halfway through.
7. When cooking is complete, the cutlets should be crispy and golden brown.
8. Serve with parsley on top.

Chapter 4 Fish and Seafood

Bacon-Wrapped Herb Rainbow Trout

Prep time: 10 minutes | Cook time: 20 minutes | Serves 4

4 (8- to 10-ounce / 227- to 283-g)
  rainbow trout, butterflied and
  boned
2 teaspoons kosher salt, divided
1 tablespoon extra-virgin olive oil,
  divided
1 tablespoon freshly squeezed lemon
  juice, divided
2 tablespoons chopped fresh parsley,
  divided
2 tablespoons chopped fresh chives,
  divided
8 thin bacon slices
Lemon wedges, for serving

1. Lightly oil a sheet pan.
2. Sprinkle the inside and outside of each trout with the salt. Brush the inside with the oil and drizzle with the lemon juice. Scatter the parsley and chives on one side of each butterflied trout. Fold the trout closed and wrap each one with two slices of bacon. Transfer to the sheet pan.
3. Select Bake. Set temperature to 400°F (205°C) and set time to 20 minutes. Select Start to begin preheating.
4. Once preheated, slide the pan into the oven. Flip the trout halfway through the cooking time.
5. When done, the bacon will be crisp.
6. Serve with lemon wedges.

Crab Cheese Enchiladas

Prep time: 10 minutes | Cook time: 25 minutes | Serves 4

8 (6-inch) corn tortillas
Nonstick cooking spray or vegetable
  oil, for brushing
2 cups mild tomatillo salsa or green
  enchilada sauce
½ cup heavy (whipping) cream
8 ounces (227 g) lump crab meat,
  picked through to remove any
  shells
3 or 4 scallions, chopped
8 ounces (227 g) Monterey Jack
  cheese, shredded

1. Spray the tortillas on both sides with cooking spray or brush lightly with oil. Arrange on a sheet pan, overlapping as little as possible.
2. Select Bake. Set temperature to 350°F (180°C) and set time to 5 minutes. Select Start to begin preheating.
3. Once preheated, slide the pan into the oven.
4. When done, the tortillas will be warm and flexible.
5. Meanwhile, stir together the salsa and cream in a shallow, microwave-safe bowl and heat in the microwave until very warm, about 45 seconds.
6. Pour a quarter of the salsa mixture into a baking pan. Place a tortilla in the sauce, turning it over to coat thoroughly. Spoon a heaping tablespoon of crab down the middle of the tortilla, then top with a teaspoon of scallions and a heaping tablespoon of cheese. Roll up the tortilla and place it seam-side down at one end of the pan. Repeat with the remaining tortillas, forming a row of enchiladas in the pan. Spoon most or all of the remaining sauce over the enchiladas so they are nicely coated but not drowning. Sprinkle the remaining cheese over the top.
7. Bake for 18 to 20 minutes, until the cheese is melted and the sauce is bubbling.

Salmon Fillet with Spinach, and Beans

Prep time: 10 minutes | Cook time: 35 minutes | Serves 4

2 tablespoons olive oil, divided
1 garlic clove, thinly sliced
1 (9- to 10-ounce / 255- to 283-g) bag baby spinach
1 (15-ounce / 425-g) can cannellini or navy beans, rinsed and drained
1½ teaspoons kosher salt, divided
½ teaspoon ground cumin
½ teaspoon ground coriander
¼ teaspoon red pepper flakes
4 (6-ounce / 170-g) skinless salmon fillets

1. Heat 1 tablespoon of oil in a large, oven-safe skillet over medium-high heat. Add the garlic and cook, stirring, until fragrant, about 30 seconds. Add the spinach a handful at a time and cook, tossing, until slightly wilted, adding more as you have room. Stir in the beans, ¾ teaspoon of salt, cumin, coriander, and red pepper flakes.
2. Season the salmon with the remaining ¾ teaspoon of salt. Place the fillets in a single layer on top of the spinach mixture and drizzle with the remaining 1 tablespoon of oil.
3. Select Bake. Set temperature to 300°F (150°C) and set time to 35 minutes. Select Start to begin preheating.
4. Once preheated, put the skillet in the oven.
5. When done, the salmon will be opaque in the center.

Sherry Tilapia and Mushroom Rice

Prep time: 15 minutes | Cook time: 25 minutes | Serves 4

4 tablespoons unsalted butter
12 ounces (340 g) cremini or white button mushrooms, trimmed and sliced
4 to 6 scallions, chopped
1 teaspoon kosher salt, divided
2 tablespoons all-purpose flour
¾ cup dry sherry or dry white wine
¾ cup low-sodium vegetable or fish broth
3 tablespoons heavy (whipping) cream
1 tablespoon chopped fresh parsley, divided
2 cups cooked white or brown rice
4 (6-ounce / 170-g) tilapia fillets
⅛ teaspoon freshly ground black pepper

1. In a large cast-iron or other oven-safe skillet, melt the butter over medium heat until foaming. Sauté the mushrooms and scallions until the mushrooms are soft. Stir in ½ teaspoon of salt and the flour. Cook for 1 minute, stirring constantly. Gradually stir in the sherry. Let the sauce simmer for 3 to 5 minutes, until some of the alcohol evaporates. Add the broth, cream, and 1½ teaspoons of parsley and bring back to a simmer.
2. Stir the rice into the sauce. Place the fish fillets in a single layer on top of the rice and sauce. Sprinkle the fish with the remaining ½ teaspoon of salt and the pepper, then spoon a little of the sauce over the fillets.
3. Select Bake. Set temperature to 325°F (163°C) and set time to 20 minutes. Select Start to begin preheating.
4. Once preheated, put the skillet in the oven.
5. When done, the fish will flake with a fork.
6. To serve, spoon some rice onto each plate and top with a fillet. Sprinkle with the remaining 1½ teaspoons of parsley.

Marinated Catfish Fillet

Prep time: 10 minutes | Cook time: 15 minutes | Serves 4

4 (6-ounce / 170-g) catfish fillets
Marinade Ingredients:
1 tablespoon olive oil
1 tablespoon lemon juice
¼ dry white wine
1 tablespoon garlic powder
1 tablespoon soy sauce

1. Combine the marinade ingredients in an ovenproof baking dish. Add the fillets and let stand for 10 minutes, spooning the marinade over the fillets every 2 minutes.
2. Select Broil. Set temperature to 400°F (205°C) and set time to 15 minutes. Select Start to begin preheating.
3. Once preheated, place the baking dish in the oven.
4. When done, the fish will flake easily with a fork.

Mackerel with Mango and Chili Salad

Prep time: 15 minutes | Cook time: 20 minutes | Serves 4

For the Fish:
2 garlic cloves, finely grated
1½in fresh ginger, peeled and finely grated
¾ teaspoon ground turmeric
1½ teaspoons ground cumin
½ teaspoon ground fenugreek
2½ tablespoons tamarind paste
¼ cup lime juice, plus more to serve, plus
    lime wedges to serve
1 tablespoon light brown sugar
2 tablespoons peanut oil
Sea salt flakes and freshly ground black
    pepper, to taste
4 whole Boston mackerel, gutted and washed
Rice, or warmed naan bread and plain yogurt,
    to serve

For the Salad:
2 just-ripe or slightly under- ripe mangoes
Juice of 2 limes
1 red Fresno chili and 1 green chili, halved, seeded, and very finely shredded
½ cup cilantro leaves and stalks (make sure the stalks aren't too long or thick)

1. Mix together the garlic, ginger, and all the spices for the mackerel, adding the lime juice, sugar, oil, and seasoning. Spread this all over each fish, inside and out. Cover and put in the refrigerator for about 15 minutes.
2. Now make the salad. Peel the mangoes and cut off the 'cheeks' (the fleshy bits that lie alongside the stone). Cut the cheeks into neat slices.
3. Put the mango slices in a serving bowl and add the lime juice, chilies, some salt, and the cilantro, and toss.
4. Line a baking pan with foil or parchment paper and put the mackerel in it.
5. Select Bake. Set temperature to 400°F (205°C) and set time to 20 minutes. Select Start to begin preheating.
6. Once preheated, slide the pan into the oven.
7. When done, squeeze some lime juice over the fish and serve with rice, or warmed naan bread and yogurt, lime wedges, and the mango and chili salad.

Lemony Shrimp with Arugula

Prep time: 10 minutes | Cook time: 10 minutes | Serves 4

4 tablespoons unsalted butter, melted
2 tablespoons extra-virgin olive oil
1 teaspoon kosher salt
6 garlic cloves, minced
¼ cup chopped fresh parsley, divided
2 pounds (907 g) large shrimp, peeled
    and deveined
2 tablespoons freshly squeezed lemon
    juice
1 (9- to 10-ounce / 255- to 283-g) bag
    arugula

1. In a baking pan, add the butter, oil, salt, garlic, and half the parsley. Stir well. Add the shrimp and toss to coat, then arrange the shrimp in a single layer.
2. Select Bake. Set temperature to 375°F (190°C) and set time to 5 minutes. Select Start to begin preheating.
3. Once preheated, slide the pan into the oven.
4. When done, the shrimp will be opaque and pink.
5. Remove the pan from the oven. Add the lemon juice, arugula, and remaining parsley. Toss well to wilt the arugula. Serve immediately.

Broiled Lemony Salmon Steak

Prep time: 10 minutes | Cook time: 20 minutes | Serves 2

2 (6-ounce / 170-g) salmon steaks
Brushing Mixture:
2 tablespoons lemon juice
2 tablespoons olive oil
1 tablespoon soy sauce
1 teaspoon dried dill or dill weed
½ teaspoon garlic powder
1 teaspoon soy sauce

1. Combine the brushing mixture ingredients in a small bowl and brush the salmon steak tops, skin side down, liberally, reserving the remaining mixture. Let the steaks sit at room temperature for 10 minutes, then place on a broiling rack with a pan underneath.
2. Select Broil. Set temperature to 400°F (205°C) and set time to 20 minutes. Select Start to begin preheating.
3. Once preheated, slide the pan into the oven.
4. After 15 minutes, remove from the oven, and brush the steaks with the remaining mixture. Broil again for 5 minutes, or until the meat flakes easily with a fork.

Crispy Fish Fillet

Prep time: 10 minutes | Cook time: 14 minutes | Serves 4

4 (6-ounce / 170-g) fish fillets, approximately ¼- to ½-inch thick
2 tablespoons vegetable oil
Coating Ingredients:
1 cup cornmeal
1 teaspoon garlic powder
1 teaspoon ground cumin
1 teaspoon paprika
Salt, to taste

1. Combine the coating ingredients in a small bowl, blending well. Transfer to a large plate, spreading evenly over the surface. Brush the fillets with vegetable oil and press both sides of each fillet into the coating.
2. Place the fillets in an oiled or nonstick square baking (cake) pan, laying them flat.
3. Select Broil. Set temperature to 400°F (205°C) and set time to 14 minutes. Select Start to begin preheating.
4. Once preheated, slide the pan into the oven.
5. Broil for 7 minutes, then remove the pan from the oven and carefully turn the fillets with a spatula. Broil for another 7 minutes, or until the fish flakes easily with a fork and the coating is crisped to your preference. Serve immediately.

Mediterranean Baked Fish Fillet

Prep time: 10 minutes | Cook time: 25 minutes | Serves 4

4 (6-ounce / 170-g) fish fillets (red snapper, cod, whiting, sole, or mackerel)
Mixture Ingredients:
1 tablespoon olive oil
2 tablespoons tomato paste
3 plum tomatoes, chopped
2 garlic cloves, minced
2 tablespoons capers
2 tablespoons pitted and chopped black olives
2 tablespoons chopped fresh basil leaves
2 tablespoons chopped fresh parsley

1. Combine the baking mixture ingredients in a small bowl. Set aside.
2. Layer the fillets in an oiled or nonstick square baking (cake) pan, overlapping them if necessary, and spoon the baking mixture over the fish.
3. Select Bake. Set temperature to 350°F (180°C) and set time to 25 minutes. Select Start to begin preheating.
4. Once preheated, slide the pan into the oven.
5. When done, the fish will flake easily with a fork.

Swordfish Steaks with Lemon

Prep time: 5 minutes | Cook time: 10 minutes | Serves 4

1 pound (454 g) swordfish steaks
2 tablespoons olive oil
2 tablespoons chopped fresh mint leaves
3 tablespoons fresh lemon juice
1 teaspoon garlic powder
½ teaspoon shallot powder
Sea salt and freshly ground black pepper, to taste

1. Start by preheating the air fryer to 400°F (205°C).
2. Toss the swordfish steaks with the remaining ingredients and place them in a lightly oiled crisper tray.
3. Place the crisper tray in the corresponding position in the air fryer. Select Air Fry and cook the swordfish steaks for about 10 minutes, turning them over halfway through the cooking time.
4. Bon appétit!

Mackerel Patties Muffins

Prep time: 10 minutes | Cook time: 14 minutes | Serves 4

1 pound (454 g) mackerel fillet, boneless and chopped
1 tablespoon olive oil
½ onion, chopped
2 garlic cloves, crushed
1 teaspoon hot paprika
1 tablespoon chopped fresh cilantro
2 tablespoons chopped fresh parsley
Sea salt and ground black pepper, to taste
4 English muffins, toasted

1. Start by preheating the air fryer to 400ºF (205ºC).
2. Mix all ingredients , except for the English muffins, in a bowl. Shape the mixture into four patties and place them in a lightly oiled crisper tray.
3. Place the crisper tray in the corresponding position in the air fryer. Select Air Fry and cook the fish patties for about 14 minutes, turning them over halfway through the cooking time.
4. Serve on English muffins and enjoy!

Calamari with Lemon

Prep time: 15 minutes | Cook time: 5 minutes | Serves 4

1 pound (454 g) calamari, sliced into rings
2 garlic cloves, minced
1 teaspoon red pepper flakes
2 tablespoons dry white wine
2 tablespoons olive oil
2 tablespoons fresh lemon juice
1 teaspoon chopped basil
1 teaspoon chopped dill
1 teaspoon chopped parsley
Coarse sea salt and freshly cracked black pepper, to taste

1. Start by preheating the air fryer to 400ºF (205ºC).
2. Toss all ingredients in a lightly greased crisper tray.
3. Place the crisper tray in the corresponding position in the air fryer. Select Air Fry and cook the calamari for 5 minutes, tossing crisper tray halfway through the cooking time.
4. Bon appétit!

Pollock Fishcakes

Prep time: 8 minutes | Cook time: 14 minutes | Serves 4

1 pound (454 g) pollock, chopped
1 teaspoon chili sauce
Sea salt and ground black pepper, to taste
4 tablespoons all-purpose flour
1 teaspoon smoked paprika
2 tablespoons olive oil
4 ciabatta buns

1. Start by preheating the air fryer to 400ºF (205ºC).
2. Mix all ingredients , except for the ciabatta buns, in a bowl. Shape the mixture into four patties and place them in a lightly oiled crisper tray.
3. Place the crisper tray in the corresponding position in the air fryer. Select Air Fry and cook the fish patties for about 14 minutes, turning them over halfway through the cooking time.
4. Serve on hamburger buns and enjoy!

Squid Tubes with Cheese

Prep time: 6 minutes | Cook time: 5 minutes | Serves 4

1½ pounds (680 g) small squid tubes
2 tablespoons butter, melted
1 chili pepper, chopped
2 garlic cloves, minced
1 teaspoon red pepper flakes
Sea salt and ground black pepper, to taste
¼ cup dry white wine
2 tablespoons fresh lemon juice
1 teaspoon Mediterranean herb mix
2 tablespoons grated Parmigiano-Reggiano cheese

1. Start by preheating the air fryer to 400ºF (205ºC).
2. Toss all ingredients , except for the Parmigiano-Reggiano cheese, in a lightly greased crisper tray.
3. Place the crisper tray in the corresponding position in the air fryer. Select Air Fry and cook the squid for 5 minutes, tossing crisper tray halfway through the cooking time.
4. Top the warm squid with the cheese. Bon appétit!

Shrimp Scampi in White Wine

Prep time: 20 minutes | Cook time: 5 minutes | Serves 2 to 4

16 to 20 raw large shrimp, peeled, deveined and tails
    removed
½ cup white wine
Freshly ground black pepper
¼ cup plus 1 tablespoon cashew butter, divided
1 clove garlic, sliced
1 teaspoon olive oil
Salt, to taste
Juice of ½ lemon
¼ cup chopped fresh parsley

1. Start by marinating the shrimp in the white wine and freshly ground black pepper for at least 30 minutes, or as long as 2 hours in the refrigerator.
2. Preheat the air fryer to 400°F (204°C).
3. Heat ¼ cup of cashew butter in a small saucepan on the stovetop. Add the garlic and let the butter simmer, but be sure to not let it burn.
4. Pour the shrimp and marinade into the air fryer, letting the marinade drain through to the bottom drawer. Drizzle the olive oil on the shrimp and season well with salt. Air fry at 400°F (204°C) for 3 minutes. Turn the shrimp over (don't shake the basket because the marinade will splash around) and pour the garlic butter over the shrimp. Air fry for another 2 minutes.
5. Remove the shrimp from the air fryer basket and transfer them to a bowl. Squeeze lemon juice over all the shrimp and toss with the chopped parsley and remaining tablespoon of butter. Season to taste with salt and serve over rice or pasta, or on their own with some crusty bread.

Sea Bass with Butter

Prep time: 5 minutes | Cook time: 10 minutes | Serves 3

2 tablespoons butter, room temperature
1 pound (454 g) sea bass
¼ cup dry white wine
¼ cup all-purpose flour
Sea salt and ground black pepper, to taste
1 teaspoon mustard seeds
1 teaspoon fennel seeds
2 cloves garlic, minced

1. Start by preheating the air fryer to 400°F (205°C).
2. Toss the fish with the remaining ingredients; place them in a lightly oiled crisper tray.
3. Place the crisper tray in the corresponding position in the air fryer. Select Air Fry and cook the fish for about 10 minutes, turning them over halfway through the cooking time.
4. Bon appétit!

Lemony Salmon Fillets

Prep time: 6 minutes | Cook time: 12 minutes | Serves 4

1½ pounds (680 g) salmon fillets
2 sprigs fresh rosemary
1 tablespoon fresh basil
1 tablespoon fresh thyme
1 tablespoon fresh dill
1 small lemon, juiced
2 tablespoons olive oil
Sea salt and ground black pepper, to taste
1 teaspoon stone-ground mustard
2 cloves garlic, chopped

1. Start by preheating the air fryer to 380°F (193°C).
2. Toss the salmon with the remaining ingredients; place them in a lightly oiled crisper tray.
3. Place the crisper tray in the corresponding position in the air fryer. Select Roast and cook the salmon fillets for about 12 minutes, turning them over halfway through the cooking time.
4. Serve immediately and enjoy!

Chili Calamari

Prep time: 10 minutes | Cook time: 5 minutes | Serves 4

½ cup milk
1 cup all-purpose flour
2 tablespoons olive oil
1 teaspoon turmeric powder
Sea salt flakes and ground black, to taste
1 teaspoon paprika
1 red chili, minced
1 pound (454 g) calamari, cut into rings

1. Start by preheating the air fryer to 400°F (205°C).
2. In a mixing bowl, thoroughly combine the milk, flour, olive oil, turmeric powder, salt, black pepper, paprika, and red chili. Mix to combine well.
3. Now, dip the calamari into the flour mixture to coat. Place the calamari in the crisper tray.
4. Place the crisper tray in the corresponding position in the air fryer. Select Air Fry and cook the calamari for 5 minutes, turning them over halfway through the cooking time.
5. Bon appétit!

Baked Sea Bass with Olive-Onion Relish

Prep time: 5 minutes | Cook time: 10 minutes | Serves 2

2 (6-ounce / 170-g) sea bass fillets
3 tablespoons extra-virgin olive oil
½ teaspoon kosher salt
½ teaspoon black pepper
½ teaspoon ground cumin
¼ cup finely diced onion
⅓ cup pitted green olives, diced
1 teaspoon chopped capers
Olive oil spray

1. Preheat the air fryer to 325°F (163°C). Spritz the air fryer basket with olive oil spray.
2. Drizzle the fish fillets with the olive oil and season with the salt, pepper, and cumin.
3. Arrange the fish fillets in the air fryer basket and bake for 10 minutes, or until the fish flakes easily with a fork.
4. Meanwhile, stir together the onion, olives, and capers in a small bowl.
5. Serve the fish fillets topped with the relish.

Halibut Steaks with Vermouth

Prep time: 5 minutes | Cook time: 10 minutes | Serves 4

1 pound (454 g) halibut steaks
¼ cup vegetable oil
2½ tablespoons Worcester sauce
2 tablespoons honey
2 tablespoons vermouth
1 tablespoon freshly squeezed lemon juice
1 tablespoon fresh parsley leaves, coarsely chopped
Salt and pepper, to taste
1 teaspoon dried basil

1. Put all the ingredients in a large mixing dish and gently stir until the fish is coated evenly. Transfer the fish to the air fry basket.
2. Select Roast, Super Convection, set temperature to 390°F (199°C), and set time to 10 minutes. Select Start/Stop to begin preheating.
3. Once preheated, place the basket on the roast position. Flip the fish halfway through cooking time.
4. When cooking is complete, the fish should reach an internal temperature of at least 145°F (63°C) on a meat thermometer. Remove from the oven and let the fish cool for 5 minutes before serving.

Catfish Fillets with Pecan

Prep time: 5 minutes | Cook time: 12 minutes | Serves 4

½ cup pecan meal
1 teaspoon fine sea salt
¼ teaspoon ground black pepper
4 (4-ounce / 113-g) catfish fillets
Avocado oil spray
For Garnish (Optional):
Fresh oregano
Pecan halves

1. Spray the air fry basket with avocado oil spray.
2. Combine the pecan meal, sea salt, and black pepper in a large bowl. Dredge each catfish fillet in the meal mixture, turning until well coated. Spritz the fillets with avocado oil spray, then transfer to the air fry basket.
3. Select Air Fry, Super Convection, set temperature to 375ºF (190ºC), and set time to 12 minutes. Select Start/Stop to begin preheating.
4. Once preheated, place the basket on the air fry position. Flip the fillets halfway through the cooking time.
5. When cooking is complete, the fish should be cooked through and no longer translucent. Remove from the oven and sprinkle the oregano sprigs and pecan halves on top for garnish, if desired. Serve immediately.

Breaded Catfish Nuggets

Prep time: 10 minutes | Cook time: 7 to 8 minutes | Serves 4

2 medium catfish fillets, cut into chunks (approximately 1 × 2 inch)
Salt and pepper, to taste
2 eggs
2 tablespoons skim milk
½ cup cornstarch
1 cup panko bread crumbs
Cooking spray

1. In a medium bowl, season the fish chunks with salt and pepper to taste.
2. In a small bowl, beat together the eggs with milk until well combined.
3. Place the cornstarch and bread crumbs into separate shallow dishes.
4. Dredge the fish chunks one at a time in the cornstarch, coating well on both sides, then dip in the egg mixture, shaking off any excess, finally press well into the bread crumbs. Spritz the fish chunks with cooking spray.
5. Arrange the fish chunks in the air fry basket in a single layer.
6. Select Air Fry, Super Convection, set temperature to 390ºF (199ºC), and set time to 8 minutes. Select Start/Stop to begin preheating.
7. Once preheated, place the basket on the air fry position. Flip the fish chunks halfway through the cooking time.
8. When cooking is complete, they should be no longer translucent in the center and golden brown. Remove the fish chunks from the oven to a plate. Serve warm.

Tilapia with Garlic Aioli

Prep time: 5 minutes | Cook time: 15 minutes | Serves 4

Tilapia:
4 tilapia fillets
1 tablespoon extra-virgin olive oil
1 teaspoon garlic powder
1 teaspoon paprika
1 teaspoon dried basil
A pinch of lemon-pepper seasoning
Garlic Aioli:
2 garlic cloves, minced
1 tablespoon mayonnaise
Juice of ½ lemon
1 teaspoon extra-virgin olive oil
Salt and pepper, to taste

1. On a clean work surface, brush both sides of each fillet with the olive oil. Sprinkle with the garlic powder, paprika, basil, and lemon-pepper seasoning. Place the fillets in the air fry basket.
2. Select Bake, Super Convection, set temperature to 400ºF (205ºC), and set time to 15 minutes. Select Start/Stop to begin preheating.
3. Once preheated, place the basket on the bake position. Flip the fillets halfway through.
4. Meanwhile, make the garlic aioli: Whisk together the garlic, mayo, lemon juice, olive oil, salt, and pepper in a small bowl until smooth.
5. When cooking is complete, the fish should flake apart with a fork and no longer translucent in the center. Remove the fish from the oven and serve with the garlic aioli on the side.

Shrimp Salad with Cheese

Prep time: 10 minutes | Cook time: 15 minutes | Serves 4

½ baguette, cut into 1-inch cubes (about 2½ cups)
4 tablespoons extra-virgin olive oil, divided
¼ teaspoon granulated garlic
¼ teaspoon kosher salt
¾ cup Caesar dressing, divided
2 romaine lettuce hearts, cut in half lengthwise and ends trimmed
1 pound (454 g) medium shrimp, peeled and deveined
2 ounces (57 g) Parmesan cheese, coarsely grated

1. Make the croutons: Put the bread cubes in a medium bowl and drizzle 3 tablespoons of olive oil over top. Season with granulated garlic and salt and toss to coat. Transfer to the air fry basket in a single layer.
2. Select Air Fry, Super Convection, set temperature to 400°F (205°C), and set time to 4 minutes. Select Start/Stop to begin preheating.
3. Once the oven has preheated, place the basket on the air fry position. Toss the croutons halfway through the cooking time.
4. When done, remove the air fry basket from the oven and set aside.
5. Brush 2 tablespoons of Caesar dressing on the cut side of the lettuce. Set aside.
6. Toss the shrimp with the ¼ cup of Caesar dressing in a large bowl until well coated. Set aside.
7. Coat the sheet pan with the remaining 1 tablespoon of olive oil. Arrange the romaine halves on the coated pan, cut side down. Brush the tops with the remaining 2 tablespoons of Caesar dressing.
8. Select Roast, Super Convection, set temperature to 375°F (190°C), and set time to 10 minutes. Select Start/Stop to begin preheating.
9. Once the oven has preheated, place the pan on the roast position.
10. After 5 minutes, remove the pan from the oven and flip the romaine halves. Spoon the shrimp around the lettuce. Return the pan to the oven and continue cooking.
11. When done, remove the sheet pan from the oven. If they are not quite cooked through, roast for another 1 minute.
12. On each of four plates, put a romaine half. Divide the shrimp among the plates and top with croutons and grated Parmesan cheese. Serve immediately.

Tilapia with Lemon

Prep time: 10 minutes | Cook time: 12 minutes | Serves 4

1 tablespoon olive oil
1 tablespoon lemon juice
1 teaspoon minced garlic
½ teaspoon chili powder
4 tilapia fillets

1. Line a baking pan with parchment paper.
2. In a shallow bowl, stir together the olive oil, lemon juice, garlic, and chili powder to make a marinade. Put the tilapia fillets in the bowl, turning to coat evenly.
3. Place the fillets in the baking pan in a single layer.
4. Select Air Fry, Super Convection, set temperature to 375°F (190°C), and set time to 12 minutes. Select Start/Stop to begin preheating.
5. Once preheated, slide the pan into the oven.
6. When cooked, the fish will flake apart with a fork. Remove from the oven to a plate and serve hot.

Shrimp and Sausage with Potato

Prep time: 10 minutes | Cook time: 15 minutes | Serves 4

1 pound (454 g) small red potatoes, halved
2 ears corn, shucked and cut into rounds, 1 to 1½ inches thick
2 tablespoons Old Bay or similar seasoning
½ cup unsalted butter, melted
1 (12- to 13-ounce / 340- to 369-g) package kielbasa or other smoked sausages
3 garlic cloves, minced
1 pound (454 g) medium shrimp, peeled and deveined

1. Place the potatoes and corn in a large bowl.
2. Stir together the butter and Old Bay seasoning in a small bowl. Drizzle half the butter mixture over the potatoes and corn, tossing to coat. Spread out the vegetables on a sheet pan.
3. Select Roast, Super Convection, set temperature to 350°F (180°C), and set time to 15 minutes. Select Start/Stop to begin preheating.
4. Once the oven has preheated, place the pan on the roast position.
5. Meanwhile, cut the sausages into 2-inch lengths, then cut each piece in half lengthwise. Put the sausages and shrimp in a medium bowl and set aside.
6. Add the garlic to the bowl of remaining butter mixture and stir well.
7. After 10 minutes, remove the sheet pan and pour the vegetables into the large bowl. Drizzle with the garlic butter and toss until well coated. Arrange the vegetables, sausages, and shrimp on the sheet pan.
8. Return to the oven and continue cooking. After 5 minutes, check the shrimp for doneness. The shrimp should be pink and opaque. If they are not quite cooked through, roast for an additional 1 minute.
9. When done, remove from the oven and serve on a plate.

Breaded Fish Sticks

Prep time: 10 minutes | Cook time: 8 minutes | Makes 8 fish sticks

8 ounces (227 g) fish fillets (pollock or cod), cut into ½×3-inch strips
Salt, to taste (optional)
½ cup plain bread crumbs
Cooking spray

1. Season the fish strips with salt to taste, if desired.
2. Place the bread crumbs on a plate. Roll the fish strips in the bread crumbs to coat. Spritz the fish strips with cooking spray.
3. Arrange the fish strips in the air fry basket in a single layer.
4. Select Air Fry, Super Convection, set temperature to 390ºF (199ºC), and set time to 8 minutes. Select Start/Stop to begin preheating.
5. Once preheated, place the basket on the air fry position.
6. When cooking is complete, they should be golden brown. Remove from the oven and cool for 5 minutes before serving.

Cheese Hake with Garlic Sauce

Prep time: 5 minutes | Cook time: 10 minutes | Serves 3

Fish:
6 tablespoons mayonnaise
1 tablespoon fresh lime juice
1 teaspoon Dijon mustard
1 cup grated Parmesan cheese
Salt, to taste
¼ teaspoon ground black pepper, or more to taste
3 hake fillets, patted dry
Nonstick cooking spray
Garlic Sauce:
¼ cup plain Greek yogurt
2 tablespoons olive oil
2 cloves garlic, minced
½ teaspoon minced tarragon leaves

1. Mix the mayo, lime juice, and mustard in a shallow bowl and whisk to combine. In another shallow bowl, stir together the grated Parmesan cheese, salt, and pepper.
2. Dredge each fillet in the mayo mixture, then roll them in the cheese mixture until they are evenly coated on both sides.
3. Spray the air fry basket with nonstick cooking spray. Place the fillets in the basket.
4. Select Air Fry, Super Convection, set temperature to 395ºF (202ºC), and set time to 10 minutes. Select Start/Stop to begin preheating.
5. Once preheated, place the basket on the air fry position. Flip the fillets halfway through the cooking time.
6. Meanwhile, in a small bowl, whisk all the ingredients for the sauce until well incorporated.
7. When cooking is complete, the fish should flake apart with a fork. Remove the fillets from the oven and serve warm alongside the sauce.

Prawns with Cayenne

Prep time: 10 minutes | Cook time: 8 minutes | Serves 2

8 prawns, cleaned
Salt and black pepper, to taste
½ teaspoon ground cayenne pepper
½ teaspoon garlic powder
½ teaspoon ground cumin
½ teaspoon red chili flakes
Cooking spray

1. Spritz the air fry basket with cooking spray.
2. Toss the remaining ingredients in a large bowl until the prawns are well coated.
3. Spread the coated prawns evenly in the air fry basket and spray them with cooking spray.
4. Select Air Fry, Super Convection, set temperature to 340ºF (171ºC), and set time to 8 minutes. Select Start/Stop to begin preheating.
5. Once preheated, place the basket on the air fry position. Flip the prawns halfway through the cooking time.
6. When cooking is complete, the prawns should be pink. Remove the prawns from the oven to a plate.

Crunchy Fish Sticks with Tartar Sauce

Prep time: 15 minutes | Cook time: 6 minutes | Serves 2

½ cup flour
½ teaspoon paprika
Salt and freshly ground black pepper,
    to taste
2 eggs
1½ cups panko bread crumbs
1 teaspoon salt
12 ounces (340 g) cod or flounder,
    cut into ¾-inch-thick sticks
Vegetable oil spray
Tartar Sauce:
¼ cup mayonnaise
2 teaspoons lemon juice
2 tablespoons finely chopped sweet pickles
Salt and freshly ground black pepper, to taste

1. Preheat the air fryer to 400ºF (204ºC). Spray the air fryer basket with vegetable oil spray.
2. Thoroughly combine the flour, paprika, salt, and pepper in a shallow dish. Beat the eggs lightly in a second shallow dish. Mix the bread crumbs and salt in a third shallow dish.
3. Dip the fish sticks in the flour mixture, then in the beaten egg, and finally in the bread crumbs to coat, pressing the crumbs firmly onto the fish.
4. Lay the fish sticks in the basket and air fry for 4 minutes. Flip the sticks and air fry for 2 minutes more.
5. Meanwhile, whisk together all the ingredients for the tartar sauce in a bowl.
6. Remove the fish sticks from the basket and serve alongside the tartar sauce.

Buttermilk Catfish Cakes with Cheese

Prep time: 5 minutes | Cook time: 15 minutes | Serves 4

2 catfish fillets
3 ounces (85 g) butter
1 cup shredded Parmesan cheese
1 cup shredded Swiss cheese
½ cup buttermilk
1 teaspoon baking powder
1 teaspoon baking soda
1 teaspoon Cajun seasoning

1. Bring a pot of salted water to a boil. Add the catfish fillets to the boiling water and let them boil for 5 minutes until they become opaque.
2. Remove the fillets from the pot to a mixing bowl and flake them into small pieces with a fork.
3. Add the remaining ingredients to the bowl of fish and stir until well incorporated.
4. Divide the fish mixture into 12 equal portions and shape each portion into a patty. Place the patties in the air fry basket.
5. Select Air Fry, Super Convection, set temperature to 380ºF (193ºC), and set time to 15 minutes. Select Start/Stop to begin preheating.
6. Once preheated, place the basket on the air fry position. Flip the patties halfway through the cooking time.
7. When cooking is complete, the patties should be golden brown and cooked through. Remove from the oven. Let the patties sit for 5 minutes and serve.

Fish and Tomato Curry

Prep time: 10 minutes | Cook time: 22 minutes | Serves 4

2 tablespoons sunflower oil,
    divided
1 pound (454 g) fish, chopped
1 ripe tomato, puréed
2 red chilies, chopped
1 shallot, minced
1 garlic clove, minced
1 cup coconut milk
1 tablespoon coriander powder
1 teaspoon red curry paste
½ teaspoon fenugreek seeds
Salt and white pepper, to taste

1. Coat the air fry basket with 1 tablespoon of sunflower oil. Place the fish in the air fry basket.
2. Select Air Fry, Super Convection, set temperature to 380ºF (193ºC), and set time to 10 minutes. Select Start/Stop to begin preheating.
3. Once preheated, place the basket on the air fry position. Flip the fish halfway through the cooking time.
4. When cooking is complete, transfer the cooked fish to a baking pan greased with the remaining 1 tablespoon of sunflower oil. Stir in the remaining ingredients.
5. Select Air Fry, Super Convection, set temperature to 350ºF (180ºC), and set time to 12 minutes. Select Start/Stop to begin preheating.
6. Once preheated, place the pan on the air fry position.
7. When cooking is complete, they should be heated through. Cool for 5 to 8 minutes before serving.

Shrimp Spring Rolls with Cabbage

Prep time: 10 minutes | Cook time: 20 minutes | Serves 4

1 tablespoon olive oil
2 teaspoons minced garlic
1 cup matchstick cut carrots
2 cups finely sliced cabbage
2 (4-ounce / 113-g) cans tiny
  shrimp, drained
4 teaspoons soy sauce
Salt and freshly ground black
  pepper, to taste
16 square spring roll
  wrappers
Cooking spray

1. Spray the air fry basket with cooking spray. Set aside.
2. Heat the olive oil in a medium skillet over medium heat until it shimmers.
3. Add the garlic to the skillet and cook for 30 seconds. Stir in the cabbage and carrots and sauté for about 5 minutes, stirring occasionally, or until the vegetables are lightly tender.
4. Fold in the shrimp and soy sauce and sprinkle with salt and pepper, then stir to combine. Sauté for another 2 minutes, or until the moisture is evaporated. Remove from the heat and set aside to cool.
5. Put a spring roll wrapper on a work surface and spoon 1 tablespoon of the shrimp mixture onto the lower end of the wrapper.
6. Roll the wrapper away from you halfway, and then fold in the right and left sides, like an envelope. Continue to roll to the very end, using a little water to seal the edge. Repeat with the remaining wrappers and filling.
7. Place the spring rolls in the air fry basket in a single layer, leaving space between each spring roll. Mist them lightly with cooking spray.
8. Select Air Fry, Super Convection, set temperature to 375°F (190°C), and set time to 10 minutes. Select Start/Stop to begin preheating.
9. Once preheated, place the basket on the air fry position. Flip the rolls halfway through the cooking time.
10. When cooking is complete, the spring rolls will be heated through and start to brown. If necessary, continue cooking for 5 minutes more. Remove from the oven and cool for a few minutes before serving.

Tangy Shrimp

Prep time: 40 minutes | Cook time: 12 minutes | Serves 4

⅓ cup orange juice
3 teaspoons minced garlic
1 teaspoon Old Bay seasoning
¼ to ½ teaspoon cayenne pepper
1 pound (454 g) medium shrimp,
  thawed, deveined, peeled, with
  tails off, and patted dry
Cooking spray

1. Stir together the orange juice, garlic, Old Bay seasoning, and cayenne pepper in a medium bowl. Add the shrimp to the bowl and toss to coat well.
2. Cover the bowl with plastic wrap and marinate in the refrigerator for 30 minutes.
3. Spritz the air fry basket with cooking spray. Place the shrimp in the pan and spray with cooking spray.
4. Select Air Fry, Super Convection, set temperature to 400°F (205°C), and set time to 12 minutes. Select Start/Stop to begin preheating.
5. Once preheated, place the basket on the air fry position. Flip the shrimp halfway through the cooking time.
6. When cooked, the shrimp should be opaque and crisp. Remove from the oven and serve hot.

Baked Flounder Fillets

Prep time: 8 minutes | Cook time: 12 minutes | Serves 2

2 flounder fillets, patted dry
1 egg
½ teaspoon Worcestershire sauce
¼ cup almond flour
¼ cup coconut flour
½ teaspoon coarse sea salt
½ teaspoon lemon pepper
¼ teaspoon chili powder
Cooking spray

1. In a shallow bowl, beat together the egg with Worcestershire sauce until well incorporated.
2. In another bowl, thoroughly combine the almond flour, coconut flour, sea salt, lemon pepper, and chili powder.
3. Dredge the fillets in the egg mixture, shaking off any excess, then roll in the flour mixture to coat well.
4. Spritz the air fry basket with cooking spray. Place the fillets in the pan.
5. Select Bake, Super Convection, set temperature to 390°F (199°C), and set time to 12 minutes. Select Start/Stop to begin preheating.
6. Once preheated, place the basket on the bake position.
7. After 7 minutes, remove from the oven and flip the fillets and spray with cooking spray. Return the basket to the oven and continue cooking for 5 minutes, or until the fish is flaky.
8. When cooking is complete, remove from the oven and serve warm.

Shrimp with Paprika

Prep time: 5 minutes | Cook time: 10 minutes | Serves 4

1 pound (454 g) tiger shrimp
2 tablespoons olive oil
½ tablespoon old bay seasoning
¼ tablespoon smoked paprika
¼ teaspoon cayenne pepper
A pinch of sea salt

1. Toss all the ingredients in a large bowl until the shrimp are evenly coated.
2. Arrange the shrimp in the air fry basket.
3. Select Air Fry, Super Convection, set temperature to 380ºF (193ºC), and set time to 10 minutes. Select Start/Stop to begin preheating.
4. Once preheated, place the basket on the air fry position.
5. When cooking is complete, the shrimp should be pink and cooked through. Remove from the oven and serve hot.

Beer Coconut Prawns

Prep time: 15 minutes | Cook time: 8 minutes | Serves 4

12 prawns, cleaned and deveined
1 teaspoon fresh lemon juice
½ teaspoon cumin powder
Salt and ground black pepper, to taste
1 medium egg
⅓ cup beer
½ cup flour, divided
1 tablespoon curry powder
1 teaspoon baking powder
½ teaspoon grated fresh ginger
1 cup flaked coconut

1. In a large bowl, toss the prawns with the lemon juice, cumin powder, salt, and pepper until well coated. Set aside.
2. In a shallow bowl, whisk together the egg, beer, ¼ cup of flour, curry powder, baking powder, and ginger until combined.
3. In a separate shallow bowl, put the remaining ¼ cup of flour, and on a plate, place the flaked coconut.
4. Dip the prawns in the flour, then in the egg mixture, finally roll in the flaked coconut to coat well. Transfer the prawns to a baking sheet.
5. Select Air Fry, Super Convection, set temperature to 350ºF (180ºC), and set time to 8 minutes. Select Start/Stop to begin preheating.
6. Once preheated, place the baking sheet into the oven.
7. After 5 minutes, remove from the oven and flip the prawns. Return to the oven and continue cooking for 3 minutes more.
8. When cooking is complete, remove from the oven and serve warm.

Shrimp with Lemon

Prep time: 10 minutes | Cook time: 8 minutes | Serves 4

1 pound (454 g) shrimp, deveined
4 tablespoons olive oil
1½ tablespoons lemon juice
1½ tablespoons fresh parsley, roughly chopped
2 cloves garlic, finely minced
1 teaspoon crushed red pepper flakes, or more to taste
Garlic pepper, to taste
Sea salt flakes, to taste

1. Toss all the ingredients in a large bowl until the shrimp are coated on all sides.
2. Arrange the shrimp in the air fry basket.
3. Select Air Fry, Super Convection, set temperature to 385ºF (196ºC), and set time to 8 minutes. Select Start/Stop to begin preheating.
4. Once preheated, place the basket on the air fry position.
5. When cooking is complete, the shrimp should be pink and cooked through. Remove from the oven and serve warm.

Shrimp and Cherry Tomato Kebabs

Prep time: 15 minutes | Cook time: 5 minutes | Serves 4

1½ pounds (680 g) jumbo shrimp, cleaned, shelled and deveined
1 pound (454 g) cherry tomatoes
2 tablespoons butter, melted
1 tablespoons Sriracha sauce
Sea salt and ground black pepper, to taste
1 teaspoon dried parsley flakes
½ teaspoon dried basil
½ teaspoon dried oregano
½ teaspoon mustard seeds
½ teaspoon marjoram

Special Equipment:
4 to 6 wooden skewers, soaked in water for 30 minutes

1. Put all the ingredients in a large bowl and toss to coat well.
2. Make the kebabs: Thread, alternating jumbo shrimp and cherry tomatoes, onto the wooden skewers. Place the kebabs in the air fry basket.
3. Select Air Fry, Super Convection, set temperature to 400°F (205°C), and set time to 5 minutes. Select Start/Stop to begin preheating.
4. Once preheated, place the basket on the air fry position.
5. When cooking is complete, the shrimp should be pink and the cherry tomatoes should be softened. Remove from the oven. Let the shrimp and cherry tomato kebabs cool for 5 minutes and serve hot.

Shrimp with Butter Sauce

Prep time: 5 minutes | Cook time: 8 minutes | Serves 4

Sauce:
¼ cup unsalted butter
2 tablespoons fish stock or chicken broth
2 cloves garlic, minced
2 tablespoons chopped fresh basil leaves
1 tablespoon lemon juice
1 tablespoon chopped fresh parsley, plus more for garnish
1 teaspoon red pepper flakes
Shrimp:
1 pound (454 g) large shrimp, peeled and deveined, tails removed
Fresh basil sprigs, for garnish

1. Put all the ingredients for the sauce in a baking pan and stir to incorporate.
2. Select Air Fry, Super Convection, set temperature to 350°F (180°C), and set time to 8 minutes. Select Start/Stop to begin preheating.
3. Once preheated, place the baking pan into the oven.
4. After 3 minutes, remove from the oven and add the shrimp to the baking pan, flipping to coat in the sauce. Return the pan to the oven and continue cooking for 5 minutes until the shrimp are pink and opaque. Stir the shrimp twice during cooking.
5. When cooking is complete, remove the pan from the oven. Serve garnished with the parsley and basil sprigs.

Garlic Shrimp with Parsley

Prep time: 10 minutes | Cook time: 5 minutes | Serves 4

18 shrimp, shelled and deveined
2 garlic cloves, peeled and minced
2 tablespoons extra-virgin olive oil
2 tablespoons freshly squeezed lemon juice
½ cup fresh parsley, coarsely chopped
1 teaspoon onion powder
1 teaspoon lemon-pepper seasoning
½ teaspoon hot paprika
½ teaspoon salt
¼ teaspoon cumin powder

1. Toss all the ingredients in a mixing bowl until the shrimp are well coated.
2. Cover and allow to marinate in the refrigerator for 30 minutes.
3. When ready, transfer the shrimp to the air fry basket.
4. Select Air Fry, Super Convection, set temperature to 400°F (205°C), and set time to 5 minutes. Select Start/Stop to begin preheating.
5. Once preheated, place the basket on the air fry position.
6. When cooking is complete, the shrimp should be pink on the outside and opaque in the center. Remove from the oven and serve warm.

Mushroom Scallops with Snow Peas

Prep time: 10 minutes | Cook time: 8 minutes | Serves 4

1 pound (454 g) sea scallops
3 tablespoons hoisin sauce
½ cup toasted sesame seeds
6 ounces (170 g) snow peas, trimmed
3 teaspoons vegetable oil, divided
1 teaspoon soy sauce
1 teaspoon sesame oil
1 cup roasted mushrooms

1. Brush the scallops with the hoisin sauce. Put the sesame seeds in a shallow dish. Roll the scallops in the sesame seeds until evenly coated.
2. Combine the snow peas with 1 teaspoon of vegetable oil, the sesame oil, and soy sauce in a medium bowl and toss to coat.
3. Grease the sheet pan with the remaining 2 teaspoons of vegetable oil. Put the scallops in the middle of the pan and arrange the snow peas around the scallops in a single layer.
4. Select Roast, Super Convection, set temperature to 375°F (190°C), and set time to 8 minutes. Select Start/Stop to begin preheating.
5. Once the oven has preheated, place the pan on the roast position.
6. After 5 minutes, remove the pan and flip the scallops. Fold in the mushrooms and stir well. Return the pan to the oven and continue cooking.
7. When done, remove the pan from the oven and cool for 5 minutes. Serve warm.

King Prawns with Garlic

Prep time: 10 minutes | Cook time: 8 minutes | Serves 2

12 king prawns, rinsed
1 tablespoon coconut oil
Salt and ground black pepper, to taste
1 teaspoon onion powder
1 teaspoon garlic paste
1 teaspoon curry powder
½ teaspoon piri piri powder
½ teaspoon cumin powder

1. Combine all the ingredients in a large bowl and toss until the prawns are completely coated. Place the prawns in the air fry basket.
2. Select Air Fry, Super Convection, set temperature to 360°F (182°C), and set time to 8 minutes. Select Start/Stop to begin preheating.
3. Once preheated, place the basket on the air fry position. Flip the prawns halfway through the cooking time.
4. When cooking is complete, the prawns will turn pink. Remove from the oven and serve hot

Panko Crab Sticks with Mayo Sauce

Prep time: 5 minutes | Cook time: 12 minutes | Serves 4

Crab Sticks:
2 eggs
1 cup flour
⅓ cup panko bread crumbs
1 tablespoon old bay seasoning
1 pound (454 g) crab sticks
Cooking spray
Mayo Sauce:
½ cup mayonnaise
1 lime, juiced
2 garlic cloves, minced

1. In a bowl, beat the eggs. In a shallow bowl, place the flour. In another shallow bowl, thoroughly combine the panko bread crumbs and old bay seasoning.
2. Dredge the crab sticks in the flour, shaking off any excess, then in the beaten eggs, finally press them in the bread crumb mixture to coat well.
3. Arrange the crab sticks in the air fry basket and spray with cooking spray.
4. Select Air Fry, Super Convection, set temperature to 390°F (199°C), and set time to 12 minutes. Select Start/Stop to begin preheating.
5. Once preheated, place the basket on the air fry position. Flip the crab sticks halfway through the cooking time.
6. Meanwhile, make the sauce by whisking together the mayo, lime juice, and garlic in a small bowl.
7. When cooking is complete, remove the basket from the oven. Serve the crab sticks with the mayo sauce on the side.

Coconut Shrimp with Pineapple

Prep time: 15 minutes | Cook time: 5 to 7 minutes | Serves 4

1 (8-ounce / 227-g) can crushed pineapple
½ cup plain Greek yogurt
¼ cup pineapple preserves
2 egg whites
⅔ cup cornstarch
⅔ cup unsweetened coconut
1 cup whole wheat bread crumbs
1 pound (454 g) uncooked large shrimp, thawed if frozen, deveined and shelled
Olive oil for misting

1. Drain the crushed pineapple well, reserving the juice.
2. In a small bowl, combine the pineapple, plain Greek yogurt, and preserves, and mix well. Set aside.
3. In a shallow bowl, beat the egg whites with 2 tablespoons of the reserved pineapple liquid. Place the cornstarch on a plate. Combine the coconut and bread crumbs on another plate.
4. Dip the shrimp into the cornstarch, shake it off, then dip into the egg white mixture and finally into the coconut mixture.
5. Place the shrimp in the air fryer basket and mist with oil. Air fry at 400°F (204°C) for 5 to 7 minutes or until the shrimp are crisp and golden brown.

Jumbo Shrimp with Mayo

Prep time: 5 minutes | Cook time: 7 minutes | Serves 4

Shrimp
12 jumbo shrimp
½ teaspoon garlic salt
¼ teaspoon freshly cracked mixed peppercorns
Sauce:
4 tablespoons mayonnaise
1 teaspoon grated lemon rind
1 teaspoon Dijon mustard
1 teaspoon chipotle powder
½ teaspoon cumin powder

1. In a medium bowl, season the shrimp with garlic salt and cracked mixed peppercorns.
2. Place the shrimp in the air fry basket.
3. Select Air Fry, Super Convection, set temperature to 395°F (202°C), and set time to 7 minutes. Select Start/Stop to begin preheating.
4. Once preheated, place the basket on the air fry position.
5. After 5 minutes, remove from the oven and flip the shrimp. Return the basket to the oven and continue cooking for 2 minutes more, or until they are pink and no longer opaque.
6. Meanwhile, stir together all the ingredients for the sauce in a small bowl until well mixed.
7. When cooking is complete, remove the shrimp from the oven and serve alongside the sauce.

Roasted Salmon with Asparagus

Prep time: 10 minutes | Cook time: 15 minutes | Serves 4

4 (6-ounce / 170 g) salmon fillets, patted dry
1 teaspoon kosher salt, divided
1 tablespoon honey
2 tablespoons unsalted butter, melted
2 teaspoons Dijon mustard
2 pounds (907 g) asparagus, trimmed
Lemon wedges, for serving

1. Season both sides of the salmon fillets with ½ teaspoon of kosher salt.
2. Whisk together the honey, 1 tablespoon of butter, and mustard in a small bowl. Set aside.
3. Arrange the asparagus on a sheet pan. Drizzle the remaining 1 tablespoon of butter all over and season with the remaining ½ teaspoon of salt, tossing to coat. Move the asparagus to the outside of the sheet pan.
4. Put the salmon fillets on the sheet pan, skin-side down. Brush the fillets generously with the honey mixture.
5. Select Roast, Super Convection, set temperature to 375°F (190°C), and set time to 15 minutes. Select Start/Stop to begin preheating.
6. Once the oven has preheated, place the pan on the roast position. Toss the asparagus once halfway through the cooking time.
7. When done, transfer the salmon fillets and asparagus to a plate. Serve warm with a squeeze of lemon juice.

Easy Salmon Patties

Prep time: 5 minutes | Cook time: 11 minutes | Makes 6 patties

1 (14.75-ounce / 418-g) can Alaskan pink salmon, drained and bones removed
½ cup bread crumbs
1 egg, whisked
2 scallions, diced
1 teaspoon garlic powder
Salt and pepper, to taste
Cooking spray

1. Stir together the salmon, bread crumbs, whisked egg, scallions, garlic powder, salt, and pepper in a large bowl until well incorporated.
2. Divide the salmon mixture into six equal portions and form each into a patty with your hands.
3. Arrange the salmon patties in the air fry basket and spritz them with cooking spray.
4. Select Air Fry, Super Convection, set temperature to 400°F (205°C), and set time to 10 minutes. Select Start/Stop to begin preheating.
5. Once preheated, place the basket on the air fry position. Flip the patties once halfway through.
6. When cooking is complete, the patties should be golden brown and cooked through. Remove the patties from the oven and serve on a plate.

Basil Salmon with Tomatoes

Prep time: 10 minutes | Cook time: 15 minutes | Serves 4

4 (6-ounce / 170-g) salmon fillets, patted dry
1 teaspoon kosher salt, divided
2 pints cherry or grape tomatoes, halved if large, divided
3 tablespoons extra-virgin olive oil, divided
2 garlic cloves, minced
1 small red bell pepper, deseeded and chopped
2 tablespoons chopped fresh basil, divided

1. Season both sides of the salmon with ½ teaspoon of kosher salt.
2. Put about half of the tomatoes in a large bowl, along with the remaining ½ teaspoon of kosher salt, 2 tablespoons of olive oil, garlic, bell pepper, and 1 tablespoon of basil. Toss to coat and then transfer to the sheet pan.
3. Arrange the salmon fillets on the sheet pan, skin-side down. Brush them with the remaining 1 tablespoon of olive oil.
4. Select Roast, Super Convection, set temperature to 375°F (190°C), and set time to 15 minutes. Select Start/Stop to begin preheating.
5. Once preheated, place the pan on the roast position.
6. After 7 minutes, remove the pan and fold in the remaining tomatoes. Return the pan to the oven and continue cooking.
7. When cooked, remove the pan from the oven. Serve sprinkled with the remaining 1 tablespoon of basil.

Teriyaki Salmon

Prep time: 15 minutes | Cook time: 15 minutes | Serves 4

¾ cup Teriyaki sauce, divided
4 (6-ounce / 170-g) skinless salmon fillets
4 heads baby bok choy, root ends trimmed off and cut in half lengthwise through the root
1 teaspoon sesame oil
1 tablespoon vegetable oil
1 tablespoon toasted sesame seeds

1. Set aside ¼ cup of Teriyaki sauce and pour the remaining sauce into a resealable plastic bag. Put the salmon into the bag and seal, squeezing as much air out as possible. Allow the salmon to marinate for at least 10 minutes.
2. Arrange the bok choy halves on the sheet pan. Drizzle the oils over the vegetables, tossing to coat. Drizzle about 1 tablespoon of the reserved Teriyaki sauce over the bok choy, then push them to the sides of the sheet pan.
3. Put the salmon fillets in the middle of the sheet pan.
4. Select Roast, Super Convection, set temperature to 375°F (190°C), and set time to 15 minutes. Select Start/Stop to begin preheating.
5. Once the oven has preheated, place the pan on the roast position.
6. When done, remove the pan and brush the salmon with the remaining Teriyaki sauce. Serve garnished with the sesame seeds.

Lemon-Honey Snapper with Fruit

Prep time: 15 minutes | Cook time: 12 minutes | Serves 4

4 (4-ounce / 113-g) red snapper fillets
2 teaspoons olive oil
3 plums, halved and pitted
3 nectarines, halved and pitted
1 cup red grapes
1 tablespoon freshly squeezed lemon juice
1 tablespoon honey
½ teaspoon dried thyme

1. Arrange the red snapper fillets in the air fry basket and drizzle the olive oil over the top.
2. Select Air Fry, Super Convection, set temperature to 390°F (199°C), and set time to 12 minutes. Select Start/Stop to begin preheating.
3. Once preheated, place the basket on the air fry position.
4. After 4 minutes, remove the basket from the oven. Top the fillets with the plums and nectarines. Scatter the red grapes all over the fillets. Drizzle with the lemon juice and honey and sprinkle the thyme on top. Return the basket to the oven and continue cooking for 8 minutes, or until the fish is flaky.
5. When cooking is complete, remove from the oven and serve warm.

Asian-Inspired Swordfish Steaks

Prep time: 10 minutes | Cook time: 8 minutes | Serves 4

4 (4-ounce / 113-g) swordfish steaks
½ teaspoon toasted sesame oil
1 jalapeño pepper, finely minced
2 garlic cloves, grated
2 tablespoons freshly squeezed lemon juice
1 tablespoon grated fresh ginger
½ teaspoon Chinese five-spice powder
⅛ teaspoon freshly ground black pepper

1. On a clean work surface, place the swordfish steaks and brush both sides of the fish with the sesame oil.
2. Combine the jalapeño, garlic, lemon juice, ginger, five-spice powder, and black pepper in a small bowl and stir to mix well. Rub the mixture all over the fish until completely coated. Allow to sit for 10 minutes.
3. When ready, arrange the swordfish steaks in the air fry basket.
4. Select Air Fry, Super Convection, set temperature to 380°F (193°C), and set time to 8 minutes. Select Start/Stop to begin preheating.
5. Once preheated, place the basket on the air fry position. Flip the steaks halfway through.
6. When cooking is complete, remove from the oven and cool for 5 minutes before serving.

Butter-Wine Baked Salmon

Prep time: 5 minutes | Cook time: 10 minutes | Serves 4

4 tablespoons butter, melted
2 cloves garlic, minced
Sea salt and ground black pepper, to taste
¼ cup dry white wine
1 tablespoon lime juice
1 teaspoon smoked paprika
½ teaspoon onion powder
4 salmon steaks
Cooking spray

1. Place all the ingredients except the salmon and oil in a shallow dish and stir to mix well.
2. Add the salmon steaks, turning to coat well on both sides. Transfer the salmon to the refrigerator to marinate for 30 minutes.
3. When ready, put the salmon steaks in the air fry basket, discarding any excess marinade. Spray the salmon steaks with cooking spray.
4. Select Air Fry, Super Convection, set temperature to 360°F (182°C), and set time to 10 minutes. Select Start/Stop to begin preheating.
5. Once preheated, place the basket on the air fry position. Flip the salmon steaks halfway through.
6. When cooking is complete, remove from the oven and divide the salmon steaks among four plates. Serve warm.

Golden Beer-Battered Cod

Prep time: 5 minutes | Cook time: 15 minutes | Serves 4

2 eggs
1 cup malty beer
1 cup all-purpose flour
½ cup cornstarch
1 teaspoon garlic powder
Salt and pepper, to taste
4 (4-ounce / 113-g) cod fillets
Cooking spray

1. In a shallow bowl, beat together the eggs with the beer. In another shallow bowl, thoroughly combine the flour and cornstarch. Sprinkle with the garlic powder, salt, and pepper.
2. Dredge each cod fillet in the flour mixture, then in the egg mixture. Dip each piece of fish in the flour mixture a second time.
3. Spritz the air fry basket with cooking spray. Arrange the cod fillets in the basket in a single layer.
4. Select Air Fry, Super Convection, set temperature to 400ºF (205ºC), and set time to 15 minutes. Select Start/Stop to begin preheating.
5. Once preheated, place the basket on the air fry position. Flip the fillets halfway through the cooking time.
6. When cooking is complete, the cod should reach an internal temperature of 145ºF (63ºC) on a meat thermometer and the outside should be crispy. Let the fish cool for 5 minutes and serve.

Garlicky Cod Fillets

Prep time: 10 minutes | Cook time: 12 minutes | Serves 4

1 teaspoon olive oil
4 cod fillets
¼ teaspoon fine sea salt
¼ teaspoon ground black pepper, or more to taste
1 teaspoon cayenne pepper
½ cup fresh Italian parsley, coarsely chopped
½ cup nondairy milk
1 Italian pepper, chopped
4 garlic cloves, minced
1 teaspoon dried basil
½ teaspoon dried oregano

1. Lightly coat the sides and bottom of a baking dish with the olive oil. Set aside.
2. In a large bowl, sprinkle the fillets with salt, black pepper, and cayenne pepper.
3. In a food processor, pulse the remaining ingredients until smoothly puréed.
4. Add the purée to the bowl of fillets and toss to coat, then transfer to the prepared baking dish.
5. Select Bake, Super Convection, set temperature to 380ºF (193ºC), and set time to 12 minutes. Select Start/Stop to begin preheating.
6. Once preheated, place the baking dish on the bake position.
7. When cooking is complete, the fish should flake when pressed lightly with a fork. Remove from the oven and serve warm.

Spiced Red Snapper

Prep time: 13 minutes | Cook time: 10 minutes | Serves 4

1 teaspoon olive oil
1½ teaspoons black pepper
¼ teaspoon garlic powder
¼ teaspoon thyme
⅛ teaspoon cayenne pepper
4 (4-ounce / 113-g) red snapper fillets, skin on
4 thin slices lemon
Nonstick cooking spray

1. Spritz the air fry basket with nonstick cooking spray.
2. In a small bowl, stir together the olive oil, black pepper, garlic powder, thyme, and cayenne pepper. Rub the mixture all over the fillets until completely coated.
3. Lay the fillets, skin-side down, in the air fry basket and top each fillet with a slice of lemon.
4. Select Bake, Super Convection, set temperature to 390ºF (199ºC), and set time to 10 minutes. Select Start/Stop to begin preheating.
5. Once preheated, place the basket on the bake position. Flip the fillets halfway through.
6. When cooking is complete, the fish should be cooked through. Let the fish cool for 5 minutes and serve.

Snapper with Tomatoes and Olives

Prep time: 9 minutes | Cook time: 18 minutes | Serves 4

2 tablespoons extra-virgin olive oil
2 large garlic cloves, minced
½ onion, finely chopped
1 (14.5-ounce / 411-g) can diced
   tomatoes, drained
¼ cup sliced green olives
3 tablespoons capers, divided
2 tablespoons chopped fresh parsley,
   divided
½ teaspoon dried oregano
4 (6-ounce / 170-g) snapper fillets
½ teaspoon kosher salt

1. Grease the sheet pan generously with olive oil, then place the pan on the roast position.
2. Select Roast, Super Convection, set temperature to 375ºF (190ºC), and set time to 18 minutes. Select Start/Stop to begin preheating.
3. When the oven has preheated, remove the pan and add the garlic and onion to the olive oil in the pan, stirring to coat. Return the pan to the oven and continue cooking.
4. After 2 minutes, remove the pan from the oven. Stir in the tomatoes, olives, 1½ tablespoons of capers, 1 tablespoon of parsley, and oregano. Return the pan to the oven and continue cooking for 6 minutes until heated through.
5. Meanwhile, rub the fillets with the salt on both sides.
6. After another 6 minutes, remove the pan. Put the fillets in the center of the sheet pan and spoon some of the sauce over them. Return the pan to the oven and continue cooking, or until the fish is flaky.
7. When cooked, remove the pan from the oven. Scatter the remaining 1½ tablespoons of capers and 1 tablespoon of parsley on top of the fillets, then serve.

Tex-Mex Salmon Bowl

Prep time: 115 minutes | Cook time: 12 minutes | Serves 4

12 ounces (340 g) salmon fillets, cut
   into 1½-inch cubes
1 red onion, chopped
1 jalapeño pepper, minced
1 red bell pepper, chopped
¼ cup low-sodium salsa
2 teaspoons peanut oil or safflower
   oil
2 tablespoons low-sodium tomato
   juice
1 teaspoon chili powder

1. Mix together the salmon cubes, red onion, jalapeño, red bell pepper, salsa, peanut oil, tomato juice, chili powder in a medium metal bowl and stir until well incorporated.
2. Select Bake, Super Convection, set temperature to 370ºF (188ºC), and set time to 12 minutes. Select Start/Stop to begin preheating.
3. Once preheated, place the metal bowl on the bake position. Stir the ingredients once halfway through the cooking time.
4. When cooking is complete, the salmon should be cooked through and the veggies should be fork-tender. Serve warm.

Parmesan-Crusted Halibut Fillets

Prep time: 5 minutes | Cook time: 10 minutes | Serves 4

2 medium-sized halibut fillets
Dash of tabasco sauce
1 teaspoon curry powder
½ teaspoon ground coriander
½ teaspoon hot paprika
Kosher salt and freshly cracked
   mixed peppercorns, to taste
2 eggs
1½ tablespoons olive oil
½ cup grated Parmesan cheese

1. On a clean work surface, drizzle the halibut fillets with the tabasco sauce. Sprinkle with the curry powder, coriander, hot paprika, salt, and cracked mixed peppercorns. Set aside.
2. In a shallow bowl, beat the eggs until frothy. In another shallow bowl, combine the olive oil and Parmesan cheese.
3. One at a time, dredge the halibut fillets in the beaten eggs, shaking off any excess, then roll them over the Parmesan cheese until evenly coated.
4. Arrange the halibut fillets in the air fry basket in a single layer.
5. Select Roast, Super Convection, set temperature to 365ºF (185ºC), and set time to 10 minutes. Select Start/Stop to begin preheating.
6. Once preheated, place the basket on the roast position.
7. When cooking is complete, the fish should be golden brown and crisp. Cool for 5 minutes before serving.

Cajun and Lemon Pepper Cod

Prep time: 5 minutes | Cook time: 12 minutes | Makes 2 cod fillets

1 tablespoon Cajun seasoning
1 teaspoon salt
½ teaspoon lemon pepper
½ teaspoon freshly ground black
    pepper
2 (8-ounce / 227-g) cod fillets, cut to
    fit into the air fry basket
Cooking spray
2 tablespoons unsalted butter,
    melted
1 lemon, cut into 4 wedges

1. Spritz the air fry basket with cooking spray.
2. Thoroughly combine the Cajun seasoning, salt, lemon pepper, and black pepper in a small bowl. Rub this mixture all over the cod fillets until completely coated.
3. Put the fillets in the air fry basket and brush the melted butter over both sides of each fillet.
4. Select Bake, Super Convection, set temperature to 360ºF (182ºC), and set time to 12 minutes. Select Start/Stop to begin preheating.
5. Once preheated, place the basket on the bake position. Flip the fillets halfway through the cooking time.
6. When cooking is complete, the fish should flake apart with a fork. Remove the fillets from the oven and serve with fresh lemon wedges.

Roasted Halibut Steaks with Parsley

Prep time: 5 minutes | Cook time: 10 minutes | Serves 4

1 pound (454 g) halibut steaks
¼ cup vegetable oil
2½ tablespoons Worcester sauce
2 tablespoons honey
2 tablespoons vermouth
1 tablespoon freshly squeezed lemon
    juice
1 tablespoon fresh parsley leaves,
    coarsely chopped
Salt and pepper, to taste
1 teaspoon dried basil

1. Put all the ingredients in a large mixing dish and gently stir until the fish is coated evenly. Transfer the fish to the air fry basket.
2. Select Roast, Super Convection, set temperature to 390ºF (199ºC), and set time to 10 minutes. Select Start/Stop to begin preheating.
3. Once preheated, place the basket on the roast position. Flip the fish halfway through cooking time.
4. When cooking is complete, the fish should reach an internal temperature of at least 145ºF (63ºC) on a meat thermometer. Remove from the oven and let the fish cool for 5 minutes before serving.

Salmon with Balsamic Maple Glaze

Prep time: 5 minutes | Cook time: 10 minutes | Serves 4

4 (6-ounce / 170-g) fillets of salmon
Salt and freshly ground black pepper
Olive oil
¼ cup pure maple syrup
3 tablespoons balsamic vinegar
1 teaspoon Dijon mustard

1. Preheat the air fryer to 400ºF (204ºC).
2. Season the salmon well with salt and freshly ground black pepper. Spray or brush the bottom of the air fryer basket with vegetable oil and place the salmon fillets inside. Air fry the salmon for 5 minutes.
3. While the salmon is air frying, combine the maple syrup, balsamic vinegar and Dijon mustard in a small saucepan over medium heat and stir to blend well. Let the mixture simmer while the fish is cooking. It should start to thicken slightly, but keep your eye on it so it doesn't burn.
4. Brush the glaze on the salmon fillets and air fry for an additional 5 minutes. The salmon should feel firm to the touch when finished and the glaze should be nicely browned on top. Brush a little more glaze on top before removing and serving with rice and vegetables, or a nice green salad.

Chili-Lemon Sockeye Salmon

Prep time: 5 minutes | Cook time: 5 minutes | Serves 4

4 wild sockeye salmon fillets
¼ cup lemon juice
2 tablespoons assorted chili pepper seasoning
Salt and ground black pepper, to taste
1 cup water

1. Drizzle the salmon fillets with lemon juice. Season with the chili pepper seasoning, salt, and pepper.
2. Pour the water into the Instant Pot and add a steamer basket. Put the salmon fillets in the steamer basket.
3. Secure the lid. Select the Pressure Cook mode and set the cooking time for 5 minutes at High Pressure.
4. Once cooking is complete, do a quick pressure release. Carefully open the lid.
5. Remove from the Instant Pot and serve.

Lemon Red Snapper with Thyme

Prep time: 13 minutes | Cook time: 10 minutes | Serves 4

1 teaspoon olive oil
1½ teaspoons black pepper
¼ teaspoon garlic powder
¼ teaspoon thyme
⅛ teaspoon cayenne pepper
4 (4-ounce / 113-g) red snapper fillets, skin on
4 thin slices lemon
Nonstick cooking spray

1. Spritz the perforated pan with nonstick cooking spray.
2. In a small bowl, stir together the olive oil, black pepper, garlic powder, thyme, and cayenne pepper. Rub the mixture all over the fillets until completely coated.
3. Lay the fillets, skin-side down, in the perforated pan and top each fillet with a slice of lemon.
4. Select Bake. Set temperature to 390°F (199°C) and set time to 10 minutes. Press Start to begin preheating.
5. Once preheated, place the pan into the oven. Flip the fillets halfway through.
6. When cooking is complete, the fish should be cooked through. Let the fish cool for 5 minutes and serve.

Snapper Fillets with Capers

Prep time: 9 minutes | Cook time: 18 minutes | Serves 4

2 tablespoons extra-virgin olive oil
2 large garlic cloves, minced
½ onion, finely chopped
1 (14.5-ounce / 411-g) can diced tomatoes, drained
¼ cup sliced green olives
3 tablespoons capers, divided
2 tablespoons chopped fresh parsley, divided
½ teaspoon dried oregano
4 (6-ounce / 170-g) snapper fillets
½ teaspoon kosher salt

1. Grease the sheet pan generously with olive oil, then place the pan into the oven.
2. Select Roast. Set temperature to 375°F (190°C) and set time to 18 minutes. Press Start to begin preheating.
3. When the oven has preheated, remove the pan and add the garlic and onion to the olive oil in the pan, stirring to coat. Return the pan to the oven and continue cooking.
4. After 2 minutes, remove the pan from the oven. Stir in the tomatoes, olives, 1½ tablespoons of capers, 1 tablespoon of parsley, and oregano. Return the pan to the oven and continue cooking for 6 minutes until heated through.
5. Meanwhile, rub the fillets with the salt on both sides.
6. After another 6 minutes, remove the pan. Put the fillets in the center of the sheet pan and spoon some of the sauce over them. Return the pan to the oven and continue cooking, or until the fish is flaky.
7. When cooked, remove the pan from the oven. Scatter the remaining 1½ tablespoons of capers and 1 tablespoon of parsley on top of the fillets, then serve.

Salmon and Pepper Bowl

Prep time: 115 minutes | Cook time: 12 minutes | Serves 4

12 ounces (340 g) salmon fillets, cut into 1½-inch cubes
1 red onion, chopped
1 jalapeño pepper, minced
1 red bell pepper, chopped
¼ cup low-sodium salsa
2 teaspoons peanut oil or safflower oil
2 tablespoons low-sodium tomato juice
1 teaspoon chili powder

1. Mix together the salmon cubes, red onion, jalapeño, red bell pepper, salsa, peanut oil, tomato juice, chili powder in a medium metal bowl and stir until well incorporated.
2. Select Bake. Set temperature to 370°F (188°C) and set time to 12 minutes. Press Start to begin preheating.
3. Once preheated, place the metal bowl into the oven. Stir the ingredients once halfway through the cooking time.
4. When cooking is complete, the salmon should be cooked through and the veggies should be fork-tender. Serve warm.

Curried Halibut Fillets with Parmesan

Prep time: 5 minutes | Cook time: 10 minutes | Serves 4

2 medium-sized halibut fillets
Dash of tabasco sauce
1 teaspoon curry powder
½ teaspoon ground coriander
½ teaspoon hot paprika
Kosher salt and freshly cracked mixed peppercorns, to taste
2 eggs
1½ tablespoons olive oil
½ cup grated Parmesan cheese

1. On a clean work surface, drizzle the halibut fillets with the tabasco sauce. Sprinkle with the curry powder, coriander, hot paprika, salt, and cracked mixed peppercorns. Set aside.
2. In a shallow bowl, beat the eggs until frothy. In another shallow bowl, combine the olive oil and Parmesan cheese.
3. One at a time, dredge the halibut fillets in the beaten eggs, shaking off any excess, then roll them over the Parmesan cheese until evenly coated.
4. Arrange the halibut fillets in the perforated pan in a single layer.
5. Select Roast. Set temperature to 365°F (185°C) and set time to 10 minutes. Press Start to begin preheating.
6. Once preheated, place the pan into the oven.
7. When cooking is complete, the fish should be golden brown and crisp. Cool for 5 minutes before serving.

Cajun Cod Fillets with Lemon Pepper

Prep time: 5 minutes | Cook time: 12 minutes | Makes 2 cod fillets

1 tablespoon Cajun seasoning
1 teaspoon salt
½ teaspoon lemon pepper
½ teaspoon freshly ground black pepper
2 (8-ounce / 227-g) cod fillets, cut to fit into the perforated pan
Cooking spray
2 tablespoons unsalted butter, melted
1 lemon, cut into 4 wedges

1. Spritz the perforated pan with cooking spray.
2. Thoroughly combine the Cajun seasoning, salt, lemon pepper, and black pepper in a small bowl. Rub this mixture all over the cod fillets until completely coated.
3. Put the fillets in the perforated pan and brush the melted butter over both sides of each fillet.
4. Select Bake. Set temperature to 360°F (182°C) and set time to 12 minutes. Press Start to begin preheating.
5. Once preheated, place the pan into the oven. Flip the fillets halfway through the cooking time.
6. When cooking is complete, the fish should flake apart with a fork. Remove the fillets from the oven and serve with fresh lemon wedges.

Tuna Casserole with Basil

Prep time: 10 minutes | Cook time: 16 minutes | Serves 4

½ tablespoon sesame oil
⅓ cup yellow onions, chopped
½ bell pepper, seeded and chopped
2 cups canned tuna, chopped
Cooking spray
5 eggs, beaten
½ chili pepper, deveined and finely minced
1½ tablespoons sour cream
⅓ teaspoon dried basil
⅓ teaspoon dried oregano
Fine sea salt and ground black pepper, to taste

1. Heat the sesame oil in a nonstick skillet over medium heat until it shimmers.
2. Add the onions and bell pepper and sauté for 4 minutes, stirring occasionally, or until tender.
3. Add the canned tuna and keep stirring until the tuna is heated through.
4. Meanwhile, coat a baking dish lightly with cooking spray.
5. Transfer the tuna mixture to the baking dish, along with the beaten eggs, chili pepper, sour cream, basil, and oregano. Stir to combine well. Season with sea salt and black pepper.
6. Select Bake. Set temperature to 325°F (163°C) and set time to 12 minutes. Press Start to begin preheating.
7. Once preheated, place the baking dish into the oven.
8. When cooking is complete, the eggs should be completely set and the top lightly browned. Remove from the oven and serve on a plate.

Cajun Tilapia Tacos

Prep time: 10 minutes | Cook time: 10 to 15 minutes | Serves 6

1 tablespoon avocado oil
1 tablespoon Cajun seasoning
4 (5 to 6 ounce / 142 to 170 g) tilapia fillets
1 (14-ounce / 397-g) package coleslaw mix
12 corn tortillas
2 limes, cut into wedges

1. Line a baking pan with parchment paper.
2. In a shallow bowl, stir together the avocado oil and Cajun seasoning to make a marinade. Place the tilapia fillets into the bowl, turning to coat evenly.
3. Put the fillets in the baking pan in a single layer.
4. Select Air Fry. Set temperature to 375°F (190°C) and set time to 10 minutes. Press Start to begin preheating.
5. Once preheated, slide the pan into the oven.
6. When cooked, the fish should be flaky. If necessary, continue cooking for 5 minutes more. Remove the fish from the oven to a plate.
7. Assemble the tacos: Spoon some of the coleslaw mix into each tortilla and top each with ⅓ of a tilapia fillet. Squeeze some lime juice over the top of each taco and serve immediately.

Hoisin Tuna with Lemongrass

Prep time: 15 minutes | Cook time: 5 minutes | Serves 4

½ cup hoisin sauce
2 tablespoons rice wine vinegar
2 teaspoons sesame oil
2 teaspoons dried lemongrass
1 teaspoon garlic powder
¼ teaspoon red pepper flakes
½ small onion, quartered and thinly sliced
8 ounces (227 g) fresh tuna, cut into 1-inch cubes
Cooking spray
3 cups cooked jasmine rice

1. In a small bowl, whisk together the hoisin sauce, vinegar, sesame oil, lemongrass, garlic powder, and red pepper flakes.
2. Add the sliced onion and tuna cubes and gently toss until the fish is evenly coated.
3. Arrange the coated tuna cubes in the perforated pan in a single layer.
4. Select Air Fry. Set temperature to 390°F (199°C) and set time to 5 minutes. Press Start to begin preheating.
5. Once preheated, place the pan into the oven. Flip the fish halfway through the cooking time.
6. When cooking is complete, the fish should begin to flake. Continue cooking for 1 minute, if necessary. Remove from the oven and serve over hot jasmine rice.

Tilapia Meunière with Parsley

Prep time: 10 minutes | Cook time: 20 minutes | Serves 4

10 ounces (283 g) Yukon Gold
   potatoes, sliced ¼-inch thick
5 tablespoons unsalted butter,
   melted, divided
1 teaspoon kosher salt, divided
4 (8-ounce / 227-g) tilapia fillets
½ pound (227 g) green beans,
   trimmed
Juice of 1 lemon
2 tablespoons chopped fresh parsley,
   for garnish

1. In a large bowl, drizzle the potatoes with 2 tablespoons of melted butter and ¼ teaspoon of kosher salt. Transfer the potatoes to the sheet pan.
2. Select Roast. Set temperature to 375°F (190°C) and set time to 20 minutes. Press Start to begin preheating.
3. Once the oven has preheated, place the pan into the oven.
4. Meanwhile, season both sides of the fillets with ½ teaspoon of kosher salt. Put the green beans in the medium bowl and sprinkle with the remaining ¼ teaspoon of kosher salt and 1 tablespoon of butter, tossing to coat.
5. After 10 minutes, remove the pan and push the potatoes to one side. Put the fillets in the middle of the pan and add the green beans on the other side. Drizzle the remaining 2 tablespoons of butter over the fillets. Return the pan to the oven and continue cooking, or until the fish flakes easily with a fork and the green beans are crisp-tender.
6. When cooked, remove the pan from the oven. Drizzle the lemon juice over the fillets and sprinkle the parsley on top for garnish. Serve hot.

Tuna and Fruit Kebabs with Honey Glaze

Prep time: 15 minutes | Cook time: 10 minutes | Serves 4

Kebabs:
1 pound (454 g) tuna steaks, cut into
   1-inch cubes
½ cup canned pineapple chunks,
   drained, juice reserved
½ cup large red grapes
Marinade:
1 tablespoon honey
1 teaspoon olive oil
2 teaspoons grated fresh ginger
Pinch cayenne pepper

Special Equipment:
4 metal skewers

1. Make the kebabs: Thread, alternating tuna cubes, pineapple chunks, and red grapes, onto the metal skewers.
2. Make the marinade: Whisk together the honey, olive oil, ginger, and cayenne pepper in a small bowl. Brush generously the marinade over the kebabs and allow to sit for 10 minutes.
3. When ready, transfer the kebabs to the perforated pan.
4. Select Air Fry. Set temperature to 370°F (188°C) and set time to 10 minutes. Press Start to begin preheating.
5. Once preheated, place the pan into the oven.
6. After 5 minutes, remove from the oven and flip the kebabs and brush with the remaining marinade. Return the pan to the oven and continue cooking for an additional 5 minutes.
7. When cooking is complete, the kebabs should reach an internal temperature of 145°F (63°C) on a meat thermometer. Remove from the oven and discard any remaining marinade. Serve hot.

Breaded Fish Fillets with Mustard

Prep time: 20 minutes | Cook time: 7 minutes | Serves 4

1 pound (454 g) fish fillets
1 tablespoon coarse brown mustard
1 teaspoon Worcestershire sauce
½ teaspoon hot sauce
Salt, to taste
Cooking spray
Crumb Coating:
¾ cup panko bread crumbs
¼ cup stone-ground cornmeal
¼ teaspoon salt

1. On your cutting board, cut the fish fillets crosswise into slices, about 1 inch wide.
2. In a small bowl, stir together the mustard, Worcestershire sauce, and hot sauce to make a paste and rub this paste on all sides of the fillets. Season with salt to taste.
3. In a shallow bowl, thoroughly combine all the ingredients for the crumb coating and spread them on a sheet of wax paper.
4. Roll the fish fillets in the crumb mixture until thickly coated. Spritz all sides of the fish with cooking spray, then arrange them in the perforated pan in a single layer.
5. Select Air Fry. Set temperature to 400°F (205°C) and set time to 7 minutes. Press Start to begin preheating.
6. Once preheated, place the perforated pan into the oven.
7. When cooking is complete, the fish should flake apart with a fork. Remove from the oven and serve warm.

Chapter 5 Rice and Grains

Air Fried Tofu

Prep time: 5 minutes | Cook time: 13 minutes | Serves 3

8 ounces (227 g) firm tofu, pressed and cut into bite-sized cubes
1 tablespoon tamari sauce
1 teaspoon peanut oil
½ teaspoon garlic powder
½ teaspoon onion powder

1. Toss the tofu cubes with tamari sauce, peanut oil, garlic powder and onion powder.
2. Cook your tofu in the preheated Air Fryer at 380ºF (193ºC) for about 13 minutes, shaking the basket once or twice to ensure even browning. Enjoy!

Four-Cheese Pizza

Prep time: 10 minutes | Cook time: 10 minutes | Serves 4

1 (11-ounce / 312-g) can refrigerated thin pizza crust
½ cup tomato pasta sauce
2 tablespoons scallions, chopped
¼ cup Parmesan cheese, grated
1 cup Provolone cheese, shredded
1 cup Mozzarella cheese. sliced
4 slices Cheddar cheese
1 tablespoon olive oil

1. Stretch the dough on a work surface lightly dusted with flour.
2. Spread with a layer of tomato pasta sauce. Top with the scallions and cheese. Place on the baking tray that is previously greased with olive oil.
3. Bake in the preheated Air Fryer at 390ºF (199ºC) for 5 minutes.
4. Rotate the baking tray and bake for a further 5 minutes.
5. Serve immediately.

Cinnamon Apple Rolls

Prep time: 5 minutes | Cook time: 13 minutes | Serves 4

1 (10-ounce / 283-g) can buttermilk biscuits
1 apple, cored and chopped
¼ cup powdered sugar
1 teaspoon cinnamon
1 tablespoon coconut oil, melted

1. Line the bottom of the Air Fryer cooking basket with a parchment paper.
2. Separate the dough into biscuits and cut each of them into 2 layers. Mix the remaining ingredients in a bowl.
3. Divide the apple/cinnamon mixture between biscuits and roll them up. Brush the biscuits with coconut oil and transfer them to the Air Fryer cooking basket.
4. Cook the rolls at 330ºF (166ºC) for about 13 minutes, turning them over halfway through the cooking time. Enjoy!

Aromatic Shrimp Pilaf

Prep time: 10 minutes | Cook time: 36 minutes | Serves 2

1 cup jasmine rice
Salt and black pepper, to taste
1 bay leaf
1 small yellow onion, chopped
1 small garlic clove, finely chopped
1 teaspoon butter, melted
4 tablespoons cream of mushroom soup
½ pound (227 g) shrimp, divined and sliced

1. Bring 2 cups of a lightly salted water to a boil in a medium saucepan over medium-high heat. Add in the jasmine rice, turn to a simmer and cook, covered, for about 18 minutes until water is absorbed. Let the jasmine rice stand covered for 5 to 6 minutes; fluff with a fork and transfer to a lightly greased Air Fryer safe pan.
2. Stir in the salt, black pepper, bay leaf, yellow onion, garlic, butter and cream of mushroom soup; stir until everything is well incorporated.
3. Cook the rice at 350°F (177°C) for about 13 minutes. Stir in the shrimp and continue to cook for a further 5 minutes.
4. Check the rice for softness. If necessary, cook for a few minutes more. Enjoy!

Brussels Sprouts with Sesame Seeds

Prep time: 10 minutes | Cook time: 15 minutes | Serves 3

1 pound (454 g) Brussels sprouts, trimmed and halved
1 teaspoon coconut oil
2 tablespoons Shoyu sauce
1 tablespoon agave syrup
1 teaspoon rice vinegar
½ teaspoon Gochujang paste
1 clove garlic, minced
2 scallion stalks, chopped
1 tablespoon sesame seeds, toasted

1. Toss the Brussels sprouts with coconut oil, Shoyu sauce, agave syrup, rice vinegar, Gochujang paste and garlic.
2. Cook the Brussels sprouts in the preheated Air Fryer at 380°F (193°C) for 15 minutes, shaking the basket halfway through the cooking time.
3. Place the roasted Brussels sprouts on a serving platter and garnish with scallions and sesame seeds.
4. Serve immediately!

Prosciutto and Basil Bruschetta

Prep time: 5 minutes | Cook time: 8 minutes | Serves 3

3 slices sourdough bread
½ cup marinara sauce
3 slices Mozzarella
6 slices prosciutto
6 fresh basil leaves

1. Using a rolling pin, flatten the bread slightly.
2. Spread the marinara sauce on top of each slice of bread, then, top with Mozzarella and prosciutto.
3. Now, bake your bruschetta at 360°F (182°C) for about 8 minutes until the cheese is melted and golden.
4. Garnish with basil leaves and serve.

Oatmeal with Two Berries

Prep time: 10 minutes | Cook time: 12 minutes | Serves 4

1 cup fresh strawberries
½ cup dried cranberries
1½ cups rolled oats
½ teaspoon baking powder
A pinch of sea salt
A pinch of grated nutmeg
½ teaspoon ground cinnamon
½ teaspoon vanilla extract
4 tablespoons agave syrup
1½ cups coconut milk

1. Spritz a baking pan with cooking spray. Place ½ cup of strawberries on the bottom of the pan; place the cranberries over that.
2. In a mixing bowl, thoroughly combine the rolled oats, baking powder, salt, nutmeg, cinnamon, vanilla, agave syrup, and milk.
3. Pour the oatmeal mixtures over the fruits; allow it to soak for 15 minutes. Top with the remaining fruits.
4. Bake at 330°F (166°C) for 12 minutes. Serve warm or at room temperature. Enjoy!

Baked Peppery Tortilla Chips

Prep time: 5 minutes | Cook time: 8 minutes | Serves 3

6 (6-inch) corn tortillas
1 teaspoon canola oil
1 teaspoon salt
¼ teaspoon ground white pepper
½ teaspoon ground cumin
½ teaspoon ancho chili powder

1. Slice the tortillas into quarters.
2. Brush the tortilla pieces with the canola oil until well coated. Toss with the spices and transfer to the Air Fryer basket.
3. Bake at 360°F (182°C) for 8 minutes or until lightly golden. Work in batches. Enjoy!

Spiced Roasted Almonds

Prep time: 10 minutes | Cook time: 6 minutes | Serves 6

1½ cups raw almonds
Sea salt and ground black pepper, to taste
¼ teaspoon garlic powder
¼ teaspoon mustard powder
½ teaspoon cumin powder
¼ teaspoon smoked paprika
1 tablespoon olive oil

1. Toss all ingredients in a mixing bowl. Line the Air Fryer basket with baking parchment.
2. Spread out the coated almonds in a single layer in the basket.
3. Roast at 350°F (177°C) for 6 to 8 minutes, shaking the basket once or twice.
4. Work in batches. Enjoy!

Honey Seeds Granola

Prep time: 5 minutes | Cook time: 25 minutes | Serves 12

½ cup rolled oats
1 cup walnuts, chopped
3 tablespoons sunflower seeds
3 tablespoons pumpkin seeds
1 teaspoon coarse sea salt
2 tablespoons honey

1. Thoroughly combine all ingredients and spread the mixture onto the Air Fryer trays.
2. Spritz with nonstick cooking spray.
Bake at 230°F (110°C) for 25 minutes; rotate the trays and bake 10 to 15 minutes more. This granola can be kept in an airtight container for up to 2 weeks. Enjoy!

Doughnut Bread Pudding

Prep time: 8 minutes | Cook time: 20 minutes | Serves 6

2 cups diced doughnuts
2 eggs, whisked
1 cup milk
1 cup half-and-half
4 tablespoons honey
1 teaspoon vanilla extract
A pinch of salt
A pinch of grated nutmeg

1. Place the doughnuts in a lightly greased baking pan.
2. In a mixing bowl, thoroughly combine the remaining ingredients.
3. Pour the custard mixture over the doughnuts. Set aside for 15 minutes to soak.
4. Preheat the air fryer to 350°F (180°C).
5. Place the baking pan in the corresponding position in the air fryer. Select Bake and cook the bread pudding for about 20 minutes or until the custard is set but still a little wobbly.
6. Serve at room temperature. Bon appétit!

Curry Basmati Rice

Prep time: 10 minutes | Cook time: 10 minutes | Serves 4

3 tablespoons olive oil
3 cloves garlic, chopped
1 large onion, peeled and chopped
1 sprigs fresh curry leaves, chopped
2 cups basmati rice, cooked
1 teaspoon cayenne pepper
Kosher salt and ground black pepper, to taste

1. Start by preheating the air fryer to 360ºF (182ºC).
2. Thoroughly combine all ingredients in a lightly greased baking pan. Pour 1 cup of boiling water over the rice.
3. Place the baking pan in the corresponding position in the air fryer. Select Bake and cook for about 10 minutes or until cooked through.
4. Bon appétit!

Cheesy Butter Macaroni

Prep time: 5 minutes | Cook time: 15 minutes | Serves 4

1 cups macaroni
1 cup cream of onion soup
2 tablespoons butter
4 ounces (113 g) Ricotta cheese
6 ounces (170 g) Mozzarella cheese, crumbled
Kosher salt and ground white pepper, to taste
½ teaspoon ground cumin
1 teaspoon dry mustard
1 teaspoon red chili powder

1. Start by preheating the air fryer to 360ºF (182ºC).
2. Cook the macaroni according to the package directions.
3. Drain the macaroni and place them in a lightly greased baking pan.
4. Fold in the remaining ingredients and stir to combine.
5. Place the baking pan in the corresponding position in the air fryer. Select Bake and cook the mac and cheese for about 15 minutes. Serve garnished with fresh Italian herbs, if desired.
6. Bon appétit!

Blueberry Cheese Rolls

Prep time: 5 minutes | Cook time: 10 minutes | Serves 6

1 (8-ounce / 227-g) can refrigerated crescent dinner rolls
6 ounces (170 g) cream cheese, room temperature
4 tablespoons granulated sugar
1 teaspoon grated lemon zest
1 cup fresh blueberries
1 cup powdered sugar
¼ teaspoon ground cinnamon

1. Start by preheating the air fryer to 300ºF (150ºC).
2. Separate the dough into rectangles. Mix the remaining ingredients until well combined.
3. Spread each rectangle with the cheese mixture; roll them up tightly.
4. Place the rolls in the baking pan.
5. Place the baking pan in the corresponding position in the air fryer. Select Bake and cook the rolls for about 5 minutes; turn them over and bake for a further 5 minutes.
6. Bon appétit!

Juicy Quinoa Porridge

Prep time: 10 minutes | Cook time: 12 minutes | Serves 4

½ cup old-fashioned oats
½ cup quinoa flakes
¼ cup chopped almonds
¼ cup chopped pecans
2 cups orange juice
4 tablespoons honey
2 tablespoons coconut oil
4 tablespoons chopped dried apricots

1. Start by preheating the air fryer to 380ºF (193ºC).
2. Thoroughly combine all ingredients in a mixing bowl. Spoon the mixture into lightly greased mugs.
3. Then, place the mugs in the baking pan.
4. Place the baking pan in the corresponding position in the air fryer. Select Bake and cook the porridge for about 12 minutes.
5. Serve immediately. Bon appétit!

Biryani with Butter

Prep time: 5 minutes | Cook time: 10 minutes | Serves 4

2 cups jasmine rice, cooked
1 cup water
1 teaspoon ginger-garlic paste
2 tablespoons chopped shallots
½ teaspoon ground cinnamon
2 tablespoons butter
½ teaspoon cumin seeds
1 teaspoon garam masala
½ teaspoon turmeric powder

1. Start by preheating the air fryer to 360°F (182°C).
2. Thoroughly combine all ingredients in a lightly greased baking pan.
3. Place the baking pan in the corresponding position in the air fryer. Select Bake and cook for about 10 minutes or until cooked through.
4. Bon appétit!

Pecans Oatmeal Cups

Prep time: 6 minutes | Cook time: 12 minutes | Serves 4

1 cup full-fat milk
1 cup unsweetened applesauce
1 egg, beaten
½ cup pure maple syrup
1 cup old-fashioned oats
1 teaspoon baking powder
1 teaspoon pure vanilla extract
½ teaspoon ground cinnamon
¼ teaspoon freshly grated nutmeg
A pinch of kosher salt
½ cup chopped pecans

1. Start by preheating the air fryer to 380°F (193°C).
2. Thoroughly combine all ingredients in a mixing bowl. Spoon the mixture into lightly greased mugs.
3. Then, place the mugs in the baking pan.
4. Place the baking pan in the corresponding position in the air fryer. Select Bake and cook the oatmeal for about 12 minutes.
5. Bon appétit!

Pumpkin Porridge with Chocolate

Prep time: 5 minutes | Cook time: 12 minutes | Serves 5

½ cup old-fashioned oats
½ cup quinoa flakes
¼ cup chopped pecans
2 tablespoons ground chia seeds
2 tablespoons ground flax seeds
1 teaspoon vanilla essence
2 ounces (57 g) dark chocolate chips
½ cup canned pumpkin
½ cup almond milk

1. Start by preheating the air fryer to 380°F (193°C).
2. Thoroughly combine all ingredients in a mixing bowl. Spoon the mixture into a lightly greased baking pan.
3. Place the baking pan in the corresponding position in the air fryer. Select Bake and cook the porridge for about 12 minutes.
4. Serve immediately. Bon appétit!

Chawal ke Pakore with Cheese

Prep time: 5 minutes | Cook time: 15 minutes | Serves 4

1 cup rice flour
½ onion, chopped
2 garlic cloves, minced
2 tablespoons butter, room
   temperature
1 teaspoon paprika
1 teaspoon cumin powder
½ cup crumbled Paneer cheese

1. Start by preheating the air fryer to 380°F (193°C).
2. Mix all ingredients until everything is well combined. Form the mixture into patties. Transfer to the crisper tray.
3. Place the crisper tray in the corresponding position in the air fryer. Select Air Fry and cook the patties for about 15 minutes or until cooked through. Turn them over halfway through the cooking time.
4. Bon appétit!

Rice Cheese Casserole

Prep time: 10 minutes | Cook time: 10 minutes | Serves 4

1 small shallot, minced
2 garlic cloves, minced
2 tablespoons olive oil
½ teaspoon paprika
2 eggs, whisked
1 cup half-and-half
1 cup shredded Cheddar cheese
2 cups cooked brown rice
1 tablespoon chopped Italian parsley leaves
1 cup cream of celery soup
Sea salt and freshly ground black pepper, to taste

1. Start by preheating the air fryer to 360°F (182°C).
2. Thoroughly combine all ingredients in a lightly greased baking pan.
3. Place the baking pan in the corresponding position in the air fryer. Select Bake and cook for about 10 minutes or until cooked through.
4. Bon appétit!

French Toast

Prep time: 5 minutes | Cook time: 8 minutes | Serves 4

2 eggs, beaten
¼ cup milk
2 tablespoons coconut oil, room
   temperature
½ teaspoon bourbon vanilla extract
½ teaspoon ground cinnamon
4 slices bread

1. Start by preheating the air fryer to 330°F (166°C).
2. In a mixing bowl, thoroughly combine the eggs, milk, coconut oil, vanilla, and cinnamon.
3. Then dip each piece of bread into the egg mixture; place the bread slices in a lightly greased baking pan.
4. Place the baking pan in the corresponding position in the air fryer. Select Bake and cook the bread slices for about 4 minutes; turn them over and cook for a further 3 to 4 minutes. Enjoy!

Chapter 6 Appetizers and Snacks

Charred Whole Peppers

Prep time: 5 minutes | Cook time: 8 minutes | Serves 4

3 cups whole peppers
2 tablespoons vegetable oil
Flaky sea salt, for garnish

1. Insert the Grill Grate and close the hood. Select GRILL, set the temperature to MAX, and set the time to 10 minutes. Select START/STOP to begin preheating.
2. While the unit is preheating, in a medium bowl, toss the peppers in the oil until evenly coated.
3. When the unit beeps to signify it has preheated, place the peppers on the Grill Grate. Gently press the peppers down to maximize grill marks. Close the hood and grill for 8 to 10 minutes, until they are blistered on all sides.
4. When cooking is complete, place the peppers in a serving dish and top with the flaky sea salt. Serve immediately.

Lemony Artichokes

Prep time: 5 minutes | Cook time: 8 minutes | Serves 4

Juice of ½ lemon
½ cup canola oil
3 garlic cloves, chopped
Sea salt, to taste
Freshly ground black pepper, to taste
2 large artichokes, trimmed and halved

1. Insert the Grill Grate and close the hood. Select GRILL, set the temperature to MAX, and set the time to 10 minutes. Select START/STOP to begin preheating.
2. While the unit is preheating, in a medium bowl, combine the lemon juice, oil, and garlic. Season with salt and pepper, then brush the artichoke halves with the lemon-garlic mixture.
3. When the unit beeps to signify it has preheated, place the artichokes on the Grill Grate, cut side down. Gently press them down to maximize grill marks. Close the hood and grill for 8 to 10 minutes, occasionally basting generously with the lemon-garlic mixture throughout cooking, until blistered on all sides.

Blistered Beans with Red Pepper Flakes

Prep time: 5 minutes | Cook time: 8 minutes | Serves 4

1 pound (454 g) haricots verts or green beans, trimmed
2 tablespoons vegetable oil
Juice of 1 lemon
Pinch red pepper flakes
Flaky sea salt
Freshly ground black pepper, to taste

1. Insert the Grill Grate and close the hood. Select GRILL, set the temperature to MAX, and set the time to 10 minutes. Select START/STOP to begin preheating.
2. While the unit is preheating, in a medium bowl, toss the green beans in oil until evenly coated.
3. When the unit beeps to signify it has preheated, place the green beans on the Grill Grate. Close the hood and grill for 8 to 10 minutes, tossing frequently until blistered on all sides.
4. When cooking is complete, place the green beans on a large serving platter. Squeeze lemon juice over the green beans, top with red pepper flakes, and season with sea salt and black pepper.

Brussels Sprouts with Bacon

Prep time: 5 minutes | Cook time: 12 minutes | Serves 4

1 pound (454 g) Brussels sprouts, trimmed and halved
2 tablespoons extra-virgin olive oil
1 teaspoon sea salt
½ teaspoon freshly ground black pepper
6 slices bacon, chopped

1. Insert the Crisper Basket and close the hood. Select AIR CRISP, set the temperature to 390°F (199°C), and set the time to 12 minutes. Select START/STOP to begin preheating.
2. Meanwhile, in a large bowl, toss the Brussels sprouts with the olive oil, salt, pepper, and bacon.
3. When the unit beeps to signify it has preheated, add the Brussels sprouts to the basket. Close the hood and cook for 10 minutes.
4. After 6 minutes, shake the basket of Brussels sprouts. Place the basket back in the unit and close the hood to resume cooking.
5. After 6 minutes, check for desired crispness. Continue cooking up to 2 more minutes, if necessary.

Buttery Honey-Glazed Grilled Carrots

Prep time: 5 minutes | Cook time: 10 minutes | Serves 4

6 medium carrots, peeled and cut lengthwise
1 tablespoon canola oil
2 tablespoons unsalted butter, melted
¼ cup brown sugar, melted
¼ cup honey
⅛ teaspoon sea salt

1. Insert the Grill Grate and close the hood. Select GRILL, set the temperature to MAX, and set the time to 10 minutes. Select START/STOP to begin preheating.
2. In a large bowl, toss the carrots and oil until well coated.
3. When the unit beeps to signify it has preheated, place carrots on the center of the Grill Grate. Close the hood and cook for 5 minutes.
4. Meanwhile, in a small bowl, whisk together the butter, brown sugar, honey, and salt.
5. After 5 minutes, open the hood and baste the carrots with the glaze. Using tongs, turn the carrots and baste the other side. Close the hood and cook for another 5 minutes.
6. When cooking is complete, serve immediately.

Parma Prosciutto-Wrapped Pears

Prep time: 5 minutes | Cook time: 2 minutes | Serves 8

2 large ripe Anjou pears
4 thin slices Parma prosciutto (about 2 ounces)
2 teaspoons aged balsamic vinegar

1. Peel the pears. Slice into 6 or 8 wedges (depending on the size of the pears) and cut out the core from each wedge.
2. Cut the prosciutto into long strips (one strip per pear wedge). Wrap each pear wedge with a strip of prosciutto. Place the wrapped pears on the sheet pan.
3. Select AIR BROIL, set temperature HIGH, and set time to 6 minutes. Select START/PAUSE to begin preheating.
4. Once the unit has preheated, slide the pan into the oven.
5. After 2 or 3 minutes, check the pears. The pears should be turned over if the prosciutto is beginning to crisp up and brown. Return the pan to the oven and continue cooking.
6. When cooking is complete, remove the pan from the oven. Serve the pears warm or at room temperature with a drizzle of the balsamic vinegar.

Sweet Cinnamon Peaches

Prep time: 5 minutes | Cook time: 10 minutes | Serves 4

2 tablespoons sugar
¼ teaspoon ground cinnamon
4 peaches, cut into wedges
Cooking spray

1. Spritz the air fry basket with cooking spray.
2. In a large bowl, stir together the sugar and cinnamon. Add the peaches to the bowl and toss to coat evenly.
3. Spread the coated peaches in a single layer in the air fry basket.
4. Select Air Fry, set temperature to 350°F (180°C) and set time to 10 minutes. Select Start/Stop to begin preheating.
5. Once preheated, place the basket on the air fry position.
6. After 5 minutes, remove the basket from the oven. Use tongs to turn the peaches skin side down. Lightly mist them with cooking spray. Return the basket to the oven to continue cooking.
7. When cooking is complete, the peaches will be lightly browned and caramelized. Remove the basket from the oven and let rest for 5 minutes before serving.

Salty Baked Almonds

Prep time: 5 minutes | Cook time: 25 minutes | Serves 4

1 cup raw almonds
1 egg white, beaten
½ teaspoon coarse sea salt

1. Spread the almonds on the sheet pan in an even layer.
2. Select Bake, set temperature to 350°F (180°C) and set time to 20 minutes. Select Start/Stop to begin preheating.
3. When the unit has preheated, place the pan on the bake position.
4. When cooking is complete, the almonds should be lightly browned and fragrant. Remove the pan from the oven.
5. Coat the almonds with the egg white and sprinkle with the salt. Return the pan to the oven.
6. Select Bake, set temperature to 350°F (180°C) and set time to 5 minutes.
7. When cooking is complete, the almonds should be dried. Cool completely before serving.

Baked Sardines with Tomato Sauce

Prep time: 10 minutes | Cook time: 20 minutes | Serves 4

2 pounds (907 g) fresh sardines
3 tablespoons olive oil, divided
4 Roma tomatoes, peeled and chopped
1 small onion, sliced thinly
Zest of 1 orange
Sea salt and freshly ground pepper, to taste
2 tablespoons whole-wheat bread crumbs
½ cup white wine

1. Brush the sheet pan with a little olive oil. Set aside.
2. Rinse the sardines under running water. Slit the belly, remove the spine and butterfly the fish. Set aside.
3. Heat the remaining olive oil in a large skillet. Add the tomatoes, onion, orange zest, salt and pepper to the skillet and simmer for 20 minutes, or until the mixture thicken and softens.
4. Place half the sauce in the bottom of the sheet pan. Arrange the sardines on top and spread the remaining half the sauce over the fish. Sprinkle with the bread crumbs and drizzle with the white wine.
5. Select Bake, set temperature to 425°F (220°C) and set time to 20 minutes. Select Start/Stop to begin preheating.
6. When the unit has preheated, place the pan on the bake position.
7. When cooking is complete, remove the pan from the oven. Serve immediately.

Air Fried Lemon-Pepper Wings

Prep time: 5 minutes | Cook time: 24 minutes | Serves 10

2 pounds (907 g) chicken wings
4½ teaspoons salt-free lemon pepper seasoning
1½ teaspoons baking powder
1½ teaspoons kosher salt

1. In a large bowl, toss together all the ingredients until well coated. Place the wings on the sheet pan, making sure they don't crowd each other too much.
2. Select Air Fry, set temperature to 375°F (190°C) and set time to 24 minutes. Select Start/Stop to begin preheating.
3. Once preheated, slide the pan into the oven.
4. After 12 minutes, remove the pan from the oven. Use tongs to turn the wings over. Rotate the pan and return the pan to the oven to continue cooking.
5. When cooking is complete, the wings should be dark golden brown and a bit charred in places. Remove the pan from the oven and let rest for 5 minutes before serving.

Air Fried Yam Sticks

Prep time: 10 minutes | Cook time: 15 minutes | Serves 2

1 large-sized yam, peeled and cut into ¼-inch sticks
1 tablespoon olive oil
Kosher salt and red pepper, to taste

1. Start by preheating the air fryer to 360°F (182°C).
2. Toss the yam with the remaining ingredients and place them in the crisper tray.
3. Place the crisper tray in the corresponding position in the air fryer. Select Air Fry and cook the yam sticks for 15 minutes, tossing halfway through the cooking time and working in batches.
4. Enjoy!

Syrupy Chicken Wings

Prep time: 6 minutes | Cook time: 18 minutes | Serves 5

2 pounds (907 g) chicken wings
¼ cup agave syrup
2 tablespoons soy sauce
2 tablespoons chopped scallions
2 tablespoons olive oil
1 teaspoon peeled and grated ginger
2 cloves garlic, minced
Sea salt and ground black pepper, to taste

1. Start by preheating the air fryer to 380°F (193°C).
2. Toss the chicken wings with the remaining ingredients. Transfer to the crisper tray.
3. Place the crisper tray in the corresponding position in the air fryer. Select Roast and cook the chicken wings for 18 minutes, turning them over halfway through the cooking time.
4. Bon appétit!

Potato Chips with Peppercorns

Prep time: 10 minutes | Cook time: 16 minutes | Serves 3

2 large-sized potatoes, peeled and thinly sliced
2 tablespoons olive oil
1 teaspoon Sichuan peppercorns
1 teaspoon garlic powder
½ teaspoon Chinese five-spice powder
Sea salt, to taste

1. Start by preheating the air fryer to 360°F (182°C).
2. Toss the potatoes with the remaining ingredients and place them in the crisper tray.
3. Place the crisper tray in the corresponding position in the air fryer. Select Air Fry and cook the potato chips for 16 minutes, shaking the crisper tray halfway through the cooking time and working in batches.
4. Enjoy!

Zucchini with Cheese

Prep time: 10 minutes | Cook time: 10 minutes | Serves 4

1 pound (454 g) zucchini, cut into sticks
1 egg, whisked
¼ cup grated Parmesan cheese
½ cup bread crumbs
1 teaspoon garlic powder
½ teaspoon onion powder
Sea salt and ground black pepper, to taste

1. Start by preheating the air fryer to 390°F (199°C).
2. Toss the zucchini sticks with the remaining ingredients and arrange them in a single layer in the crisper tray.
3. Place the crisper tray in the corresponding position in the air fryer. Select Air Fry and cook the zucchini sticks for about 10 minutes, shaking the crisper tray halfway through the cooking time. Work in batches.
4. Bon appétit!

Rice Cereal with Dill

Prep time: 5 minutes | Cook time: 7 minutes | Serves 8

4 cups crispy rice cereal
¼ teaspoon salt
2 teaspoons dill
3 tablespoons grated Parmesan-style topping
1 tablespoon soy sauce

1. In a medium bowl, stir all ingredients together to coat well.
2. Pour into the air fryer baking pan.
3. Cook at 360°F (182°C) for 5 minutes.
4. Stir and cook for 2 more minutes.

Wax Beans with Cumin

Prep time: 6 minutes | Cook time: 6 minutes | Serves 4

1 pound (454 g) fresh wax beans, trimmed
2 teaspoons olive oil
½ teaspoon onion powder
1 teaspoon garlic powder
½ teaspoon cumin powder
Sea salt and ground black pepper, to taste

1. Start by preheating the air fryer to 390°F (199°C).
2. Toss the wax beans with the remaining ingredients. Transfer to the crisper tray.
3. Place the crisper tray in the corresponding position in the air fryer. Select Air Fry and cook the wax beans for about 6 minutes, tossing the crisper tray halfway through the cooking time.
4. Enjoy!

Cilantro and Onion Pakoras

Prep time: 5 minutes | Cook time: 10 minutes per batch | Serves 2

½ cup chopped fresh cilantro
2 medium yellow onions, sliced (2 cups)
1 tablespoon chickpea flour
1 tablespoon rice flour
1 teaspoon ground turmeric
1 teaspoon cumin seeds
2 tablespoons vegetable oil
1 teaspoon kosher salt
½ teaspoon cayenne pepper
Cooking spray

1. In a large bowl, combine the cilantro, onions, chickpea flour, rice flour, turmeric, cumin seeds, oil, salt, and cayenne. Stir to combine. Cover and let stand for 30 minutes or up to overnight.
2. Preheat the air fryer to 350°F (177°C). Spritz the air fryer basket with cooking spray.
3. Drop half of the batter in 6 heaping tablespoons into the basket. Air fry for 8 minutes. Carefully turn the pakoras over and air fry for 2 more minutes, or until the batter is cooked through and crisp.
4. Repeat with remaining batter to make 6 more pakoras. Serve hot.

Eggplant with Paprika

Prep time: 5 minutes | Cook time: 15 minutes | Serves 3

¾ pound (340 g) eggplant
Sea salt and ground black pepper,
    to taste
½ teaspoon paprika
2 tablespoons olive oil
2 tablespoons balsamic vinegar

1. Start by preheating the air fryer to 400ºF (205ºC).
2. Toss the eggplant pieces with the remaining ingredients until they are well coated on all sides.
3. Arrange the eggplant in the crisper tray.
4. Place the crisper tray in the corresponding position in the air fryer. Select Air Fry and cook the eggplant for about 15 minutes, shaking the crisper tray halfway through the cooking time.
5. Bon appétit!

Tomato Chips with Cheese

Prep time: 5 minutes | Cook time: 15 minutes | Serves 3

1 large-sized beefsteak tomatoes
2 tablespoons olive oil
½ teaspoon paprika
Sea salt, to taste
1 teaspoon garlic powder
1 tablespoon chopped fresh cilantro
4 tablespoons grated Pecorino
    cheese

1. Start by preheating the air fryer to 360ºF (182ºC).
2. Toss the tomato slices with the olive oil and spices until they are well coated on all sides.
3. Arrange the tomato slices in the crisper tray.
4. Place the crisper tray in the corresponding position in the air fryer. Select Air Fry and cook the tomato slices for about 10 minutes.
5. Reduce the temperature to 330ºF (166ºC). Top the tomato slices with the cheese and continue to cook for a further 5 minutes.
6. Bon appétit!

Cinnamon Mixed Nuts

Prep time: 5 minutes | Cook time: 6 minutes | Serves 4

1 egg white, lightly beaten
½ cup pecan halves
½ cup almonds
½ cup walnuts
Sea salt and cayenne pepper, to taste
1 teaspoon chili powder
½ teaspoon ground cinnamon
½ teaspoon ground allspice

1. Start by preheating the air fryer to 330ºF (166ºC).
2. Mix the nuts with the rest of the ingredients and place them in the crisper tray.
3. Place the crisper tray in the corresponding position in the air fryer. Select Air Fry and cook the nuts for 6 minutes, shaking the crisper tray halfway through the cooking time and working in batches.
4. Enjoy!

Pasta Chips

Prep time: 7 minutes | Cook time: 10 minutes | Serves 4

2 cups (152 g) dry whole wheat bow
    tie pasta (use brown rice pasta)
1 tablespoon (15 ml) olive oil (or use
    aquafaba)
1 tablespoon (7 g) nutritional yeast
1½ teaspoon (3 g) italian seasoning
    blend
½ teaspoon salt

1. Cook the pasta according to your package directions with the important exception of only cooking it for half the time listed, then drain the pasta well.
2. Toss the drained pasta with the olive oil (or aquafaba), nutritional yeast, italian seasoning blend and salt.
3. Place about half of the mixture in your air fryer basket if yours is small; larger ones may be able to cook in one batch. Cook on 390ºF (199ºC) (200ºC) for 5 minutes. Shake the basket and cook 3 to 5 minutes more or until crunchy.

Paprika Beet Chips

Prep time: 10 minutes | Cook time: 30 minutes | Serves 2

½ pound (227 g) golden beets, peeled and thinly sliced
Kosher salt and ground black pepper, to taste
1 teaspoon paprika
2 tablespoons olive oil
½ teaspoon garlic powder
1 teaspoon ground turmeric

1. Start by preheating the air fryer to 330ºF (166ºC).
2. Toss the beets with the remaining ingredients and place them in the crisper tray.
3. Place the crisper tray in the corresponding position in the air fryer. Select Air Fry and cook the chips for 30 minutes, shaking the crisper tray occasionally and working in batches.
4. Enjoy!

Carrot with Butter

Prep time: 5 minutes | Cook time: 15 minutes | Serves 4

1 pound (454 g) baby carrots
2 tablespoons butter
Kosher salt and ground white pepper, to taste
1 teaspoon paprika
1 teaspoon dried oregano

1. Start by preheating the air fryer to 380ºF (193ºC).
2. Toss the carrots with the remaining ingredients; then, arrange the carrots in the crisper tray.
3. Place the crisper tray in the corresponding position in the air fryer. Select Air Fry and cook the carrots for 15 minutes, shaking the crisper tray halfway through the cooking time.
4. Bon appétit!

Olive Nuggets

Prep time: 20 minutes | Cook time: 15 minutes | Serves 24 to 26 nuggets

1 (7-ounce / 198-g) jar pimento-stuffed green olives
1 cup Monterey Jack & Cheddar–style shreds
1 cup self-rising flour
1½ tablespoons all-vegetable shortening
3 tablespoons almond milk
Oil for misting
Strawberry jam (optional)

1. Drain the olives and blot them dry on paper towels.
2. Chop the cheese shreds and place them in a medium bowl.
3. Add the flour to the cheese shreds and mix together with your hands.
4. Still using your hands, work the shortening into the mixture until it's well blended.
5. Work in the milk until a dough forms.
6. Using 1½ teaspoons of dough for each olive, roll the dough into a ball, then flatten the ball into a disc about 2½ inches in diameter.
7. Lay the olive in the center of the dough and wrap the dough around the olive, squeezing and pinching to seal it.
8. Repeat to make 12 or 13 nuggets.
9. Mist the nuggets with oil and place them in the air fryer basket in a single layer.
10. Cook at 390ºF (199ºC) for 13 to 15 minutes, until they brown.
11. Repeat steps 6 through 10 to cook the remaining nuggets.
12. Serve with Strawberry Jam for dipping if you like.

Lime Avocado Chips

Prep time: 15 minutes | Cook time: 10 minutes | Serves 4

1 egg
1 tablespoon lime juice
⅛ teaspoon hot sauce
2 tablespoons flour
¾ cup panko bread crumbs
¼ cup cornmeal
¼ teaspoon salt
1 large avocado, pitted, peeled, and
    cut into ½-inch slices
Cooking spray

1. Whisk together the egg, lime juice, and hot sauce in a small bowl.
2. On a sheet of wax paper, place the flour. In a separate sheet of wax paper, combine the bread crumbs, cornmeal, and salt.
3. Dredge the avocado slices one at a time in the flour, then in the egg mixture, finally roll them in the bread crumb mixture to coat well.
4. Place the breaded avocado slices in the air fry basket and mist them with cooking spray.
5. Select Air Fry, Super Convection, set temperature to 390°F (199°C), and set time to 10 minutes. Select Start/Stop to begin preheating.
6. Once preheated, place the basket on the air fry position.
7. When cooking is complete, the slices should be nicely browned and crispy. Transfer the avocado slices to a plate and serve.

Cinnamon Apple Wedges with Yogurt

Prep time: 5 minutes | Cook time: 12 minutes | Serves 4

2 medium apples, cored and sliced
    into ¼-inch wedges
1 teaspoon canola oil
2 teaspoons peeled and grated fresh
    ginger
½ teaspoon ground cinnamon
½ cup low-fat Greek vanilla yogurt,
    for serving

1. In a large bowl, toss the apple wedges with the canola oil, ginger, and cinnamon until evenly coated. Put the apple wedges in the air fry basket.
2. Select Air Fry, Super Convection, set temperature to 360°F (182°C), and set time to 12 minutes. Select Start/Stop to begin preheating.
3. Once preheated, place the basket on the air fry position.
4. When cooking is complete, the apple wedges should be crisp-tender. Remove the apple wedges from the oven and serve drizzled with the yogurt.

Corn and Black Bean Chunky Salsa

Prep time: 10 minutes | Cook time: 10 minutes | Serves 4

½ (15-ounce / 425-g) can corn,
    drained and rinsed
½ (15-ounce / 425-g) can black beans,
    drained and rinsed
¼ cup chunky salsa
2 ounces (57 g) reduced-fat cream
    cheese, softened
¼ cup shredded reduced-fat
    Cheddar cheese
½ teaspoon paprika
½ teaspoon ground cumin
Salt and freshly ground black pepper, to taste

1. Combine the corn, black beans, salsa, cream cheese, Cheddar cheese, paprika, and cumin in a medium bowl. Sprinkle with salt and pepper and stir until well blended.
2. Pour the mixture into a baking dish.
3. Select Air Fry, Super Convection, set temperature to 325°F (163°C), and set time to 10 minutes. Select Start/Stop to begin preheating.
4. Once preheated, place the baking dish in the oven.
5. When cooking is complete, the mixture should be heated through. Rest for 5 minutes and serve warm.

Simple Carrot Chips

Prep time: 5 minutes | Cook time: 10 minutes | Serves 4

4 to 5 medium carrots, trimmed and thinly sliced
1 tablespoon olive oil, plus more for greasing
1 teaspoon seasoned salt

1. Toss the carrot slices with 1 tablespoon of olive oil and salt in a medium bowl until thoroughly coated.
2. Grease the air fry basket with the olive oil. Place the carrot slices in the greased pan.
3. Select Air Fry, Super Convection, set temperature to 390°F (199°C), and set time to 10 minutes. Select Start/Stop to begin preheating.
4. Once preheated, place the basket on the air fry position. Stir the carrot slices halfway through the cooking time.
5. When cooking is complete, the chips should be crisp-tender. Remove the basket from the oven and allow to cool for 5 minutes before serving.

Smoky Sausage and Mushroom Empanadas

Prep time: 5 minutes | Cook time: 12 minutes | Serves 4

½ pound (227 g) Kielbasa smoked sausage, chopped
4 chopped canned mushrooms
2 tablespoons chopped onion
½ teaspoon ground cumin
¼ teaspoon paprika
Salt and black pepper, to taste
½ package puff pastry dough, at room temperature
1 egg, beaten
Cooking spray

1. Combine the sausage, mushrooms, onion, cumin, paprika, salt, and pepper in a bowl and stir to mix well.
2. Make the empanadas: Place the puff pastry dough on a lightly floured surface. Cut circles into the dough with a glass. Place 1 tablespoon of the sausage mixture into the center of each pastry circle. Fold each in half and pinch the edges to seal. Using a fork, crimp the edges. Brush them with the beaten egg and mist with cooking spray.
3. Spritz the air fry basket with cooking spray. Place the empanadas in the air fry basket.
4. Select Air Fry, Super Convection, set temperature to 360°F (182°C), and set time to 12 minutes. Select Start/Stop to begin preheating.
5. Once preheated, place the basket on the air fry position. Flip the empanadas halfway through the cooking time.
6. When cooking is complete, the empanadas should be golden brown. Remove the basket from the oven. Allow them to cool for 5 minutes and serve hot.

Hot Chickpeas

Prep time: 5 minutes | Cook time: 18 minutes | Serves 4

½ teaspoon chili powder
½ teaspoon ground cumin
¼ teaspoon cayenne pepper
¼ teaspoon salt
1 (19-ounce / 539-g) can chickpeas, drained and rinsed
Cooking spray

1. Lina the air fry basket with parchment paper and lightly spritz with cooking spray.
2. Mix the chili powder, cumin, cayenne pepper, and salt in a small bowl.
3. Place the chickpeas in a medium bowl and lightly mist with cooking spray.
4. Add the spice mixture to the chickpeas and toss until evenly coated. Transfer the chickpeas to the parchment.
5. Select Air Fry, Super Convection, set temperature to 390°F (199°C), and set time to 18 minutes. Select Start/Stop to begin preheating.
6. Once preheated, place the basket on the air fry position. Stir the chickpeas twice during cooking.
7. When cooking is complete, the chickpeas should be crunchy. Remove the basket from the oven. Let the chickpeas cool for 5 minutes before serving.

Edamame

Prep time: 5 minutes | Cook time: 9 minutes | Serves 4

1 (16-ounce / 454-g) bag frozen edamame in pods
2 tablespoon olive oil, divided
½ teaspoon garlic salt
½ teaspoon salt
¼ teaspoon freshly ground black pepper
½ teaspoon red pepper flakes (optional)

1. Place the edamame in a medium bowl and drizzle with 1 tablespoon of olive oil. Toss to coat well.
2. Stir together the garlic salt, salt, pepper, and red pepper flakes (if desired) in a small bowl. Pour the mixture into the bowl of edamame and toss until the edamame is fully coated.
3. Grease the air fry basket with the remaining 1 tablespoon of olive oil.
4. Place the edamame in the greased basket.
5. Select Air Fry, Super Convection, set temperature to 375ºF (190ºC), and set time to 9 minutes. Select Start/Stop to begin preheating.
6. Once preheated, place the basket on the air fry position. Stir the edamame once halfway through the cooking time.
7. When cooking is complete, the edamame should be crisp. Remove from the oven to a plate and serve warm.

Hawaiian Beef Meatballs

Prep time: 12 minutes | Cook time: 11 to 24 minutes | Serves 2

For the Glaze:
1 tablespoon chili-garlic sauce
1 teaspoon honey
3 tablespoons mayonnaise
1 teaspoon pineapple juice
For the Meatballs:
1 pound (454 g) lean ground beef
1 egg, lightly beaten
2 tablespoons milk
⅓ cup bread crumbs
1 tablespoon soy sauce
2 teaspoons dried minced onion
½ teaspoon ground ginger
1 teaspoon minced garlic
1 teaspoon sesame oil
½ teaspoon salt

To make the glaze
1. In a small bowl, combine the chili-garlic sauce, honey, mayonnaise, and pineapple juice. Whisk well and set aside.
To make the meatballs
2. Preheat the air fryer to 400ºF (204ºC).
3. In a large bowl, combine the ingredients for the meatballs. Stir to mix well.
4. Separate and roll the mixture into 16 equal meatballs.
5. Place the meatballs in a baking pan, then place the pan in the air fryer basket.
6. Bake for about 12 minutes, or until well browned. Flip the meatballs and baste with glaze mixture halfway through.
7. Serve immediately.

Apple Chips

Prep time: 10 minutes | Cook time: 10 minutes | Serves 4

4 medium apples (any type will work), cored and thinly sliced
¼ teaspoon nutmeg
¼ teaspoon cinnamon
Cooking spray

1. Place the apple slices in a large bowl and sprinkle the spices on top. Toss to coat.
2. Put the apple slices in the air fry basket in a single layer and spray them with cooking spray.
3. Select Air Fry, Super Convection, set temperature to 360ºF (182ºC), and set time to 10 minutes. Select Start/Stop to begin preheating.
4. Once preheated, place the basket on the air fry position. Stir the apple slices halfway through.
5. When cooking is complete, the apple chips should be crispy. Transfer the apple chips to a paper towel-lined plate and rest for 5 minutes before serving.

Bruschetta with Parmesan Tomato

Prep time: 5 minutes | Cook time: 3 minutes | Serves 6

4 tomatoes, diced
⅓ cup shredded fresh basil
¼ cup shredded Parmesan cheese
1 tablespoon balsamic vinegar
1 tablespoon minced garlic
1 teaspoon olive oil
1 teaspoon salt
1 teaspoon freshly ground black
  pepper
1 loaf French bread, cut into 1-inch-
  thick slices
Cooking spray

1. Mix together the tomatoes and basil in a medium bowl. Add the cheese, vinegar, garlic, olive oil, salt, and pepper and stir until well incorporated. Set aside.
2. Spritz the air fry basket with cooking spray and lay the bread slices in the pan in a single layer. Spray the slices with cooking spray.
3. Select Bake, Super Convection, set temperature to 250°F (121°C), and set time to 3 minutes. Select Start/Stop to begin preheating.
4. Once preheated, place the basket on the bake position.
5. When cooking is complete, remove from the oven to a plate. Top each slice with a generous spoonful of the tomato mixture and serve.

Hush Puppies

Prep time: 7 minutes | Cook time: 20 minutes | Serves 2

¼ cup plus 2 tablespoons all-purpose
  flour
½ cup yellow cornmeal
2 tablespoons dried minced onion
¾ teaspoon baking powder
⅛ teaspoon granulated sugar
¼ teaspoon salt
1 egg
¼ cup plus 2 tablespoons milk
Cooking spray

1. Preheat the air fryer to 350°F (177°C).
2. In a large bowl, combine the flour, cornmeal, dried minced onion, baking powder, sugar, and salt. Whisk in the egg and the milk.
3. Divide and roll the mixture into tablespoon-size into balls.
4. Place the balls in the air fryer basket, and spritz with cooking spray. Air fry for 20 minutes or until golden brown. Flip the balls halfway through.
5. Serve hot.

Sesame Kale Chips

Prep time: 15 minutes | Cook time: 8 minutes | Serves 5

8 cups deribbed kale leaves, torn into
  2-inch pieces
1½ tablespoons olive oil
¾ teaspoon chili powder
¼ teaspoon garlic powder
½ teaspoon paprika
2 teaspoons sesame seeds

1. In a large bowl, toss the kale with the olive oil, chili powder, garlic powder, paprika, and sesame seeds until well coated.
2. Transfer the kale to the air fry basket.
3. Select Air Fry, Super Convection, set temperature to 350°F (180°C), and set time to 8 minutes. Select Start/Stop to begin preheating.
4. Once preheated, place the basket on the air fry position. Flip the kale twice during cooking.
5. When cooking is complete, the kale should be crispy. Remove from the oven and serve warm.

Spicy Corn Tortilla Chips

Prep time: 5 minutes | Cook time: 5 minutes | Serves 4

½ teaspoon ground cumin
½ teaspoon paprika
½ teaspoon chili powder
½ teaspoon salt
Pinch cayenne pepper
8 (6-inch) corn tortillas, each cut
    into 6 wedges
Cooking spray

1. Lightly spritz the air fry basket with cooking spray.
2. Stir together the cumin, paprika, chili powder, salt, and pepper in a small bowl.
3. Place the tortilla wedges in the air fry basket in a single layer. Lightly mist them with cooking spray. Sprinkle the seasoning mixture on top of the tortilla wedges.
4. Select Air Fry, Super Convection, set temperature to 375°F (190°C), and set time to 5 minutes. Select Start/Stop to begin preheating.
5. Once preheated, place the basket on the air fry position. Stir the tortilla wedges halfway through the cooking time.
6. When cooking is complete, the chips should be lightly browned and crunchy. Remove the basket from the oven. Let the tortilla chips cool for 5 minutes and serve.

Lush Snack Mix

Prep time: 10 minutes | Cook time: 12 minutes | Serves 10

½ cup honey
3 tablespoons butter, melted
1 teaspoon salt
2 cups sesame sticks
2 cup pumpkin seeds
2 cups granola
1 cup cashews
2 cups crispy corn puff cereal
2 cup mini pretzel crisps

1. In a bowl, combine the honey, butter, and salt.
2. In another bowl, mix the sesame sticks, pumpkin seeds, granola, cashews, corn puff cereal, and pretzel crisps.
3. Combine the contents of the two bowls.
4. Preheat the air fryer oven to 370°F (188°C).
5. Put the mixture in the air fryer basket. Place the air fryer basket onto the baking pan and slide into Rack Position 2, select Air Fry and set time to 12 minutes. Shake the basket frequently during cooking.
6. Put the snack mix on a cookie sheet and allow it to cool completely. Serve immediately.

Caramelized Cinnamon Peaches

Prep time: 5 minutes | Cook time: 10 to 13 minutes | Serves 4

2 tablespoons sugar
¼ teaspoon ground cinnamon
4 peaches, cut into wedges
Cooking spray

1. Toss the peaches with the sugar and cinnamon in a medium bowl until evenly coated.
2. Lightly spray the air fry basket with cooking spray. Place the peaches in the air fry basket in a single layer. Lightly mist the peaches with cooking spray.
3. Select Air Fry, Super Convection, set temperature to 350°F (180°C), and set time to 10 minutes. Select Start/Stop to begin preheating.
4. Once preheated, place the basket on the air fry position.
5. After 5 minutes, remove from the oven and flip the peaches. Return to the oven and continue cooking for 5 minutes.
6. When cooking is complete, the peaches should be caramelized. If necessary, continue cooking for 3 minutes. Remove the basket from the oven. Let the peaches cool for 5 minutes and serve warm.

Mozzarella Chicken Sausage Pizza

Prep time: 10 minutes | Cook time: 8 minutes | Serves 1

1 piece naan bread
¼ cup barbecue sauce
¼ cup shredded Monterrey Jack cheese
¼ cup shredded Mozzarella cheese
½ chicken herby sausage, sliced
2 tablespoons red onion, thinly sliced
Chopped cilantro or parsley, for garnish
Cooking spray

1. Spritz the bottom of naan bread with cooking spray, then transfer to the air fry basket.
2. Brush with the Barbecue sauce. Top with the cheeses, sausage, and finish with the red onion.
3. Select Air Fry, Super Convection, set temperature to 400°F (205°C), and set time to 8 minutes. Select Start/Stop to begin preheating.
4. Once preheated, place the basket on the air fry position.
5. When cooking is complete, the cheese should be melted. Remove the basket from the oven. Garnish with the chopped cilantro or parsley before slicing to serve.

Panko- Crusted Artichoke Bites

Prep time: 5 minutes | Cook time: 8 minutes | Serves 4

14 whole artichoke hearts packed in water
½ cup all-purpose flour
1 egg
⅓ cup panko bread crumbs
1 teaspoon Italian seasoning
Cooking spray

1. Drain the artichoke hearts and dry thoroughly with paper towels.
2. Place the flour on a plate. Beat the egg in a shallow bowl until frothy. Thoroughly combine the bread crumbs and Italian seasoning in a separate shallow bowl.
3. Dredge the artichoke hearts in the flour, then in the beaten egg, and finally roll in the bread crumb mixture until evenly coated.
4. Place the artichoke hearts in the air fry basket and mist them with cooking spray.
5. Select Air Fry, Super Convection, set temperature to 375°F (190°C), and set time to 8 minutes. Select Start/Stop to begin preheating.
6. Once preheated, place the basket on the air fry position. Flip the artichoke hearts halfway through the cooking time.
7. When cooking is complete, the artichoke hearts should start to brown and the edges should be crispy. Remove the basket from the oven. Let the artichoke hearts sit for 5 minutes before serving.

Easy Muffuletta Sliders with Olives

Prep time: 10 minutes | Cook time: 6 minutes | Makes 8 sliders

¼ pound (113 g) thinly sliced deli ham
¼ pound (113 g) thinly sliced pastrami
4 ounces (113 g) low-fat Mozzarella cheese, grated
8 slider buns, split in half
Cooking spray
1 tablespoon sesame seeds
Olive Mix:
½ cup sliced green olives with pimentos
¼ cup sliced black olives
¼ cup chopped kalamata olives
1 teaspoon red wine vinegar
¼ teaspoon basil
⅛ teaspoon garlic powder

1. Combine all the ingredients for the olive mix in a small bowl and stir well.
2. Stir together the ham, pastrami, and cheese in a medium bowl and divide the mixture into 8 equal portions.
3. Assemble the sliders: Top each bottom bun with 1 portion of meat and cheese, 2 tablespoons of olive mix, finished by the remaining buns. Lightly spritz the tops with cooking spray. Scatter the sesame seeds on top.
4. Arrange the sliders in the air fry basket.
5. Select Bake, Super Convection, set temperature to 360°F (182°C), and set time to 6 minutes. Select Start/Stop to begin preheating.
6. Once preheated, place the basket on the bake position.
7. When cooking is complete, the cheese should be melted. Remove the basket from the oven and serve.

Crab Melts

Prep time: 10 minutes | Cook time: 5 minutes | Makes 15 to 18 toasts

1 (6-ounce / 170-g) can flaked crab meat, well drained
3 tablespoons light mayonnaise
¼ cup shredded Parmesan cheese
¼ cup shredded Cheddar cheese
1 teaspoon Worcestershire sauce
½ teaspoon lemon juice
1 loaf artisan bread, French bread, or baguette, cut into ⅜-inch-thick slices

1. In a large bowl, stir together all the ingredients except the bread slices.
2. On a clean work surface, lay the bread slices. Spread ½ tablespoon of crab mixture onto each slice of bread.
3. Arrange the bread slices in the air fry basket in a single layer.
4. Select Bake, Super Convection, set temperature to 360ºF (182ºC), and set time to 5 minutes. Select Start/Stop to begin preheating.
5. Once preheated, place the basket on the bake position.
6. When cooking is complete, the tops should be lightly browned. Remove the basket from the oven. Serve warm.

Buttermilk Fried Chicken Wings

Prep time: 10 minutes | Cook time: 18 minutes | Serves 4

2 pounds (907 g) chicken wings
Cooking spray
Marinade:
1 cup buttermilk
½ teaspoon salt
½ teaspoon black pepper
Coating:
1 cup flour
1 cup panko bread crumbs
2 tablespoons poultry seasoning
2 teaspoons salt

1. Whisk together all the ingredients for the marinade in a large bowl.
2. Add the chicken wings to the marinade and toss well. Transfer to the refrigerator to marinate for at least an hour.
3. Spritz the air fry basket with cooking spray. Set aside.
4. Thoroughly combine all the ingredients for the coating in a shallow bowl.
5. Remove the chicken wings from the marinade and shake off any excess. Roll them in the coating mixture.
6. Place the chicken wings in the air fry basket in a single layer. Mist the wings with cooking spray.
7. Select Air Fry, Super Convection, set temperature to 360ºF (182ºC), and set time to 18 minutes. Select Start/Stop to begin preheating.
8. Once preheated, place the basket on the air fry position. Flip the wings halfway through the cooking time.
9. When cooking is complete, the wings should be crisp and golden brown on the outside. Remove from the oven to a plate and serve hot.

Cuban Pork and Turkey Sandwiches

Prep time: 10 minutes | Cook time: 8 minutes | Makes 4 sandwiches

8 slices ciabatta bread, about ¼-inch thick
Cooking spray
1 tablespoon brown mustard
Toppings:
6 to 8 ounces (170 to 227 g) thinly sliced leftover roast pork
4 ounces (113 g) thinly sliced deli turkey
⅓ cup bread and butter pickle slices
2 to 3 ounces (57 to 85 g) Pepper Jack cheese slices

1. On a clean work surface, spray one side of each slice of bread with cooking spray. Spread the other side of each slice of bread evenly with brown mustard.
2. Top 4 of the bread slices with the roast pork, turkey, pickle slices, cheese, and finish with remaining bread slices. Transfer to the air fry basket.
3. Select Air Fry, Super Convection, set temperature to 390ºF (199ºC), and set time to 8 minutes. Select Start/Stop to begin preheating.
4. Once preheated, place the basket on the air fry position.
5. When cooking is complete, remove the basket from the oven. Cool for 5 minutes and serve warm.

Breaded Green Tomatoes with Horseradish

Prep time: 15 minutes | Cook time: 13 minutes | Serves 4

2 eggs

¼ cup buttermilk

½ cup bread crumbs

½ cup cornmeal

¼ teaspoon salt

1½ pounds (680 g) firm green tomatoes, cut into ¼-inch slices

Cooking spray

Horseradish Sauce:

¼ cup sour cream

¼ cup mayonnaise

2 teaspoons prepared horseradish

½ teaspoon lemon juice

½ teaspoon Worcestershire sauce

⅛ teaspoon black pepper

1. Spritz the air fry basket with cooking spray. Set aside.
2. In a small bowl, whisk together all the ingredients for the horseradish sauce until smooth. Set aside.
3. In a shallow dish, beat the eggs and buttermilk.
4. In a separate shallow dish, thoroughly combine the bread crumbs, cornmeal, and salt.
5. Dredge the tomato slices, one at a time, in the egg mixture, then roll in the bread crumb mixture until evenly coated.
6. Place the tomato slices in the air fry basket in a single layer. Spray them with cooking spray.
7. Select Air Fry, Super Convection, set temperature to 390°F (199°C), and set time to 13 minutes. Select Start/Stop to begin preheating.
8. Once preheated, place the basket on the air fry position. Flip the tomato slices halfway through the cooking time.
9. When cooking is complete, the tomato slices should be nicely browned and crisp. Remove from the oven to a platter and serve drizzled with the prepared horseradish sauce.

Spinach and Mushroom Cheese Calzones

Prep time: 15 minutes | Cook time: 26 to 27 minutes | Serves 4

2 tablespoons olive oil

1 onion, chopped

2 garlic cloves, minced

¼ cup chopped mushrooms

1 pound (454 g) spinach, chopped

1 tablespoon Italian seasoning

½ teaspoon oregano

Salt and black pepper, to taste

1½ cups marinara sauce

1 cup ricotta cheese, crumbled

1 (13-ounce / 369-g) pizza crust

Cooking spray

Make the Filling:

1. Heat the olive oil in a pan over medium heat until shimmering.
2. Add the onion, garlic, and mushrooms and sauté for 4 minutes, or until softened.
3. Stir in the spinach and sauté for 2 to 3 minutes, or until the spinach is wilted. Sprinkle with the Italian seasoning, oregano, salt, and pepper and mix well.
4. Add the marinara sauce and cook for about 5 minutes, stirring occasionally, or until the sauce is thickened.
5. Remove the pan from the heat and stir in the ricotta cheese. Set aside.

Make the Calzones:

6. Spritz the air fry basket with cooking spray. Set aside.
7. Roll the pizza crust out with a rolling pin on a lightly floured work surface, then cut it into 4 rectangles.
8. Spoon ¼ of the filling into each rectangle and fold in half. Crimp the edges with a fork to seal. Mist them with cooking spray. Transfer the calzones to the air fry basket.
9. Select Air Fry, Super Convection, set temperature to 375°F (190°C), and set time to 15 minutes. Select Start/Stop to begin preheating.
10. Once preheated, place the basket on the air fry position. Flip the calzones halfway through the cooking time.
11. When cooking is complete, the calzones should be golden brown and crisp. Transfer the calzones to a paper towel-lined plate and serve.

Turkey Bacon-Wrapped Almond Stuffed Dates

Prep time: 10 minutes | Cook time: 6 minutes | Makes 16 appetizers

16 whole dates, pitted

16 whole almonds

6 to 8 strips turkey bacon, cut in half

Special Equipment:

16 toothpicks, soaked in water for at least 30 minutes

1. On a flat work surface, stuff each pitted date with a whole almond.
2. Wrap half slice of bacon around each date and secure it with a toothpick.
3. Place the bacon-wrapped dates in the air fry basket.
4. Select Air Fry, Super Convection, set temperature to 390°F (199°C), and set time to 6 minutes. Select Start/Stop to begin preheating.
5. Once preheated, place the basket on the air fry position.
6. When cooking is complete, transfer the dates to a paper towel-lined plate to drain. Serve hot.

Brie Pear Sandwiches

Prep time: 5 minutes | Cook time: 6 minutes | Serves 4 to 8

8 ounces (227 g) Brie
8 slices oat nut bread
1 large ripe pear, cored and cut into
    ½-inch-thick slices
2 tablespoons butter, melted

1. Make the sandwiches: Spread each of 4 slices of bread with ¼ of the Brie. Top the Brie with the pear slices and remaining 4 bread slices.
2. Brush the melted butter lightly on both sides of each sandwich.
3. Arrange the sandwiches in the air fry basket.
4. Select Bake, Super Convection, set temperature to 360ºF (182ºC), and set time to 6 minutes. Select Start/Stop to begin preheating.
5. Once preheated, place the basket on the bake position.
6. When cooking is complete, the cheese should be melted. Remove the basket from the oven and serve warm.

Muffuletta with Mozzarella Olives Topping

Prep time: 15 minutes | Cook time: 6 minutes | Makes 8 sliders

¼ pound (113 g) thinly sliced deli ham
¼ pound (113 g) thinly sliced
    pastrami
4 ounces (113 g) low-fat Mozzarella
    cheese, grated
8 slider buns, split in half
Cooking spray
1 tablespoon sesame seeds
Olive Mix:
½ cup sliced green olives with
    pimentos
¼ cup sliced black olives
¼ cup chopped kalamata olives
1 teaspoon red wine vinegar
¼ teaspoon basil
⅛ teaspoon garlic powder

8. Combine all the ingredients for the olive mix in a small bowl and stir well.
9. Stir together the ham, pastrami, and cheese in a medium bowl and divide the mixture into 8 equal portions.
10. Assemble the sliders: Top each bottom bun with 1 portion of meat and cheese, 2 tablespoons of olive mix, finished by the remaining buns. Lightly spritz the tops with cooking spray. Scatter the sesame seeds on top.
11. Arrange the sliders in the air fry basket.
12. Select Bake, Super Convection, set temperature to 360ºF (182ºC), and set time to 6 minutes. Select Start/Stop to begin preheating.
13. Once preheated, place the basket on the bake position.
14. When cooking is complete, the cheese should be melted. Remove the basket from the oven and serve.

Crispy Breaded Beef Cubes

Prep time: 10 minutes | Cook time: 8 minutes | Serves 4

1 pound (454 g) sirloin tip, cut into
    1-inch cubes
1 cup cheese pasta sauce
1½ cups soft bread crumbs
2 tablespoons olive oil
½ teaspoon dried marjoram

1. Preheat the air fryer oven to 360ºF (182ºC).
2. In a medium bowl, toss the beef with the pasta sauce to coat.
3. In a shallow bowl, combine the bread crumbs, oil, and marjoram, and stir well. Drop the beef cubes, one at a time, into the bread crumb mixture to coat thoroughly. Transfer the beef to the air fryer basket.
4. Place the air fryer basket onto the baking pan and slide into Rack Position 2, select Air Fry and set time to 8 minutes, or until the beef is at least 145ºF (63ºC) and the outside is crisp and brown. Shake the basket once during cooking time.
5. Serve hot.

Honey Chocolate Lava Cake

Prep time: 5 minutes | Cook time: 10 minutes | Serves 4

Olive oil cooking spray
¼ cup whole wheat flour
1 tablespoon unsweetened dark
    chocolate cocoa powder
⅛ teaspoon salt
½ teaspoon baking powder
¼ cup honey
1 egg
2 tablespoons olive oil

1. Preheat the air fryer to 380°F (193°C). Lightly coat the insides of four ramekins with olive oil cooking spray.
2. In a medium bowl, combine the flour, cocoa powder, salt, baking powder, honey, egg, and olive oil.
3. Divide the batter evenly among the ramekins.
4. Place the filled ramekins inside the air fryer and bake for 10 minutes.
5. Remove the lava cakes from the air fryer and slide a knife around the outside edge of each cake. Turn each ramekin upside down on a saucer and serve.

Pineapple with Lime and Mint

Prep time: 5 minutes | Cook time: 30 minutes | Serves 4

1 pineapple
4 tablespoons cashew butter
2 tablespoons plus 2 teaspoons coconut
    sugar
2 tablespoons fresh mint, cut into ribbons
1 lime

1. Cut off the top and bottom of the pineapple and stand it on a cut end. Slice off the outer skin, cutting deeply enough to remove the eyes of the pineapple. Cut off any pointy edges to make the pineapple nice and round. Cut the peeled pineapple into 8 circles, approximately ½ to ¾ inch (1.3 to 2 cm) thick. Remove the core of each slice using a small, circular cookie or biscuit cutter, or simply cut out the core using a paring knife. Place the pineapple rings on a plate.
2. Brush both sides of the pineapple rings with the cashew butter. Working in 2 batches, arrange 4 slices in a single layer in the basket of the air fryer. Sprinkle ½ teaspoon coconut sugar on the top of each ring. Cook at 400°F (204°C) until the top side is browned and caramelized, about 10 minutes. With tongs, carefully flip each ring and sprinkle coconut sugar on the second side. Cook for an additional 5 minutes until the second side is browned and caramelized. Remove the cooked pineapple and repeat with the remaining pineapple rings.
3. Arrange all the cooked pineapple rings on a serving plate or platter. Sprinkle with mint and spritz with the juice of the lime. Serve warm.

Turkey Bacon-
Wrapped Dates

Prep time: 10 minutes | Cook time: 6 minutes | Makes 16 appetizers

16 whole dates, pitted
16 whole almonds
6 to 8 strips turkey bacon, cut in half

Special Equipment:
16 toothpicks, soaked in water for at least
    30 minutes

7. On a flat work surface, stuff each pitted date with a whole almond.
8. Wrap half slice of bacon around each date and secure it with a toothpick.
9. Place the bacon-wrapped dates in the air fry basket.
10. Select Air Fry, Super Convection, set temperature to 390°F (199°C), and set time to 6 minutes. Select Start/Stop to begin preheating.
11. Once preheated, place the basket on the air fry position.
12. When cooking is complete, transfer the dates to a paper towel-lined plate to drain. Serve hot.

Italian Rice Balls

Prep time: 20 minutes | Cook time: 10 minutes | Makes 8 rice balls

1½ cups cooked sticky rice
½ teaspoon Italian seasoning blend
¾ teaspoon salt, divided
8 black olives, pitted
1 ounce (28 g) Mozzarella cheese, cut into tiny pieces (small enough to stuff into olives)
2 eggs
⅓ cup Italian bread crumbs
¾ cup panko bread crumbs
Cooking spray

1. Stuff each black olive with a piece of Mozzarella cheese.
2. In a bowl, combine the cooked sticky rice, Italian seasoning blend, and ½ teaspoon of salt and stir to mix well. Form the rice mixture into a log with your hands and divide it into 8 equal portions. Mold each portion around a black olive and roll into a ball.
3. Transfer to the freezer to chill for 10 to 15 minutes until firm.
4. In a shallow dish, place the Italian bread crumbs. In a separate shallow dish, whisk the eggs. In a third shallow dish, combine the panko bread crumbs and remaining salt.
5. One by one, roll the rice balls in the Italian bread crumbs, then dip in the whisked eggs, finally coat them with the panko bread crumbs.
6. Arrange the rice balls in the air fry basket and spritz both sides with cooking spray.
7. Select Air Fry, Super Convection, set temperature to 390°F (199°C), and set time to 10 minutes. Select Start/Stop to begin preheating.
8. Once preheated, place the basket on the air fry position. Flip the balls halfway through the cooking time.
9. When cooking is complete, the rice balls should be golden brown. Remove from the oven and serve warm.

Crispy Cod Fingers

Prep time: 5 minutes | Cook time: 12 minutes | Serves 4

2 eggs
2 tablespoons milk
2 cups flour
1 cup cornmeal
1 teaspoon seafood seasoning
Salt and black pepper, to taste
1 cup bread crumbs
1 pound (454 g) cod fillets, cut into 1-inch strips

1. Beat the eggs with the milk in a shallow bowl. In another shallow bowl, combine the flour, cornmeal, seafood seasoning, salt, and pepper. On a plate, place the bread crumbs.
2. Dredge the cod strips, one at a time, in the flour mixture, then in the egg mixture, finally roll in the bread crumb to coat evenly.
3. Transfer the cod strips to the air fry basket.
4. Select Air Fry, Super Convection, set temperature to 400°F (205°C), and set time to 12 minutes. Select Start/Stop to begin preheating.
5. Once preheated, place the basket on the air fry position.
6. When cooking is complete, the cod strips should be crispy. Remove from the oven to a paper towel-lined plate and serve warm.

Lemony Potato Cubes

Prep time: 5 minutes | Cook time: 10 minutes | Serves 2

2½ medium potatoes, scrubbed and cubed
1 tablespoon chopped fresh rosemary
½ tablespoon olive oil
Freshly ground black pepper, to taste
1 tablespoon fresh lemon juice
½ cup vegetable broth

1. Put the potatoes, rosemary, oil, and pepper to the Instant Pot. Stir to mix well.
2. Set to the Pressure Cook mode and sauté for 4 minutes.
3. Fold in the remaining ingredients.
4. Secure the lid and select the Pressure Cook mode. Set the cooking time for 6 minutes at High Pressure.
5. Once cooking is complete, do a quick release, then open the lid.
6. Serve warm.

Mushroom Stuffed Tomatoes

Prep time: 20 minutes | Cook time: 10 minutes | Serves 4

4 tomatoes
1 tablespoon ghee
2 tablespoons celery, chopped
1 yellow onion, chopped
½ cup mushrooms, chopped
1 tablespoon parsley, chopped
1 cup cottage cheese
Salt and black pepper, to taste
¼ teaspoon caraway seeds
½ cup water

1. On a clean work surface, remove the tops of each tomato about 1 inch, then scoop the tomato pulp out and reserve in a small bowl. Set aside.
2. Set the Instant Pot on Sauté mode. Add the ghee and heat until melted.
3. Add the celery and onion. Sauté for 3 minutes or until softened.
4. Add the mushrooms, tomato pulp, parsley, cheese, salt, pepper, and caraway seeds, then stir well. Sauté for 3 minutes more. Stuff the hollowed tomatoes with the mixture.
5. Pour the water in the Instant Pot, then arrange the steamer basket in the pot. Place the stuffed tomatoes inside.
6. Seal the Instant Pot lid and set to the Pressure Cook mode. Set the cooking time for 4 minutes on High Pressure.
7. Once cooking is complete, perform a quick pressure release. Carefully open the lid.
8. Arrange the stuffed tomatoes on a platter and serve immediately.

Port Wined Short Ribs

Prep time: 20 minutes | Cook time: 1 hour 45 minutes | Serves 4

½ tablespoon lard
1 pound (454 g) short ribs
¼ cup port wine
1 tablespoon rice vinegar
1 tablespoon molasses
1 thyme sprig
1 rosemary sprig
1 garlic clove
½ cup beef bone broth
½ teaspoon cayenne pepper
Sea salt and ground black pepper, to
    season

1. Press the Sauté button and melt the lard in the Instant Pot.
2. Add the short ribs and cook for 4 to 5 minutes, flipping periodically to ensure even cooking.
3. Add the remaining ingredients and stir to mix well.
4. Secure the lid. Choose the Pressure Cook mode and set the cooking time for 90 minutes at High pressure.
5. Once cooking is complete, perform a natural pressure release for 30 minutes, then release any remaining pressure. Carefully open the lid.
6. Transfer the short ribs into the broiler and broil for 10 minutes or until crispy. Transfer the ribs to a platter and serve immediately.

Queso Fundido

Prep time: 15 minutes | Cook time: 6 minutes | Serves 4 to 6

1 pound (454 g) chorizo sausage,
    chopped
½ cup tomato salsa
1 red onion, chopped
1 cup cream cheese
1 teaspoon Mexican oregano
½ teaspoon cayenne pepper
½ cup water
¼ teaspoon ground black pepper
1 teaspoon coriander
1 cup Cotija cheese

1. Combine the sausage, tomato salsa, red onion, cream cheese, oregano, cayenne pepper, water, black pepper, and coriander in the Instant Pot.
2. Secure the lid. Choose the Pressure Cook mode and set the cooking time for 6 minutes at High Pressure.
3. Once cooking is complete, perform a natural pressure release for 5 minutes, then release any remaining pressure. Carefully open the lid.
4. Add the Cotija cheese and press the Sauté button. Sauté until heated through. Serve warm.

Roasted Nuts, Chickpeas, and Seeds

Prep time: 10 minutes | Cook time: 11 minutes | Serves 2 to 4

2 tablespoons pecans halves
¼ cup canned chickpeas
2 tablespoons almonds
1 tablespoon pumpkin seeds
1 tablespoon sunflower seeds
¼ teaspoon grated nutmeg
¼ teaspoon ground ginger
2 tablespoons maple syrup
1 tablespoon butter
¼ teaspoon kosher salt
¼ cup Sultanas

1. Place all ingredients, except for the Sultanas, in the Instant Pot. Stir to combine well.
2. Press the Sauté button and sauté for 1 minute until the butter melts and the nuts are well coated.
3. Secure the lid. Choose the Pressure Cook mode and set the cooking time for 10 minutes at High pressure.
4. Once cooking is complete, perform a quick pressure release. Carefully open the lid.
5. Transfer them on a baking pan and bake in the preheated oven at 375°F (190°C) for about 8 minutes.
6. Remove the pan from the oven. Add the Sultanas and stir to combine. Serve immediately.

Super Pickles Deviled Eggs

Prep time: 15 minutes | Cook time: 4 minutes | Makes 12 deviled eggs

1 cup water
6 large eggs
1 teaspoon finely diced dill pickles
½ teaspoon dill pickle juice
1 teaspoon yellow mustard
3 tablespoons mayonnaise
⅛ teaspoon smoked paprika
⅛ teaspoon salt
⅛ teaspoon ground black pepper
½ cup crushed dill pickle flavored potato chips

1. Add water to the Instant Pot and insert a steamer basket. Place the eggs in the basket. Lock the lid.
2. Select the Pressure Cook mode and set the cook time for 4 minutes on High Pressure. When timer beeps, quick release pressure, and then unlock the lid.
3. Transfer the eggs in a large bowl of ice water. Peel the eggs under the water. Slice each egg in half lengthwise and place yolks in a small bowl. Place egg white halves on a serving tray.
4. Add the diced pickles, pickle juice, mustard, mayonnaise, smoked paprika, salt, and pepper to the small bowl with yolks. Stir until smooth.
5. Spoon the yolk mixture into egg white halves. Sprinkle with crushed chips. Serve immediately.

Sausage Stuffed Bella Mushrooms

Prep time: 10 minutes | Cook time: 7 minutes | Makes 10 mushrooms

1 tablespoon olive oil
4 ounces (113 g) ground pork sausage
1 tablespoon diced yellow onion
1 tablespoon horseradish
1 tablespoon bread crumbs
1 teaspoon yellow mustard
2 tablespoons cream cheese, at room temperature
¼ teaspoon garlic salt
1 cup water
8 ounces (227 g) whole baby bella mushrooms, stem removed
2 tablespoons chopped fresh Italian flat-leaf parsley

1. Press the Sauté button on the Instant Pot and heat the olive oil until shimmering.
2. Add the sausage and onion to the pot. Sauté for 5 minutes until the sausage is lightly browned.
3. Transfer the sausage and onion to a small bowl and use paper towels to pat dry. Add the horseradish, bread crumbs, yellow mustard, cream cheese, and garlic salt.
4. Pour the water into the Instant Pot. Stuff the sausage mixture into each mushroom cap and place in a steamer basket. Insert the steamer basket in the pot and lock the lid.
5. Select the Pressure Cook mode and set the cook time for 2 minutes on Low Pressure. When timer beeps, quick release the pressure. Unlock lid.
6. Transfer the stuffed mushrooms to a serving dish. Garnish with chopped parsley. Serve warm.

Eggplant and Olive Spread

Prep time: 20 minutes | Cook time: 8 minutes | Serves 6

¼ cup olive oil

2 pounds (907 g) eggplant, peeled and cut into medium chunks

4 garlic cloves, minced

½ cup water

Salt and black pepper, to taste

1 tablespoon sesame seed paste

¼ cup lemon juice

1 bunch thyme, chopped

3 olives, pitted and sliced

1. Set the Instant Pot on Sauté mode. Add the olive oil and heat until shimmering.
2. Add eggplant pieces and Sauté for 5 minutes. Add the garlic, water, salt and pepper, then stir well.
3. Close the lid, set to the Pressure Cook mode and set the cooking time for 3 minutes on High Pressure.
4. Once cooking is complete, perform a quick pressure release. Carefully open the lid.
5. Transfer to a blender, then add sesame seed paste, lemon juice and thyme, pulse to combine well.
6. Transfer to bowls, sprinkle olive slices on top and serve.

Hearty Red Pepper Hummus

Prep time: 10 minutes | Cook time: 30 minutes | Makes 1½ cups

½ cup dried chickpeas

2 cups water

1 cup jarred roasted red peppers with liquid, chopped and divided

1 tablespoon tahini paste

1 tablespoon lemon juice

1 teaspoon lemon zest

¼ teaspoon ground cumin

2 cloves garlic, minced

¼ teaspoon smoked paprika

⅛ teaspoon cayenne pepper

¼ teaspoon salt

1 teaspoon sesame oil

1 tablespoon olive oil

1. Add chickpeas and water to the Instant Pot. Drain liquid from the roasted peppers into the pot. Set aside the drained peppers.
2. Lock the lid. Press the Beans / Chili button and set the time to 30 minutes on High Pressure. When the timer beeps, let pressure release naturally for 5 minutes, then release any remaining pressure. Unlock the lid.
3. Drain pot, reserving the liquid in a small bowl.
4. Make the hummus: Transfer the chickpeas into a food processor. Add ¼ cup of chopped red peppers, tahini paste, lemon juice and zest, cumin, garlic, smoked paprika, cayenne pepper, salt, sesame oil, and olive oil. If consistency is too thick, slowly add reserved liquid, 1 tablespoon at a time until it has a loose paste consistency.
5. Transfer the hummus to a serving dish. Garnish with remaining chopped roasted red peppers and serve.

Beery Shrimp with Thai Sauce

Prep time: 10 minutes | Cook time: 10 minutes | Serves 10

Thai Sauce:

¼ cup Thai sweet chili sauce

1 tablespoon Sriracha sauce

¼ cup sour cream

2 teaspoons lime juice

½ cup mayonnaise

Shrimp:

1 (12-ounce / 340-g) bottle beer

4 pounds (1.8 kg) large shrimp, shelled and deveined

1. Combine ingredients for the Thai sauce in a small bowl. Cover the bowl in plastic and refrigerate until ready to serve.
2. Pour the beer into the Instant Pot and insert the steamer basket. Place shrimp in basket.
3. Lock the lid. Press the Steam button and set the cook time for 10 minutes on Low Pressure.
4. When timer beeps, quick release the pressure and then unlock the lid.
5. Transfer shrimp to a serving dish and serve with the Thai sauce.

Bacon Stuffed Mini Peppers

Prep time: 15 minutes | Cook time: 16 minutes | Serves 4

1 ounce (28 g) bacon, chopped
1 garlic clove, minced
2 tablespoons chopped onion
½ teaspoon Worcestershire sauce
2 ounces (57 g) Mexican cheese blend, crumbled
½ teaspoon Taco seasoning
4 mini sweet bell peppers, deseeded and membranes removed
1 cup water
1 tablespoon fresh cilantro, chopped

1. Press the Sauté button of the Instant Pot. Add and cook the bacon for 8 minutes or until it is crisp. Flip the bacon halfway through and crumble with a spatula. Set aside.
2. Add and cook the garlic and onion for 3 minutes or until tender and fragrant.
3. Add the Worcestershire sauce, cheese, and Taco seasoning. Stir in the reserved bacon.
4. Divide the mixture among the peppers on a clean work surface.
5. Pour the water in the Instant Pot. Arrange a trivet over the water. Place the stuffed peppers onto the trivet.
6. Secure the lid. Choose the Pressure Cook mode and set the cooking time for 5 minutes at High pressure.
7. Once cooking is complete, perform a natural pressure release for 5 minutes, then release any remaining pressure. Carefully open the lid.
8. Serve the bacon stuffed pepper on a platter garnished with fresh cilantro.

Simple Cinnamon Popcorn

Prep time: 5 minutes | Cook time: 1 minute | Serves 2

1 tablespoon coconut oil
¼ cup popcorn kernels
½ tablespoon ground cinnamon
3 tablespoons icing sugar

1. Press the Sauté button and melt the coconut oil in the Instant Pot.
2. Stir in the popcorn kernels and stir to cover. Cook for about a minute or until the popping slows down.
3. Transfer the popped corn to a large bowl and toss with cinnamon and icing sugar to coat well. Serve immediately.

Cheesy Rutabaga and Bacon Bites

Prep time: 10 minutes | Cook time: 5 minutes | Serves 8

1 cup water
½ pound (227 g) rutabaga, grated
7 ounces (198 g) Gruyère cheese, shredded
4 slices meaty bacon, chopped
3 eggs, lightly beaten
3 tablespoons almond flour
1 teaspoon shallot powder
1 teaspoon granulated garlic
Sea salt and ground black pepper, to taste

1. Pour the water into the Instant Pot and insert a trivet.
2. Stir together the remaining ingredients in a bowl until well combined. Pour the mixture into a greased silicone pod tray and cover with a sheet of aluminum foil. Place it on top of the trivet.
3. Lock the lid. Select the Pressure Cook mode and set the cooking time for 5 minutes at Low Pressure.
4. When the timer beeps, perform a quick pressure release. Carefully remove the lid.
5. Allow to cool for 5 minutes before serving.

Cajun Shrimp and Asparagus

Prep time: 7 minutes | Cook time: 3 minutes | Serves 4

1 cup water
1 pound (454 g) shrimp, peeled and deveined
1 bunch asparagus, trimmed
½ tablespoon Cajun seasoning
1 teaspoon extra virgin olive oil

1. Pour the water into the Instant Pot and insert a steamer basket. Put the shrimp and asparagus in the basket. Sprinkle with the Cajun seasoning and drizzle with the olive oil. Toss a bit.
2. Secure the lid. Select the Pressure Cook mode and set the cooking time for 3 minutes at High Pressure.
3. Once cooking is complete, do a quick pressure release. Carefully open the lid.
4. Remove from the basket to a plate and serve.

Chapter 7 Vegetables and Side Dishes

Lemony Wax Beans

Prep time: 5 minutes | Cook time: 12 minutes | Serves 4

2 pounds (907 g) wax beans
2 tablespoons extra-virgin olive oil
Salt and freshly ground black pepper, to taste
Juice of ½ lemon, for serving

1. Line a baking sheet with aluminum foil.
2. Toss the wax beans with the olive oil in a large bowl. Lightly season with salt and pepper.
3. Spread out the wax beans on the sheet pan.
4. Select Roast, , set temperature to 400°F (205°C), and set time to 12 minutes. Select Start/Stop to begin preheating.
5. Once preheated, place the baking sheet on the roast position.
6. When done, the beans will be caramelized and tender. Remove from the oven to a plate and serve sprinkled with the lemon juice.

Brussels Sprouts with Tomatoes

Prep time: 15 minutes | Cook time: 20 minutes | Serves 4

1 pound (454 g) Brussels sprouts, trimmed and halved
1 tablespoon extra-virgin olive oil
Sea Salt and freshly ground black pepper, to taste
½ cup sun-dried tomatoes, chopped
2 tablespoons freshly squeezed lemon juice
1 teaspoon lemon zest

1. Line a large baking sheet with aluminum foil.
2. Toss the Brussels sprouts with the olive oil in a large bowl. Sprinkle with salt and black pepper.
3. Spread the Brussels sprouts in a single layer on the baking sheet.
4. Select Roast, , set temperature to 400°F (205°C), and set time to 20 minutes. Select Start/Stop to begin preheating.
5. Once preheated, place the baking sheet on the roast position.
6. When done, the Brussels sprouts should be caramelized. Remove from the oven to a serving bowl, along with the tomatoes, lemon juice, and lemon zest. Toss to combine. Serve immediately.

Pecan Granola with Maple Syrup

Prep time: 5 minutes | Cook time: 20 minutes | Serves 4

1½ cups rolled oats
¼ cup maple syrup
¼ cup pecan pieces
1 teaspoon vanilla extract
½ teaspoon ground cinnamon

1. Line a baking sheet with parchment paper.
2. Mix together the oats, maple syrup, pecan pieces, vanilla, and cinnamon in a large bowl and stir until the oats and pecan pieces are completely coated. Spread the mixture evenly on the baking sheet.
3. Select Bake, set temperature to 300°F (150°C), and set time to 20 minutes. Select Start/Stop to begin preheating.
4. Once preheated, place the baking sheet on the bake position. Stir once halfway through the cooking time.
5. When done, remove from the oven and cool for 30 minutes before serving. The granola may still be a bit soft right after removing, but it will gradually firm up as it cools.

Broccoli with Sauce

Prep time: 10 minutes | Cook time: 15 to 20 minutes | Serves 4

½ teaspoon olive oil, plus more for greasing
1 pound (454 g) fresh broccoli, cut into florets
½ tablespoon minced garlic
Salt, to taste
Sauce:
1½ tablespoons soy sauce
2 teaspoons hot sauce
1½ teaspoons honey
1 teaspoon white vinegar
Freshly ground black pepper, to taste

1. Grease the air fry basket with olive oil.
2. Add the broccoli florets, ½ teaspoon of olive oil, and garlic to a large bowl and toss well. Season with salt to taste.
3. Put the broccoli in the air fry basket in a single layer.
4. Select Air Fry, , set temperature to 400°F (205°C), and set time to 15 minutes. Select Start/ Stop to begin preheating.
5. Once preheated, place the air fry basket on the air fry position. Stir the broccoli florets three times during cooking.
6. Meanwhile, whisk together all the ingredients for the sauce in a small bowl until well incorporated. If the honey doesn't incorporate well, microwave the sauce for 10 to 20 seconds until the honey is melted.
7. When cooking is complete, the broccoli should be lightly browned and crispy. Continue cooking for 5 minutes, if desired. Remove from the oven to a serving bowl. Pour over the sauce and toss to combine. Add more salt and pepper, if needed. Serve warm.

Celery Roots with Butter

Prep time: 10 minutes | Cook time: 20 minutes | Serves 4

2 celery roots, peeled and diced
1 teaspoon extra-virgin olive oil
1 teaspoon butter, melted
½ teaspoon ground cinnamon
Sea salt and freshly ground black pepper, to taste

1. Line a baking sheet with aluminum foil.
2. Toss the celery roots with the olive oil in a large bowl until well coated. Transfer them to the prepared baking sheet.
3. Select Roast, set temperature to 350°F (180°C), and set time to 20 minutes. Select Start/Stop to begin preheating.
4. Once preheated, place the baking sheet on the roast position.
5. When done, the celery roots should be very tender. Remove from the oven to a serving bowl. Stir in the butter and cinnamon and mash them with a potato masher until fluffy.
6. Season with salt and pepper to taste. Serve immediately.

Cheesy Broccoli Tots

Prep time: 20 minutes | Cook time: 15 minutes | Serves 4

12 ounces (340 g) frozen broccoli, thawed, drained, and patted dry
1 large egg, lightly beaten
½ cup seasoned whole-wheat bread crumbs
¼ cup shredded reduced-fat sharp Cheddar cheese
¼ cup grated Parmesan cheese
1½ teaspoons minced garlic
Salt and freshly ground black pepper, to taste
Cooking spray

1. Spritz the air fry basket lightly with cooking spray.
2. Place the remaining ingredients into a food processor and process until the mixture resembles a coarse meal. Transfer the mixture to a bowl.
3. Using a tablespoon, scoop out the broccoli mixture and form into 24 oval "tater tot" shapes with your hands.
4. Put the tots in the prepared basket in a single layer, spacing them 1 inch apart. Mist the tots lightly with cooking spray.
5. Select Air Fry, set temperature to 375°F (190°C), and set time to 15 minutes. Select Start/Stop to begin preheating.
6. Once preheated, place the air fry basket on the air fry position. Flip the tots halfway through the cooking time.
7. When done, the tots will be lightly browned and crispy. Remove from the oven and serve on a plate.

Cauliflower with Paprika

Prep time: 10 minutes | Cook time: 20 minutes | Serves 4

1 large head cauliflower, broken into small florets
2 teaspoons smoked paprika
1 teaspoon garlic powder
Salt and freshly ground black pepper, to taste
Cooking spray

1. Spray the air fry basket with cooking spray.
2. In a medium bowl, toss the cauliflower florets with the smoked paprika and garlic powder until evenly coated. Sprinkle with salt and pepper.
3. Place the cauliflower florets in the air fry basket and lightly mist with cooking spray.
4. Select Air Fry, set temperature to 400°F (205°C), and set time to 20 minutes. Select Start/Stop to begin preheating.
5. Once preheated, place the air fry basket on the air fry position. Stir the cauliflower four times during cooking.
6. Remove the cauliflower from the oven and serve hot.

Tortellini with Peas and Asparagus

Prep time: 10 minutes | Cook time: 16 minutes | Serves 4

8 ounces (227 g) sugar snap peas, trimmed
½ pound (227 g) asparagus, trimmed and cut into 1-inch pieces
2 teaspoons kosher salt or 1 teaspoon fine salt, divided
1 tablespoon extra-virgin olive oil
1½ cups water
1 (20-ounce / 340-g) package frozen cheese tortellini
2 garlic cloves, minced
1 cup heavy (whipping) cream
1 cup cherry tomatoes, halved
½ cup grated Parmesan cheese
¼ cup chopped fresh parsley or basil

1. Add the peas and asparagus to a large bowl. Add ½ teaspoon of kosher salt and the olive oil and toss until well coated. Place the veggies in the sheet pan.
2. Select Bake, set the temperature to 450°F (235°C), and set the time for 4 minutes. Select Start/Stop to begin preheating.
3. Once the unit has preheated, place the pan on the bake position.
4. Meanwhile, dissolve 1 teaspoon of kosher salt in the water.
5. Once cooking is complete, remove the pan from the oven and arrange the tortellini on the pan. Pour the salted water over the tortellini. Transfer the pan back to the oven.
6. Select Bake, set temperature to 450°F (235°C), and set time for 7 minutes. Place the pan on the bake position.
7. Meantime, stir together the garlic, heavy cream, and remaining ½ teaspoon of kosher salt in a small bowl.
8. Once cooking is complete, remove the pan from the oven. Blot off any remaining water with a paper towel. Gently stir the ingredients. Drizzle the cream over and top with the tomatoes.
9. Select Roast, set the temperature to 375°F (190°C), and set the time for 5 minutes. Place the pan on the roast position.
10. Once the unit has preheated, place the pan in the oven.
11. After 4 minutes, remove the pan from the oven.
12. Add the Parmesan cheese and stir until the cheese is melted
13. Serve topped with the parsley.

Carrot Tofu with Peanuts

Prep time: 10 minutes | Cook time: 10 minutes | Serves 4

⅓ cup Asian-Style sauce
1 teaspoon cornstarch
½ teaspoon red pepper flakes, or more to taste
1 pound (454 g) firm or extra-firm tofu, cut into 1-inch cubes
1 small carrot, peeled and cut into ¼-inch-thick coins
1 small green bell pepper, cut into bite-size pieces
3 scallions, sliced, whites and green parts separated
3 tablespoons roasted unsalted peanuts

1. In a large bowl, whisk together the sauce, cornstarch, and red pepper flakes. Fold in the tofu, carrot, pepper, and the white parts of the scallions and toss to coat. Spread the mixture evenly on the sheet pan.
2. Select Roast, set temperature to 375°F (190°C), and set time to 10 minutes. Select Start/Stop to begin preheating.
3. Once preheated, place the pan on the roast position. Stir the ingredients once halfway through the cooking time.
4. When done, remove the pan from the oven. Serve sprinkled with the peanuts and scallion greens.

Cabbage and Peas with Mango

Prep time: 10 minutes | Cook time: 8 minutes | Serves 4

1 small head Napa cabbage, shredded, divided
1 medium carrot, cut into thin coins
8 ounces (227 g) snow peas
1 red or green bell pepper, sliced into thin strips
1 tablespoon vegetable oil
2 tablespoons soy sauce
1 tablespoon sesame oil
2 tablespoons brown sugar
2 tablespoons freshly squeezed lime juice
2 teaspoons red or green Thai curry paste
1 serrano chili, deseeded and minced
1 cup frozen mango slices, thawed
½ cup chopped roasted peanuts or cashews

1. Put half the Napa cabbage in a large bowl, along with the carrot, snow peas, and bell pepper. Drizzle with the vegetable oil and toss to coat. Spread them evenly on the sheet pan.
2. Select Roast, set temperature to 375ºF (190ºC), and set time to 8 minutes. Select Start/Stop to begin preheating.
3. Once preheated, place the pan on the roast position.
4. Meanwhile, whisk together the soy sauce, sesame oil, brown sugar, lime juice, and curry paste in a small bowl.
5. When done, the vegetables should be tender and crisp. Remove the pan and put the vegetables back into the bowl. Add the chili, mango slices, and the remaining cabbage. Pour over the dressing and toss to coat. Top with the roasted nuts and serve.

Eggplant with Basil

Prep time: 15 minutes | Cook time: 20 minutes | Serves 2

1 small eggplant, halved and sliced
1 yellow bell pepper, cut into thick strips
1 red bell pepper, cut into thick strips
2 garlic cloves, quartered
1 red onion, sliced
1 tablespoon extra-virgin olive oil
Salt and freshly ground black pepper, to taste
½ cup chopped fresh basil, for garnish
Cooking spray

1. Grease a nonstick baking dish with cooking spray.
2. Place the eggplant, bell peppers, garlic, and red onion in the greased baking dish. Drizzle with the olive oil and toss to coat well. Spritz any uncoated surfaces with cooking spray.
3. Select Bake, set temperature to 350ºF (180ºC), and set time to 20 minutes. Select Start/Stop to begin preheating.
4. Once preheated, place the baking dish on the bake position. Flip the vegetables halfway through the cooking time.
5. When done, remove from the oven and sprinkle with salt and pepper.
6. Sprinkle the basil on top for garnish and serve.

Bell Peppers with Chili

Prep time: 5 minutes | Cook time: 15 minutes | Serves 3

1 pound (454 g) bell peppers, seeded and halved
1 chili pepper, seeded
2 tablespoons olive oil
Kosher salt and ground black pepper, to taste
1 teaspoon granulated garlic

1. Start by preheating the air fryer to 400ºF (205ºC).
2. Toss the peppers with the remaining ingredients; place them in the crisper tray.
3. Place the crisper tray in the corresponding position in the air fryer. Select Air Fry and cook the peppers for about 15 minutes, shaking crisper tray halfway through the cooking time.
4. Taste, adjust the seasonings and serve at room temperature. Bon appétit!

Mushrooms with Tamari Sauce

Prep time: 5 minutes | Cook time: 7 minutes | Serves 4

1 pound (454 g) brown mushrooms, quartered
2 tablespoons sesame oil
1 tablespoon tamari sauce
1 garlic clove, pressed
Sea salt and ground black pepper, to taste

1. Start by preheating the air fryer to 400°F (205°C).
2. Toss the mushrooms with the remaining ingredients. Toss until they are well coated on all sides.
3. Arrange the mushrooms in the crisper tray.
4. Place the crisper tray in the corresponding position in the air fryer. Select Roast and cook the mushrooms for about 7 minutes, shaking crisper tray halfway through the cooking time.
5. Bon appétit!

Carrot and Parsnip

Prep time: 15 minutes | Cook time: 15 minutes | Serves 4

1 carrot, trimmed and sliced
1 parsnip, trimmed and sliced
1 celery stalk, trimmed and sliced
1 onion, peeled and diced
2 tablespoons olive oil
Sea salt and ground black pepper, to taste
1 teaspoon crushed red pepper flakes

1. Start by preheating the air fryer to 380°F (193°C).
2. Toss all ingredients in the crisper tray.
3. Place the crisper tray in the corresponding position in the air fryer. Select Air Fry and cook for about 15 minutes, shaking crisper tray halfway through the cooking time.
4. Bon appétit!

Green Beans and Spinach Salad

Prep time: 10 minutes | Cook time: 7 minutes | Serves 3

¾ pound (340 g) fresh green beans, washed and trimmed
2 tablespoons olive oil
½ cup thinly sliced green onions
2 cups baby spinach
1 tablespoon chopped fresh basil
1 green pepper, sliced
2 tablespoons fresh lemon juice
Sea salt and ground black pepper, to taste

1. Start by preheating the air fryer to 375°F (190°C).
2. Toss the green beans with 1 tablespoon of the olive oil. Arrange the green beans in the crisper tray.
3. Place the crisper tray in the corresponding position in the air fryer. Select Air Fry and cook the green beans for 7 minutes; make sure to check the green beans halfway through the cooking time.
4. Add the green beans to a salad bowl; add in the remaining ingredients and stir to combine well. Enjoy!

Buttery Brussels Sprouts

Prep time: 5 minutes | Cook time: 10 minutes | Serves 3

¾ pound (340 g) Brussels sprouts, trimmed
1 tablespoon butter, melted
1 teaspoon crushed red pepper flakes
Kosher salt and ground black pepper, to taste

1. Start by preheating the air fryer to 380°F (193°C).
2. Toss the Brussels sprouts with the butter and spices until they are well coated on all sides; then, arrange the Brussels sprouts in the crisper tray.
3. Place the crisper tray in the corresponding position in the air fryer. Select Roast and cook the Brussels sprouts for 10 minutes, shaking crisper tray halfway through the cooking time.
4. Serve warm and enjoy!

Breaded Eggplant

Prep time: 5 minutes | Cook time: 13 minutes | Serves 3

Sea salt and freshly ground
    black pepper, to taste
½ cup all-purpose flour
2 eggs
¾ pound (340 g) eggplant,
    sliced
½ cup bread crumbs

1. Start by preheating the air fryer to 400ºF (205ºC).
2. In a shallow bowl, mix the salt, black pepper, and flour. Whisk the eggs in the second bowl, and place the bread crumbs in the third bowl.
3. Dip the eggplant slices in the flour mixture, then in the whisked eggs; finally, roll the eggplant slices over the bread crumbs until they are well coated on all sides.
4. Arrange the eggplant in the crisper tray.
5. Place the crisper tray in the corresponding position in the air fryer. Select Air Fry and cook the eggplant for about 13 minutes, shaking crisper tray halfway through the cooking time.
6. Bon appétit!

Breaded Mushrooms

Prep time: 5 minutes | Cook time: 7 minutes | Serves 3

½ cup flour
2 eggs
1 cup seasoned bread crumbs
1 teaspoon smoked paprika
Sea salt and ground black
    pepper, to taste
¾ pound (340 g) portobello
    mushrooms, sliced

1. Start by preheating the air fryer to 400ºF (205ºC).
2. Place the flour in a plate. Whisk the eggs in a shallow bowl. In a third bowl, mix the bread crumbs, paprika, salt, and black pepper.
3. Dip the mushrooms in the flour, then dunk them in the whisked eggs, and finally toss them in the bread crumb mixture. Toss until well coated on all sides. Arrange the mushrooms in the crisper tray.
4. Place the crisper tray in the corresponding position in the air fryer. Select Air Fry and cook the mushrooms for about 7 minutes, turning them halfway through the cooking time.
5. Bon appétit!

Tomato and Cheese Stuffed Peppers

Prep time: 5 minutes | Cook time: 15 minutes | Serves 3

3 bell peppers, seeded and halved
1 tablespoon olive oil
1 small onion, chopped
2 garlic cloves, minced
Sea salt and ground black pepper,
    to taste
1 cup tomato sauce
2 ounces (57 g) Cheddar cheese,
    shredded

1. Start by preheating the air fryer to 400ºF (205ºC).
2. Toss the peppers with the oil; place them in the crisper tray.
3. Mix the onion, garlic, salt, black pepper, and tomato sauce. Spoon the sauce into the pepper halves.
4. Place the crisper tray in the corresponding position in the air fryer. Select Roast and cook the peppers for about 10 minutes. Top the peppers with the cheese. Continue to cook for 5 minutes more.
5. Bon appétit!

Parsnip Burgers

Prep time: 8 minutes | Cook time: 15 minutes | Serves 3

¾ pound (340 g) peeled parsnips, shredded
¼ cup all-purpose flour
¼ cup cornflour
1 egg, lightly beaten
1 teaspoon cayenne pepper
Sea salt and ground black pepper, to taste

1. Start by preheating the air fryer to 380ºF (193ºC).
2. Mix all ingredients until everything is well combined. Form the mixture into three patties.
3. Arrange the patties in the crisper tray.
4. Place the crisper tray in the corresponding position in the air fryer. Select Air Fry and cook the burgers for about 15 minutes or until cooked through.
5. Bon appétit!

Broccoli Salad with Cranberry

Prep time: 5 minutes | Cook time: 6 minutes | Serves 3

¾ pound (340 g) broccoli florets
¼ cup raw sunflower seeds
1 clove garlic, peeled and minced
1 small red onion, thinly sliced
¼ cup dried cranberries
¼ cup extra-virgin olive oil
2 tablespoons fresh lemon juice
1 tablespoon Dijon mustard
Sea salt and ground black pepper, to taste

1. Start by preheating the air fryer to 395°F (202°C).
2. Place the broccoli florets in a lightly greased crisper tray.
3. Place the crisper tray in the corresponding position in the air fryer. Select Air Fry and cook the broccoli florets for 6 minutes, shaking crisper tray halfway through the cooking time.
4. Toss the broccoli florets with the remaining ingredients. Serve at room temperature.
5. Bon appétit!

Potato with Cheese

Prep time: 10 minutes | Cook time: 15 minutes | Serves 3

¾ pound (340 g) potatoes, diced
1 tablespoon olive oil
1 teaspoon smoked paprika
1 teaspoon crushed red pepper flakes
Sea salt and ground black pepper, to taste
2 ounces (57 g) Parmesan cheese, grated

1. Start by preheating the air fryer to 400°F (205°C).
2. Toss the potatoes with the olive oil and spices until well coated on all sides.
3. Arrange the potatoes in the crisper tray.
4. Place the crisper tray in the corresponding position in the air fryer. Select Air Fry and cook the potatoes for about 15 minutes, shaking crisper tray halfway through the cooking time.
5. Top the warm potatoes with cheese and serve immediately. Enjoy!

Chermoula Beet

Prep time: 15 minutes | Cook time: 25 minutes | Serves 4

Chermoula:
1 cup packed fresh cilantro leaves
½ cup packed fresh parsley leaves
6 cloves garlic, peeled
2 teaspoons smoked paprika
2 teaspoons ground cumin
1 teaspoon ground coriander
½ to 1 teaspoon cayenne pepper
Pinch of crushed saffron (optional)
½ cup extra-virgin olive oil
Kosher salt, to taste
Beets:
3 medium beets, trimmed, peeled, and cut into 1-inch chunks
2 tablespoons chopped fresh cilantro
2 tablespoons chopped fresh parsley

1. In a food processor, combine the cilantro, parsley, garlic, paprika, cumin, coriander, and cayenne. Pulse until coarsely chopped. Add the saffron, if using, and process until combined. With the food processor running, slowly add the olive oil in a steady stream; process until the sauce is uniform. Season with salt.
2. Preheat the air fryer oven to 375°F (191°C).
3. In a large bowl, drizzle the beets with ½ cup of the chermoula to coat. Arrange the beets in the air fryer basket.
4. Place the air fryer basket onto the baking pan and slide into Rack Position 2, select Air Fry and set time to 25 minutes, or until the beets are tender.
5. Transfer the beets to a serving platter. Sprinkle with the chopped cilantro and parsley and serve.

Green Beans with Sesame Seeds

Prep time: 5 minutes | Cook time: 8 minutes | Serves 4

1 tablespoon reduced-sodium soy sauce or tamari
½ tablespoon Sriracha sauce
4 teaspoons toasted sesame oil, divided
12 ounces (340 g) trimmed green beans
½ tablespoon toasted sesame seeds

1. Whisk together the soy sauce, Sriracha sauce, and 1 teaspoon of sesame oil in a small bowl until smooth. Set aside.
2. Toss the green beans with the remaining sesame oil in a large bowl until evenly coated.
3. Place the green beans in the air fry basket in a single layer.
4. Select Air Fry, Super Convection, set temperature to 375ºF (190ºC), and set time to 8 minutes. Select Start/Stop to begin preheating.
5. Once preheated, place the basket on the air fry position. Stir the green beans halfway through the cooking time.
6. When cooking is complete, the green beans should be lightly charred and tender. Remove from the oven to a platter. Pour the prepared sauce over the top of green beans and toss well. Serve sprinkled with the toasted sesame seeds.

Corn Cheese Casserole

Prep time: 5 minutes | Cook time: 15 minutes | Serves 4

2 cups frozen yellow corn
1 egg, beaten
3 tablespoons flour
½ cup grated Swiss or Havarti cheese
½ cup light cream
¼ cup milk
Pinch salt
Freshly ground black pepper, to taste
2 tablespoons butter, cut into cubes
Nonstick cooking spray

1. Spritz a baking pan with nonstick cooking spray.
2. Stir together the remaining ingredients except the butter in a medium bowl until well incorporated. Transfer the mixture to the prepared baking pan and scatter with the butter cubes.
3. Select Bake, Super Convection, set temperature to 320ºF (160ºC), and set time to 15 minutes. Select Start/Stop to begin preheating.
4. Once preheated, place the pan on the bake position.
5. When cooking is complete, the top should be golden brown and a toothpick inserted in the center should come out clean. Remove the pan from the oven. Let the casserole cool for 5 minutes before slicing into wedges and serving.

Corn on the Cob

Prep time: 10 minutes | Cook time: 15 minutes | Serves 4

2 tablespoon olive oil, divided
2 tablespoons grated Parmesan cheese
1 teaspoon garlic powder
1 teaspoon chili powder
1 teaspoon ground cumin
1 teaspoon paprika
1 teaspoon salt
¼ teaspoon cayenne pepper (optional)
4 ears fresh corn, shucked

1. Grease the air fry basket with 1 tablespoon of olive oil. Set aside.
2. Combine the Parmesan cheese, garlic powder, chili powder, cumin, paprika, salt, and cayenne pepper (if desired) in a small bowl and stir to mix well.
3. Lightly coat the ears of corn with the remaining 1 tablespoon of olive oil. Rub the cheese mixture all over the ears of corn until completely coated.
4. Arrange the ears of corn in the greased basket in a single layer.
5. Select Air Fry, Super Convection, set temperature to 400ºF (205ºC), and set time to 15 minutes. Select Start/Stop to begin preheating.
6. Once preheated, place the basket on the air fry position. Flip the ears of corn halfway through the cooking time.
7. When cooking is complete, they should be lightly browned. Remove from the oven and let them cool for 5 minutes before serving.

Squash with Cinnamon

Prep time: 5 minutes | Cook time: 15 minutes | Serves 2

1 medium acorn squash, halved crosswise and deseeded
1 teaspoon coconut oil
1 teaspoon light brown sugar
Few dashes of ground cinnamon
Few dashes of ground nutmeg

1. On a clean work surface, rub the cut sides of the acorn squash with coconut oil. Scatter with the brown sugar, cinnamon, and nutmeg.
2. Put the squash halves in the air fry basket, cut-side up.
3. Select Air Fry, Super Convection, set temperature to 325°F (163°C), and set time to 15 minutes. Select Start/Stop to begin preheating.
4. Once preheated, place the basket on the air fry position.
5. When cooking is complete, the squash halves should be just tender when pierced in the center with a paring knife. Remove the basket from the oven. Rest for 5 to 10 minutes and serve warm.

Potato with Yogurt

Prep time: 5 minutes | Cook time: 35 minutes | Serves 4

4 (7-ounce / 198-g) russet potatoes, rinsed
Olive oil spray
½ teaspoon kosher salt, divided
½ cup 2% plain Greek yogurt
¼ cup minced fresh chives
Freshly ground black pepper, to taste

1. Pat the potatoes dry and pierce them all over with a fork. Spritz the potatoes with olive oil spray. Sprinkle with ¼ teaspoon of the salt.
2. Transfer the potatoes to the air fry basket.
3. Select Bake, Super Convection, set temperature to 400°F (205°C), and set time to 35 minutes. Select Start/Stop to begin preheating.
4. Once preheated, place the basket on the bake position.
5. When cooking is complete, the potatoes should be fork-tender. Remove from the oven and split open the potatoes. Top with the yogurt, chives, the remaining ¼ teaspoon of salt, and finish with the black pepper. Serve immediately.

Panko Cheese Asparagus

Prep time: 15 minutes | Cook time: 6 minutes | Serves 4

2 egg whites
¼ cup water
¼ cup plus 2 tablespoons grated Parmesan cheese, divided
¾ cup panko bread crumbs
¼ teaspoon salt
12 ounces (340 g) fresh asparagus spears, woody ends trimmed
Cooking spray

1. In a shallow dish, whisk together the egg whites and water until slightly foamy. In a separate shallow dish, thoroughly combine ¼ cup of Parmesan cheese, bread crumbs, and salt.
2. Dip the asparagus in the egg white, then roll in the cheese mixture to coat well.
3. Place the asparagus in the air fry basket in a single layer, leaving space between each spear. Spritz the asparagus with cooking spray.
4. Select Air Fry, Super Convection, set temperature to 390°F (199°C), and set time to 6 minutes. Select Start/Stop to begin preheating.
5. Once preheated, place the basket on the air fry position.
6. When cooking is complete, the asparagus should be golden brown and crisp. Remove the basket from the oven. Sprinkle with the remaining 2 tablespoons of cheese and serve hot.

Asparagus with Garlic

Prep time: 5 minutes | Cook time: 10 minutes | Serves 4

1 pound (454 g) asparagus,
  woody ends trimmed
2 tablespoons olive oil
1 tablespoon balsamic vinegar
2 teaspoons minced garlic
Salt and freshly ground black
  pepper, to taste

1. In a large shallow bowl, toss the asparagus with the olive oil, balsamic vinegar, garlic, salt, and pepper until thoroughly coated. Put the asparagus in the air fry basket.
2. Select Roast, Super Convection, set temperature to 400°F (205°C), and set time to 10 minutes. Select Start/Stop to begin preheating.
3. Once preheated, place the basket on the roast position. Flip the asparagus with tongs halfway through the cooking time.
4. When cooking is complete, the asparagus should be crispy. Remove the basket from the oven and serve warm.

Buttered Broccoli with Parmesan

Prep time: 5 minutes | Cook time: 4 minutes | Serves 4

1 pound (454 g) broccoli florets
1 medium shallot, minced
2 tablespoons olive oil
2 tablespoons unsalted butter, melted
2 teaspoons minced garlic
¼ cup grated Parmesan cheese

1. Combine the broccoli florets with the shallot, olive oil, butter, garlic, and Parmesan cheese in a medium bowl and toss until the broccoli florets are thoroughly coated.
2. Place the broccoli florets in the air fry basket in a single layer.
3. Select Roast, Super Convection, set temperature to 360°F (182°C), and set time to 4 minutes. Select Start/Stop to begin preheating.
4. Once preheated, place the basket on the roast position.
5. When cooking is complete, the broccoli florets should be crisp-tender. Remove from the oven and serve warm.

Lemony Kale Cheese Salad

Prep time: 10 minutes | Cook time: 3 minutes | Serves 2

1½ cups cubed whole
  grain bread
2 teaspoons olive oil
6 cups chopped kale
⅓ cup shredded vegan
  Parmesan-style
  cheese

The Dressing:
2 tablespoons vegan mayonnaise
1 tablespoon olive oil
Juice of 1 lemon
2 teaspoons white miso paste
1 garlic clove, minced
½ teaspoon Dijon mustard
½ teaspoon kosher salt
½ teaspoon freshly ground black
  pepper

1. Set the air fryer temp to 390°F (199°C).
2. In a medium bowl, make the dressing by whisking together the ingredients. Taste for seasoning and adjust as needed. Set aside.
3. In a large bowl, combine the bread and olive oil.
4. Place the bread in the fryer basket and cook until toasted, about 2 to 3 minutes. Remove the croutons from the fryer basket and set aside to cool slightly.
5. In a large bowl, place the kale and Parmesan. Top with the croutons. Drizzle the dressing over the top. Toss well to coat. Divide the salad into 2 bowls before serving.

Air Fryer Corn on the Cob

Prep time: 10 minutes | Cook time: 10 minutes | Serves 4

4 ears corn, shucked and halved crosswise
1 tablespoon extra-virgin olive oil
Salt
Pepper

1. Place the corn in a large bowl. Coat with the olive oil and season with salt and pepper to taste.
2. Place the corn in the air fryer. Cook at 390°F (199°C) for 6 minutes.
3. Cool before serving.

Chapter 8 Vegan and Vegetarian

Roasted Veggie and Tofu

Prep time: 10 minutes | Cook time: 10 minutes | Serves 4

⅓ cup Asian-Style sauce
1 teaspoon cornstarch
½ teaspoon red pepper flakes, or more to taste
1 pound (454 g) firm or extra-firm tofu, cut into 1-inch cubes
1 small carrot, peeled and cut into ¼-inch-thick coins
1 small green bell pepper, cut into bite-size pieces
3 scallions, sliced, whites and green parts separated
3 tablespoons roasted unsalted peanuts

1. In a large bowl, whisk together the sauce, cornstarch, and red pepper flakes. Fold in the tofu, carrot, pepper, and the white parts of the scallions and toss to coat. Spread the mixture evenly on the sheet pan.
2. Select Roast. Set temperature to 375ºF (190ºC) and set time to 10 minutes. Press Start to begin preheating.
3. Once preheated, place the pan into the oven. Stir the ingredients once halfway through the cooking time.
4. When done, remove the pan from the oven. Serve sprinkled with the peanuts and scallion greens.

Black Bean and Salsa Tacos

Prep time: 12 minutes | Cook time: 7 minutes | Serves 4

1 (15-ounce / 425-g) can black beans, drained and rinsed
½ cup prepared salsa
1½ teaspoons chili powder
4 ounces (113 g) grated Monterey Jack cheese
2 tablespoons minced onion
8 (6 inch) flour tortillas
2 tablespoons vegetable or extra-virgin olive oil
Shredded lettuce, for serving

1. In a medium bowl, add the beans, salsa and chili powder. Coarsely mash them with a potato masher. Fold in the cheese and onion and stir until combined.
2. Arrange the flour tortillas on a cutting board and spoon 2 to 3 tablespoons of the filling into each tortilla. Fold the tortillas over, pressing lightly to even out the filling. Brush the tacos on one side with half the olive oil and put them, oiled side down, on the sheet pan. Brush the top side with the remaining olive oil.
3. Select Air Fry. Set temperature to 400ºF (205ºC) and set time to 7 minutes. Press Start to begin preheating.
4. Once preheated, place the pan into the oven. Flip the tacos halfway through the cooking time.
5. Remove the pan from the oven and allow to cool for 5 minutes. Serve with the shredded lettuce on the side.

Thai Curried Veggies

Prep time: 10 minutes | Cook time: 8 minutes | Serves 4

1 small head Napa cabbage, shredded, divided
1 medium carrot, cut into thin coins
8 ounces (227 g) snow peas
1 red or green bell pepper, sliced into thin strips
1 tablespoon vegetable oil
2 tablespoons soy sauce
1 tablespoon sesame oil
2 tablespoons brown sugar
2 tablespoons freshly squeezed lime juice
2 teaspoons red or green Thai curry paste
1 serrano chile, deseeded and minced
1 cup frozen mango slices, thawed
½ cup chopped roasted peanuts or cashews

1. Put half the Napa cabbage in a large bowl, along with the carrot, snow peas, and bell pepper. Drizzle with the vegetable oil and toss to coat. Spread them evenly on the sheet pan.
2. Select Roast. Set temperature to 375ºF (190ºC) and set time to 8 minutes. Press Start to begin preheating.
3. Once preheated, place the pan into the oven.
4. Meanwhile, whisk together the soy sauce, sesame oil, brown sugar, lime juice, and curry paste in a small bowl.
5. When done, the vegetables should be tender and crisp. Remove the pan and put the vegetables back into the bowl. Add the chile, mango slices, and the remaining cabbage. Pour over the dressing and toss to coat. Top with the roasted nuts and serve.

Eggplant and Bell Peppers with Basil

Prep time: 15 minutes | Cook time: 20 minutes | Serves 2

1 small eggplant, halved and sliced
1 yellow bell pepper, cut into thick strips
1 red bell pepper, cut into thick strips
2 garlic cloves, quartered
1 red onion, sliced
1 tablespoon extra-virgin olive oil
Salt and freshly ground black pepper, to taste
½ cup chopped fresh basil, for garnish
Cooking spray

1. Grease a nonstick baking dish with cooking spray.
2. Place the eggplant, bell peppers, garlic, and red onion in the greased baking dish. Drizzle with the olive oil and toss to coat well. Spritz any uncoated surfaces with cooking spray.
3. Select Bake. Set temperature to 350ºF (180ºC) and set time to 20 minutes. Press Start to begin preheating.
4. Once preheated, place the baking dish into the oven. Flip the vegetables halfway through the cooking time.
5. When done, remove from the oven and sprinkle with salt and pepper.
6. Sprinkle the basil on top for garnish and serve.

Vinegary Asparagus

Prep time: 15 minutes | Cook time: 10 minutes | Serves 4

4 tablespoons olive oil, plus more for greasing
4 tablespoons balsamic vinegar
1½ pounds (680 g) asparagus spears, trimmed
Salt and freshly ground black pepper, to taste

1. Grease the perforated pan with olive oil.
2. In a shallow bowl, stir together the 4 tablespoons of olive oil and balsamic vinegar to make a marinade.
3. Put the asparagus spears in the bowl so they are thoroughly covered by the marinade and allow to marinate for 5 minutes.
4. Put the asparagus in the greased pan in a single layer and season with salt and pepper.
5. Select Air Fry. Set temperature to 350ºF (180ºC) and set time to 10 minutes. Press Start to begin preheating.
6. Once preheated, place the pan into the oven. Flip the asparagus halfway through the cooking time.
7. When done, the asparagus should be tender and lightly browned. Cool for 5 minutes before serving.

Baked Eggs with Spinach and Basil

Prep time: 10 minutes | Cook time: 10 minutes | Serves 2

2 tablespoons olive oil

4 eggs, whisked

5 ounces (142 g) fresh spinach, chopped

1 medium-sized tomato, chopped

1 teaspoon fresh lemon juice

½ teaspoon ground black pepper

½ teaspoon coarse salt

½ cup roughly chopped fresh basil leaves, for garnish

1. Generously grease a baking pan with olive oil.
2. Stir together the remaining ingredients except the basil leaves in the greased baking pan until well incorporated.
3. Select Bake. Set temperature to 280°F (137°C) and set time to 10 minutes. Press Start to begin preheating.
4. Once preheated, place the pan into the oven.
5. When cooking is complete, the eggs should be completely set and the vegetables should be tender. Remove from the oven and serve garnished with the fresh basil leaves.

Cheesy Broccoli with Rosemary

Prep time: 5 minutes | Cook time: 18 minutes | Serves 4

1 large-sized head broccoli, stemmed and cut into small florets

2½ tablespoons canola oil

2 teaspoons dried basil

2 teaspoons dried rosemary

Salt and ground black pepper, to taste

⅓ cup grated yellow cheese

1. Bring a pot of lightly salted water to a boil. Add the broccoli florets to the boiling water and let boil for about 3 minutes.
2. Drain the broccoli florets well and transfer to a large bowl. Add the canola oil, basil, rosemary, salt, and black pepper to the bowl and toss until the broccoli is fully coated. Place the broccoli in the perforated pan.
3. Select Air Fry. Set temperature to 390°F (199°C) and set time to 15 minutes. Press Start to begin preheating.
4. Once preheated, place the pan into the oven. Stir the broccoli halfway through the cooking time.
5. When cooking is complete, the broccoli should be crisp. Remove the pan from the oven. Serve the broccoli warm with grated cheese sprinkled on top.

Kale with Tahini-Lemon Dressing

Prep time: 5 minutes | Cook time: 15 minutes | Serves 2 to 4

Dressing:

¼ cup tahini

¼ cup fresh lemon juice

2 tablespoons olive oil

1 teaspoon sesame seeds

½ teaspoon garlic powder

¼ teaspoon cayenne pepper

Kale:

4 cups packed torn kale leaves (stems and ribs removed and leaves torn into palm-size pieces)

Kosher salt and freshly ground black pepper, to taste

1. Make the dressing: Whisk together the tahini, lemon juice, olive oil, sesame seeds, garlic powder, and cayenne pepper in a large bowl until well mixed.
2. Add the kale and massage the dressing thoroughly all over the leaves. Sprinkle the salt and pepper to season.
3. Place the kale in the perforated pan in a single layer.
4. Select Air Fry. Set temperature to 350°F (180°C) and set time to 15 minutes. Press Start to begin preheating.
5. Once preheated, place the pan into the oven.
6. When cooking is complete, the leaves should be slightly wilted and crispy. Remove from the oven and serve on a plate.

Vegetable Mélange with Garlic

Prep time: 10 minutes | Cook time: 16 minutes | Serves 4

1 (8-ounce / 227-g) package sliced mushrooms
1 yellow summer squash, sliced
1 red bell pepper, sliced
3 cloves garlic, sliced
1 tablespoon olive oil
½ teaspoon dried basil
½ teaspoon dried thyme
½ teaspoon dried tarragon

1. Toss the mushrooms, squash, and bell pepper with the garlic and olive oil in a large bowl until well coated. Mix in the basil, thyme, and tarragon and toss again.
2. Spread the vegetables evenly in the perforated pan.
3. Select Roast. Set temperature to 350°F (180°C) and set time to 16 minutes. Press Start to begin preheating.
4. Once preheated, place the pan into the oven.
5. When cooking is complete, the vegetables should be fork-tender. Remove the pan from the oven. Cool for 5 minutes before serving.

Garlic Carrots with Sesame Seeds

Prep time: 5 minutes | Cook time: 16 minutes | Serves 4 to 6

1 pound (454 g) baby carrots
1 tablespoon sesame oil
½ teaspoon dried dill
Pinch salt
Freshly ground black pepper, to taste
6 cloves garlic, peeled
3 tablespoons sesame seeds

1. In a medium bowl, drizzle the baby carrots with the sesame oil. Sprinkle with the dill, salt, and pepper and toss to coat well.
2. Place the baby carrots in the perforated pan.
3. Select Roast. Set temperature to 380°F (193°C) and set time to 16 minutes. Press Start to begin preheating.
4. Once preheated, place the pan into the oven.
5. After 8 minutes, remove the pan from the oven and stir in the garlic. Return the pan to the oven and continue roasting for 8 minutes more.
6. When cooking is complete, the carrots should be lightly browned. Remove the pan from the oven and serve sprinkled with the sesame seeds.

Thai-Flavored Brussels Sprouts

Prep time: 5 minutes | Cook time: 20 minutes | Serves 2

¼ cup Thai sweet chili sauce
2 tablespoons black vinegar or balsamic vinegar
½ teaspoon hot sauce
2 small shallots, cut into ¼-inch-thick slices
8 ounces (227 g) Brussels sprouts, trimmed (large sprouts halved)
Kosher salt and freshly ground black pepper, to taste
2 teaspoons lightly packed fresh cilantro leaves, for garnish

1. Place the chili sauce, vinegar, and hot sauce in a large bowl and whisk to combine.
2. Add the shallots and Brussels sprouts and toss to coat. Sprinkle with the salt and pepper. Transfer the Brussels sprouts and sauce to a baking pan.
3. Select Roast. Set temperature to 390°F (199°C) and set time to 20 minutes. Press Start to begin preheating.
4. Once preheated, place the pan into the oven. Stir the Brussels sprouts twice during cooking.
5. When cooking is complete, the Brussels sprouts should be crisp-tender. Remove from the oven. Sprinkle the cilantro on top for garnish and serve warm.

Honey Eggplant with Yogurt Sauce

Prep time: 5 minutes | Cook time: 15 minutes | Serves 2

1 medium eggplant, quartered and cut crosswise into ½-inch-thick slices
2 tablespoons vegetable oil
Kosher salt and freshly ground black pepper, to taste
½ cup plain yogurt (not Greek)
2 tablespoons harissa paste
1 garlic clove, grated
2 teaspoons honey

1. Toss the eggplant slices with the vegetable oil, salt, and pepper in a large bowl until well coated.
2. Lay the eggplant slices in the perforated pan.
3. Select Air Fry. Set temperature to 400°F (205°C) and set time to 15 minutes. Press Start to begin preheating.
4. Once preheated, place the pan into the oven. Stir the slices two to three times during cooking.
5. Meanwhile, make the yogurt sauce by whisking together the yogurt, harissa paste, and garlic in a small bowl.
6. When cooking is complete, the eggplant slices should be golden brown. Spread the yogurt sauce on a platter, and pile the eggplant slices over the top. Serve drizzled with the honey.

Parmesan Cabbage Wedges

Prep time: 5 minutes | Cook time: 20 minutes | Serves 4

4 tablespoons melted butter
1 head cabbage, cut into wedges
1 cup shredded Parmesan cheese
Salt and black pepper, to taste
½ cup shredded Mozzarella cheese

1. Brush the melted butter over the cut sides of cabbage wedges and sprinkle both sides with the Parmesan cheese. Season with salt and pepper to taste.
2. Place the cabbage wedges in the perforated pan.
3. Select Air Fry. Set temperature to 380°F (193°C) and set time to 20 minutes. Press Start to begin preheating.
4. Once preheated, place the pan into the oven. Flip the cabbage halfway through the cooking time.
5. When cooking is complete, the cabbage wedges should be lightly browned. Transfer the cabbage wedges to a plate and serve with the Mozzarella cheese sprinkled on top.

Sesame Mushrooms with Thyme

Prep time: 5 minutes | Cook time: 15 minutes | Serves 2

1 tablespoon soy sauce
2 teaspoons toasted sesame oil
3 teaspoons vegetable oil, divided
1 garlic clove, minced
7 ounces (198 g) maitake (hen of the woods) mushrooms
½ teaspoon flaky sea salt
½ teaspoon sesame seeds
½ teaspoon finely chopped fresh thyme leaves

1. Whisk together the soy sauce, sesame oil, 1 teaspoon of vegetable oil, and garlic in a small bowl.
2. Arrange the mushrooms in the perforated pan in a single layer. Drizzle the soy sauce mixture over the mushrooms.
3. Select Roast. Set temperature to 300°F (150°C) and set time to 15 minutes. Press Start to begin preheating.
4. Once preheated, place the pan into the oven.
5. After 10 minutes, remove the pan from the oven. Flip the mushrooms and sprinkle the sea salt, sesame seeds, and thyme leaves on top. Drizzle the remaining 2 teaspoons of vegetable oil all over. Return to the oven and continue roasting for an additional 5 minutes.
6. When cooking is complete, remove the mushrooms from the oven to a plate and serve hot.

Ratatouille with Bread Crumb Topping

Prep time: 10 minutes | Cook time: 12 minutes | Serves 6

1 medium zucchini, sliced ½-inch thick

1 small eggplant, peeled and sliced ½-inch thick

2 teaspoons kosher salt, divided

4 tablespoons extra-virgin olive oil, divided

3 garlic cloves, minced

1 small onion, chopped

1 small red bell pepper, cut into ½-inch chunks

1 small green bell pepper, cut into ½-inch chunks

½ teaspoon dried oregano

¼ teaspoon freshly ground black pepper

1 pint cherry tomatoes

2 tablespoons minced fresh basil

1 cup panko bread crumbs

½ cup grated Parmesan cheese (optional)

1. Season one side of the zucchini and eggplant slices with ¾ teaspoon of salt. Put the slices, salted side down, on a rack set over a baking sheet. Sprinkle the other sides with ¾ teaspoon of salt. Allow to sit for 10 minutes, or until the slices begin to exude water. When ready, rinse and dry them. Cut the zucchini slices into quarters and the eggplant slices into eighths.
2. Pour the zucchini and eggplant into a large bowl, along with 2 tablespoons of olive oil, garlic, onion, bell peppers, oregano, and black pepper. Toss to coat well. Arrange the vegetables on the sheet pan.
3. Select Roast. Set temperature to 375°F (190°C) and set time to 12 minutes. Press Start to begin preheating.
4. Once preheated, place the pan into the oven.
5. Meanwhile, add the tomatoes and basil to the large bowl. Sprinkle with the remaining ½ teaspoon of salt and 1 tablespoon of olive oil. Toss well and set aside.
6. Stir together the remaining 1 tablespoon of olive oil, panko, and Parmesan cheese (if desired) in a small bowl.
7. After 6 minutes, remove the pan and add the tomato mixture to the sheet pan and stir to mix well. Scatter the panko mixture on top. Return the pan to the oven and continue cooking for 6 minutes, or until the vegetables are softened and the topping is golden brown.
8. Cool for 5 minutes before serving.

Butternut Squash and Parsnip with Thyme

Prep time: 5 minutes | Cook time: 16 minutes | Serves 2

1 parsnip, sliced

1 cup sliced butternut squash

1 small red onion, cut into wedges

½ chopped celery stalk

1 tablespoon chopped fresh thyme

2 teaspoons olive oil

Salt and black pepper, to taste

1. Toss all the ingredients in a large bowl until the vegetables are well coated.
2. Transfer the vegetables to the perforated pan.
3. Select Air Fry. Set temperature to 380°F (193°C) and set time to 16 minutes. Press Start to begin preheating.
4. Once preheated, place the pan into the oven. Stir the vegetables halfway through the cooking time.
5. When cooking is complete, the vegetables should be golden brown and tender. Remove from the oven and serve warm.

Butternut Squash with Goat Cheese

Prep time: 5 minutes | Cook time: 20 minutes | Serves 2

1 pound (454 g) butternut squash, cut into wedges

2 tablespoons olive oil

1 tablespoon dried rosemary

Salt, to salt

1 cup crumbled goat cheese

1 tablespoon maple syrup

1. Toss the squash wedges with the olive oil, rosemary, and salt in a large bowl until well coated.
2. Transfer the squash wedges to the perforated pan, spreading them out in as even a layer as possible.
3. Select Air Fry. Set temperature to 350°F (180°C) and set time to 20 minutes. Press Start to begin preheating.
4. Once preheated, place the pan into the oven.
5. After 10 minutes, remove from the oven and flip the squash. Return the pan to the oven and continue cooking for 10 minutes.
6. When cooking is complete, the squash should be golden brown. Remove the pan from the oven. Sprinkle the goat cheese on top and serve drizzled with the maple syrup.

Ginger-Pepper Broccoli

Prep time: 5 minutes | Cook time: 10 minutes | Serves 2

12 ounces (340 g) broccoli florets
2 tablespoons Asian hot chili oil
1 teaspoon ground Sichuan peppercorns (or black pepper)
2 garlic cloves, finely chopped
1 (2-inch) piece fresh ginger, peeled and finely chopped
Kosher salt and freshly ground black pepper

1. Toss the broccoli florets with the chili oil, Sichuan peppercorns, garlic, ginger, salt, and pepper in a mixing bowl until thoroughly coated.
2. Transfer the broccoli florets to the perforated pan.
3. Select Air Fry. Set temperature to 375ºF (190ºC) and set time to 10 minutes. Press Start to begin preheating.
4. Once preheated, place the pan into the oven. Stir the broccoli florets halfway through the cooking time.
5. When cooking is complete, the broccoli florets should be lightly browned and tender. Remove the broccoli from the oven and serve on a plate.

Parmesan Brussels Sprouts

Prep time: 10 minutes | Cook time: 20 minutes | Serves 4

1 pound (454 g) fresh Brussels sprouts, trimmed
1 tablespoon olive oil
½ teaspoon salt
⅛ teaspoon pepper
¼ cup grated Parmesan cheese

1. In a large bowl, combine the Brussels sprouts with olive oil, salt, and pepper and toss until evenly coated.
2. Spread the Brussels sprouts evenly in the perforated pan.
3. Select Air Fry. Set temperature to 330ºF (166ºC) and set time to 20 minutes. Press Start to begin preheating.
4. Once preheated, place the pan into the oven. Stir the Brussels sprouts twice during cooking.
5. When cooking is complete, the Brussels sprouts should be golden brown and crisp. Remove the pan from the oven. Sprinkle the grated Parmesan cheese on top and serve warm.

Cayenne Green Beans

Prep time: 5 minutes | Cook time: 15 minutes | Serves 4

½ cup flour
2 eggs
1 cup panko bread crumbs
½ cup grated Parmesan cheese
1 teaspoon cayenne pepper
Salt and black pepper, to taste
1½ pounds (680 g) green beans

1. In a bowl, place the flour. In a separate bowl, lightly beat the eggs. In a separate shallow bowl, thoroughly combine the bread crumbs, cheese, cayenne pepper, salt, and pepper.
2. Dip the green beans in the flour, then in the beaten eggs, finally in the bread crumb mixture to coat well. Transfer the green beans to the perforated pan.
3. Select Air Fry. Set temperature to 400ºF (205ºC) and set time to 15 minutes. Press Start to begin preheating.
4. Once preheated, place the pan into the oven. Stir the green beans halfway through the cooking time.
5. When cooking is complete, remove from the oven to a bowl and serve.

Honey Baby Carrots with Dill

Prep time: 5 minutes | Cook time: 12 minutes | Serves 4

1 pound (454 g) baby carrots
2 tablespoons olive oil
1 tablespoon honey
1 teaspoon dried dill
Salt and black pepper, to taste

1. Place the carrots in a large bowl. Add the olive oil, honey, dill, salt, and pepper and toss to coat well.
2. Transfer the carrots to the perforated pan.
3. Select Roast. Set temperature to 350ºF (180ºC) and set time to 12 minutes. Press Start to begin preheating.
4. Once preheated, place the pan into the oven. Stir the carrots once during cooking.
5. When cooking is complete, the carrots should be crisp-tender. Remove from the oven and serve warm.

Cheese Stuffed Peppers

Prep time: 10 minutes | Cook time: 15 minutes | Serves 3

6 Italian peppers, seeded and stems removed
2 garlic cloves, minced
1 tablespoon taco seasoning mix
½ cup grated vegan Cheddar cheese
Sea salt and red pepper flakes, to taste
2 tablespoons olive oil

1. Start by preheating the air fryer to 400°F (205°C).
2. Arrange the peppers in the crisper tray.
3. Mix the remaining ingredients until well combined. Dived the filling between the peppers.
4. Place the crisper tray in the corresponding position in the air fryer. Select Air Fry and cook the peppers for about 15 minutes.
5. Bon appétit!

White Beans Sausage

Prep time: 5 minutes | Cook time: 15 minutes | Serves 3

1 cup canned white beans, drained and rinsed
1 medium onion, chopped
2 cloves garlic, chopped
2 tablespoons olive oil
1 teaspoon liquid smoke
2 tablespoons buckwheat flour

1. Start by preheating the air fryer to 390°F (199°C).
2. Pulse all the ingredients in the food processor until everything is well incorporated.
3. Shape the mixture into three sausages and place them in a lightly greased crisper tray.
4. Place the crisper tray in the corresponding position in the air fryer. Select Air Fry and cook the sausage for about 15 minutes, shaking the crisper tray halfway through the cooking time.
5. Bon appétit!

Polenta with Marinara Sauce

Prep time: 5 minutes | Cook time: 15 minutes | Serves 2

½ pound (227 g) polenta
2 tablespoons olive oil, plus more as needed
1 teaspoon dried basil
1 teaspoon dried oregano
¼ cup marinara sauce

1. Start by preheating the air fryer to 350°F (180°C).
2. Cut the polenta into pieces. Toss each piece with the olive oil, basil, oregano, and marinara sauce. Transfer to the crisper tray.
3. Place the crisper tray in the corresponding position in the air fryer. Select Air Fry and cook the polenta bites for about 15 minutes, turning them over halfway through the cooking time.
4. Enjoy!

Zucchini with Mushrooms and Chickpeas

Prep time: 10 minutes | Cook time: 13 minutes | Serves 2

2 medium zucchinis, halved
2 tablespoons olive oil
1 teaspoon minced garlic
1 shallot, minced
2 tablespoons marinara sauce
2 ounces (57 g) canned chickpeas, drained and rinsed
2 ounces (57 g) button mushrooms, chopped
Sea salt and ground black pepper, to taste

1. Start by preheating the air fryer to 390°F (199°C).
2. Arrange the zucchini halves in the crisper tray.
3. Mix the remaining ingredients until well combined. Dived the filling between the zucchini halves.
4. Place the crisper tray in the corresponding position in the air fryer. Select Air Fry and cook the zucchini halves for about 13 minutes.
5. Bon appétit!

Chickpeas Meatballs

Prep time: 10 minutes | Cook time: 15 minutes | Serves 4

16 ounces (454 g) canned chickpeas, rinsed and drained
1 shallot, chopped
4 cloves garlic, roughly chopped
¼ cup roughly chopped fresh parsley
¼ cup roughly chopped fresh coriander
½ teaspoon stone-ground mustard
½ teaspoon ground cumin
2 tablespoons tahini
Kosher salt and ground black pepper, to taste

1. Start by preheating the air fryer to 380ºF (193ºC).
2. Pulse all ingredients in the food processor until everything is well incorporated.
3. Form the mixture into balls and place them in a lightly greased crisper tray.
4. Place the crisper tray in the corresponding position in the air fryer. Select Air Fry and cook the meatballs for about 15 minutes, shaking the crisper tray occasionally to ensure even cooking.
5. Serve in pita bread with toppings of the choice. Enjoy!

Tomato Stuffed Eggplant

Prep time: 8 minutes | Cook time: 15 minutes | Serves 2

2 small eggplants, halved lengthwise
1 tablespoon olive oil
1 small shallot, chopped
2 garlic cloves, minced
1 bell pepper, chopped
1 medium tomato, chopped
2 tablespoons minced fresh parsley
1 tablespoon minced fresh basil
Sea salt and ground black pepper, to taste

1. Start by preheating the air fryer to 400ºF (205ºC).
2. Toss the eggplants with the oil; place them in the crisper tray.
3. Mix the remaining ingredients to make the filling. Spoon the filling into the eggplant halves.
4. Place the crisper tray in the corresponding position in the air fryer. Select Air Fry and cook the stuffed eggplants for about 15 minutes.
5. Serve warm and enjoy!

Butternut Squash with Cheese

Prep time: 5 minutes | Cook time: 20 minutes | Serves 2

1 pound (454 g) butternut squash, cut into wedges
2 tablespoons olive oil
1 tablespoon dried rosemary
Salt, to salt
1 cup crumbled goat cheese
1 tablespoon maple syrup

1. Toss the squash wedges with the olive oil, rosemary, and salt in a large bowl until well coated.
2. Transfer the squash wedges to the air fry basket, spreading them out in as even a layer as possible.
3. Select Air Fry, Super Convection, set temperature to 350ºF (180ºC), and set time to 20 minutes. Select Start/Stop to begin preheating.
4. Once preheated, place the air fry basket on the air fry position.
5. After 10 minutes, remove from the oven and flip the squash. Return the basket to the oven and continue cooking for 10 minutes.
6. When cooking is complete, the squash should be golden brown. Remove the basket from the oven. Sprinkle the goat cheese on top and serve drizzled with the maple syrup.

Broccoli with Peppercorn

Prep time: 5 minutes | Cook time: 10 minutes | Serves 2

12 ounces (340 g) broccoli florets
2 tablespoons Asian hot chili oil
1 teaspoon ground Sichuan peppercorns (or black pepper)
2 garlic cloves, finely chopped
1 (2-inch) piece fresh ginger, peeled and finely chopped
Kosher salt and freshly ground black pepper

1. Toss the broccoli florets with the chili oil, Sichuan peppercorns, garlic, ginger, salt, and pepper in a mixing bowl until thoroughly coated.
2. Transfer the broccoli florets to the air fry basket.
3. Select Air Fry, Super Convection, set temperature to 375°F (190°C), and set time to 10 minutes. Select Start/Stop to begin preheating.
4. Once preheated, place the air fry basket on the air fry position. Stir the broccoli florets halfway through the cooking time.
5. When cooking is complete, the broccoli florets should be lightly browned and tender. Remove the broccoli from the oven and serve on a plate.

Pea and Mushroom with Rice

Prep time: 5 minutes | Cook time: 12 minutes | Serves 4

2 teaspoons melted butter
1 cup chopped mushrooms
1 cup cooked rice
1 cup peas
1 carrot, chopped
1 red onion, chopped
1 garlic clove, minced
Salt and black pepper, to taste
2 hard-boiled eggs, grated
1 tablespoon soy sauce

1. Coat a baking dish with melted butter.
2. Stir together the mushrooms, cooked rice, peas, carrot, onion, garlic, salt, and pepper in a large bowl until well mixed. Pour the mixture into the prepared baking dish.
3. Select Roast, Super Convection, set temperature to 380°F (193°C), and set time to 12 minutes. Select Start/Stop to begin preheating.
4. Once preheated, place the baking dish on the roast position.
5. When cooking is complete, remove from the oven. Divide the mixture among four plates. Serve warm with a sprinkle of grated eggs and a drizzle of soy sauce.

Crispy Tofu Strips

Prep time: 5 minutes | Cook time: 14 minutes | Serves 4

2 tablespoons olive oil, divided
½ cup flour
½ cup crushed cornflakes
Salt and black pepper, to taste
14 ounces (397 g) firm tofu, cut into ½-inch-thick strips

1. Grease the air fry basket with 1 tablespoon of olive oil.
2. Combine the flour, cornflakes, salt, and pepper on a plate.
3. Dredge the tofu strips in the flour mixture until they are completely coated. Transfer the tofu strips to the greased basket.
4. Drizzle the remaining 1 tablespoon of olive oil over the top of tofu strips.
5. Select Air Fry, Super Convection, set temperature to 360°F (182°C), and set time to 14 minutes. Select Start/Stop to begin preheating.
6. Once preheated, place the basket on the air fry position. Flip the tofu strips halfway through the cooking time.
7. When cooking is complete, the tofu strips should be crispy. Remove from the oven and serve warm.

Breaded Eggplant Slices

Prep time: 5 minutes | Cook time: 12 minutes | Serves 4

1 cup flour
4 eggs
Salt, to taste
2 cups bread crumbs
1 teaspoon Italian seasoning
2 eggplants, sliced
2 garlic cloves, sliced
2 tablespoons chopped parsley
Cooking spray

1. Spritz the air fry basket with cooking spray. Set aside.
2. On a plate, place the flour. In a shallow bowl, whisk the eggs with salt. In another shallow bowl, combine the bread crumbs and Italian seasoning.
3. Dredge the eggplant slices, one at a time, in the flour, then in the whisked eggs, finally in the bread crumb mixture to coat well.
4. Lay the coated eggplant slices in the air fry basket.
5. Select Air Fry, Super Convection, set temperature to 390°F (199°C), and set time to 12 minutes. Select Start/Stop to begin preheating.
6. Once preheated, place the basket on the air fry position. Flip the eggplant slices halfway through the cooking time.
7. When cooking is complete, the eggplant slices should be golden brown and crispy. Transfer the eggplant slices to a plate and sprinkle the garlic and parsley on top before serving.

Panko-Crusted Cheese Green Beans

Prep time: 5 minutes | Cook time: 15 minutes | Serves 4

½ cup flour
2 eggs
1 cup panko bread crumbs
½ cup grated Parmesan cheese
1 teaspoon cayenne pepper
Salt and black pepper, to taste
1½ pounds (680 g) green beans

1. In a bowl, place the flour. In a separate bowl, lightly beat the eggs. In a separate shallow bowl, thoroughly combine the bread crumbs, cheese, cayenne pepper, salt, and pepper.
2. Dip the green beans in the flour, then in the beaten eggs, finally in the bread crumb mixture to coat well. Transfer the green beans to the air fry basket.
3. Select Air Fry, Super Convection, set temperature to 400°F (205°C), and set time to 15 minutes. Select Start/Stop to begin preheating.
4. Once preheated, place the basket on the air fry position. Stir the green beans halfway through the cooking time.
5. When cooking is complete, remove from the oven to a bowl and serve.

Carrots with Dill

Prep time: 5 minutes | Cook time: 12 minutes | Serves 4

1 pound (454 g) baby carrots
2 tablespoons olive oil
1 tablespoon honey
1 teaspoon dried dill
Salt and black pepper, to taste

1. Place the carrots in a large bowl. Add the olive oil, honey, dill, salt, and pepper and toss to coat well.
2. Transfer the carrots to the air fry basket.
3. Select Roast, Super Convection, set temperature to 350°F (180°C), and set time to 12 minutes. Select Start/Stop to begin preheating.
4. Once preheated, place the basket on the roast position. Stir the carrots once during cooking.
5. When cooking is complete, the carrots should be crisp-tender. Remove from the oven and serve warm.

Baked Tofu

Prep time: 5 minutes | Cook time: 10 minutes | Serves 2

1 tablespoon soy sauce
1 tablespoon water
⅓ teaspoon garlic powder
⅓ teaspoon onion powder
⅓ teaspoon dried oregano
⅓ teaspoon dried basil
Black pepper, to taste
6 ounces (170 g) extra firm tofu, pressed and cubed

1. In a large mixing bowl, whisk together the soy sauce, water, garlic powder, onion powder, oregano, basil, and black pepper. Add the tofu cubes, stirring to coat, and let them marinate for 10 minutes.
2. Arrange the tofu in the air fry basket.
3. Select Bake, Super Convection. Set temperature to 390ºF (199ºC) and set time to 10 minutes. Select Start/Stop to begin preheating.
4. Once preheated, place the basket on the bake position. Flip the tofu halfway through the cooking time.
5. When cooking is complete, the tofu should be crisp.
6. Remove from the oven to a plate and serve.

Zucchini Cheese Quesadilla

Prep time: 5 minutes | Cook time: 10 minutes | Serves 1

1 teaspoon olive oil
2 flour tortillas
¼ zucchini, sliced
¼ yellow bell pepper, sliced
¼ cup shredded gouda cheese
1 tablespoon chopped cilantro
½ green onion, sliced

1. Coat the air fry basket with 1 teaspoon of olive oil.
2. Arrange a flour tortilla in the air fry basket and scatter the top with zucchini, bell pepper, gouda cheese, cilantro, and green onion. Place the other flour tortilla on top.
3. Select Air Fry, Super Convection, set temperature to 390ºF (199ºC), and set time to 10 minutes. Select Start/Stop to begin preheating.
4. Once preheated, place the basket on the air fry position.
5. When cooking is complete, the tortillas should be lightly browned and the vegetables should be tender. Remove from the oven and cool for 5 minutes before slicing into wedges.

Cauliflower with Yogurt and Cashew

Prep time: 5 minutes | Cook time: 12 minutes | Serves 2

4 cups cauliflower florets (about half a large head)
1 tablespoon olive oil
1 teaspoon curry powder
Salt, to taste
½ cup toasted, chopped cashews, for garnish
Yogurt Sauce:
¼ cup plain yogurt
2 tablespoons sour cream
1 teaspoon honey
1 teaspoon lemon juice
Pinch cayenne pepper
Salt, to taste
1 tablespoon chopped fresh cilantro, plus leaves for garnish

1. In a large mixing bowl, toss the cauliflower florets with the olive oil, curry powder, and salt.
2. Place the cauliflower florets in the air fry basket.
3. Select Air Fry, Super Convection, set temperature to 400ºF (205ºC) and set time to 12 minutes. Select Start/Stop to begin preheating.
4. Once preheated, place the basket on the air fry position. Stir the cauliflower florets twice during cooking.
5. When cooking is complete, the cauliflower should be golden brown.
6. Meanwhile, mix all the ingredients for the yogurt sauce in a small bowl and whisk to combine.
7. Remove the cauliflower from the oven and drizzle with the yogurt sauce. Scatter the toasted cashews and cilantro on top and serve immediately.

Carrot and Potato with Thyme

Prep time: 10 minutes | Cook time: 22 minutes | Serves 4

2 carrots, sliced
2 potatoes, cut into chunks
1 rutabaga, cut into chunks
1 turnip, cut into chunks
1 beet, cut into chunks
8 shallots, halved
2 tablespoons olive oil
Salt and black pepper, to taste
2 tablespoons tomato pesto
2 tablespoons water
2 tablespoons chopped fresh thyme

1. Toss the carrots, potatoes, rutabaga, turnip, beet, shallots, olive oil, salt, and pepper in a large mixing bowl until the root vegetables are evenly coated.
2. Place the root vegetables in the air fry basket.
3. Select Air Fry, Super Convection, set temperature to 400°F (205°C) and set time to 22 minutes. Select Start/Stop to begin preheating.
4. Once preheated, place the basket on the air fry position. Stir the vegetables twice during cooking.
5. When cooking is complete, the vegetables should be tender.
6. Meanwhile, in a small bowl, whisk together the tomato pesto and water until smooth.
7. When ready, remove the root vegetables from the oven to a platter. Drizzle with the tomato pesto mixture and sprinkle with the thyme. Serve immediately.

Okra with Sour Cream

Prep time: 5 minutes | Cook time: 10 minutes | Serves 4

3 tablespoons sour cream
2 tablespoons flour
2 tablespoons semolina
½ teaspoon red chili powder
Salt and black pepper, to taste
1 pound (454 g) okra, halved
Cooking spray

1. Spray the air fry basket with cooking spray. Set aside.
2. In a shallow bowl, place the sour cream. In another shallow bowl, thoroughly combine the flour, semolina, red chili powder, salt, and pepper.
3. Dredge the okra in the sour cream, then roll in the flour mixture until evenly coated. Transfer the okra to the air fry basket.
4. Select Air Fry, Super Convection, set temperature to 400°F (205°C), and set time to 10 minutes. Select Start/Stop to begin preheating.
5. Once preheated, place the basket on the air fry position. Flip the okra halfway through the cooking time.
6. When cooking is complete, the okra should be golden brown and crispy. Remove the basket from the oven. Cool for 5 minutes before serving.

Lemony Chickpea Oat Meatballs

Prep time: 15 minutes | Cook time: 18 minutes | Serves 3

½ cup grated carrots
½ cup sweet onions
2 tablespoons olive oil
1 cup rolled oats
½ cup roasted cashews
2 cups cooked chickpeas
Juice of 1 lemon
2 tablespoons soy sauce
1 tablespoon flax meal
1 teaspoon garlic powder
1 teaspoon cumin
½ teaspoon turmeric

1. Mix the carrots, onions, and olive oil in a baking dish and stir to combine.
2. Select Roast, Super Convection, set temperature to 350°F (180°C) and set time to 6 minutes. Select Start/Stop to begin preheating.
3. Once preheated, place the baking dish on the roast position. Stir the vegetables halfway through.
4. When cooking is complete, the vegetables should be tender.
5. Meanwhile, put the oats and cashews in a food processor or blender and pulse until coarsely ground. Transfer the mixture to a large bowl. Add the chickpeas, lemon juice, and soy sauce to the food processor and pulse until smooth. Transfer the chickpea mixture to the bowl of oat and cashew mixture.
6. Remove the carrots and onions from the oven to the bowl of chickpea mixture. Add the flax meal, garlic powder, cumin, and turmeric and stir to incorporate.
7. Scoop tablespoon-sized portions of the veggie mixture and roll them into balls with your hands. Transfer the balls to the air fry basket.
8. Increase the temperature to 370°F (188°C) and set time to 12 minutes on Bake, Super Convection. Place the basket on the bake position. Flip the balls halfway through the cooking time.
9. When cooking is complete, the balls should be golden brown.
10. Serve warm.

Bell Peppers with Garlic

Prep time: 10 minutes | Cook time: 22 minutes | Serves 4

1 green bell pepper, sliced into 1-inch strips
1 red bell pepper, sliced into 1-inch strips
1 orange bell pepper, sliced into 1-inch strips
1 yellow bell pepper, sliced into 1-inch strips
2 tablespoons olive oil, divided
½ teaspoon dried marjoram
Pinch salt
Freshly ground black pepper, to taste
1 head garlic

1. Toss the bell peppers with 1 tablespoon of olive oil in a large bowl until well coated. Season with the marjoram, salt, and pepper. Toss again and set aside.
2. Cut off the top of a head of garlic. Place the garlic cloves on a large square of aluminum foil. Drizzle the top with the remaining 1 tablespoon of olive oil and wrap the garlic cloves in foil.
3. Transfer the garlic to the air fry basket.
4. Select Roast, Super Convection, set temperature to 330°F (166°C) and set time to 15 minutes. Select Start/Stop to begin preheating.
5. Once preheated, place the basket on the roast position.
6. After 15 minutes, remove the air fry basket from the oven and add the bell peppers. Return to the oven and set time to 7 minutes.
7. When cooking is complete or until the garlic is soft and the bell peppers are tender.
8. Transfer the cooked bell peppers to a plate. Remove the garlic and unwrap the foil. Let the garlic rest for a few minutes. Once cooled, squeeze the roasted garlic cloves out of their skins and add them to the plate of bell peppers. Stir well and serve immediately.

Tofu Carrot and Cauliflower Rice

Prep time: 10 minutes | Cook time: 22 minutes | Serves 4

½ block tofu, crumbled
1 cup diced carrot
½ cup diced onions
2 tablespoons soy sauce
1 teaspoon turmeric
Cauliflower:
3 cups cauliflower rice
½ cup chopped broccoli
½ cup frozen peas
2 tablespoons soy sauce
1 tablespoon minced ginger
2 garlic cloves, minced
1 tablespoon rice vinegar
1½ teaspoons toasted sesame oil

1. Mix the tofu, carrot, onions, soy sauce, and turmeric in a baking dish and stir until well incorporated.
2. Select Roast, Super Convection, set temperature to 370°F (188°C) and set time to 10 minutes. Select Start/Stop to begin preheating.
3. Once preheated, place the baking dish on the roast position. Flip the tofu and carrot halfway through the cooking time.
4. When cooking is complete, the tofu should be crisp.
5. Meanwhile, in a large bowl, combine all the ingredients for the cauliflower and toss well.
6. Remove the dish from the oven and add the cauliflower mixture to the tofu and stir to combine.
7. Return the baking dish to the oven and set time to 12 minutes on Roast, Super Convection. Place the baking dish on the roast position
8. When cooking is complete, the vegetables should be tender.
9. Cool for 5 minutes before serving.

Zucchini and Carrot with Cheese

Prep time: 5 minutes | Cook time: 14 minutes | Serves 2

2 zucchinis, cut into even chunks
1 large eggplant, peeled, cut into chunks
1 large carrot, cut into chunks
6 ounces (170 g) halloumi cheese, cubed
2 teaspoons olive oil
Salt and black pepper, to taste
1 teaspoon dried mixed herbs

1. Combine the zucchinis, eggplant, carrot, cheese, olive oil, salt, and pepper in a large bowl and toss to coat well.
2. Spread the mixture evenly in the air fry basket.
3. Select Air Fry, Super Convection, set temperature to 340°F (171°C), and set time to 14 minutes. Select Start/Stop to begin preheating.
4. Once preheated, place the basket on the air fry position. Stir the mixture once during cooking.
5. When cooking is complete, they should be crispy and golden. Remove from the oven and serve topped with mixed herbs.

Breaded Zucchini Chips

Prep time: 5 minutes | Cook time: 14 minutes | Serves 4

2 egg whites
Salt and black pepper, to taste
½ cup seasoned bread crumbs
2 tablespoons grated Parmesan cheese
¼ teaspoon garlic powder
2 medium zucchini, sliced
Cooking spray

1. Spritz the air fry basket with cooking spray.
2. In a bowl, beat the egg whites with salt and pepper. In a separate bowl, thoroughly combine the bread crumbs, Parmesan cheese, and garlic powder.
3. Dredge the zucchini slices in the egg white, then coat in the bread crumb mixture.
4. Arrange the zucchini slices in the air fry basket.
5. Select Air Fry, Super Convection. Set temperature to 400ºF (205ºC) and set time to 14 minutes. Select Start/Stop to begin preheating.
6. Once preheated, place the basket on the air fry position. Flip the zucchini halfway through.
7. When cooking is complete, the zucchini should be tender.
8. Remove from the oven to a plate and serve.

Glazed Red Potato and Mushrooms

Prep time: 15 minutes | Cook time: 20 minutes | Makes 3 cups

Glaze:
2 tablespoons raw honey
2 teaspoons minced garlic
¼ teaspoon dried marjoram
¼ teaspoon dried basil
¼ teaspoon dried oregano
⅛ teaspoon dried sage
⅛ teaspoon dried rosemary
⅛ teaspoon dried thyme
½ teaspoon salt
¼ teaspoon ground black pepper
Veggies:
3 to 4 medium red potatoes, cut into 1- to 2-inch pieces
1 small zucchini, cut into 1- to 2-inch pieces
1 small carrot, sliced into ¼-inch rounds
1 (10.5-ounce / 298-g) package cherry tomatoes, halved
1 cup sliced mushrooms
3 tablespoons olive oil

1. Combine the honey, garlic, marjoram, basil, oregano, sage, rosemary, thyme, salt, and pepper in a small bowl and stir to mix well. Set aside.
2. Place the red potatoes, zucchini, carrot, cherry tomatoes, and mushroom in a large bowl. Drizzle with the olive oil and toss to coat.
3. Pour the veggies into the air fry basket.
4. Select Roast, Super Convection, set temperature to 380ºF (193ºC) and set time to 15 minutes. Select Start/Stop to begin preheating.
5. Once preheated, place the basket on the roast position. Stir the veggies halfway through.
6. When cooking is complete, the vegetables should be tender.
7. When ready, transfer the roasted veggies to the large bowl. Pour the honey mixture over the veggies, tossing to coat.
8. Spread out the veggies in a baking pan and place in the oven.
9. Increase the temperature to 390ºF (199ºC) and set time to 5 minutes on Roast, Super Convection. Place the basket on the roast position.
10. When cooking is complete, the veggies should be tender and glazed. Serve warm.

Zucchini and Tomato Ratatouille

Prep time: 15 minutes | Cook time: 16 minutes | Serves 2

2 Roma tomatoes, thinly sliced
1 zucchini, thinly sliced
2 yellow bell peppers, sliced
2 garlic cloves, minced
2 tablespoons olive oil
2 tablespoons herbes de Provence
1 tablespoon vinegar
Salt and black pepper, to taste

1. Place the tomatoes, zucchini, bell peppers, garlic, olive oil, herbes de Provence, and vinegar in a large bowl and toss until the vegetables are evenly coated. Sprinkle with salt and pepper and toss again. Pour the vegetable mixture into a baking dish.
2. Select Roast, Super Convection, set temperature to 390ºF (199ºC) and set time to 16 minutes. Select Start/Stop to begin preheating.
3. Once preheated, place the baking dish on the roast position. Stir the vegetables halfway through.
4. When cooking is complete, the vegetables should be tender.
5. Let the vegetable mixture stand for 5 minutes in the oven before removing and serving.

Glazed Cauliflower

Prep time: 5 minutes | Cook time: 14 minutes | Serves 4

½ cup soy sauce
⅓ cup water
1 tablespoon brown sugar
1 teaspoon sesame oil
1 teaspoon cornstarch
2 cloves garlic, chopped
½ teaspoon chili powder
1 big cauliflower head, cut into
    florets

1. Make the teriyaki sauce: In a small bowl, whisk together the soy sauce, water, brown sugar, sesame oil, cornstarch, garlic, and chili powder until well combined.
2. Place the cauliflower florets in a large bowl and drizzle the top with the prepared teriyaki sauce and toss to coat well.
3. Put the cauliflower florets in the air fry basket.
4. Select Air Fry, Super Convection, set temperature to 340°F (171°C) and set time to 14 minutes. Select Start/Stop to begin preheating.
5. Once preheated, place the basket on the air fry position. Stir the cauliflower halfway through.
6. When cooking is complete, the cauliflower should be crisp-tender.
7. Let the cauliflower cool for 5 minutes before serving.

Garlic Stuffed Mushrooms

Prep time: 5 minutes | Cook time: 12 minutes | Serves 2

18 medium-sized white mushrooms
1 small onion, peeled and chopped
4 garlic cloves, peeled and minced
2 tablespoons olive oil
2 teaspoons cumin powder
A pinch ground allspice
Fine sea salt and freshly ground
    black pepper, to taste

1. On a clean work surface, remove the mushroom stems. Using a spoon, scoop out the mushroom gills and discard.
2. Thoroughly combine the onion, garlic, olive oil, cumin powder, allspice, salt, and pepper in a mixing bowl. Stuff the mushrooms evenly with the mixture.
3. Place the stuffed mushrooms in the air fry basket.
4. Select Roast, Super Convection, set temperature to 345°F (174°C) and set time to 12 minutes. Select Start/Stop to begin preheating.
5. Once preheated, place the basket on the roast position.
6. When cooking is complete, the mushroom should be browned.
7. Cool for 5 minutes before serving.

Turnip and Zucchini

Prep time: 5 minutes | Cook time: 18 minutes | Serves 4

3 turnips, sliced
1 large zucchini, sliced
1 large red onion, cut into rings
2 cloves garlic, crushed
1 tablespoon olive oil
Salt and black pepper, to taste

1. Put the turnips, zucchini, red onion, and garlic in a baking pan. Drizzle the olive oil over the top and sprinkle with the salt and pepper.
2. Select Bake, Super Convection, set temperature to 330°F (166°C), and set time to 18 minutes. Select Start/Stop to begin preheating.
3. Once preheated, place the pan on the bake position.
4. When cooking is complete, the vegetables should be tender. Remove from the oven and serve on a plate.

Rosemary Beets with Glaze

Prep time: 5 minutes | Cook time: 10 minutes | Serves 2

Beet:
2 beets, cubed
2 tablespoons olive oil
2 springs rosemary, chopped
Salt and black pepper, to taste
Balsamic Glaze:
⅓ cup balsamic vinegar
1 tablespoon honey

1. Combine the beets, olive oil, rosemary, salt, and pepper in a mixing bowl and toss until the beets are completely coated.
2. Place the beets in the air fry basket.
3. Select Air Fry, Super Convection. Set temperature to 400°F (205°C) and set time to 10 minutes. Select Start/Stop to begin preheating.
4. Once preheated, place the basket on the air fry position. Stir the vegetables halfway through.
5. When cooking is complete, the beets should be crisp and browned at the edges.
6. Meanwhile, make the balsamic glaze: Place the balsamic vinegar and honey in a small saucepan and bring to a boil over medium heat. When the sauce boils, reduce the heat to medium-low heat and simmer until the liquid is reduced by half.
7. When ready, remove the beets from the oven to a platter. Pour the balsamic glaze over the top and serve immediately.

Walnut and Cheese Stuffed Mushrooms

Prep time: 5 minutes | Cook time: 10 minutes | Serves 4

4 large portobello mushrooms
1 tablespoon canola oil
½ cup shredded Mozzarella cheese
⅓ cup minced walnuts
2 tablespoons chopped fresh parsley
Cooking spray

1. Spritz the air fry basket with cooking spray.
2. On a clean work surface, remove the mushroom stems. Scoop out the gills with a spoon and discard. Coat the mushrooms with canola oil. Top each mushroom evenly with the shredded Mozzarella cheese, followed by the minced walnuts.
3. Arrange the mushrooms in the air fry basket.
4. Select Roast, Super Convection, set temperature to 350°F (180°C) and set time to 10 minutes. Select Start/Stop to begin preheating.
5. Once preheated, place the basket on the roast position.
6. When cooking is complete, the mushroom should be golden brown.
7. Transfer the mushrooms to a plate and sprinkle the parsley on top for garnish before serving.

Bean, Salsa, and Cheese Tacos

Prep time: 12 minutes | Cook time: 7 minutes | Serves 4

1 (15-ounce / 425-g) can black beans, drained and rinsed
½ cup prepared salsa
1½ teaspoons chili powder
4 ounces (113 g) grated Monterey Jack cheese
2 tablespoons minced onion
8 (6-inch) flour tortillas
2 tablespoons vegetable or extra-virgin olive oil
Shredded lettuce, for serving

1. In a medium bowl, add the beans, salsa and chili powder. Coarsely mash them with a potato masher. Fold in the cheese and onion and stir until combined.
2. Arrange the flour tortillas on a cutting board and spoon 2 to 3 tablespoons of the filling into each tortilla. Fold the tortillas over, pressing lightly to even out the filling. Brush the tacos on one side with half the olive oil and put them, oiled side down, on the sheet pan. Brush the top side with the remaining olive oil.
3. Select Air Fry, Super Convection, set temperature to 400°F (205°C), and set time to 7 minutes. Select Start/Stop to begin preheating.
4. Once preheated, place the pan into the oven. Flip the tacos halfway through the cooking time.
5. Remove the pan from the oven and allow to cool for 5 minutes. Serve with the shredded lettuce on the side.

Spicy Thai-Style Vegetables

Prep time: 10 minutes | Cook time: 8 minutes | Serves 4

1 small head Napa cabbage, shredded, divided
1 medium carrot, cut into thin coins
8 ounces (227 g) snow peas
1 red or green bell pepper, sliced into thin strips
1 tablespoon vegetable oil
2 tablespoons soy sauce
1 tablespoon sesame oil
2 tablespoons brown sugar
2 tablespoons freshly squeezed lime juice
2 teaspoons red or green Thai curry paste
1 serrano chile, deseeded and minced
1 cup frozen mango slices, thawed
½ cup chopped roasted peanuts or cashews

1. Put half the Napa cabbage in a large bowl, along with the carrot, snow peas, and bell pepper. Drizzle with the vegetable oil and toss to coat. Spread them evenly on the sheet pan.
2. Select Roast, Super Convection, set temperature to 375°F (190°C), and set time to 8 minutes. Select Start/Stop to begin preheating.
3. Once preheated, place the pan on the roast position.
4. Meanwhile, whisk together the soy sauce, sesame oil, brown sugar, lime juice, and curry paste in a small bowl.
5. When done, the vegetables should be tender and crisp. Remove the pan and put the vegetables back into the bowl. Add the chile, mango slices, and the remaining cabbage. Pour over the dressing and toss to coat. Top with the roasted nuts and serve.

Roasted Vegetables with Basil

Prep time: 15 minutes | Cook time: 20 minutes | Serves 2

1 small eggplant, halved and sliced
1 yellow bell pepper, cut into thick strips
1 red bell pepper, cut into thick strips
2 garlic cloves, quartered
1 red onion, sliced
1 tablespoon extra-virgin olive oil
Salt and freshly ground black pepper, to taste
½ cup chopped fresh basil, for garnish
Cooking spray

1. Grease a nonstick baking dish with cooking spray.
2. Place the eggplant, bell peppers, garlic, and red onion in the greased baking dish. Drizzle with the olive oil and toss to coat well. Spritz any uncoated surfaces with cooking spray.
3. Select Bake, Super Convection, set temperature to 350°F (180°C), and set time to 20 minutes. Select Start/Stop to begin preheating.
4. Once preheated, place the baking dish on the bake position. Flip the vegetables halfway through the cooking time.
5. When done, remove from the oven and sprinkle with salt and pepper.
6. Sprinkle the basil on top for garnish and serve.

Balsamic Asparagus

Prep time: 15 minutes | Cook time: 10 minutes | Serves 4

4 tablespoons olive oil, plus more for greasing
4 tablespoons balsamic vinegar
1½ pounds (680 g) asparagus spears, trimmed
Salt and freshly ground black pepper, to taste

1. Grease the air fry basket with olive oil.
2. In a shallow bowl, stir together the 4 tablespoons of olive oil and balsamic vinegar to make a marinade.
3. Put the asparagus spears in the bowl so they are thoroughly covered by the marinade and allow to marinate for 5 minutes.
4. Put the asparagus in the greased basket in a single layer and season with salt and pepper.
5. Select Air Fry, Super Convection, set temperature to 350°F (180°C), and set time to 10 minutes. Select Start/Stop to begin preheating.
6. Once preheated, place the air fry basket on the air fry position. Flip the asparagus halfway through the cooking time.
7. When done, the asparagus should be tender and lightly browned. Cool for 5 minutes before serving.

Mediterranean Baked Eggs with Spinach

Prep time: 10 minutes | Cook time: 10 minutes | Serves 2

2 tablespoons olive oil
4 eggs, whisked
5 ounces (142 g) fresh spinach, chopped
1 medium-sized tomato, chopped
1 teaspoon fresh lemon juice
½ teaspoon ground black pepper
½ teaspoon coarse salt
½ cup roughly chopped fresh basil leaves, for garnish

1. Generously grease a baking pan with olive oil.
2. Stir together the remaining ingredients except the basil leaves in the greased baking pan until well incorporated.
3. Select Bake, Super Convection, set temperature to 280°F (137°C), and set time to 10 minutes. Select Start/Stop to begin preheating.
4. Once preheated, place the pan on the bake position.
5. When cooking is complete, the eggs should be completely set and the vegetables should be tender. Remove from the oven and serve garnished with the fresh basil leaves.

Herbed Broccoli with Cheese

Prep time: 5 minutes | Cook time: 18 minutes | Serves 4

1 large-sized head broccoli, stemmed and cut into small florets
2½ tablespoons canola oil
2 teaspoons dried basil
2 teaspoons dried rosemary
Salt and ground black pepper, to taste
⅓ cup grated yellow cheese

1. Bring a pot of lightly salted water to a boil. Add the broccoli florets to the boiling water and let boil for about 3 minutes.
2. Drain the broccoli florets well and transfer to a large bowl. Add the canola oil, basil, rosemary, salt, and black pepper to the bowl and toss until the broccoli is fully coated. Place the broccoli in the air fry basket.
3. Select Air Fry, Super Convection, set temperature to 390°F (199°C), and set time to 15 minutes. Select Start/Stop to begin preheating.
4. Once preheated, place the air fry basket on the air fry position. Stir the broccoli halfway through the cooking time.
5. When cooking is complete, the broccoli should be crisp. Remove the basket from the oven. Serve the broccoli warm with grated cheese sprinkled on top.

Cayenne Tahini Kale

Prep time: 5 minutes | Cook time: 15 minutes | Serves 2 to 4

Dressing:
¼ cup tahini
¼ cup fresh lemon juice
2 tablespoons olive oil
1 teaspoon sesame seeds
½ teaspoon garlic powder
¼ teaspoon cayenne pepper
Kale:
4 cups packed torn kale leaves (stems and ribs removed and leaves torn into palm-size pieces)
Kosher salt and freshly ground black pepper, to taste

1. Make the dressing: Whisk together the tahini, lemon juice, olive oil, sesame seeds, garlic powder, and cayenne pepper in a large bowl until well mixed.
2. Add the kale and massage the dressing thoroughly all over the leaves. Sprinkle the salt and pepper to season.
3. Place the kale in the air fry basket in a single layer.
4. Select Air Fry, Super Convection, set temperature to 350°F (180°C), and set time to 15 minutes. Select Start/Stop to begin preheating.
5. Once preheated, place the air fry basket on the air fry position.
6. When cooking is complete, the leaves should be slightly wilted and crispy. Remove from the oven and serve on a plate.

Roasted Vegetable Mélange with Herbs

Prep time: 10 minutes | Cook time: 16 minutes | Serves 4

1 (8-ounce / 227-g) package sliced mushrooms
1 yellow summer squash, sliced
1 red bell pepper, sliced
3 cloves garlic, sliced
1 tablespoon olive oil
½ teaspoon dried basil
½ teaspoon dried thyme
½ teaspoon dried tarragon

1. Toss the mushrooms, squash, and bell pepper with the garlic and olive oil in a large bowl until well coated. Mix in the basil, thyme, and tarragon and toss again.
2. Spread the vegetables evenly in the air fry basket.
3. Select Roast, Super Convection, set temperature to 350ºF (180ºC), and set time to 16 minutes. Select Start/Stop to begin preheating.
4. Once preheated, place the basket on the roast position.
5. When cooking is complete, the vegetables should be fork-tender. Remove the basket from the oven. Cool for 5 minutes before serving.

Garlicky Sesame Carrots

Prep time: 5 minutes | Cook time: 16 minutes | Serves 4 to 6

1 pound (454 g) baby carrots
1 tablespoon sesame oil
½ teaspoon dried dill
Pinch salt
Freshly ground black pepper, to taste
6 cloves garlic, peeled
3 tablespoons sesame seeds

1. In a medium bowl, drizzle the baby carrots with the sesame oil. Sprinkle with the dill, salt, and pepper and toss to coat well.
2. Place the baby carrots in the air fry basket.
3. Select Roast, Super Convection, set temperature to 380ºF (193ºC), and set time to 16 minutes. Select Start/Stop to begin preheating.
4. Once preheated, place the basket on the roast position.
5. After 8 minutes, remove the basket from the oven and stir in the garlic. Return the basket to the oven and continue roasting for 8 minutes more.
6. When cooking is complete, the carrots should be lightly browned. Remove the basket from the oven and serve sprinkled with the sesame seeds.

Sweet-and-Sour Brussels Sprouts

Prep time: 5 minutes | Cook time: 20 minutes | Serves 2

¼ cup Thai sweet chili sauce
2 tablespoons black vinegar or balsamic vinegar
½ teaspoon hot sauce
2 small shallots, cut into ¼-inch-thick slices
8 ounces (227 g) Brussels sprouts, trimmed (large sprouts halved)
Kosher salt and freshly ground black pepper, to taste
2 teaspoons lightly packed fresh cilantro leaves, for garnish

1. Place the chili sauce, vinegar, and hot sauce in a large bowl and whisk to combine.
2. Add the shallots and Brussels sprouts and toss to coat. Sprinkle with the salt and pepper. Transfer the Brussels sprouts and sauce to a baking pan.
3. Select Roast, Super Convection, set temperature to 390ºF (199ºC), and set time to 20 minutes. Select Start/Stop to begin preheating.
4. Once preheated, place the pan on the roast position. Stir the Brussels sprouts twice during cooking.
5. When cooking is complete, the Brussels sprouts should be crisp-tender. Remove from the oven. Sprinkle the cilantro on top for garnish and serve warm.

Chapter 9 Desserts

Rum-Plums with Brown Sugar Cream

Prep time: 10 minutes | Cook time: 20 minutes | Serves 6

For the Cream:

¾ cup plus 2 tablespoons heavy cream

⅔ cup Greek yogurt

3 to 4 heaping tablespoons dark brown sugar

For the Plums:

1¾ pounds (793 g) plums (preferably crimson-fleshed), halved and pitted

2 slices of crystallized ginger, very finely chopped

½ cup light brown sugar

½ teaspoon ground ginger

3 broad strips of lime zest, plus juice of 1 lime

⅔ cup dark rum, plus 3 tablespoons

1. Make the cream about 12 hours before you want to serve it. Lightly whip the heavy cream, then fold in the yogurt. Put this in a bowl and sprinkle evenly with the sugar. Cover with plastic wrap and refrigerate. The sugar will become soft and molasses-like.
2. Put the plums into a baking pan in a single layer. Arrange the fruits so they are cut sides up. Scatter the crystallized ginger around the plums. Mix the sugar with the ground ginger and sprinkle it over the top. Squeeze the lime juice over and tuck the pieces of lime zest under the fruits, then pour the ⅔ cup rum around them.
3. Select Bake. Set temperature to 375°F (190°C) and set time to 20 minutes. Select Start to begin preheating.
4. Once preheated, slide the pan into the oven.
5. When done, the fruit should be tender when pierced with a sharp knife, but not collapsing. Leave to cool completely; the juices should thicken as they cool. If they aren't thick enough, drain off the juices and boil them in a saucepan until they become more syrupy. Add the remaining 3 tablespoons of rum. Serve the plums, at room temperature, with the brown sugar cream.

Rhubarb with Sloe Gin and Rosemary

Prep time: 10 minutes | Cook time: 30 minutes | Serves 44

1½ pounds (680 g) hothouse or main crop rhubarb stalks, all about the same thickness

½ cup granulated sugar

Finely grated zest of ½ orange

7 tablespoons sloe gin

3 tablespoons orange juice

2 rosemary sprigs, bruised

Whipped cream or heavy cream, to serve

1. Remove any leaves from the rhubarb and trim the bottoms. Cut into 1¼in lengths and put them into a large ovenproof baking dish. Scatter the sugar and zest on top and turn it all over with your hands, then pour in the sloe gin, orange juice, and 2 tablespoons of water, and finally tuck the rosemary sprigs under the rhubarb. Cover tightly with foil.
2. Select Bake. Set temperature to 350°F (180°C) and set time to 30 minutes. Select Start to begin preheating.
3. Once preheated, slide the baking dish into the oven.
4. When done, the rhubarb should be tender, but holding its shape and not collapsing.
5. Remove from the oven and leave to cool a bit in the dish. Eat warm, at room temperature, or chilled, with whipped cream or heavy cream.

Glazed Sweet Bundt Cake

Prep time: 10 minutes | Cook time: 55 minutes | Serves 8

For the Cake:
1½ cups unsalted butter, at room temperature, plus more for preparing the pan
2 cups light brown sugar
1 cup sugar
5 large eggs
3 cups all-purpose flour, plus more for preparing the pan
1 teaspoon table salt
1 cup sour cream, at room temperature
1 tablespoon vanilla extract

For the Glaze:
1 cup confectioners' sugar
2 tablespoons milk

Make the Cake
1. Butter and flour a 10-cup Bundt pan.
2. In a large bowl, using a wooden spoon or an electric mixer, cream together the butter, brown sugar, and sugar until the mixture is pale yellow and fluffy.
3. Add the eggs, one at a time, mixing after each addition until incorporated.
4. Add the flour, salt, sour cream, and vanilla and beat until just combined. Transfer the batter to the prepared pan.
5. Select Bake. Set temperature to 300ºF (150ºC) and set time to 55 minutes. Select Start to begin preheating.
6. Once preheated, slide the pan into the oven.
7. Remove the cake from the oven and set on a wire rack to cool for 10 minutes before inverting it onto a cake platter and letting it cool completely.

Make the Glaze
8. In a small bowl, whisk the confectioners' sugar and milk until smooth. Drizzle the glaze over the completely cooled cake.

Mexican Brownie Squares

Prep time: 10 minutes | Cook time: 25 minutes | Serves 8

½ cup unsalted butter, plus more for greasing
8 ounces (227 g) dark chocolate (60 to 72 percent cocoa)
1 cup sugar
2 teaspoons vanilla extract
Pinch salt
2 large eggs, at room temperature
1 teaspoon ground cinnamon
¼ teaspoon cayenne
¾ cup all-purpose flour

1. Line a square baking pan with aluminum foil, with the ends extending over the edges of the pan on two sides. Butter the foil and pan.
2. In a small saucepan, gently melt the butter and chocolate together over low heat, stirring, just until melted. Remove from the heat and let cool slightly. Pour into a large bowl.
3. Stir in the sugar, vanilla, and salt. Add the eggs, one at a time, and stir until completely blended.
4. Mix the cinnamon and cayenne into the flour until evenly dispersed. Add the flour to the chocolate mixture and beat until incorporated, about a minute. The batter may be a bit grainy looking.
5. Pour the batter into the prepared pan.
6. Select Bake. Set temperature to 350ºF (180ºC) and set time to 25 minutes. Select Start to begin preheating.
7. Once preheated, slide the pan into the oven.
8. When done, a toothpick inserted into the center should come out with crumbs but no raw batter sticking to it. Let cool for about 10 minutes. Pick up the edges of the foil and carefully lift the brownies out of the pan. Peel off the foil and let cool for another 5 minutes. Cut into squares.

Easy Nutmeg Butter Cookies

Prep time: 10 minutes | Cook time: 11 minutes | Makes 4 dozen

½ cup (1 stick) unsalted butter, melted
1 cup sugar
1 teaspoon vanilla extract
¼ teaspoon kosher salt
1 large egg
1 cup all-purpose flour
1½ teaspoons freshly grated nutmeg

1. Line two sheet pans with silicone baking mats (or use one sheet pan and bake in batches).
2. In a large bowl, mix together the butter and sugar. Stir in the vanilla and salt. Add the egg and beat until the mixture is smooth.
3. In a small bowl, whisk together the flour and nutmeg. Stir the flour mixture into the sugar and butter mixture just until blended.
4. Drop the batter by level teaspoons onto the prepared pans, leaving about 2 inches around the dough balls.
5. Select Bake. Set temperature to 350ºF (180ºC) and set time to 11 minutes. Select Start to begin preheating.
6. Once preheated, slide the pans into the oven.
7. When done, the cookies will spread, the edges will be golden brown, and the tops will start to collapse. Let cool on the pans for a few minutes, then transfer to a rack to cool completely.

Blueberry and Peach Crisp

Prep time: 15 minutes | Cook time: 30 minutes | Serves 4

For the Filling:
Nonstick cooking spray
5 ripe yellow peaches
1 cup fresh or frozen blueberries
⅓ cup granulated sugar
1 tablespoon all-purpose flour
1 teaspoon grated lemon zest
For the Topping:
½ cup quick-cooking oatmeal
⅓ cup brown sugar
⅓ cup all-purpose flour
¼ cup blanched slivered almonds
1 teaspoon ground cinnamon
½ teaspoon ground cardamom
Pinch salt
4 tablespoons unsalted butter or vegan margarine

1. Spray a square baking pan with cooking spray.
2. Peel and pit the peaches. Slice them about ½-inch thick, then cut the slices in half. You should have about 4 cups of slices. Put them in a medium bowl and add the blueberries, sugar, flour, and lemon zest. Toss gently. Pour into the prepared baking pan.
3. For the topping, mix together the oatmeal, brown sugar, flour, almonds, cinnamon, cardamom, and salt. With a pastry cutter or a large fork, cut in the butter until the mixture is crumbly.
4. Sprinkle the topping over the fruit.
5. Select Bake. Set temperature to 350°F (180°C) and set time to 30 minutes. Select Start to begin preheating.
6. Once preheated, slide the pan into the oven.
7. When done, the top is lightly browned and the peaches are bubbling. Let cool for about 15 minutes before cutting. Serve warm.

Vanilla Coconut Cookies with Pecans

Prep time: 10 minutes | Cook time: 25 minutes | Serves 10

1½ cups coconut flour
1½ cups extra-fine almond flour
½ teaspoon baking powder
⅓ teaspoon baking soda
3 eggs plus an egg yolk, beaten
¾ cup coconut oil, at room temperature
1 cup unsalted pecan nuts, roughly chopped
¾ cup monk fruit
¼ teaspoon freshly grated nutmeg
⅓ teaspoon ground cloves
½ teaspoon pure vanilla extract
½ teaspoon pure coconut extract
⅛ teaspoon fine sea salt

1. Line the perforated pan with parchment paper.
2. Mix the coconut flour, almond flour, baking powder, and baking soda in a large mixing bowl.
3. In another mixing bowl, stir together the eggs and coconut oil. Add the wet mixture to the dry mixture.
4. Mix in the remaining ingredients and stir until a soft dough forms.
5. Drop about 2 tablespoons of dough on the parchment paper for each cookie and flatten each biscuit until it's 1 inch thick.
6. Select Bake. Set temperature to 370°F (188°C) and set time to 25 minutes. Press Start to begin preheating.
7. Once the oven has preheated, place the pan into the oven.
8. When cooking is complete, the cookies should be golden and firm to the touch.
9. Remove from the oven to a plate. Let the cookies cool to room temperature and serve.

Peach and Apple Crisp with Oatmeal

Prep time: 10 minutes | Cook time: 10 to 12 minutes | Serves 4

2 peaches, peeled, pitted, and chopped
1 apple, peeled and chopped
2 tablespoons honey
3 tablespoons packed brown sugar
2 tablespoons unsalted butter, at room temperature
½ cup quick-cooking oatmeal
⅓ cup whole-wheat pastry flour
½ teaspoon ground cinnamon

1. Place the peaches, apple, and honey in a baking pan and toss until thoroughly combined.
2. Mix together the brown sugar, butter, oatmeal, pastry flour, and cinnamon in a medium bowl and stir until crumbly. Sprinkle this mixture generously on top of the peaches and apples.
3. Select Bake. Set temperature to 380°F (193°C) and set time to 10 minutes. Press Start to begin preheating.
4. Once the unit has preheated, place the pan into the oven.
5. Bake until the fruit is bubbling and the topping is golden brown.
6. Once cooking is complete, remove the pan from the oven and allow to cool for 5 minutes before serving.

Mixed Berry Bake with Almond Topping

Prep time: 5 minutes | Cook time: 17 minutes | Serves 3

½ cup mixed berries
Cooking spray
Topping:
1 egg, beaten
3 tablespoons almonds, slivered
3 tablespoons chopped pecans
2 tablespoons chopped walnuts
3 tablespoons granulated Swerve
2 tablespoons cold salted butter, cut into pieces
½ teaspoon ground cinnamon

1. Lightly spray a baking dish with cooking spray.
2. Make the topping: In a medium bowl, stir together the beaten egg, nuts, Swerve, butter, and cinnamon until well blended.
3. Put the mixed berries in the bottom of the baking dish and spread the topping over the top.
4. Select Bake. Set temperature to 340ºF (171ºC) and set time to 17 minutes. Press Start to begin preheating.
5. Once the oven has preheated, place the baking dish into the oven.
6. When cooking is complete, the fruit should be bubbly and topping should be golden brown.
7. Allow to cool for 5 to 10 minutes before serving.

Peach and Blueberry Galette

Prep time: 10 minutes | Cook time: 20 minutes | Serves 6

1 pint blueberries, rinsed and picked through (about 2 cups)
2 large peaches or nectarines, peeled and cut into ½-inch slices (about 2 cups)
⅓ cup plus 2 tablespoons granulated sugar, divided
2 tablespoons unbleached all-purpose flour
½ teaspoon grated lemon zest (optional)
¼ teaspoon ground allspice or cinnamon
Pinch kosher or fine salt
1 (9-inch) refrigerated piecrust (or use homemade)
2 teaspoons unsalted butter, cut into pea-size pieces
1 large egg, beaten

1. Mix together the blueberries, peaches, ⅓ cup of sugar, flour, lemon zest (if desired) allspice, and salt in a medium bowl.
2. Unroll the crust on the sheet pan, patching any tears if needed. Place the fruit in the center of the crust, leaving about 1½ inches of space around the edges. Scatter the butter pieces over the fruit. Fold the outside edge of the crust over the outer circle of the fruit, making pleats as needed.
3. Brush the egg over the crust. Sprinkle the crust and fruit with the remaining 2 tablespoons of sugar.
4. Select Bake. Set temperature to 350ºF (180ºC) and set time to 20 minutes. Press Start to begin preheating.
5. Once the unit has preheated, place the pan into the oven.
6. After about 15 minutes, check the pancake, rotating the pan if the crust is not browning evenly. Continue cooking until the crust is deep golden brown and the fruit is bubbling.
7. When cooking is complete, remove the pan from the oven and allow to cool for 10 minutes before slicing and serving.

Banana Goreng Pisang

Prep time: 6 minutes | Cook time: 13 minutes | Serves 2

4 tablespoons rice flour
4 tablespoons all-purpose flour
¼ teaspoon ground cinnamon
A pinch of sea salt
A pinch of grated nutmeg
4 tablespoons coconut flakes
2 teaspoons coconut oil
2 eggs, whisked
2 bananas, peeled and sliced

1. Start by preheating the air fryer to 390ºF (199ºC).
2. In a mixing dish, thoroughly combine the flour, cinnamon, salt, nutmeg, and coconut flakes.
3. Now, add in the coconut oil and eggs. Roll each slice of banana over the egg mixture. Transfer to the baking pan.
4. Place the baking pan in the corresponding position in the air fryer. Select Bake and cook the bananas for approximately 13 minutes, turning them over halfway through the cooking time. Bon appétit!

French Baguette

Prep time: 5 minutes | Cook time: 8 minutes | Serves 2

2 eggs
2 tablespoons coconut oil, melted
¼ cup milk
½ teaspoon vanilla extract
¼ teaspoon ground cinnamon
⅛ teaspoon ground nutmeg
4 thick slices baguette

1. Start by preheating the air fryer to 330°F (166°C).
2. In a mixing bowl, thoroughly combine the eggs, coconut oil, milk, vanilla, cinnamon, and nutmeg.
3. Then, dip each piece of bread into the egg mixture; place the bread slices in a lightly greased baking pan.
4. Place the baking pan in the corresponding position in the air fryer. Select Bake and cook the bread slices for about 4 minutes; turn them over and cook for a further 3 to 4 minutes. Enjoy!

Eggs and Butter Crullers

Prep time: 5 minutes | Cook time: 20 minutes | Serves 4

¾ cup all-purpose flour
¼ cup butter
¼ cup water
½ cup full-fat milk
¼ teaspoon kosher salt
A pinch of grated nutmeg
3 eggs, beaten

1. Start by preheating the air fryer to 360°F (182°C).
2. In a mixing bowl, thoroughly combine all ingredients. Place the batter in a piping bag fitted with a large open star tip.
3. Pipe the crullers into circles and lower them onto the greased baking pan.
4. Place the baking pan in the corresponding position in the air fryer. Select Bake and cook the crullers for 10 minutes, flipping them halfway through the cooking time.
5. Repeat with the remaining batter and serve immediately. Enjoy!

Cocoa Cupcakes with Raisins

Prep time: 5 minutes | Cook time: 15 minutes | Serves 4

¾ cup all-purpose flour
½ teaspoon baking powder
½ cup unsweetened cocoa powder
A pinch of kosher salt
¼ teaspoon grated nutmeg
½ teaspoon ground cinnamon
4 tablespoons coconut oil
¾ cup brown sugar
2 eggs, whisked
½ teaspoon vanilla extract
¾ cup yogurt
2 tablespoons raisins

1. Start by preheating the air fryer to 330°F (166°C).
2. Mix all the ingredients in a bowl. Scrape the batter into silicone baking molds; place them in the baking pan.
3. Place the baking pan in the corresponding position in the air fryer. Select Bake and cook the cupcakes for about 15 minutes or until a tester comes out dry and clean.
4. Allow the cupcakes to cool before unmolding and serving. Bon appétit!

Walnuts and Yogurt Stuffed Pears

Prep time: 5 minutes | Cook time: 17 minutes | Serves 2

2 pears
¼ teaspoon cloves
⅛ teaspoon grated nutmeg
¼ teaspoon ground cinnamon
2 tablespoons honey
2 tablespoons chopped walnuts
2 ounces (57 g) Greek yogurt

1. Start by preheating the air fryer to 340°F (171°C).
2. Cut the pears in half and spoon out some of the flesh.
3. In a mixing bowl, thoroughly combine the remaining ingredients. Stuff the pear halves.
4. Pour ¼ cup of water into the baking pan. Place the pears in the pan.
5. Place the baking pan in the corresponding position in the air fryer. Select Bake and cook the apples for 17 minutes. Serve at room temperature. Bon appétit!

Strawberry Fritters

Prep time: 5 minutes | Cook time: 15 minutes | Serves 4

¾ cup all-purpose flour
½ teaspoon baking powder
2 tablespoons butter, melted
¼ cup coconut milk
2 eggs, whisked
1 teaspoon lime juice
½ cup strawberries
2 tablespoons powdered sugar

1. Start by preheating the air fryer to 360°F (182°C).
2. In a mixing bowl, thoroughly combine all the ingredients.
3. Drop a spoonful of batter onto the greased baking pan.
4. Place the baking pan in the corresponding position in the air fryer. Select Bake and cook for 10 minutes, flipping them halfway through the cooking time.
5. Repeat with the remaining batter and serve warm. Enjoy!

Roasted Cherries

Prep time: 10 minutes | Cook time: 20 minutes | Serves 4

2 cups pitted cherries
4 tablespoons brown sugar
1 tablespoon coconut oil
2 tablespoons bourbon
¼ teaspoon ground cinnamon

1. Start by preheating the air fryer to 370°F (188°C).
2. Toss the cherries with the remaining ingredients; place the cherries in a lightly greased crisper tray.
3. Place the crisper tray in the corresponding position in the air fryer. Select Roast and cook the cherries in the preheated air fryer for approximately 20 minutes.
4. Serve at room temperature. Bon appétit!

Hearty Honey Yeast Rolls

Prep time: 10 minutes | Cook time: 12 minutes | Makes 8 rolls

¼ cup whole milk, heated to 115°F (46°C) in the microwave
½ teaspoon active dry yeast
1 tablespoon honey
⅔ cup all-purpose flour, plus more for dusting
½ teaspoon kosher salt
2 tablespoons unsalted butter, at room temperature, plus more for greasing
Flaky sea salt, to taste

1. In a large bowl, whisk together the milk, yeast, and honey and let stand until foamy, about 10 minutes.
2. Stir in the flour and salt until just combined. Stir in the butter until absorbed. Scrape the dough onto a lightly floured work surface and knead until smooth, about 6 minutes. Transfer the dough to a lightly greased bowl, cover loosely with a sheet of plastic wrap or a kitchen towel, and let sit until nearly doubled in size, about 1 hour.
3. Uncover the dough, lightly press it down to expel the bubbles, then portion it into 8 equal pieces. Prep the work surface by wiping it clean with a damp paper towel (if there is flour on the work surface, it will prevent the dough from sticking lightly to the surface, which helps it form a ball). Roll each piece into a ball by cupping the palm of the hand around the dough against the work surface and moving the heel of the hand in a circular motion while using the thumb to contain the dough and tighten it into a perfectly round ball. Once all the balls are formed, nestle them side by side in the air fryer basket.
4. Cover the rolls loosely with a kitchen towel or a sheet of plastic wrap and let sit until lightly risen and puffed, 20 to 30 minutes.
5. Preheat the air fryer oven to 270°F (132°C).
6. Uncover the rolls and gently brush with more butter, being careful not to press the rolls too hard.
7. Place the air fryer basket onto the baking pan and slide into Rack Position 2, select Air Fry and set time to 12 minutes, until the rolls are light golden brown and fluffy.
8. Remove the rolls from the oven and brush liberally with more butter, if you like, and sprinkle each roll with a pinch of sea salt. Serve warm.

Chocolate Chips Mug Cake

Prep time: 5 minutes | Cook time: 20 minutes | Serves 2

2 tablespoons coconut flour
2 tablespoons almond flour
2 tablespoons all-purpose flour
½ teaspoon baking powder
4 tablespoons unsweetened cocoa
 powder
2 ounces (57 g) chocolate chips
A pinch of salt
A pinch of grated nutmeg
2 tablespoons coconut oil
4 tablespoons coconut milk
½ teaspoon pure almond extract

1. Start by preheating the air fryer to 350°F (180°C).
2. Thoroughly combine all the ingredients; mix until well combined.
3. Divide the mixture between two mugs and place them in the baking pan.
4. Place the baking pan in the corresponding position in the air fryer. Select Bake and cook the mug cakes for approximately 20 minutes. Bon appétit!

Caramelized Fruity Kebabs

Prep time: 10 minutes | Cook time: 4 minutes | Serves 4

2 peaches, peeled, pitted, and thickly
 sliced
3 plums, halved and pitted
3 nectarines, halved and pitted
1 tablespoon honey
½ teaspoon ground cinnamon
¼ teaspoon ground allspice
Pinch cayenne pepper

Special Equipment:
8 metal skewers

1. Thread, alternating peaches, plums, and nectarines onto the metal skewers that fit into the oven.
2. Thoroughly combine the honey, cinnamon, allspice, and cayenne in a small bowl. Brush generously the glaze over the fruit skewers.
3. Transfer the fruit skewers to the air fry basket.
4. Select Air Fry, Super Convection, set temperature to 400°F (205°C), and set time to 4 minutes. Select Start/Stop to begin preheating.
5. Once the oven has preheated, place the basket on the air fry position.
6. When cooking is complete, the fruit should be caramelized.
7. Remove the fruit skewers from the oven and let rest for 5 minutes before serving.

Pound Cake

Prep time: 10 minutes | Cook time: 30 minutes | Serves 8

1 stick butter, at room temperature
1 cup Swerve
4 eggs
1½ cups coconut flour
½ cup buttermilk
½ teaspoon baking soda
½ teaspoon baking powder
¼ teaspoon salt
1 teaspoon vanilla essence
A pinch of ground star anise
A pinch of freshly grated nutmeg
Cooking spray

1. Spray a baking pan with cooking spray.
2. With an electric mixer or hand mixer, beat the butter and Swerve until creamy. One at a time, mix in the eggs and whisk until fluffy. Add the remaining ingredients and stir to combine.
3. Transfer the batter to the prepared baking pan.
4. Select Bake, Super Convection, set temperature to 320°F (160°C), and set time to 30 minutes. Select Start/Stop to begin preheating.
5. Once the oven has preheated, place the pan on the bake position. Rotate the pan halfway through the cooking time.
6. When cooking is complete, the center of the cake should be springy.
7. Allow the cake to cool in the pan for 10 minutes before removing and serving.

Pumpkin Pudding with Vanilla Wafers Topping

Prep time: 10 minutes | Cook time: 15 minutes | Serves 4

1 cup canned no-salt-added pumpkin purée (not pumpkin pie filling)
¼ cup packed brown sugar
3 tablespoons all-purpose flour
1 egg, whisked
2 tablespoons milk
1 tablespoon unsalted butter, melted
1 teaspoon pure vanilla extract
4 low-fat vanilla wafers, crumbled
Cooking spray

1. Coat a baking pan with cooking spray. Set aside.
2. Mix the pumpkin purée, brown sugar, flour, whisked egg, milk, melted butter, and vanilla in a medium bowl and whisk to combine. Transfer the mixture to the baking pan.
3. Select Bake, Super Convection, set temperature to 350°F (180°C), and set time to 15 minutes. Select Start/Stop to begin preheating.
4. Once the oven has preheated, place the pan on the bake position.
5. When cooking is complete, the pudding should be set.
6. Remove the pudding from the oven to a wire rack to cool.
7. Divide the pudding into four bowls and serve with the vanilla wafers sprinkled on top.

Ricotta Cheesecake

Prep time: 5 minutes | Cook time: 25 minutes | Serves 6

17.5 ounces (496 g) ricotta cheese
5.4 ounces (153 g) sugar
3 eggs, beaten
3 tablespoons flour
1 lemon, juiced and zested
2 teaspoons vanilla extract

1. In a large mixing bowl, stir together all the ingredients until the mixture reaches a creamy consistency.
2. Pour the mixture into a baking pan and place in the oven.
3. Select Bake, Super Convection, set temperature to 320°F (160°C), and set time to 25 minutes. Select Start/Stop to begin preheating.
4. Once the oven has preheated, place the pan on the bake position.
5. When cooking is complete, a toothpick inserted in the center should come out clean.
6. Allow to cool for 10 minutes on a wire rack before serving.

Cinnamon Candy Covered Apple

Prep time: 15 minutes | Cook time: 12 minutes | Serves 4

1 cup packed light brown sugar
2 teaspoons ground cinnamon
2 medium Granny Smith apples, peeled and diced

1. Thoroughly combine the brown sugar and cinnamon in a medium bowl.
2. Add the apples to the bowl and stir until well coated. Transfer the apples to a baking pan.
3. Select Bake, Super Convection, set temperature to 350°F (180°C), and set time to 12 minutes. Select Start/Stop to begin preheating.
4. Once the oven has preheated, place the pan on the bake position.
5. After about 9 minutes, stir the apples and bake for an additional 3 minutes. When cooking is complete, the apples should be softened.
6. Serve warm.

Southern Fudge Pie

Prep time: 10 minutes | Cook time: 26 minutes | Serves 8

1½ cups sugar
½ cup self-rising flour
⅓ cup unsweetened cocoa powder
3 large eggs, beaten
12 tablespoons (1½ sticks) butter, melted
1½ teaspoons vanilla extract
1 (9-inch) unbaked pie crust
¼ cup confectioners' sugar (optional)

1. Thoroughly combine the sugar, flour, and cocoa powder in a medium bowl. Add the beaten eggs and butter and whisk to combine. Stir in the vanilla.
2. Pour the prepared filling into the pie crust and transfer to the air fry basket.
3. Select Bake, Super Convection, set temperature to 350°F (180°C), and set time to 26 minutes. Select Start/Stop to begin preheating.
4. Once the oven has preheated, place the basket on the bake position.
5. When cooking is complete, the pie should be set.
6. Allow the pie to cool for 5 minutes. Sprinkle with the confectioners' sugar, if desired. Serve warm.

Orange and Ginger Cookie

Prep time: 20 minutes | Cook time: 15 minutes | Serves 2

Cookie:
1 cup plus 2 tablespoons all-purpose flour
1 tablespoon grated orange zest
1 teaspoon crushed aniseeds
1 teaspoon ground ginger
¼ teaspoon kosher salt
4 tablespoons (½ stick) unsalted butter, at room temperature
½ cup granulated sugar, plus more for sprinkling
3 tablespoons dark molasses
1 large egg
Vegetable oil spray
Icing:
½ cup confectioners' sugar
2 to 3 teaspoons milk

1. Preheat the air fryer to 325°F (163°C). Spray a baking pan generously with vegetable oil spray.
2. Whisk together the flour, orange zest, aniseeds, ginger, and salt in a medium bowl.
3. In a medium bowl, using a hand mixer, beat the butter and sugar on medium-high speed until well mixed, about 2 minutes. Add the molasses and egg and beat until light, about 2 minutes. Add the flour mixture and mix on low until just incorporated. Using a rubber spatula, scrape the dough into the baking pan, spreading it to the edges and smoothing the top. Sprinkle the sugar on top. Transfer the baking pan to the air fryer basket.
4. Bake until the sides are browned, but the center is still soft, about 15 minutes.
5. Remove from the air fryer and place on a wire rack to cool for 15 minutes.
6. Meanwhile, make the icing: Whisk together the sugar and 2 teaspoons of milk until well incorporated. Stir in 1 teaspoon of milk if needed for the desired consistency. Drizzle the icing onto the cookie before serving.

Blackberry Goden Cobbler

Prep time: 10 minutes | Cook time: 20 to 25 minutes | Serves 6

3 cups fresh or frozen blackberries
1¾ cups sugar, divided
1 teaspoon vanilla extract
8 tablespoons (1 stick) butter, melted
1 cup self-rising flour
Cooking spray

1. Spritz a baking pan with cooking spray.
2. Mix the blackberries, 1 cup of sugar, and vanilla in a medium bowl and stir to combine.
3. Stir together the melted butter, remaining sugar, and flour in a separate medium bowl.
4. Spread the blackberry mixture evenly in the prepared pan and top with the butter mixture.
5. Select Bake, Super Convection, set temperature to 350°F (180°C), and set time to 25 minutes. Select Start/Stop to begin preheating.
6. Once the oven has preheated, place the pan on the bake position.
7. After about 20 minutes, check if the cobbler has a golden crust and you can't see any batter bubbling while it cooks. If needed, bake for another 5 minutes.
8. Remove from the oven and place on a wire rack to cool to room temperature. Serve immediately.

Black and White Chocolate Cake

Prep time: 10 minutes | Cook time: 20 minutes | Makes 1 dozen brownies

1 egg
¼ cup brown sugar
2 tablespoons white sugar
2 tablespoons safflower oil
1 teaspoon vanilla
⅓ cup all-purpose flour
¼ cup cocoa powder
¼ cup white chocolate chips
Nonstick cooking spray

1. Spritz a baking pan with nonstick cooking spray.
2. Whisk together the egg, brown sugar, and white sugar in a medium bowl. Mix in the safflower oil and vanilla and stir to combine.
3. Add the flour and cocoa powder and stir just until incorporated. Fold in the white chocolate chips.
4. Scrape the batter into the prepared baking pan.
5. Select Bake, Super Convection, set temperature to 340ºF (171ºC), and set time to 20 minutes. Select Start/Stop to begin preheating.
6. Once the oven has preheated, place the pan on the bake position.
7. When done, the brownie should spring back when touched lightly with your fingers.
8. Transfer to a wire rack and let cool for 30 minutes before slicing to serve.

White Chocolate Cookies

Prep time: 10 minutes | Cook time: 11 minutes | Serves 10

8 ounces (227 g) unsweetened white chocolate
2 eggs, well beaten
¾ cup butter, at room temperature
1⅔ cups almond flour
½ cup coconut flour
¾ cup granulated Swerve
2 tablespoons coconut oil
⅓ teaspoon grated nutmeg
⅓ teaspoon ground allspice
⅓ teaspoon ground anise star
¼ teaspoon fine sea salt

1. Line a baking sheet with parchment paper.
2. Combine all the ingredients in a mixing bowl and knead for about 3 to 4 minutes, or until a soft dough forms. Transfer to the refrigerator to chill for 20 minutes.
3. Make the cookies: Roll the dough into 1-inch balls and transfer to the parchment-lined baking sheet, spacing 2 inches apart. Flatten each with the back of a spoon.
4. Select Bake, Super Convection, set temperature to 350ºF (180ºC), and set time to 11 minutes. Select Start/Stop to begin preheating.
5. Once the oven has preheated, place the baking sheet on the bake position.
6. When cooking is complete, the cookies should be golden and firm to the touch.
7. Transfer to a wire rack and let the cookies cool completely. Serve immediately.

Chocolate Bread Pudding

Prep time: 10 minutes | Cook time: 10 minutes | Serves 8

1 egg
1 egg yolk
¾ cup chocolate milk
3 tablespoons brown sugar
3 tablespoons peanut butter
2 tablespoons cocoa powder
1 teaspoon vanilla
5 slices firm white bread, cubed
Nonstick cooking spray

1. Spritz a baking pan with nonstick cooking spray.
2. Whisk together the egg, egg yolk, chocolate milk, brown sugar, peanut butter, cocoa powder, and vanilla until well combined.
3. Fold in the bread cubes and stir to mix well. Allow the bread soak for 10 minutes.
4. When ready, transfer the egg mixture to the prepared baking pan.
5. Select Bake, Super Convection, set temperature to 330ºF (166ºC), and set time to 10 minutes. Select Start/Stop to begin preheating.
6. Once the oven has preheated, place the pan on the bake position.
7. When done, the pudding should be just firm to the touch.
8. Serve at room temperature.

Coconut Flake-Coated Pineapple Rings

Prep time: 10 minutes | Cook time: 7 minutes | Serves 6

1 cup rice milk
⅔ cup flour
½ cup water
¼ cup unsweetened flaked coconut
4 tablespoons sugar
½ teaspoon baking soda
½ teaspoon baking powder
½ teaspoon vanilla essence
½ teaspoon ground cinnamon
¼ teaspoon ground anise star
Pinch of kosher salt
1 medium pineapple, peeled and sliced

1. In a large bowl, stir together all the ingredients except the pineapple.
2. Dip each pineapple slice into the batter until evenly coated.
3. Arrange the pineapple slices in the air fry basket.
4. Select Air Fry, Super Convection, set temperature to 380°F (193°C), and set time to 7 minutes. Select Start/Stop to begin preheating.
5. Once the oven has preheated, place the basket on the air fry position.
6. When cooking is complete, the pineapple rings should be golden brown.
7. Remove from the oven to a plate and cool for 5 minutes before serving.

Balsamic Roasted Strawberry Tart

Prep time: 5 minutes | Cook time: 25 to 30 minutes | Serves 2

1 pound (454 g) strawberries, hulled and thinly sliced
1 tablespoon honey
1 tablespoon balsamic vinegar
1 sprig basil
1 sheet frozen puff pastry, thawed
1 egg, beaten with 1 tablespoon water

1. Preheat the air fryer to 325°F (163°C). Put the strawberries in a baking pan.
2. Whisk together the honey and balsamic vinegar in a small bowl. Drizzle the mixture over the strawberries. Slice the leaves from the sprig of basil into ribbons and scatter them over the strawberries.
3. Cut out an 8-inch square from the sheet of puff pastry. Drape the pastry over the strawberries in the pan. Poke holes in the puff pastry with the tines of a fork. Brush the top of the pastry with the egg wash. Put the baking pan in the air fryer basket.
4. Bake for 25 to 30 minutes until the top of the pastry is golden brown and glossy.
5. Cool for 5 minutes before serving.

Desiccated Coconut-Pineapple Sticks

Prep time: 5 minutes | Cook time: 10 minutes | Serves 4

½ fresh pineapple, cut into sticks
¼ cup desiccated coconut

1. Place the desiccated coconut on a plate and roll the pineapple sticks in the coconut until well coated.
2. Lay the pineapple sticks in the air fry basket.
3. Select Air Fry, Super Convection, set temperature to 400°F (205°C), and set time to 10 minutes. Select Start/Stop to begin preheating.
4. Once the oven has preheated, place the basket on the air fry position.
5. When cooking is complete, the pineapple sticks should be crisp-tender.
6. Serve warm.

Cinnamon Pumpkin Seeds

Prep time: 10 minutes | Cook time: 17 to 18 minutes | Serves 2

1 cup pumpkin raw seeds
1 tablespoon ground cinnamon
2 tablespoons sugar
1 cup water
1 tablespoon olive oil

1. In a frying pan, combine the pumpkin seeds, cinnamon and water.
2. Boil the mixture over a high heat for 2 to 3 minutes.
3. Pour out the water and place the seeds on a clean kitchen towel, allowing them to dry for 20 to 30 minutes.
4. Preheat the air fryer to 340°F (171°C).
5. In a bowl, mix together the sugar, dried seeds, a pinch of cinnamon and olive oil.
6. Place the seed mixture in the fryer basket and roast for 15 minutes, shaking the basket periodically.
7. Serve immediately.

Bourbon Chocolate Pecan Pie

Prep time: 20 minutes | Cook time: 25 minutes | Serves 8

1 (9-inch) unbaked pie crust
Filling:
2 large eggs
⅓ cup butter, melted
1 cup sugar
½ cup all-purpose flour
1 cup milk chocolate chips
1½ cups coarsely chopped pecans
2 tablespoons bourbon

1. Whisk the eggs and melted butter in a large bowl until creamy.
2. Add the sugar and flour and stir to incorporate. Mix in the milk chocolate chips, pecans, and bourbon and stir until well combined.
3. Use a fork to prick holes in the bottom and sides of the pie crust. Pour the prepared filling into the pie crust. Place the pie crust in the air fry basket.
4. Select Bake, Super Convection, set temperature to 350°F (180°C), and set time to 25 minutes. Select Start/Stop to begin preheating.
5. Once the oven has preheated, place the basket on the bake position.
6. When cooking is complete, a toothpick inserted in the center should come out clean.
7. Allow the pie cool for 10 minutes in the basket before serving.

Caramelized Peach with Blueberry Yogurt

Prep time: 10 minutes | Cook time: 10 minutes | Serves 6

3 peaches, peeled, halved, and pitted
2 tablespoons packed brown sugar
1 cup plain Greek yogurt
¼ teaspoon ground cinnamon
1 teaspoon pure vanilla extract
1 cup fresh blueberries

1. Arrange the peaches in the air fry basket, cut-side up. Top with a generous sprinkle of brown sugar.
2. Select Bake, Super Convection, set temperature to 380°F (193°C), and set time to 10 minutes. Select Start/Stop to begin preheating.
3. Once the oven has preheated, place the basket on the bake position.
4. Meanwhile, whisk together the yogurt, cinnamon, and vanilla in a small bowl until smooth.
5. When cooking is complete, the peaches should be lightly browned and caramelized.
6. Remove the peaches from the oven to a plate. Serve topped with the yogurt mixture and fresh blueberries.

Triple Berry Crisp

Prep time: 10 minutes | Cook time: 12 minutes | Serves 4

½ cup fresh blueberries
½ cup chopped fresh strawberries
⅓ cup frozen raspberries, thawed
1 tablespoon honey
1 tablespoon freshly squeezed lemon juice
⅔ cup whole-wheat pastry flour
3 tablespoons packed brown sugar
2 tablespoons unsalted butter, melted

1. Place the blueberries, strawberries, and raspberries in a baking pan and drizzle the honey and lemon juice over the top.
2. Combine the pastry flour and brown sugar in a small mixing bowl.
3. Add the butter and whisk until the mixture is crumbly. Scatter the flour mixture on top of the fruit.
4. Select Bake, Super Convection, set temperature to 380°F (193°C), and set time to 12 minutes. Select Start/Stop to begin preheating.
5. Once the oven has preheated, place the pan on the bake position.
6. When cooking is complete, the fruit should be bubbly and the topping should be golden brown.
7. Remove from the oven and serve on a plate.

Lemon Cream Bars

Prep time: 25 minutes | Cook time: 22 minutes | Serves 6

4 tablespoons coconut oil, melted
¼ teaspoon plus 1 pinch of kosher salt
1 teaspoon pure vanilla extract
½ cup plus 3 tablespoons granulated sugar
½ cup plus 2 tablespoons all-purpose flour
¼ cup freshly squeezed lemon juice
Zest of 1 lemon
½ cup canned coconut cream
4 tablespoons cornstarch
Powdered sugar, to taste

1. Set the air fryer temp to 350°F (180°C).
2. In a medium bowl, combine the coconut oil, ¼ teaspoon of salt, vanilla extract, and 3 tablespoons of sugar. Mix in the flour until a soft dough forms. Transfer the mixture to a baking dish and gently press the dough to cover the bottom.
3. Place the dish in the fryer basket and bake until golden, about 10 minutes. Remove the crust from the fryer basket and set aside to cool slightly.
4. In a medium saucepan on the stovetop over medium heat, combine the lemon juice and zest, coconut cream, the pinch of kosher salt, and the remaining ½ cup of sugar,. Whisk in the cornstarch and cook until thickened, about 5 minutes. Pour the lemon mixture over the crust.
5. Place the dish in the fryer basket and cook until the mixture is bubbly and almost completely set, about 10 to 12 minutes.
6. Remove the dish from the fryer basket and set aside to cool completely. Transfer the dish to the refrigerator for at least 4 hours. Dust with the powdered sugar and slice into 6 bars before serving.

Blackberry Almond Muffins

Prep time: 10 minutes | Cook time: 12 minutes | Serves 8

½ cup fresh blackberries
Dry Ingredients:
1½ cups almond flour
1 teaspoon baking powder
½ teaspoon baking soda
½ cup Swerve
¼ teaspoon kosher salt
Wet Ingredients:
2 eggs
¼ cup coconut oil, melted
½ cup milk
½ teaspoon vanilla paste

1. Line an 8-cup muffin tin with paper liners.
2. Thoroughly combine the almond flour, baking powder, baking soda, Swerve, and salt in a mixing bowl.
3. Whisk together the eggs, coconut oil, milk, and vanilla in a separate mixing bowl until smooth.
4. Add the wet mixture to the dry and fold in the blackberries. Stir with a spatula just until well incorporated.
5. Spoon the batter into the prepared muffin cups, filling each about three-quarters full.
6. Select Bake, Super Convection, set temperature to 350°F (180°C), and set time to 12 minutes. Select Start/Stop to begin preheating.
7. Once the oven has preheated, place the muffin tin on the bake position.
8. When done, the tops should be golden and a toothpick inserted in the middle should come out clean.
9. Allow the muffins to cool in the muffin tin for 10 minutes before removing and serving

Cherry Tomatoes

Prep time: 13 minutes | Cook time: 1 hour | Makes 1 pint

1 pint (280 to 310 g) cherry or grape tomatoes, halved lengthwise

1. Place the tomato halves cut-side up in your air fryer basket. Cook on 150°F (66°C) for 1 hour. Check, then cook again for 1 hour.
2. The tomato halves should be dry enough to shake now but will still need to dry out more to store them, so shake and cook 1 hour more.
3. Shake again and check for doneness. If you are using in a cooked dish, they can be a little soft, but if you're using them in the tomato powder, they need to be bone dry, so you will cook an additional 30 minutes to 1 hour more.
4. Store in an airtight container.

Cinnamon S'mores

Prep time: 5 minutes | Cook time: 3 minutes | Makes 12 s'mores

12 whole cinnamon graham crackers, halved
2 (1.55-ounce / 44-g) chocolate bars, cut into 12 pieces
12 marshmallows

1. Arrange 12 graham cracker squares in the air fry basket in a single layer.
2. Top each square with a piece of chocolate.
3. Select Bake, Super Convection, set temperature to 350°F (180°C), and set time to 3 minutes. Select Start/Stop to begin preheating.
4. Once the oven has preheated, place the basket on the bake position.
5. After 2 minutes, remove the basket and place a marshmallow on each piece of melted chocolate. Return the basket to the oven and continue to cook for another 1 minute.
6. Remove from the oven to a serving plate.
7. Serve topped with the remaining graham cracker squares

Chocolate Pecan Pie

Prep time: 20 minutes | Cook time: 25 minutes | Serves 8

1 (9-inch) unbaked pie crust
Filling:
2 large eggs
⅓ cup butter, melted
1 cup sugar
½ cup all-purpose flour
1 cup milk chocolate chips
1½ cups coarsely chopped pecans
2 tablespoons bourbon

1. Whisk the eggs and melted butter in a large bowl until creamy.
2. Add the sugar and flour and stir to incorporate. Mix in the milk chocolate chips, pecans, and bourbon and stir until well combined.
3. Use a fork to prick holes in the bottom and sides of the pie crust. Pour the prepared filling into the pie crust. Place the pie crust in the air fry basket.
4. Select Bake, Super Convection, set temperature to 350°F (180°C), and set time to 25 minutes. Select Start/Stop to begin preheating.
5. Once the oven has preheated, place the basket on the bake position.
6. When cooking is complete, a toothpick inserted in the center should come out clean.
7. Allow the pie cool for 10 minutes in the basket before serving.

Baked Peaches and Blueberries

Prep time: 10 minutes | Cook time: 10 minutes | Serves 6

3 peaches, peeled, halved, and pitted
2 tablespoons packed brown sugar
1 cup plain Greek yogurt
¼ teaspoon ground cinnamon
1 teaspoon pure vanilla extract
1 cup fresh blueberries

1. Arrange the peaches in the air fry basket, cut-side up. Top with a generous sprinkle of brown sugar.
2. Select Bake, Super Convection, set temperature to 380°F (193°C), and set time to 10 minutes. Select Start/Stop to begin preheating.
3. Once the oven has preheated, place the basket on the bake position.
4. Meanwhile, whisk together the yogurt, cinnamon, and vanilla in a small bowl until smooth.
5. When cooking is complete, the peaches should be lightly browned and caramelized.
6. Remove the peaches from the oven to a plate. Serve topped with the yogurt mixture and fresh blueberries.

Summer Berry Crisp

Prep time: 10 minutes | Cook time: 12 minutes | Serves 4

½ cup fresh blueberries
½ cup chopped fresh strawberries
⅓ cup frozen raspberries, thawed
1 tablespoon honey
1 tablespoon freshly squeezed lemon juice
⅔ cup whole-wheat pastry flour
3 tablespoons packed brown sugar
2 tablespoons unsalted butter, melted

1. Place the blueberries, strawberries, and raspberries in a baking pan and drizzle the honey and lemon juice over the top.
2. Combine the pastry flour and brown sugar in a small mixing bowl.
3. Add the butter and whisk until the mixture is crumbly. Scatter the flour mixture on top of the fruit.
4. Select Bake, Super Convection, set temperature to 380°F (193°C), and set time to 12 minutes. Select Start/Stop to begin preheating.
5. Once the oven has preheated, place the pan on the bake position.
6. When cooking is complete, the fruit should be bubbly and the topping should be golden brown.
7. Remove from the oven and serve on a plate.

Fudgy Chocolate Brownies

Prep time: 5 minutes | Cook time: 21 minutes | Serves 8

1 stick butter, melted
1 cup Swerve
2 eggs
1 cup coconut flour
½ cup unsweetened cocoa powder
2 tablespoons flaxseed meal
1 teaspoon baking powder
1 teaspoon vanilla essence
A pinch of salt
A pinch of ground cardamom
Cooking spray

1. Spray a baking pan with cooking spray.
2. Beat together the melted butter and Swerve in a large mixing dish until fluffy. Whisk in the eggs.
3. Add the coconut flour, cocoa powder, flaxseed meal, baking powder, vanilla essence, salt, and cardamom and stir with a spatula until well incorporated. Spread the mixture evenly into the prepared baking pan.
4. Select Bake, Super Convection, set temperature to 350°F (180°C), and set time to 21 minutes. Select Start/Stop to begin preheating.
5. Once the oven has preheated, place the pan on the bake position.
6. When cooking is complete, a toothpick inserted in the center should come out clean.
7. Remove from the oven and place on a wire rack to cool completely. Cut into squares and serve immediately.

Graham Cracker Cheesecake

Prep time: 10 minutes | Cook time: 20 minutes | Serves 8

1 cup graham cracker
crumbs
3 tablespoons softened
butter
1½ (8-ounce / 227-g)
packages cream
cheese, softened
⅓ cup sugar
2 eggs
1 tablespoon flour
1 teaspoon vanilla
¼ cup chocolate syrup

1. For the crust, combine the graham cracker crumbs and butter in a small bowl and mix well. Press into the bottom of a baking pan and put in the freezer to set.
2. For the filling, combine the cream cheese and sugar in a medium bowl and mix well. Beat in the eggs, one at a time. Add the flour and vanilla.
3. Preheat the air fryer oven to 450°F (232°C).
4. Remove ⅔ cup of the filling to a small bowl and stir in the chocolate syrup until combined.
5. Pour the vanilla filling into the pan with the crust. Drop the chocolate filling over the vanilla filling by the spoonful. With a clean butter knife, stir the fillings in a zigzag pattern to marbleize them.
6. Slide the baking pan into Rack Position 1, select Convection Bake and set time to 20 minutes, or until the cheesecake is just set.
7. Cool on a wire rack for 1 hour, then chill in the refrigerator until the cheesecake is firm.
8. Serve immediately.

Black Forest Pies

Prep time: 10 minutes | Cook time: 15 minutes | Serves 6

3 tablespoons milk or dark chocolate
chips
2 tablespoons thick, hot fudge sauce
2 tablespoons chopped dried
cherries
1 (10-by-15-inch) sheet frozen puff
pastry, thawed
1 egg white, beaten
2 tablespoons sugar
½ teaspoon cinnamon

1. Preheat the air fryer oven to 350°F (177°C).
2. In a small bowl, combine the chocolate chips, fudge sauce, and dried cherries.
3. Roll out the puff pastry on a floured surface. Cut into 6 squares with a sharp knife.
4. Divide the chocolate chip mixture into the center of each puff pastry square. Fold the squares in half to make triangles. Firmly press the edges with the tines of a fork to seal.
5. Brush the triangles on all sides sparingly with the beaten egg white. Sprinkle the tops with sugar and cinnamon, then transfer to a baking pan.
6. Slide the baking pan into Rack Position 1, select Convection Bake and set time to 15 minutes, or until the triangles are golden brown.
7. The filling will be hot, so cool for at least 20 minutes before serving.

Lemon Caramelized Pear Tart

Prep time: 15 minutes | Cook time: 25 minutes | Serves 8

Juice of 1 lemon
4 cups water
3 medium or 2 large ripe
or almost ripe pears
(preferably Bosc
or Anjou) peeled,
stemmed, and halved
lengthwise
1 sheet (½ package) frozen
puff pastry, thawed
All-purpose flour, for
dusting
4 tablespoons caramel
sauce such as Smucker's
Salted Caramel, divided

1. Combine the lemon juice and water in a large bowl.
2. Remove the seeds from the pears with a melon baller and cut out the blossom end. Remove any tough fibers between the stem end and the center. As you work, place the pear halves in the acidulated water.
3. On a lightly floured cutting board, unwrap and unfold the puff pastry, roll it very lightly with a rolling pin so as to press the folds together. Place it on the sheet pan.
4. Roll about ½ inch of the pastry edges up to form a ridge around the perimeter. Crimp the corners together so as to create a solid rim around the pastry to hold in the liquid as the tart cooks.
5. Brush 2 tablespoons of caramel sauce over the bottom of the pastry.
6. Remove the pear halves from the water and blot off any remaining water with paper towels.
7. Place one of the halves on the board cut-side down and cut ¼-inch-thick slices radially. Repeat with the remaining halves. Arrange the pear slices over the pastry. Drizzle the remaining 2 tablespoons of caramel sauce over the top.
8. Select Bake. Set temperature to 350°F (180°C) and set time to 25 minutes. Press Start to begin preheating.
9. Once the unit has preheated, place the pan into the oven.
10. After 15 minutes, check the tart, rotating the pan if the crust is not browning evenly. Continue cooking for another 10 minutes, or until the pastry is golden brown, the pears are soft, and the caramel is bubbling.
11. When done, remove the pan from the oven and allow to cool for about 10 minutes.
12. Served warm.

Honey Walnut and Pistachios Baklava

Prep time: 10 minutes | Cook time: 16 minutes | Serves 10

1 cup walnut pieces
1 cup shelled raw pistachios
½ cup unsalted butter, melted
¼ cup plus 2 tablespoons honey, divided
3 tablespoons granulated sugar
1 teaspoon ground cinnamon
2 (1.9-ounce / 54-g) packages frozen miniature
    phyllo tart shells

1. Place the walnuts and pistachios in the perforated pan in an even layer.
2. Select Air Fry. Set temperature to 350ºF (180ºC) and set time to 4 minutes. Press Start to begin preheating.
3. Once the unit has preheated, place the pan into the oven.
4. After 2 minutes, remove the pan and stir the nuts. Transfer the pan back to the oven and cook for another 1 to 2 minutes until the nuts are golden brown and fragrant.
5. Meanwhile, stir together the butter, ¼ cup of honey, sugar, and cinnamon in a medium bowl.
6. When done, remove the pan from the oven and place the nuts on a cutting board and allow to cool for 5minutes. Finely chop the nuts. Add the chopped nuts and all the "nut dust" to the butter mixture and stir well.
7. Arrange the phyllo cups on the pan. Evenly fill the phyllo cups with the nut mixture, mounding it up. As you work, stir the nuts in the bowl frequently so that the syrup is evenly distributed throughout the filling.
8. Select Bake. Set temperature to 350ºF (180ºC) and set time to 12 minutes.
9. Place the pan into the oven. After about 8 minutes, check the cups. Continue cooking until the cups are golden brown and the syrup is bubbling.
10. When cooking is complete, remove the baklava from the oven, drizzle each cup with about ⅛ teaspoon of the remaining honey over the top.
11. Allow to cool for 5 minutes before serving.

Monk Fruit and Hazelnut Cake

Prep time: 5 minutes | Cook time: 20 minutes | Serves 6

1 stick butter, at room temperature
5 tablespoons liquid monk fruit
2 eggs plus 1 egg yolk, beaten
⅓ cup hazelnuts, roughly chopped
3 tablespoons sugar-free orange marmalade
6 ounces (170 g) unbleached almond flour
1 teaspoon baking soda
½ teaspoon baking powder
½ teaspoon ground cinnamon
½ teaspoon ground allspice
½ ground anise seed
Cooking spray

1. Lightly spritz a baking pan with cooking spray.
2. In a mixing bowl, whisk the butter and liquid monk fruit until the mixture is pale and smooth. Mix in the beaten eggs, hazelnuts, and marmalade and whisk again until well incorporated.
3. Add the almond flour, baking soda, baking powder, cinnamon, allspice, anise seed and stir to mix well.
4. Scrape the batter into the prepared baking pan.
5. Select Bake. Set temperature to 310ºF (154ºC) and set time to 20 minutes. Press Start to begin preheating.
6. Once the oven has preheated, place the pan into the oven.
7. When cooking is complete, the top of the cake should spring back when gently pressed with your fingers.
8. Transfer to a wire rack and let the cake cool to room temperature. Serve immediately.

Blueberry and Peach Tart

Prep time: 10 minutes | Cook time: 30 minutes | Serves 6 to 8

4 peaches, pitted and sliced
1 cup fresh blueberries
2 tablespoons cornstarch
3 tablespoons sugar
1 tablespoon freshly squeezed lemon juice
Cooking spray
1 sheet frozen puff pastry, thawed
1 tablespoon nonfat or low-fat milk
Confectioners' sugar, for dusting

1. Add the peaches, blueberries, cornstarch, sugar, and lemon juice to a large bowl and toss to coat.
2. Spritz a round baking pan with cooking spray.
3. Unfold the pastry and put on the prepared baking pan.
4. Lay the peach slices on the pan, slightly overlapping them. Scatter the blueberries over the peach.
5. Drape the pastry over the outside of the fruit and press pleats firmly together. Brush the milk over the pastry.
6. Select Bake. Set temperature to 400°F (205°C) and set time to 30 minutes. Press Start to begin preheating.
7. Once the unit has preheated, place the pan into the oven.
8. Bake until the crust is golden brown and the fruit is bubbling.
9. When cooking is complete, remove the pan from the oven and allow to cool for 10 minutes.
10. Serve the tart with the confectioners' sugar sprinkled on top.

Butter Shortbread with Lemon

Prep time: 10 minutes | Cook time: 36 to 40 minutes | Makes 4 dozen cookies

1 tablespoon grated lemon zest
1 cup granulated sugar
1 pound (454 g) unsalted butter, at room temperature
¼ teaspoon fine salt
4 cups all-purpose flour
⅓ cup cornstarch
Cooking spray

1. Add the lemon zest and sugar to a stand mixer fitted with the paddle attachment and beat on medium speed for 1 to 2 minute. Let stand for about 5 minutes. Fold in the butter and salt and blend until fluffy.
2. Mix together the flour and cornstarch in a large bowl. Add to the butter mixture and mix to combine.
3. Spritz the sheet pan with cooking spray and spread a piece of parchment paper onto the pan. Scrape the dough into the pan until even and smooth.
4. Select Bake. Set temperature to 325°F (163°C) and set time to 36 minutes. Press Start to begin preheating.
5. Once the unit has preheated, place the pan into the oven.
6. After 20 minutes, check the shortbread, rotating the pan if it is not browning evenly. Continue cooking for another 16 minutes until lightly browned.
7. When done, remove the pan from the oven. Slice and allow to cool for 5 minutes before serving.

Chocolate Coconut Cake

Prep time: 5 minutes | Cook time: 15 minutes | Serves 10

1¼ cups unsweetened bakers' chocolate
1 stick butter
1 teaspoon liquid stevia
⅓ cup shredded coconut
2 tablespoons coconut milk
2 eggs, beaten
Cooking spray

1. Lightly spritz a baking pan with cooking spray.
2. Place the chocolate, butter, and stevia in a microwave-safe bowl. Microwave for about 30 seconds until melted. Let the chocolate mixture cool to room temperature.
3. Add the remaining ingredients to the chocolate mixture and stir until well incorporated. Pour the batter into the prepared baking pan.
4. Select Bake. Set temperature to 330°F (166°C) and set time to 15 minutes. Press Start to begin preheating.
5. Once the oven has preheated, place the pan into the oven.
6. When cooking is complete, a toothpick inserted in the center should come out clean.
7. Remove from the oven and allow to cool for about 10 minutes before serving.

Coffee Chocolate Cake with Cinnamon

Prep time: 5 minutes | Cook time: 30 minutes | Serves 8

Dry Ingredients:

1½ cups almond flour

½ cup coconut meal

⅔ cup Swerve

1 teaspoon baking powder

¼ teaspoon salt

Wet Ingredients:

1 egg

1 stick butter, melted

½ cup hot strongly brewed coffee

Topping:

½ cup confectioner's Swerve

¼ cup coconut flour

3 tablespoons coconut oil

1 teaspoon ground cinnamon

½ teaspoon ground cardamom

1. In a medium bowl, combine the almond flour, coconut meal, Swerve, baking powder, and salt.
2. In a large bowl, whisk the egg, melted butter, and coffee until smooth.
3. Add the dry mixture to the wet and stir until well incorporated. Transfer the batter to a greased baking pan.
4. Stir together all the ingredients for the topping in a small bowl. Spread the topping over the batter and smooth the top with a spatula.
5. Select Bake. Set temperature to 330°F (166°C) and set time to 30 minutes. Press Start to begin preheating.
6. Once the oven has preheated, place the pan into the oven.
7. When cooking is complete, the cake should spring back when gently pressed with your fingers.
8. Rest for 10 minutes before serving.

Vanilla Cookies with Chocolate Chips

Prep time: 10 minutes | Cook time: 22 minutes | Makes 30 cookies

⅓ cup (80g) organic brown sugar

⅓ cup (80g) organic cane sugar

4 ounces (112g) cashew-based vegan butter

½ cup coconut cream

1 teaspoon vanilla extract

2 tablespoons ground flaxseed

1 teaspoon baking powder

1 teaspoon baking soda

Pinch of salt

2¼ cups (220g) almond flour

½ cup (90g) dairy-free dark chocolate chips

1. Line a baking sheet with parchment paper.
2. Mix together the brown sugar, cane sugar, and butter in a medium bowl or the bowl of a stand mixer. Cream together with a mixer.
3. Fold in the coconut cream, vanilla, flaxseed, baking powder, baking soda, and salt. Stir well.
4. Add the almond flour, a little at a time, mixing after each addition until fully incorporated. Stir in the chocolate chips with a spatula.
5. Scoop the dough onto the prepared baking sheet.
6. Select Bake. Set temperature to 325°F (163°C) and set time to 22 minutes. Press Start to begin preheating.
7. Once the unit has preheated, place the baking sheet into the oven.
8. Bake until the cookies are golden brown.
9. When cooking is complete, transfer the baking sheet onto a wire rack to cool completely before serving.

Chocolate Vanilla Cheesecake

Prep time: 5 minutes | Cook time: 18 minutes | Serves 6

Crust:

½ cup butter, melted

½ cup coconut flour

2 tablespoons stevia

Cooking spray

Topping:

4 ounces (113 g) unsweetened baker's chocolate

1 cup mascarpone cheese, at room temperature

1 teaspoon vanilla extract

2 drops peppermint extract

1. Lightly coat a baking pan with cooking spray.
2. In a mixing bowl, whisk together the butter, flour, and stevia until well combined. Transfer the mixture to the prepared baking pan.
3. Select Bake. Set temperature to 350°F (180°C) and set time to 18 minutes. Press Start to begin preheating.
4. Once the oven has preheated, place the pan into the oven.
5. When done, a toothpick inserted in the center should come out clean.
6. Remove the crust from the oven to a wire rack to cool.
7. Once cooled completely, place it in the freezer for 20 minutes.
8. When ready, combine all the ingredients for the topping in a small bowl and stir to incorporate.
9. Spread this topping over the crust and let it sit for another 15 minutes in the freezer.
10. Serve chilled.

Strawberry Crumble with Rhubarb

Prep time: 10 minutes | Cook time: 12 to 17 minutes | Serves 6

1½ cups sliced fresh strawberries
⅓ cup sugar
¾ cup sliced rhubarb
⅔ cup quick-cooking oatmeal
¼ cup packed brown sugar
½ cup whole-wheat pastry flour
½ teaspoon ground cinnamon
3 tablespoons unsalted butter, melted

1. Place the strawberries, sugar, and rhubarb in a baking pan and toss to coat.
2. Combine the oatmeal, brown sugar, pastry flour, and cinnamon in a medium bowl.
3. Add the melted butter to the oatmeal mixture and stir until crumbly. Sprinkle this generously on top of the strawberries and rhubarb.
4. Select Bake. Set temperature to 370°F (188°C) and set time to 12 minutes. Press Start to begin preheating.
5. Once the unit has preheated, place the pan into the oven.
6. Bake until the fruit is bubbly and the topping is golden brown. Continue cooking for an additional 2 to 5 minutes if needed.
7. When cooking is complete, remove from the oven and serve warm.

Raspberry Muffins

Prep time: 5 minutes | Cook time: 15 minutes | Serves 6

2 cups almond flour
¾ cup Swerve
1¼ teaspoons baking powder
⅓ teaspoon ground allspice
⅓ teaspoon ground anise star
½ teaspoon grated lemon zest
¼ teaspoon salt
2 eggs
1 cup sour cream
½ cup coconut oil
½ cup raspberries

1. Line a muffin pan with 6 paper liners.
2. In a mixing bowl, mix the almond flour, Swerve, baking powder, allspice, anise, lemon zest, and salt.
3. In another mixing bowl, beat the eggs, sour cream, and coconut oil until well mixed. Add the egg mixture to the flour mixture and stir to combine. Mix in the raspberries.
4. Scrape the batter into the prepared muffin cups, filling each about three-quarters full.
5. Select Bake. Set temperature to 345°F (174°C) and set time to 15 minutes. Press Start to begin preheating.
6. Once the oven has preheated, place the muffin pan into the oven.
7. When cooking is complete, the tops should be golden and a toothpick inserted in the middle should come out clean.
8. Allow the muffins to cool for 10 minutes in the muffin pan before removing and serving.

Vanilla Walnuts Tart with Cloves

Prep time: 5 minutes | Cook time: 13 minutes | Serves 6

1 cup coconut milk
½ cup walnuts, ground
½ cup Swerve
½ cup almond flour
½ stick butter, at room temperature
2 eggs
1 teaspoon vanilla essence
¼ teaspoon ground cardamom
¼ teaspoon ground cloves
Cooking spray

1. Coat a baking pan with cooking spray.
2. Combine all the ingredients except the oil in a large bowl and stir until well blended. Spoon the batter mixture into the baking pan.
3. Select Bake. Set temperature to 360°F (182°C) and set time to 13 minutes. Press Start to begin preheating.
4. Once the oven has preheated, place the pan into the oven.
5. When cooking is complete, a toothpick inserted into the center of the tart should come out clean.
6. Remove from the oven and place on a wire rack to cool. Serve immediately.

Chapter 10 Fast and Easy Everyday Favorites

Crunchy Tortilla Chips

Prep time: 5 minutes | Cook time: 10 minutes | Serves 4

4 six-inch corn tortillas, cut in half and slice into thirds
1 tablespoon canola oil
¼ teaspoon kosher salt
Cooking spray

1. Spritz the air fry basket with cooking spray.
2. On a clean work surface, brush the tortilla chips with canola oil, then transfer the chips to the air fry basket.
3. Select Air Fry, set temperature to 360ºF (182ºC) and set time to 10 minutes. Select Start/Stop to begin preheating.
4. Once preheated, place the basket on the air fry position. Flip the chips and sprinkle with salt halfway through the cooking time.
5. When cooked, the chips will be crunchy and lightly browned. Transfer the chips to a plate lined with paper towels. Serve immediately.

Crispy Zucchini

Prep time: 5 minutes | Cook time: 10 minutes | Serves 4

1 medium zucchini, cut into 48 sticks
¼ cup seasoned bread crumbs
1 tablespoon melted buttery spread
Cooking spray

1. Spritz the air fry basket with cooking spray and set aside.
2. In 2 different shallow bowls, add the seasoned bread crumbs and the buttery spread.
3. One by one, dredge the zucchini sticks into the buttery spread, then roll in the bread crumbs to coat evenly. Arrange the crusted sticks in the air fry basket.
4. Select Air Fry, set temperature to 360ºF (182ºC) and set time to 10 minutes. Select Start/Stop to begin preheating.
5. When preheated, place the basket on the air fry position. Stir the sticks halfway through the cooking time.
6. When done, the sticks should be golden brown and crispy. Transfer the fries to a plate. Rest for 5 minutes and serve warm

Beer Battered Onion Rings

Prep time: 10 minutes | Cook time: 16 minutes | Serves 2 to 4

⅔ cup all-purpose flour
1 teaspoon paprika
½ teaspoon baking soda
1 teaspoon salt
½ teaspoon freshly ground black pepper
1 egg, beaten
¾ cup beer
1½ cups bread crumbs
1 tablespoons olive oil
1 large Vidalia onion, peeled and sliced into ½-inch rings
Cooking spray

1. Spritz the air fry basket with cooking spray.
2. Combine the flour, paprika, baking soda, salt, and ground black pepper in a bowl. Stir to mix well.
3. Combine the egg and beer in a separate bowl. Stir to mix well.
4. Make a well in the center of the flour mixture, then pour the egg mixture in the well. Stir to mix everything well.
5. Pour the bread crumbs and olive oil in a shallow plate. Stir to mix well.
6. Dredge the onion rings gently into the flour and egg mixture, then shake the excess off and put into the plate of bread crumbs. Flip to coat the both sides well. Arrange the onion rings in the air fry basket.
7. Select Air Fry, set temperature to 360ºF (182ºC) and set time to 16 minutes. Select Start/Stop to begin preheating.
8. Once preheated, place the basket on the air fry position. Flip the rings and put the bottom rings to the top halfway through.
9. When cooked, the rings will be golden brown and crunchy. Remove the pan from the oven.
10. Serve immediately.

Fast Corn on the Cob

Prep time: 10 minutes | Cook time: 10 minutes | Serves 4

2 tablespoons mayonnaise
2 teaspoons minced garlic
½ teaspoon sea salt
1 cup panko bread crumbs
4 (4-inch length) ears corn on the cob, husk and silk removed
Cooking spray

1. Spritz the air fry basket with cooking spray.
2. Combine the mayonnaise, garlic, and salt in a bowl. Stir to mix well. Pour the panko on a plate.
3. Brush the corn on the cob with mayonnaise mixture, then roll the cob in the bread crumbs and press to coat well.
4. Transfer the corn on the cob in the air fry basket and spritz with cooking spray.
5. Select Air Fry, set temperature to 400ºF (205ºC) and set time to 10 minutes. Select Start/Stop to begin preheating.
6. Once the oven has preheated, place the basket on the air fry position. Flip the corn on the cob at least three times during the cooking.
7. When cooked, the corn kernels on the cob should be almost browned. Remove the basket from the oven.
8. Serve immediately.

Butternut Squash with Fried-Hazelnuts

Prep time: 10 minutes | Cook time: 23 minutes | Makes 3 cups

2 tablespoons whole hazelnuts
3 cups butternut squash, peeled, deseeded and cubed
¼ teaspoon kosher salt
¼ teaspoon freshly ground black pepper
2 teaspoons olive oil
Cooking spray

1. Spritz the air fry basket with cooking spray. Spread the hazelnuts in the basket.
2. Select Air Fry, , set temperature to 300ºF (150ºC) and set time to 3 minutes. Select Start/Stop to begin preheating.
3. Once preheated, place the basket on the air fry position.
4. When done, the hazelnuts should be soft. Remove from the oven. Chopped the hazelnuts roughly and transfer to a small bowl. Set aside.
5. Put the butternut squash in a large bowl, then sprinkle with salt and pepper and drizzle with olive oil. Toss to coat well. Transfer the squash to the lightly greased basket.
6. Select Air Fry, set temperature to 360ºF (182ºC) and set time to 20 minutes.
7. Place the basket on the air fry position. Flip the squash halfway through the cooking time.
8. When cooking is complete, the squash will be soft. Transfer the squash to a plate and sprinkle with the chopped hazelnuts before serving.

Jalapeño Cheddar Cornbread

Prep time: 10 minutes | Cook time: 20 minutes | Serves 8

⅔ cup cornmeal
⅓ cup all-purpose flour
¾ teaspoon baking powder
2 tablespoons buttery spread,
    melted
½ teaspoon kosher salt
1 tablespoon granulated sugar
¾ cup whole milk
1 large egg, beaten
1 jalapeño pepper, thinly sliced
⅓ cup shredded sharp Cheddar
    cheese
Cooking spray

1. Spritz a baking pan with cooking spray.
2. Combine all the ingredients in a large bowl. Stir to mix well. Pour the mixture in the baking pan.
3. Select Bake , set temperature to 300ºF (150ºC) and set time to 20 minutes. Select Start/Stop to begin preheating.
4. Once preheated, place the pan on the bake position.
5. When the cooking is complete, a toothpick inserted in the center of the bread should come out clean.
6. Remove the baking pan from the oven and allow the bread to cool for 5 minutes before slicing to serve.

Quick Edamame

Prep time: 5 minutes | Cook time: 7 minutes | Serves 6

1½ pounds (680 g) unshelled
    edamame
2 tablespoons olive oil
1 teaspoon sea salt

1. Place the edamame in a large bowl, then drizzle with olive oil. Toss to coat well. Transfer the edamame to the air fry basket.
2. Select Air Fry , set temperature to 400ºF (205ºC) and set time to 7 minutes. Select Start/Stop to begin preheating.
3. Once preheated, place the basket on the air fry position. Stir the edamame at least three times during cooking.
4. When done, the edamame will be tender and warmed through.
5. Transfer the cooked edamame onto a plate and sprinkle with salt. Toss to combine well and set aside for 3 minutes to infuse before serving.

Maple Bacon Pinwheels

Prep time: 5 minutes | Cook time: 10 minutes | Makes 8 pinwheels

1 sheet puff pastry
2 tablespoons maple syrup
¼ cup brown sugar
8 slices bacon
Ground black pepper, to taste
Cooking spray

1. Spritz the air fry basket with cooking spray.
2. Roll the puff pastry into a 10-inch square with a rolling pin on a clean work surface, then cut the pastry into 8 strips.
3. Brush the strips with maple syrup and sprinkle with sugar, leaving a 1-inch far end uncovered.
4. Arrange each slice of bacon on each strip, leaving a ⅛-inch length of bacon hang over the end close to you. Sprinkle with black pepper.
5. From the end close to you, roll the strips into pinwheels, then dab the uncovered end with water and seal the rolls.
6. Arrange the pinwheels in the air fry basket and spritz with cooking spray.
7. Select Air Fry , set temperature to 360ºF (182ºC) and set time to 10 minutes. Select Start/Stop to begin preheating.
8. Once preheated, place the basket on the air fry position. Flip the pinwheels halfway through.
9. When cooking is complete, the pinwheels should be golden brown. Remove the pan from the oven.
10. Serve immediately.

French Fries with Ketchup

Prep time: 5 minutes | Cook time: 25 minutes | Serves 2

2 russet potatoes, peeled and cut
    into ½-inch sticks
2 teaspoons olive oil
Salt, to taste
¼ cup ketchup, for serving

1. Bring a pot of salted water to a boil. Put the potato sticks into the pot and blanch for 4 minutes.
2. Rinse the potatoes under running cold water and pat dry with paper towels.
3. Put the potato sticks in a large bowl and drizzle with olive oil. Toss to coat well.
4. Transfer the potato sticks to the air fry basket.
5. Select Air Fry, set temperature to 400°F (205°C) and set time to 25 minutes. Select Start/Stop to begin preheating.
6. Once the oven has preheated, place the basket on the air fry position. Stir the potato sticks and sprinkle with salt halfway through.
7. When cooked, the potato sticks will be crispy and golden brown. Remove the French fries from the oven and serve with ketchup.

Candy Coated Pecans

Prep time: 5 minutes | Cook time: 10 minutes | Makes 4 cups

2 egg whites
1 tablespoon cumin
2 teaspoons smoked paprika
½ cup brown sugar
2 teaspoons kosher salt
1 pound (454 g) pecan halves
Cooking spray

1. Spritz the air fry basket with cooking spray.
2. Combine the egg whites, cumin, paprika, sugar, and salt in a large bowl. Stir to mix well. Add the pecans to the bowl and toss to coat well.
3. Transfer the pecans to the air fry basket.
4. Select Air Fry , set temperature to 300°F (150°C) and set time to 10 minutes. Select Start/Stop to begin preheating.
5. Once the oven has preheated, place the basket on the air fry position. Stir the pecans at least two times during the cooking.
6. When cooking is complete, the pecans should be lightly caramelized. Remove the basket from the oven.
7. Serve immediately.

Lime Avocado Wedge

Prep time: 10 minutes | Cook time: 8 minutes | Makes 12 fries

1 cup all-purpose flour
3 tablespoons lime juice
¾ cup orange juice
1¼ cups plain dried bread crumbs
1 cup yellow cornmeal
1½ tablespoons chili powder
2 large Hass avocados, peeled, pitted,
    and cut into wedges
Coarse sea salt, to taste
Cooking spray

1. Spritz the air fry basket with cooking spray.
2. Pour the flour in a bowl. Mix the lime juice with orange juice in a second bowl. Combine the bread crumbs, cornmeal, and chili powder in a third bowl.
3. Dip the avocado wedges in the bowl of flour to coat well, then dredge the wedges into the bowl of juice mixture, and then dunk the wedges in the bread crumbs mixture. Shake the excess off.
4. Arrange the coated avocado wedges in a single layer in the air fry basket. Spritz with cooking spray.
5. Select Air Fry, set temperature to 400°F (205°C) and set time to 8 minutes. Select Start/Stop to begin preheating.
6. Once preheated, place the basket on the air fry position. Stir the avocado wedges and sprinkle with salt halfway through the cooking time.
7. When cooking is complete, the avocado wedges should be tender and crispy.
8. Serve immediately.

Creamy Mushroom Cheese Frittata

Prep time: 6 minutes | Cook time: 15 minutes | Serves 3

6 eggs
¼ cup sour cream
½ cup shredded Swiss cheese
Kosher salt and ground black pepper,
    to taste
1 teaspoon hot paprika
2 tablespoons olive oil
2 cloves garlic, crushed
6 ounces (170 g) brown mushrooms,
    sliced
2 tablespoons roughly chopped fresh parsley

1. Start by preheating the air fryer to 350°F (180°C).
2. Spritz the sides and bottom of the baking pan with nonstick cooking oil.
3. In a mixing bowl, thoroughly combine all the ingredients.
4. Pour the mixture into the prepared baking pan.
5. Place the baking pan in the corresponding position in the air fryer. Select Bake and cook the frittata for approximately 15 minutes, or until a toothpick comes out dry and clean.
6. Bon appétit!

Potato Cheese Sticks

Prep time: 6 minutes | Cook time: 14 minutes | Serves 4

1 cup mashed boiled potato
1 cup grated Cheddar cheese
1 tablespoon miso paste
1 cup all-purpose flour
½ teaspoon coriander seeds
Sea salt and ground black pepper,
    to taste
1 egg, beaten
1 cup bread crumbs
2 tablespoons Kewpie Japanese
    mayonnaise

1. Start by preheating the air fryer to 400°F (205°C).
2. Mix all the ingredients, except for the bread crumbs, in a bowl. Press the mixture into a parchment-lined baking pan and allow it to freeze until firm.
3. Cut the mixture into sticks and roll them into the bread crumbs; place the sticks in a lightly oiled crisper tray.
4. Place the crisper tray in the corresponding position in the air fryer. Select Air Fry and cook the sticks for about 14 minutes, shaking the crisper tray halfway through the cooking time.
5. Bon appétit!

Pork and Turkey Cheese Meatballs

Prep time: 5 minutes | Cook time: 15 minutes | Serves 4

½ pound (227 g) ground pork
½ pound (227 g) ground turkey
1 onion, minced
2 garlic cloves, minced
¼ cup Italian-style bread crumbs
¼ cup grated Parmesan cheese
1 large-sized egg, whisked
Sea salt and ground black pepper,
    to taste

1. Start by preheating the air fryer to 380°F (193°C).
2. Mix all the ingredients until everything is well combined. Form the mixture into balls. Transfer to the crisper tray.
3. Place the crisper tray in the corresponding position in the air fryer. Select Air Fry and cook the meatballs for about 15 minutes or until cooked through, shaking the crisper tray halfway through the cooking time.
4. Bon appétit!

Eggs Salad with Yogurt

Prep time: 5 minutes | Cook time: 15 minutes | Serves 4

6 eggs
4 tablespoons Greek-style yogurt
4 tablespoons mayonnaise
3 tablespoons chopped scallions
1 tablespoon Dijon mustard
Sea salt and ground black pepper, to taste

1. Start by preheating the air fryer to 270ºF (132ºC).
2. Place the eggs in the crisper tray.
3. Place the crisper tray in the corresponding position in the air fryer. Select Air Fry and cook the eggs for about 15 minutes.
4. Peel and chop the eggs; place them in a salad bowl and add in the remaining ingredients. Gently toss to combine.
5. Place the salad in the refrigerator until ready to serve. Bon appétit!

Eggs Muffins with Bacon

Prep time: 6 minutes | Cook time: 15 minutes | Serves 4

6 eggs
6 tablespoons crumbled cottage cheese
2 tablespoons chopped scallions
1 teaspoon minced garlic
3 ounces (85 g) bacon, chopped
1 teaspoon paprika
Sea salt and ground black pepper, to taste

1. Start by preheating the air fryer to 350ºF (180ºC).
2. Spritz the silicone molds with nonstick cooking oil.
3. In a mixing bowl, thoroughly combine all the ingredients.
4. Pour the mixture into the prepared silicone molds and lower them into the baking pan.
5. Place the baking pan in the corresponding position in the air fryer. Select Bake and cook the egg muffins for approximately 15 minutes, or until a toothpick comes out dry and clean.
6. Bon appétit!

Milk Rabanadas

Prep time: 5 minutes | Cook time: 8 minutes | Serves 2

4 slices baguette
½ cup full-fat milk
4 tablespoons granulated sugar
2 eggs, beaten
½ teaspoon ground cinnamon
2 tablespoons coconut oil

1. Start by preheating the air fryer to 330ºF (166ºC).
2. Toss the bread slices with the remaining ingredients. Transfer to the crisper tray.
3. Place the crisper tray in the corresponding position in the air fryer. Select Air Fry and cook the bread slices for about 4 minutes; turn them over and cook for a further 3 to 4 minutes.
4. Bon appétit!

Cauliflower Steaks

Prep time: 5 minutes | Cook time: 20 minutes | Serves 4

1 pound (454 g) cauliflower, cut into 4 steaks
4 tablespoons olive oil
1 teaspoon minced garlic
1 teaspoon cayenne pepper
½ teaspoon cumin seeds
Coarse sea salt and ground black pepper, to taste

1. Start by preheating the air fryer to 390ºF (199ºC).
2. Toss the cauliflower steaks with the remaining ingredients.
3. Place the cauliflower steaks in a lightly greased crisper tray.
4. Place the crisper tray in the corresponding position in the air fryer. Select Air Fry and cook the cauliflower steaks for about 20 minutes, turning them over halfway through the cooking time.
5. Bon appétit!

Bulgur and Mushrooms Fritters

Prep time: 8 minutes | Cook time: 15 minutes | Serves 4

1½ cups cooked bulgur
1 cup chopped brown mushrooms
1 medium onion, chopped
2 cloves garlic, finely chopped
1 cup crushed crackers
2 tablespoons butter
2 tablespoons chopped fresh parsley
Sea salt and ground black pepper,
    to taste

1. Start by preheating the air fryer to 380°F (193°C).
2. Mix all the ingredients until everything is well combined. Form the mixture into balls. Transfer to the crisper tray.
3. Place the crisper tray in the corresponding position in the air fryer. Select Air Fry and cook the balls for about 15 minutes or until cooked through, shaking the crisper tray halfway through the cooking time.
4. Bon appétit!

Southwest Lemony Corn and Bell Pepper

Prep time: 10 minutes | Cook time: 10 minutes | Serves 4

Corn:
1½ cups thawed frozen corn kernels
1 cup mixed diced bell peppers
1 jalapeño, diced
1 cup diced yellow onion
½ teaspoon ancho chile powder
1 tablespoon fresh lemon juice
1 teaspoon ground cumin
½ teaspoon kosher salt
Cooking spray
For Serving:
¼ cup feta cheese
¼ cup chopped fresh cilantro
1 tablespoon fresh lemon juice

1. Spritz the air fry basket with cooking spray.
2. Combine the ingredients for the corn in a large bowl. Stir to mix well.
3. Pour the mixture into the air fry basket.
4. Select Air Fry, Super Convection, set temperature to 375°F (190°C) and set time to 10 minutes. Select Start/Stop to begin preheating.
5. Once the oven has preheated, place the basket on the air fry position. Stir the mixture halfway through the cooking time.
6. When done, the corn and bell peppers should be soft.
7. Transfer them onto a large plate, then spread with feta cheese and cilantro. Drizzle with lemon juice and serve.

Vanilla Cinnamon Toast

Prep time: 5 minutes | Cook time: 5 minutes | Serves 6

1½ teaspoons cinnamon
1½ teaspoons vanilla extract
½ cup sugar
2 teaspoons ground black pepper
2 tablespoons melted coconut oil
12 slices whole wheat bread

1. Combine all the ingredients, except for the bread, in a large bowl. Stir to mix well.
2. Dunk the bread in the bowl of mixture gently to coat and infuse well. Shake the excess off. Arrange the bread slices in the air fry basket.
3. Select Air Fry, Super Convection, set temperature to 400°F (205°C) and set time to 5 minutes. Select Start/Stop to begin preheating.
4. Once the oven has preheated, place the basket on the air fry position. Flip the bread halfway through.
5. When cooking is complete, the bread should be golden brown.
6. Remove the bread slices from the oven and slice to serve.

Parmesan Shrimps

Prep time: 10 minutes | Cook time: 8 minutes | Serves 4 to 6

⅔ cup grated Parmesan cheese
4 minced garlic cloves
1 teaspoon onion powder
½ teaspoon oregano
1 teaspoon basil
1 teaspoon ground black pepper
2 tablespoons olive oil
2 pounds (907 g) cooked large shrimps, peeled and deveined
Lemon wedges, for topping
Cooking spray

1. Spritz the air fry basket with cooking spray.
2. Combine all the ingredients, except for the shrimps, in a large bowl. Stir to mix well.
3. Dunk the shrimps in the mixture and toss to coat well. Shake the excess off. Arrange the shrimps in the air fry basket.
4. Select Air Fry, Super Convection, set temperature to 350ºF (180ºC) and set time to 8 minutes. Select Start/Stop to begin preheating.
5. Once the oven has preheated, place the basket on the air fry position. Flip the shrimps halfway through the cooking time.
6. When cooking is complete, the shrimps should be opaque. Remove the pan from the oven.
7. Transfer the cooked shrimps on a large plate and squeeze the lemon wedges over before serving.

Manchego Cheese Wafers

Prep time: 5 minutes | Cook time: 5 minutes | Serves 2

1 cup shredded aged Manchego cheese
1 teaspoon all-purpose flour
½ teaspoon cumin seeds
¼ teaspoon cracked black pepper

1. Line the air fry basket with parchment paper.
2. Combine the cheese and flour in a bowl. Stir to mix well. Spread the mixture in the basket into a 4-inch round.
3. Combine the cumin and black pepper in a small bowl. Stir to mix well. Sprinkle the cumin mixture over the cheese round.
4. Select Air Fry, Super Convection, set temperature to 375ºF (190ºC) and set time to 5 minutes. Select Start/Stop to begin preheating.
5. Once preheated, place the basket on the air fry position.
6. When cooked, the cheese will be lightly browned and frothy.
7. Use tongs to transfer the cheese wafer onto a plate and slice to serve.

Cherry Tomato with Basil

Prep time: 5 minutes | Cook time: 5 minutes | Serves 2

2 cups cherry tomatoes
1 clove garlic, thinly sliced
1 teaspoon olive oil
⅛ teaspoon kosher salt
1 tablespoon freshly chopped basil, for topping
Cooking spray

1. Spritz a baking pan with cooking spray and set aside.
2. In a large bowl, toss together the cherry tomatoes, sliced garlic, olive oil, and kosher salt. Spread the mixture in an even layer in the prepared pan.
3. Select Bake, Super Convection, set temperature to 360ºF (182ºC) and set time to 5 minutes. Select Start/Stop to begin preheating.
4. Once the oven has preheated, place the pan on the bake position.
5. When cooking is complete, the tomatoes should be the soft and wilted.
6. Transfer to a bowl and rest for 5 minutes. Top with the chopped basil and serve warm.

Shrimp, Sausage and Corn Bake

Prep time: 10 minutes | Cook time: 18 minutes | Serves 2

1 ear corn, husk and silk removed, cut into 2-inch rounds
8 ounces (227 g) red potatoes, unpeeled, cut into 1-inch pieces
2 teaspoons Old Bay Seasoning, divided
2 teaspoons vegetable oil, divided
¼ teaspoon ground black pepper
8 ounces (227 g) large shrimps (about 12 shrimps), deveined
6 ounces (170 g) andouille or chorizo sausage, cut into 1-inch pieces
2 garlic cloves, minced
1 tablespoon chopped fresh parsley

1. Put the corn rounds and potatoes in a large bowl. Sprinkle with 1 teaspoon of Old Bay seasoning and drizzle with vegetable oil. Toss to coat well.
2. Transfer the corn rounds and potatoes onto a baking pan.
3. Select Bake, Super Convection, set temperature to 400°F (205°C) and set time to 18 minutes. Select Start/Stop to begin preheating.
4. Once preheated, place the pan on the bake position.
5. After 6 minutes, remove the pan from the oven. Stir the corn rounds and potatoes. Return the pan to the oven and continue cooking.
6. Meanwhile, cut slits into the shrimps but be careful not to cut them through. Combine the shrimps, sausage, remaining Old Bay seasoning, and remaining vegetable oil in the large bowl. Toss to coat well.
7. After 6 minutes, remove the pan from the oven. Add the shrimps and sausage to the pan. Return the pan to the oven and continue cooking for 6 minutes. Stir the shrimp mixture halfway through the cooking time.
8. When done, the shrimps should be opaque. Remove the pan from the oven.
9. Transfer the dish to a plate and spread with parsley before serving.

Chips with Lemony Cream Dip

Prep time: 10 minutes | Cook time: 15 minutes | Serves 2 to 4

2 large russet potatoes, sliced into ⅛-inch slices, rinsed
Sea salt and freshly ground black pepper, to taste
Cooking spray
Lemony Cream Dip:
½ cup sour cream
¼ teaspoon lemon juice
2 scallions, white part only, minced
1 tablespoon olive oil
¼ teaspoon salt
Freshly ground black pepper, to taste

1. Soak the potato slices in water for 10 minutes, then pat dry with paper towels.
2. Transfer the potato slices in the air fry basket. Spritz the slices with cooking spray.
3. Select Air Fry, Super Convection, set temperature to 300°F (150°C) and set time to 15 minutes. Select Start/Stop to begin preheating.
4. Once the oven has preheated, place the basket on the air fry position. Stir the potato slices three times during cooking. Sprinkle with salt and ground black pepper in the last minute.
5. Meanwhile, combine the ingredients for the dip in a small bowl. Stir to mix well.
6. When cooking is complete, the potato slices will be crispy and golden brown. Remove the basket from the oven.
7. Serve the potato chips immediately with the dip.

Air-Fried Brussels Sprouts

Prep time: 5 minutes | Cook time: 20 minutes | Serves 4

¼ teaspoon salt
⅛ teaspoon ground black pepper
1 tablespoon extra-virgin olive oil
1 pound (454 g) Brussels sprouts, trimmed and halved
Lemon wedges, for garnish

1. Combine the salt, black pepper, and olive oil in a large bowl. Stir to mix well.
2. Add the Brussels sprouts to the bowl of mixture and toss to coat well. Arrange the Brussels sprouts in the air fry basket.
3. Select Air Fry, Super Convection, set temperature to 350°F (180°C) and set time to 20 minutes. Select Start/Stop to begin preheating.
4. Once preheated, place the basket on the air fry position. Stir the Brussels sprouts two times during cooking.
5. When cooked, the Brussels sprouts will be lightly browned and wilted. Remove from the oven.
6. Transfer the cooked Brussels sprouts to a large plate and squeeze the lemon wedges on top to serve.

Buttered Knots with Parsley

Prep time: 5 minutes | Cook time: 5 minutes | Makes 8 knots

1 teaspoon dried parsley
¼ cup melted butter
2 teaspoons garlic powder
1 (11-ounce / 312-g) tube refrigerated French bread dough, cut into 8 slices

1. Combine the parsley, butter, and garlic powder in a bowl. Stir to mix well.
2. Place the French bread dough slices on a clean work surface, then roll each slice into a 6-inch long rope. Tie the ropes into knots and arrange them on a plate.
3. Transfer the knots into a baking pan. Brush the knots with butter mixture.
4. Select Air Fry, Super Convection, set temperature to 350°F (180°C) and set time to 5 minutes. Select Start/Stop to begin preheating.
5. Once the oven has preheated, slide the pan into the oven. Flip the knots halfway through the cooking time.
6. When done, the knots should be golden brown. Remove the pan from the oven.
7. Serve immediately.

Okra Chips

Prep time: 5 minutes | Cook time: 16 minutes | Serves 6

2 pounds (907 g) fresh okra pods, cut into 1-inch pieces
2 tablespoons canola oil
1 teaspoon coarse sea salt

1. Stir the oil and salt in a bowl to mix well. Add the okra and toss to coat well. Place the okra in the air fry basket.
2. Select Air Fry, Super Convection, set temperature to 400°F (205°C) and set time to 16 minutes. Select Start/Stop to begin preheating.
3. Once the oven has preheated, place the basket on the air fry position. Flip the okra at least three times during cooking.
4. When cooked, the okra should be lightly browned. Remove from the oven.
5. Serve immediately.

Baked Green Beans

Prep time: 5 minutes | Cook time: 10 minutes | Makes 2 cups

½ teaspoon lemon pepper
2 teaspoons granulated garlic
½ teaspoon salt
1 tablespoon olive oil
2 cups fresh green beans, trimmed and snapped in half

1. Combine the lemon pepper, garlic, salt, and olive oil in a bowl. Stir to mix well.
2. Add the green beans to the bowl of mixture and toss to coat well.
3. Arrange the green beans in the air fry basket.
4. Select Bake, Super Convection, set temperature to 370°F (188°C) and set time to 10 minutes. Select Start/Stop to begin preheating.
5. Once preheated, place the basket on the bake position. Stir the green beans halfway through the cooking time.
6. When cooking is complete, the green beans will be tender and crispy. Remove from the oven.
7. Serve immediately.

Salmon Fillet and Carrot Croquettes

Prep time: 15 minutes | Cook time: 10 minutes | Serves 6

2 egg whites
1 cup almond flour
1 cup panko bread crumbs
1 pound (454 g) chopped salmon
    fillet
⅔ cup grated carrots
2 tablespoons minced garlic cloves
½ cup chopped onion
2 tablespoons chopped chives
Cooking spray

1. Spritz the air fry basket with cooking spray.
2. Whisk the egg whites in a bowl. Put the flour in a second bowl. Pour the bread crumbs in a third bowl. Set aside.
3. Combine the salmon, carrots, garlic, onion, and chives in a large bowl. Stir to mix well.
4. Form the mixture into balls with your hands. Dredge the balls into the flour, then egg, and then bread crumbs to coat well.
5. Arrange the salmon balls in the air fry basket and spritz with cooking spray.
6. Select Air Fry, Super Convection, set temperature to 350ºF (180ºC) and set time to 10 minutes. Select Start/Stop to begin preheating.
7. Once preheated, place the basket on the air fry position. Flip the salmon balls halfway through cooking.
8. When cooking is complete, the salmon balls will be crispy and browned. Remove the basket from the oven.
9. Serve immediately.

Garlicky Zucchini and Summer Squash

Prep time: 10 minutes | Cook time: 10 minutes | Serves 4

2 large zucchini, peeled and
    spiralized
2 large yellow summer squash,
    peeled and spiralized
1 tablespoon olive oil, divided
½ teaspoon kosher salt
1 garlic clove, whole
2 tablespoons fresh basil, chopped
Cooking spray

1. Spritz the air fry basket with cooking spray.
2. Combine the zucchini and summer squash with 1 teaspoon of the olive oil and salt in a large bowl. Toss to coat well.
3. Transfer the zucchini and summer squash to the air fry basket and add the garlic.
4. Select Air Fry, Super Convection, set temperature to 360ºF (182ºC) and set time to 10 minutes. Select Start/Stop to begin preheating.
5. Once preheated, place the basket on the air fry position. Stir the zucchini and summer squash halfway through the cooking time.
6. When cooked, the zucchini and summer squash will be tender and fragrant. Transfer the cooked zucchini and summer squash onto a plate and set aside.
7. Remove the garlic from the oven and allow to cool for 5 minutes. Mince the garlic and combine with remaining olive oil in a small bowl. Stir to mix well.
8. Drizzle the spiralized zucchini and summer squash with garlic oil and sprinkle with basil. Toss to serve.

Kale Chips

Prep time: 5 minutes | Cook time: 5 minutes | Serves 2

4 medium kale leaves, about 1 ounce
    (28 g) each, stems removed, tear
    the leaves in thirds
2 teaspoons soy sauce
2 teaspoons olive oil

1. Toss the kale leaves with soy sauce and olive oil in a large bowl to coat well. Place the leaves in the baking pan.
2. Select Air Fry, Super Convection, set temperature to 400ºF (205ºC) and set time to 5 minutes. Select Start/Stop to begin preheating.
3. Once the oven has preheated, slide the pan into the oven. Flip the leaves with tongs gently halfway through.
4. When cooked, the kale leaves should be crispy. Remove the pan from the oven.
5. Serve immediately.

Apple Fritters with Sweet Glaze

Prep time: 10 minutes | Cook time: 8 minutes | Makes 15 fritters

Apple Fritters:
2 firm apples, peeled, cored, and diced
½ teaspoon cinnamon
Juice of 1 lemon
1 cup all-purpose flour
1½ teaspoons baking powder
½ teaspoon kosher salt
2 eggs
¼ cup milk
2 tablespoons unsalted butter, melted
2 tablespoons granulated sugar
Cooking spray
Glaze:
½ teaspoon vanilla extract
1¼ cups powdered sugar, sifted
¼ cup water

1. Line the air fry basket with parchment paper.
2. Combine the apples with cinnamon and lemon juice in a small bowl. Toss to coat well.
3. Combine the flour, baking powder, and salt in a large bowl. Stir to mix well.
4. Whisk the egg, milk, butter, and sugar in a medium bowl. Stir to mix well.
5. Make a well in the center of the flour mixture, then pour the egg mixture into the well and stir to mix well. Mix in the apple until a dough forms.
6. Use an ice cream scoop to scoop 15 balls from the dough onto the pan. Spritz with cooking spray.
7. Select Air Fry, Super Convection, set temperature to 360°F (182°C) and set time to 8 minutes. Select Start/Stop to begin preheating.
8. Once the oven has preheated, place the basket on the air fry position. Flip the apple fritters halfway through the cooking time.
9. Meanwhile, combine the ingredients for the glaze in a separate small bowl. Stir to mix well.
10. When cooking is complete, the apple fritters will be golden brown. Serve the fritters with the glaze on top or use the glaze for dipping.

Pears with Lemony Ricotta

Prep time: 10 minutes | Cook time: 8 minutes | Serves 4

2 large Bartlett pears, peeled, cut in half, cored
3 tablespoons melted butter
½ teaspoon ground ginger
¼ teaspoon ground cardamom
3 tablespoons brown sugar
½ cup whole-milk ricotta cheese
1 teaspoon pure lemon extract
1 teaspoon pure almond extract
1 tablespoon honey, plus additional for drizzling

1. Toss the pears with butter, ginger, cardamom, and sugar in a large bowl. Toss to coat well. Arrange the pears in a baking pan, cut side down.
2. Select Air Fry, Super Convection, set temperature to 375°F (190°C) and set time to 8 minutes. Select Start/Stop to begin preheating.
3. Once preheated, place the pan into the oven.
4. After 5 minutes, remove the pan and flip the pears. Return the pan to the oven and continue cooking.
5. When cooking is complete, the pears should be soft and browned. Remove the pan from the oven.
6. In the meantime, combine the remaining ingredients in a separate bowl. Whip for 1 minute with a hand mixer until the mixture is puffed.
7. Divide the mixture into four bowls, then put the pears over the mixture and drizzle with more honey to serve.

Lemony Asparagus

Prep time: 5 minutes | Cook time: 10 minutes | Makes 10 spears

10 spears asparagus (about ½ pound / 227 g in total), snap the ends off
1 tablespoon lemon juice
2 teaspoons minced garlic
½ teaspoon salt
¼ teaspoon ground black pepper
Cooking spray

1. Line the air fry basket with parchment paper.
2. Put the asparagus spears in a large bowl. Drizzle with lemon juice and sprinkle with minced garlic, salt, and ground black pepper. Toss to coat well.
3. Transfer the asparagus to the air fry basket and spritz with cooking spray.
4. Select Air Fry, Super Convection, set temperature to 400°F (205°C) and set time to 10 minutes. Select Start/Stop to begin preheating.
5. Once the oven has preheated, place the basket on the air fry position. Flip the asparagus halfway through cooking.
6. When cooked, the asparagus should be wilted and soft. Remove the basket from the oven.
7. Serve immediately.

Carrot Chips

3 large carrots, peeled and sliced into long and thick chips diagonally
1 tablespoon granulated garlic
1 teaspoon salt
¼ teaspoon ground black pepper
1 tablespoon olive oil
1 tablespoon finely chopped fresh parsley

1. Toss the carrots with garlic, salt, ground black pepper, and olive oil in a large bowl to coat well. Place the carrots in the air fry basket.
2. Select Roast, Super Convection, set temperature to 360ºF (182ºC) and set time to 15 minutes. Select Start/Stop to begin preheating.
3. Once the oven has preheated, place the basket on the roast position. Stir the carrots halfway through the cooking time.
4. When cooking is complete, the carrot chips should be soft. Remove from the oven.
5. Serve the carrot chips with parsley on top.

Old Bay Shrimp

Prep time: 10 minutes | Cook time: 10 minutes | Makes 2 cups

½ teaspoon Old Bay Seasoning
1 teaspoon ground cayenne pepper
½ teaspoon paprika
1 tablespoon olive oil
⅛ teaspoon salt
½ pound (227 g) shrimps, peeled and deveined
Juice of half a lemon

1. Combine the Old Bay Seasoning, cayenne pepper, paprika, olive oil, and salt in a large bowl, then add the shrimps and toss to coat well.
2. Put the shrimps in the air fry basket.
3. Select Air Fry, Super Convection, set temperature to 390ºF (199ºC) and set time to 10 minutes. Select Start/Stop to begin preheating.
4. Once preheated, place the basket on the air fry position. Flip the shrimps halfway through the cooking time.
5. When cooking is complete, the shrimps should be opaque. Remove from the oven.
6. Serve the shrimps with lemon juice on top.

Sweet-Sour Peanut

Prep time: 5 minutes | Cook time: 5 minutes | Serves 9

3 cups shelled raw peanuts
1 tablespoon hot red pepper sauce
3 tablespoons granulated white sugar

1. Put the peanuts in a large bowl, then drizzle with hot red pepper sauce and sprinkle with sugar. Toss to coat well.
2. Pour the peanuts in the air fry basket.
3. Select Air Fry, Super Convection, set temperature to 400ºF (205ºC) and set time to 5 minutes. Select Start/Stop to begin preheating.
4. Once preheated, place the basket on the air fry position. Stir the peanuts halfway through the cooking time.
5. When cooking is complete, the peanuts will be crispy and browned. Remove from the oven.
6. Serve immediately.

Bartlett Pears with Lemony Ricotta

Prep time: 10 minutes | Cook time: 8 minutes | Serves 4

2 large Bartlett pears, peeled, cut in half, cored
3 tablespoons melted butter
½ teaspoon ground ginger
¼ teaspoon ground cardamom
3 tablespoons brown sugar
½ cup whole-milk ricotta cheese
1 teaspoon pure lemon extract
1 teaspoon pure almond extract
1 tablespoon honey, plus additional for drizzling

1. Toss the pears with butter, ginger, cardamom, and sugar in a large bowl. Toss to coat well. Arrange the pears in a baking pan, cut side down.
2. Select Air Fry, Super Convection, set temperature to 375°F (190°C) and set time to 8 minutes. Select Start/Stop to begin preheating.
3. Once preheated, place the pan into the oven.
4. After 5 minutes, remove the pan and flip the pears. Return the pan to the oven and continue cooking.
5. When cooking is complete, the pears should be soft and browned. Remove the pan from the oven.
6. In the meantime, combine the remaining ingredients in a separate bowl. Whip for 1 minute with a hand mixer until the mixture is puffed.
7. Divide the mixture into four bowls, then put the pears over the mixture and drizzle with more honey to serve.

Lemony and Garlicky Asparagus

Prep time: 5 minutes | Cook time: 10 minutes | Makes 10 spears

10 spears asparagus (about ½ pound / 227 g in total), snap the ends off
1 tablespoon lemon juice
2 teaspoons minced garlic
½ teaspoon salt
¼ teaspoon ground black pepper
Cooking spray

1. Line the air fry basket with parchment paper.
2. Put the asparagus spears in a large bowl. Drizzle with lemon juice and sprinkle with minced garlic, salt, and ground black pepper. Toss to coat well.
3. Transfer the asparagus to the air fry basket and spritz with cooking spray.
4. Select Air Fry, Super Convection, set temperature to 400°F (205°C) and set time to 10 minutes. Select Start/Stop to begin preheating.
5. Once the oven has preheated, place the basket on the air fry position. Flip the asparagus halfway through cooking.
6. When cooked, the asparagus should be wilted and soft. Remove the basket from the oven.
7. Serve immediately.

Roasted Carrot Chips

Prep time: 5 minutes | Cook time: 15 minutes | Makes 3 cups

3 large carrots, peeled and sliced into long and thick chips diagonally
1 tablespoon granulated garlic
1 teaspoon salt
¼ teaspoon ground black pepper
1 tablespoon olive oil
1 tablespoon finely chopped fresh parsley

1. Toss the carrots with garlic, salt, ground black pepper, and olive oil in a large bowl to coat well. Place the carrots in the air fry basket.
2. Select Roast, Super Convection, set temperature to 360°F (182°C) and set time to 15 minutes. Select Start/Stop to begin preheating.
3. Once the oven has preheated, place the basket on the roast position. Stir the carrots halfway through the cooking time.
4. When cooking is complete, the carrot chips should be soft. Remove from the oven.
5. Serve the carrot chips with parsley on top.

Spicy Air Fried Old Bay Shrimp

Prep time: 10 minutes | Cook time: 10 minutes | Makes 2 cups

½ teaspoon Old Bay Seasoning
1 teaspoon ground cayenne pepper
½ teaspoon paprika
1 tablespoon olive oil
⅛ teaspoon salt
½ pound (227 g) shrimps, peeled and deveined
Juice of half a lemon

1. Combine the Old Bay Seasoning, cayenne pepper, paprika, olive oil, and salt in a large bowl, then add the shrimps and toss to coat well.
2. Put the shrimps in the air fry basket.
3. Select Air Fry, Super Convection, set temperature to 390ºF (199ºC) and set time to 10 minutes. Select Start/Stop to begin preheating.
4. Once preheated, place the basket on the air fry position. Flip the shrimps halfway through the cooking time.
5. When cooking is complete, the shrimps should be opaque. Remove from the oven.
6. Serve the shrimps with lemon juice on top.

Sweet and Sour Peanuts

Prep time: 5 minutes | Cook time: 5 minutes | Serves 9

3 cups shelled raw peanuts
1 tablespoon hot red pepper sauce
3 tablespoons granulated white sugar

1. Put the peanuts in a large bowl, then drizzle with hot red pepper sauce and sprinkle with sugar. Toss to coat well.
2. Pour the peanuts in the air fry basket.
3. Select Air Fry, Super Convection, set temperature to 400ºF (205ºC) and set time to 5 minutes. Select Start/Stop to begin preheating.
4. Once preheated, place the basket on the air fry position. Stir the peanuts halfway through the cooking time.
5. When cooking is complete, the peanuts will be crispy and browned. Remove from the oven.
6. Serve immediately.

Cheesy Potato Patties

Prep time: 5 minutes | Cook time: 10 minutes | Serves 8

2 pounds (907 g) white potatoes
½ cup finely chopped scallions
½ teaspoon freshly ground black pepper, or more to taste
1 tablespoon fine sea salt
½ teaspoon hot paprika
2 cups shredded Colby cheese
¼ cup canola oil
1 cup crushed crackers

1. Preheat the air fryer to 360ºF (182ºC).
2. Boil the potatoes until soft. Dry them off and peel them before mashing thoroughly, leaving no lumps.
3. Combine the mashed potatoes with scallions, pepper, salt, paprika, and cheese.
4. Mold the mixture into balls with your hands and press with your palm to flatten them into patties.
5. In a shallow dish, combine the canola oil and crushed crackers. Coat the patties in the crumb mixture.
6. Bake the patties for about 10 minutes, in multiple batches if necessary.
7. Serve hot.

Simple and Easy Croutons

Prep time: 5 minutes | Cook time: 8 minutes | Serves 4

2 slices friendly bread
1 tablespoon olive oil
Hot soup, for serving

1. Preheat the air fryer to 390ºF (199ºC).
2. Cut the slices of bread into medium-size chunks.
3. Brush the air fryer basket with the oil.
4. Place the chunks inside and air fry for at least 8 minutes.
5. Serve with hot soup.

Sweet Corn and Carrot Fritters

Prep time: 10 minutes | Cook time: 8 to 11 minutes | Serves 4

1 medium-sized carrot, grated
1 yellow onion, finely chopped
4 ounces (113 g) canned sweet corn
    kernels, drained
1 teaspoon sea salt flakes
1 tablespoon chopped fresh cilantro
1 medium-sized egg, whisked
2 tablespoons plain milk
1 cup grated Parmesan cheese
¼ cup flour
⅓ teaspoon baking powder
⅓ teaspoon sugar
Cooking spray

1. Preheat the air fryer to 350°F (177°C).
2. Place the grated carrot in a colander and press down to squeeze out any excess moisture. Dry it with a paper towel.
3. Combine the carrots with the remaining ingredients.
4. Mold 1 tablespoon of the mixture into a ball and press it down with your hand or a spoon to flatten it. Repeat until the rest of the mixture is used up.
5. Spritz the balls with cooking spray.
6. Arrange in the air fryer basket, taking care not to overlap any balls. Bake for 8 to 11 minutes, or until they're firm.
7. Serve warm.

Bistro Potato Wedges

Prep time: 10 minutes | Cook time: 13 minutes | Serves 4

1 pound (454 g) fingerling potatoes,
    cut into wedges
1 teaspoon extra-virgin olive oil
½ teaspoon garlic powder
Salt and pepper, to taste
½ cup raw cashews, soaked in water
    overnight
½ teaspoon ground turmeric
½ teaspoon paprika
1 tablespoon nutritional yeast
1 teaspoon fresh lemon juice
2 tablespoons to ¼ cup water

1. Preheat the air fryer to 400°F (204°C).
2. In a bowl, toss together the potato wedges, olive oil, garlic powder, and salt and pepper, making sure to coat the potatoes well.
3. Transfer the potatoes to the air fryer basket and air fry for 10 minutes.
4. In the meantime, prepare the cheese sauce. Pulse the cashews, turmeric, paprika, nutritional yeast, lemon juice, and water together in a food processor. Add more water to achieve your desired consistency.
5. When the potatoes are finished cooking, transfer to a bowl and add the cheese sauce on top. Air fry for an additional 3 minutes.
6. Serve hot.

Spinach and Carrot Balls

Prep time: 10 minutes | Cook time: 10 minutes | Serves 4

2 slices toasted bread
1 carrot, peeled and grated
1 package fresh spinach, blanched
    and chopped
½ onion, chopped
1 egg, beaten
½ teaspoon garlic powder
1 teaspoon minced garlic
1 teaspoon salt
½ teaspoon black pepper
1 tablespoon nutritional yeast
1 tablespoon flour

1. Preheat the air fryer to 390°F (199°C).
2. In a food processor, pulse the toasted bread to form bread crumbs. Transfer into a shallow dish or bowl.
3. In a bowl, mix together all the other ingredients.
4. Use your hands to shape the mixture into small-sized balls. Roll the balls in the bread crumbs, ensuring to cover them well.
5. Put in the air fryer basket and air fry for 10 minutes.
6. Serve immediately.

Simple Pea Delight

Prep time: 5 minutes | Cook time: 15 minutes | Serves 2 to 4

1 cup flour
1 teaspoon baking powder
3 eggs
1 cup coconut milk
1 cup cream cheese
3 tablespoons pea protein
½ cup chicken or turkey strips
Pinch of sea salt
1 cup Mozzarella cheese

1. Preheat the air fryer to 390°F (199°C).
2. In a large bowl, mix all ingredients together using a large wooden spoon.
3. Spoon equal amounts of the mixture into muffin cups and bake for 15 minutes.
4. Serve immediately.

Cheesy Sausage Balls

Prep time: 5 minutes | Cook time: 15 minutes | Serves 6

12 ounces (340 g) Jimmy Dean's Sausage
6 ounces (170 g) shredded Cheddar cheese
10 Cheddar cubes

1. Preheat the air fryer to 375°F (191°C).
2. Mix the shredded cheese and sausage.
3. Divide the mixture into 12 equal parts to be stuffed.
4. Add a cube of cheese to the center of the sausage and roll into balls.
5. Air fry for 15 minutes, or until crisp.
6. Serve immediately.

Bacon-Wrapped Beef Hot Dog

Prep time: 5 minutes | Cook time: 10 minutes | Serves 4

4 slices sugar-free bacon
4 beef hot dogs

1. Preheat the air fryer to 370°F (188°C).
2. Take a slice of bacon and wrap it around the hot dog, securing it with a toothpick. Repeat with the other pieces of bacon and hot dogs, placing each wrapped dog in the air fryer basket.
3. Bake for 10 minutes, turning halfway through.
4. Once hot and crispy, the hot dogs are ready to serve.

Beef Bratwursts

Prep time: 5 minutes | Cook time: 15 minutes | Serves 4

4 (3-ounce / 85-g) beef bratwursts

1. Preheat the air fryer to 375°F (191°C).
2. Place the beef bratwursts in the air fryer basket and air fry for 15 minutes, turning once halfway through.
3. Serve hot.

Easy Roasted Asparagus

Prep time: 5 minutes | Cook time: 6 minutes | Serves 4

1 pound (454 g) asparagus, trimmed and halved crosswise
1 teaspoon extra-virgin olive oil
Salt and pepper, to taste
Lemon wedges, for serving

1. Preheat the air fryer to 400ºF (204ºC).
2. Toss the asparagus with the oil, ⅛ teaspoon salt, and ⅛ teaspoon pepper in bowl. Transfer to air fryer basket.
3. Place the basket in air fryer and roast for 6 to 8 minutes, or until tender and bright green, tossing halfway through cooking.
4. Season with salt and pepper and serve with lemon wedges.

Baked Chorizo Scotch Eggs

Prep time: 5 minutes | Cook time: 15 to 20 minutes | Makes 4 eggs

1 pound (454 g) Mexican chorizo or other seasoned sausage meat
4 soft-boiled eggs plus 1 raw egg
1 tablespoon water
½ cup all-purpose flour
1 cup panko bread crumbs
Cooking spray

1. Divide the chorizo into 4 equal portions. Flatten each portion into a disc. Place a soft-boiled egg in the center of each disc. Wrap the chorizo around the egg, encasing it completely. Place the encased eggs on a plate and chill for at least 30 minutes.
2. Preheat the air fryer to 360ºF (182ºC).
3. Beat the raw egg with 1 tablespoon of water. Place the flour on a small plate and the panko on a second plate. Working with 1 egg at a time, roll the encased egg in the flour, then dip it in the egg mixture. Dredge the egg in the panko and place on a plate. Repeat with the remaining eggs.
4. Spray the eggs with oil and place in the air fryer basket. Bake for 10 minutes. Turn and bake for an additional 5 to 10 minutes, or until browned and crisp on all sides.
5. Serve immediately.

Rosemary and Orange Roasted Chickpeas

Prep time: 5 minutes | Cook time: 10 to 12 minutes | Makes 4 cups

4 cups cooked chickpeas
2 tablespoons vegetable oil
1 teaspoon kosher salt
1 teaspoon cumin
1 teaspoon paprika
Zest of 1 orange
1 tablespoon chopped fresh rosemary

1. Preheat the air fryer to 400ºF (204ºC).
2. Make sure the chickpeas are completely dry prior to roasting. In a medium bowl, toss the chickpeas with oil, salt, cumin, and paprika.
3. Working in batches, spread the chickpeas in a single layer in the air fryer basket. Air fry for 10 to 12 minutes until crisp, shaking once halfway through.
4. Return the warm chickpeas to the bowl and toss with the orange zest and rosemary. Allow to cool completely.
5. Serve.

Pomegranate Avocado Fries

Prep time: 5 minutes | Cook time: 7 to 8 minutes | Serves 4

1 cup panko bread crumbs
1 teaspoon kosher salt, plus more for sprinkling
1 teaspoon garlic powder
½ teaspoon cayenne pepper

2 ripe but firm avocados
1 egg, beaten with 1 tablespoon water
Cooking spray
Pomegranate molasses, for serving

1. Preheat the air fryer to 375°F (191°C).
2. Whisk together the panko, salt, and spices on a plate. Cut each avocado in half and remove the pit. Cut each avocado half into 4 slices and scoop the slices out with a large spoon, taking care to keep the slices intact.
3. Dip each avocado slice in the egg wash and then dredge it in the panko. Place the breaded avocado slices on a plate.
4. Working in 2 batches, arrange half of the avocado slices in a single layer in the air fryer basket. Spray lightly with oil. Bake the slices for 7 to 8 minutes, turning once halfway through. Remove the cooked slices to a platter and repeat with the remaining avocado slices.
5. Sprinkle the warm avocado slices with salt and drizzle with pomegranate molasses. Serve immediately.

Crunchy Fried Okra

Prep time: 5 minutes | Cook time: 8 to 10 minutes | Serves 4

1 cup self-rising yellow cornmeal
1 teaspoon Italian-style seasoning
1 teaspoon paprika
1 teaspoon salt
½ teaspoon freshly ground black pepper
2 large eggs, beaten
2 cups okra slices
Cooking spray

1. Preheat the air fryer to 400°F (204°C). Line the air fryer basket with parchment paper.
2. In a shallow bowl, whisk the cornmeal, Italian-style seasoning, paprika, salt, and pepper until blended. Place the beaten eggs in a second shallow bowl.
3. Add the okra to the beaten egg and stir to coat. Add the egg and okra mixture to the cornmeal mixture and stir until coated.
4. Place the okra on the parchment and spritz it with oil.
5. Air fry for 4 minutes. Shake the basket, spritz the okra with oil, and air fry for 4 to 6 minutes more until lightly browned and crispy.
6. Serve immediately.

Buttery Sweet Potatoes

Prep time: 5 minutes | Cook time: 10 minutes | Serves 4

2 tablespoons butter, melted
1 tablespoon light brown sugar
2 sweet potatoes, peeled and cut into ½-inch cubes
Cooking spray

1. Preheat the air fryer to 400°F (204°C). Line the air fryer basket with parchment paper.
2. In a medium bowl, stir together the melted butter and brown sugar until blended. Toss the sweet potatoes in the butter mixture until coated.
3. Place the sweet potatoes on the parchment and spritz with oil.
4. Air fry for 5 minutes. Shake the basket, spritz the sweet potatoes with oil, and air fry for 5 minutes more until they're soft enough to cut with a fork.
5. Serve immediately.

Corn Fritters

Prep time: 15 minutes | Cook time: 8 minutes | Serves 6

1 cup self-rising flour
1 tablespoon sugar
1 teaspoon salt
1 large egg, lightly beaten
¼ cup buttermilk
¾ cup corn kernels
¼ cup minced onion
Cooking spray

1. Preheat the air fryer to 350°F (177°C). Line the air fryer basket with parchment paper.
2. In a medium bowl, whisk the flour, sugar, and salt until blended. Stir in the egg and buttermilk. Add the corn and minced onion. Mix well. Shape the corn fritter batter into 12 balls.
3. Place the fritters on the parchment and spritz with oil. Bake for 4 minutes. Flip the fritters, spritz them with oil, and bake for 4 minutes more until firm and lightly browned.
4. Serve immediately.

Chapter 11 Rotisserie Recipes

Tri-Tip Roast with Ketchup Sauce

Prep time: 15 minutes | Cook time: 1 hour 30 minutes | Serves 8

2 tri-tip roasts, 2 pounds (907 g) each
Sauce:
¾ cup ketchup
¾ cup Dr Pepper
¼ cup packed brown sugar
2 teaspoons apple cider vinegar
¼ teaspoon freshly ground black pepper
⅛ teaspoon salt
Rub:
1 tablespoon kosher salt
1½ teaspoons freshly ground black
    pepper
1½ teaspoons paprika
1½ teaspoons mild chili powder
½ teaspoon garlic powder

1. Place one tri-tip on top of the other with the small ends on opposite sides. Fold in these ends and tie the roasts with kitchen twine, creating one single, uniform roast. Run a long sword skewer through the center of the roast lengthwise to create a pilot hole. Run the rotisserie spit through the hole and secure with the forks. Balance as necessary.
2. To make the sauce: Combine the sauce ingredients in a small saucepan and simmer over medium heat for 5 to 6 minutes, stirring often. Watch for burning and lower the heat if necessary. Remove from the heat and let sit for 15 to 30 minutes before using.
3. To make the rub: Combine the rub ingredients in a small bowl and evenly apply all over the roast.
4. Select the ROAST function and preheat AIR FRYER to 400ºF (205ºC). Press ROTATE button and set time to 85 minutes.
5. Place the roast on the preheated air fryer oven, set a drip pan underneath, and add 1 to 2 cups hot water to the pan. During the last 30 minutes of cooking time, begin basting with the sauce. Do this 6 to 8 times, until the roast is well coated with the barbecue sauce and the internal temperature reaches 140ºF (60ºC). The roast will shrink during the cooking process, so adjust the forks when appropriate.
6. Remove the roast from the air fryer oven, carefully remove the rotisserie forks and slide the spit out, and then place the roast on a large cutting board. Cover the meat with aluminum foil and let rest for 12 to 15 minutes. Cut off the twine. Separate the roasts, slice against the grain, and serve.

Tri-Tip with Chimichurri Sauce

Prep time: 20 minutes | Cook time: 1 hour 20 minutes | Serves 10 to 12

2 tri-tip roasts, 4 to 5 pounds (1.8 to 2.3 kg) each
Chimichurri Sauce:
½ cup packed fresh flat-leaf parsley, chopped
⅓ cup packed fresh cilantro leaves, chopped
3 or 4 cloves garlic
1 small shallot, chopped
2 tablespoons white vinegar
¼ teaspoon salt
¼ teaspoon freshly ground black pepper

¼ teaspoon red pepper flakes (optional)
½ cup olive oil

Rub:
1½ tablespoons kosher salt
2 teaspoons freshly ground black pepper
1 teaspoon onion powder
½ teaspoon cayenne

1. To make the chimichurri sauce: Prepare the sauce 1 to 2 hours before the meat will be finished cooking. Place all the sauce ingredients, except the oil, into a food processor. Pulse a few times. Slowly pour in the oil while pulsing 10 or so more times. You do not want to purée the chimichurri, but all the ingredients should be finely chopped and well combined with the oil. Remove the sauce from the food processor, transfer to a bowl, and set aside until ready to eat.
2. Place one tri-tip on top of the other with the small ends on opposite sides. Fold in these ends and tie the roasts with kitchen twine, creating one single, uniform roast. Run a long sword skewer through the center of the roast lengthwise to create a pilot hole. Run the rotisserie spit through the hole and secure with the forks. Balance as necessary.
3. To make the rub: Combine the rub ingredients in a small bowl and apply evenly all over the meat.
4. Select the ROAST function and preheat AIR FRYER to 400°F (205°C). Press ROTATE button and set time to 80 minutes.
5. Place the roast on the preheated air fryer oven and set a drip pan underneath. Roast until near the desired doneness. The roast will shrink during the cooking process, so adjust the forks when appropriate.
6. Carefully remove the rotisserie forks and slide the spit out, and then place the roast on a large cutting board. Cover the meat with aluminum foil and let rest for 15 minutes. Cut off the twine. Separate the roasts, slice against the grain ⅓ to ½ inch thick and serve with the chimichurri sauce.

Prime Rib Roast with Grainy Mustard

Prep time: 10 minutes | Cook time: 2 hours | Serves 8 to 10

1 4-bone prime rib roast (8 to 10 pounds / 3.6 to 4.5 kg)
Rub:
½ cup grainy mustard
¼ cup olive oil
1 large shallot, finely chopped
3 tablespoons kosher salt
1½ tablespoons chopped fresh marjoram
1 tablespoon chopped fresh thyme
1 tablespoon coarsely ground black pepper

1. Trim off any straggling pieces of meat or fat from the roast. If the fat cap is too thick, cut it down to between ¼ to ½ inch in thickness depending on how you like your prime rib.
2. To make the rub: Combine the rub ingredients in a small bowl and coat the roast thoroughly with it. Loosely cover with plastic wrap and let the roast sit at room temperature for 30 minutes.
3. Run a long sword skewer through the center of the roast lengthwise to create a pilot hole. Run the rotisserie spit through the hole and secure with the forks. Balance as necessary.
4. Select the ROAST function and preheat AIR FRYER to 400°F (205°C). Press ROTATE button and set time to 2 hours.
5. Place the roast on the preheated air fryer oven, set a drip pan underneath, and add 1 to 2 cups hot water to the pan. Add more water to the pan as necessary.
6. Roast until it is near the desired doneness: 125°F (52°C) for rare, 135°F (57°C) for medium rare, 145°F (63°C) for medium, 155°F (68°C) for medium well, or 165°F (74°C) for well done. The roast will shrink during cooking, so adjust the forks when appropriate. Remove the roast when it is 5°F to 10°F below the desired doneness. It will continue to cook during the resting phase.
7. Carefully remove the rotisserie forks and slide the spit out, and then place the roast on a large cutting board. Tent the roast with aluminum foil and a kitchen towel and let the meat rest for 15 to 20 minutes. Cut away the bones first by passing a knife against the bones and cutting through (save the bones for later). Cut the meat into thin slices.

Prime Rib Roast with Whiskey Baste

Prep time: 10 minutes | Cook time: 2 hours | Serves 8 to 10

1 4-bone prime rib roast (8 to 10 pounds / 3.6 to 4.5 kg)

Rub:
¼ cup coarse salt
1 small shallot, finely chopped
2 cloves garlic, minced
2 tablespoons olive oil
1 tablespoon coarsely ground black pepper
Zest of 1 large lemon
1 teaspoon paprika
1 teaspoon sugar

Baste:
⅓ cup whiskey
¼ cup water
Juice of 1 lemon
⅛ teaspoon salt

1. Trim off any straggling pieces of meat or fat from the roast. If the fat cap is too thick, cut it down to between ¼ to ½ inch in thickness depending on how you like your prime rib.
2. Run a long sword skewer through the center of the roast lengthwise to create a pilot hole. Run the rotisserie spit through the hole and secure with the forks. Balance as necessary.
3. To make the rub: Combine the rub ingredients in a small bowl to form an even paste. Use additional olive oil if necessary to get it to a thick but workable consistency. Apply evenly to the roast, focusing on the outer shell of the roast.
4. To make the baste: Combine the baste ingredients in a small bowl and set aside for 15 to 30 minutes to come to room temperature.
5. Select the ROAST function and preheat AIR FRYER to 400ºF (205ºC). Press ROTATE button and set time to 2 hours.
6. Place the roast on the preheated air fryer oven, set a drip pan underneath, and add 1 to 2 cups hot water to the pan. If you intend to make a gravy from the drippings, monitor the drip pan to make sure it does not run dry. Add extra water if needed.
7. During the last hour of cooking time, begin basting. Apply the baste gently so as not to wash away the seasonings on the outside of the roast. Do this 6 to 8 times, until the roast is well coated with the baste. Roast until it is near the desired doneness: 125ºF (52ºC) for rare, 135ºF (57ºC) for medium rare, 145ºF (63ºC) for medium, 155ºF (68ºC) for medium well, or 165ºF (74ºC) for well done. The roast will shrink during cooking, so adjust the forks when appropriate.
8. Carefully remove the rotisserie forks and slide the spit out, and then set the roast on a large cutting board. Tent the roast with aluminum foil and let the meat rest for 15 to 20 minutes. Cut away the bones first by passing a knife against the bones and cutting through (save the bones for later). Cut the meat into thin slices.

Chipotle Chuck Roast with Garlic

Prep time: 10 minutes | Cook time: 2½ hours | Serves 6 to 8

1 chuck roast, 3½ to 4 pounds (1.5 to 1.8 kg)

Marinade:
1 (7-ounce / 198-g) can chipotle peppers in adobo
1 cup diced onion
½ cup beef or vegetable broth
3 cloves garlic, cut into fourths
1 tablespoon ground cumin
2 tablespoons water
1 tablespoon white vinegar
1 tablespoon salt
2 teaspoons dried oregano

1. To make the marinade: Place the marinade ingredients in a food processor and pulse 8 to 10 times. Everything should be very finely chopped and combined. Reserve 1 cup of the mixture to use as a baste and refrigerate until ready to cook, then bring to room temperature before using.
2. Trim away any loose or excess pieces of fat from the roast. Place in a large glass dish or large resealable plastic bag. Pour the marinade over the meat, making sure all sides are well covered. Seal the bag or cover the dish with plastic wrap and place in the refrigerator for 12 to 24 hours.
3. Remove the roast from the bag, discarding the marinade. Lay the roast out on a large cutting board. With kitchen twine, tie the roast into a round and uniform shape, pulling tightly. Start in the center and work toward the ends until it is tied into a solid round roast. This will take four or five ties. Run a long sword skewer through the center of the roast lengthwise to create a pilot hole. Run the rotisserie spit through the hole and secure with the forks. Balance as necessary.
4. Select the ROAST function and preheat AIR FRYER to 400ºF (205ºC). Press ROTATE button and set time to 2½ hours.
5. Place the roast on the preheated air fryer oven and set a drip pan underneath. Roast until the meat reaches an internal temperature of about 160ºF (70ºC). Baste with the reserved marinade during the last 30 to 40 minutes of cooking. This roast is intentionally overcooked so that it can be shredded easily. It will be tender and juicy.
6. Remove from the heat, carefully remove the rotisserie forks and slide the spit out, and then set the roast on a large cutting board. Tent the roast with aluminum foil and let the meat rest for 20 minutes. Cut off the twine. Shred into small pieces or carve into thin slices and serve with warmed tortillas, Spanish rice, beans, and fresh salsa.

Pulled Pork with Paprika

Prep time: 10 minutes | Cook time: 6 hours | Serves 10

1 pork butt, 5 to 6 pounds (2.3 to 2.7 kg)

Rub:
2 tablespoons paprika
2 tablespoons packed brown sugar
1 tablespoon kosher salt
1 tablespoon mild chili powder
1 teaspoon freshly ground black pepper
1 teaspoon celery salt
½ teaspoon cayenne
½ teaspoon garlic powder

1. Run a long sword skewer through the center of the roast lengthwise to create a pilot hole. Run the rotisserie spit through the hole and secure with the forks. Balance as necessary.
2. To make the rub: Combine the rub ingredients in a small bowl and apply evenly all over the roast. Let sit at room temperature for 15 minutes. By this time the air fryer oven should be ready.
3. Select the ROAST function and preheat AIR FRYER to 350ºF (180ºC). Press ROTATE button and set time to 6 hours.
4. Place the roast on the preheated air fryer oven with a drip pan underneath. Roast until the internal temperature reaches 185ºF (85ºC). The roast will shrink during cooking, so adjust the forks when appropriate.
5. Remove from the heat, carefully remove the rotisserie forks and slide the spit out, and then set the pork on a large cutting board. Tent the roast with aluminum foil and let the meat rest for 20 minutes. Remove the foil and let stand for an additional 10 minutes.
6. Using two forks, check to see how easily the meat shreds. Some parts will do this more easily than others. Be sure to use heat-resistant gloves to break the roast apart. Begin shredding each large chunk one at a time. Add pieces to a large bowl and either add the barbecue sauce directly to the shredded meat or serve on the side. Keep the bowl covered as you're working on each section. This will help keep the meat warm. Serve by itself or with your favorite sides or in sandwiches.

Ham with Honey-Orange Glaze

Prep time: 10 minutes | Cook time: 45 minutes | Serves 12 to 14

1 ham, bone in and unsliced, 7 to 8 pounds (3.2 to 3.6 kg)
1 cup packed brown sugar

Glaze:
1½ cups orange juice
½ cup honey
2 tablespoons packed brown sugar
¼ teaspoon ground cinnamon
⅛ teaspoon ground nutmeg
⅛ teaspoon ground allspice
⅛ teaspoon ground cloves
⅛ teaspoon white pepper
2 tablespoons unsalted butter

1. To make the glaze: Combine the orange juice, honey, brown sugar, and spices in a saucepan and bring almost to a boil over medium-high heat. Decrease the heat to medium and simmer for 10 minutes, stirring often. The mixture should be a little runnier than real maple syrup. Remove from the heat and add the butter, stirring until melted. Let the mixture cool.
2. Run a long sword skewer through the center of the ham lengthwise to create a pilot hole. There is a bone in the middle of this ham, but generally it is just to one side. The skewer should easily go through, but feel for the bone before you start so you will know how to navigate around it. Run the rotisserie spit through the hole and secure with the forks. Balance the ham on the spit as well as possible.
3. Select the ROAST function and preheat AIR FRYER to 375ºF (190ºC). Press ROTATE button and set time to 45 minutes.
4. Place the ham on the preheated air fryer oven and set a drip pan underneath, if there is room. The ham should not take too long to heat up. Look for an internal temperature around 130ºF (54ºC). The surface should be hot.
5. Baste the ham with the glaze after 20 minutes on the air fryer oven. Repeat the process every 5 minutes and about 3 more times.
6. During the last 5 to 10 minutes of cooking time, the ham should be hot as well as sticky from the glaze. Increase the temperature to 400ºF (205ºC) and sprinkle the brown sugar evenly on the surface of the ham in small amounts until it is completely coated. Continue to cook until the sugar starts to bubble. Move quickly, as sugar tends to burn.
7. Once the sugar is bubbling rapidly, remove the ham from the heat and place on a large cutting board. Remove the rotisserie forks and slide the spit out, loosely cover the ham with aluminum foil, and let it rest for 5 minutes. Carve into thin slices and serve warm.

Pineapple and Cherry Rotisserie Ham

Prep time: 15 minutes | Cook time: 35 to 40 minutes | Serves 12 to 14

Glaze:
1 cup pineapple preserves
2½ tablespoons cherry jelly
2 tablespoons packed brown sugar
1 tablespoon water
2 teaspoons soy sauce

1 ham, unsliced, 6 to 7 pounds (2.7 to 3.2 kg)
¼ cup whole cloves (use more if necessary)

1. To make the glaze: Combine all the glaze ingredients in a saucepan over low heat and heat through. Do not boil; just bring to a low simmer until everything is melted and well blended. Remove from the heat, cover, and keep warm.
2. Select Rotisserie, Super Convection, set temperature to 375°F (191°C) and set time to 10 minutes. Select Start/Stop to begin preheating.
3. Cut diagonal lines into the surface of the ham in one direction and then again in the opposite direction, creating 1-inch squares. Do not cut too deeply. Poke a clove in the center of each square. Run a long sword skewer through the center of the ham lengthwise to create a pilot hole. Run the rotisserie rod through the hole and secure with the forks. Balance as necessary.
4. Once preheated, place the ham in the preheated air fryer basket with a drip pan underneath. Cook for 35 to 40 minutes, basting with the glaze every 5 minutes during the last 20 minutes of cooking time.
5. Remove from the heat, carefully remove the rotisserie forks and slide the rod out, and then set the ham on a large cutting board. Tent the ham with aluminum foil and let the meat rest for 5 to 10 minutes. Plate the ham with the cloves in place, but remove them before carving.

Hawaiian Pineapple Rotisserie Butt Roast

Prep time: 15 minutes | Cook time: 3 to 4 hours | Serves 8 to 10

Sauce:
1 cup pineapple juice
1 cup packed brown sugar
3 tablespoons soy sauce

1 pork butt roast, 4 to 5 pounds (1.8 to 2.3 kg)
1½ teaspoons sea salt
1 teaspoon white pepper

1. To make the sauce: Combine the sauce ingredients in a saucepan over medium-high heat and simmer for 2 minutes, stirring often. Decrease the heat to medium-low and simmer for another 4 to 5 minutes. The sauce should be a little runnier than syrup. Remove from the heat and let cool for at least 30 minutes before using. Divide into two equal portions, one for the baste and one to serve alongside the roast.
2. Trim the fat cap on the roast to ½ inch (1.3 cm) thick. Score the fat lightly with a sharp knife in a diagonal pattern.
3. Combine the sea salt and white pepper and apply all over the pork. Let sit for 15 to 20 minutes at room temperature.
4. Select Rotisserie, Super Convection, set temperature to 350°F (177°C) and set time to 8 minutes. Select Start/Stop to begin preheating.
5. Run a long sword skewer to find the best path through the center of the roast lengthwise to create a pilot hole. Run the rotisserie rod through the hole and secure with the forks. Balance as necessary. If needed, run the rod through diagonally and secure tightly with the rotisserie forks.
6. Once preheated, place the roast in the preheated air fryer basket, set a drip pan underneath, and add 1 cup hot water to the pan. Cook the roast for 3 to 4 hours, or until it reaches 185°F (85°C) in the center. The roast will shrink during cooking, so adjust the forks when appropriate. During the last half of the cooking time, baste with half of the sauce.
7. Remove from the heat, carefully remove the rotisserie forks and slide the rod out, and then set the roast on a large cutting board. Tent the roast with aluminum foil and let the meat rest for 10 to 15 minutes. Slice and place on a platter. Rewarm the reserved sauce in the microwave for 30 seconds to 1 minute and drizzle over the sliced pork. Serve.

Herbed Rotisserie Lamb Rack

Prep time: minutes | Cook time: minutes | Serves 4 to 6

2 trimmed racks of lamb, 2 to 2½ pounds (907 g to 1.1 kg) each

Rub:
⅓ cup Dijon mustard
4 cloves garlic, minced
1 tablespoon chopped fresh oregano
2½ teaspoons kosher salt
2 teaspoons chopped fresh thyme
2 teaspoons olive oil
1 teaspoon freshly ground black pepper

1. Trim off the excess fat and any hanging pieces of meat from the lamb racks. Typically there is a large fat cap on the outside of the rack. Trim this down to no more than ¼ inch in thickness.
2. To make the rub: Combine the rub ingredients in a small bowl. Apply to both racks, and tent the racks with plastic wrap. Allow to sit at room temperature for 20 minutes.
3. Select Rotisserie, Super Convection, set temperature to 375ºF (191ºC) and set time to 10 minutes. Select Start/Stop to begin preheating.
4. Remove the plastic from the racks and place one rack on top of the other so the bone ends line up. Lace the bones together and, with kitchen twine, tie both racks tightly together in several locations through the bones. Run the rotisserie rod between the racks in a balanced position and secure tightly with the rotisserie forks. Wrap the bone ends in aluminum foil and secure with kitchen twine tied perpendicular to the bones. This will prevent the bone ends from burning.
5. Once preheated, place the lamb in the preheated air fryer basket and set a drip pan underneath. Cook until the center of each rack reaches 145ºF (63ºC). Measure the internal temperature in the center of the thickest part of the meat section, away from the bone and rotisserie rod. This should take about 1 hour.
6. Remove from the air fryer, carefully remove the rotisserie forks and slide the rod out, and then set the racks on a large cutting board. Tent the racks with foil and let the meat rest for 10 minutes. Cut away the twine, slice between each bone into individual chops, and serve.

Tangerine Rotisserie Chicken

Prep time: 15 minutes | Cook time: 1 to 1½ hours | Serves 4

Marinade:
½ cup freshly squeezed tangerine juice
¼ cup freshly squeezed lime juice
3 cloves garlic, minced
2 tablespoons olive oil
1½ tablespoons packed brown sugar
1½ tablespoons chopped fresh tarragon
1½ teaspoons salt
1 teaspoon grated fresh ginger
½ teaspoon white pepper

1 whole chicken, 3 to 3½ pounds (1.4 to 1.6 kg)

1. To make the marinade: Combine the marinade ingredients in a small bowl and set aside.
2. Pat the chicken dry inside and out with paper towels. Cut off any extra, straggling skin. Place the chicken in a large resealable plastic bag or nonreactive container. Add the marinade, making sure the bird is well coated. Seal the bag or cover the container and place in the refrigerator for 3 to 4 hours.
3. Select Rotisserie, Super Convection, of the air fryer oven, set temperature to 375ºF (191ºC) and set time to 10 minutes. Select Start/Stop to begin preheating.
4. Remove the chicken from the bag and pour the marinade into a saucepan. Bring to a quick boil over high heat, decrease the heat to medium, and simmer for 3 minutes. Remove from the heat and let cool.
5. Truss the chicken with kitchen twine, run the rotisserie rod through the cavity, and secure with the rotisserie forks.
6. Once preheated, place in the preheated air fryer basket, set a drip pan underneath, and pour 1 cup hot water into the pan. Cook for 1 to 1½ hours, or until the meat in the thighs and legs reaches 175ºF (80ºC). The breasts should be 165ºF (74ºC). Baste the chicken after the first 20 minutes of cooking time with the reserved marinade and stop basting about 10 minutes before the chicken is done.
7. Remove from the heat, carefully remove the rotisserie forks and slide the rod out, and then set the chicken on a large cutting board. Tent the chicken with aluminum foil and let it rest for 10 to 12 minutes before cutting off the twine and carving.

Whiskey-Basted Prime Rib Roast

Prep time: 10 minutes | Cook time: 2 hours | Serves 8 to 10

1 4-bone prime rib roast (8 to 10 pounds / 3.6 to 4.5 kg)

Rub:
¼ cup coarse salt
1 small shallot, finely chopped
2 cloves garlic, minced
2 tablespoons olive oil
1 tablespoon coarsely ground black pepper
Zest of 1 large lemon
1 teaspoon paprika
1 teaspoon sugar

Baste:
⅓ cup whiskey
¼ cup water
Juice of 1 lemon
⅛ teaspoon salt

1. Trim off any straggling pieces of meat or fat from the roast. If the fat cap is too thick, cut it down to between ¼ to ½ inch in thickness depending on how you like your prime rib.
2. Run a long sword skewer through the center of the roast lengthwise to create a pilot hole. Run the rotisserie spit through the hole and secure with the forks. Balance as necessary.
3. To make the rub: Combine the rub ingredients in a small bowl to form an even paste. Use additional olive oil if necessary to get it to a thick but workable consistency. Apply evenly to the roast, focusing on the outer shell of the roast.
4. To make the baste: Combine the baste ingredients in a small bowl and set aside for 15 to 30 minutes to come to room temperature.
5. Select Roast, set temperature to 400°F (205°C), Rotate, and set time to 2 hours. Select Start to begin preheating.
6. Once preheated, place the prepared roast with rotisserie spit into the oven. Set a drip tray underneath, and add 1 to 2 cups hot water to the tray. If you intend to make a gravy from the drippings, monitor the drip tray to make sure it does not run dry. Add extra water if needed.
7. During the last hour of cooking time, begin basting. Apply the baste gently so as not to wash away the seasonings on the outside of the roast. Do this 6 to 8 times, until the roast is well coated with the baste. Roast until it is near the desired doneness: 125°F (52°C) for rare, 135°F (57°C) for medium rare, 145°F (63°C) for medium, 155°F (68°C) for medium well, or 165°F (74°C) for well done. The roast will shrink during cooking, so adjust the forks when appropriate.
8. When cooking is complete, remove the roast using the rotisserie lift. Carefully remove the rotisserie forks and slide the spit out, and then set the roast on a large cutting board. Tent the roast with aluminum foil and let the meat rest for 15 to 20 minutes. Cut away the bones first by passing a knife against the bones and cutting through (save the bones for later). Cut the meat into thin slices.

Paprika Pulled Pork Butt

Prep time: 10 minutes | Cook time: 6 hours | Serves 10

1 pork butt, 5 to 6 pounds (2.3 to 2.7 kg)

Rub:
2 tablespoons paprika
2 tablespoons packed brown sugar
1 tablespoon kosher salt
1 tablespoon mild chili powder
1 teaspoon freshly ground black pepper
1 teaspoon celery salt
½ teaspoon cayenne
½ teaspoon garlic powder

1. Run a long sword skewer through the center of the roast lengthwise to create a pilot hole. Run the rotisserie spit through the hole and secure with the forks. Balance as necessary.
2. To make the rub: Combine the rub ingredients in a small bowl and apply evenly all over the roast. Let sit at room temperature for 15 minutes. By this time the air fryer oven should be ready.
3. Select Roast, set temperature to 350°F (180°C), Rotate, and set time to 6 hours. Select Start to begin preheating.
4. Once preheated, place the prepared roast with rotisserie spit into the oven. Set a drip tray underneath. Roast until the internal temperature reaches 185°F (85°C). The roast will shrink during cooking, so adjust the forks when appropriate.
5. When cooking is complete, remove the roast using the rotisserie lift. Carefully remove the rotisserie forks and slide the spit out, and then set the pork on a large cutting board. Tent the roast with aluminum foil and let the meat rest for 20 minutes. Remove the foil and let stand for an additional 10 minutes.
6. Using two forks, check to see how easily the meat shreds. Some parts will do this more easily than others. Be sure to use heat-resistant gloves to break the roast apart. Begin shredding each large chunk one at a time. Add pieces to a large bowl and either add the barbecue sauce directly to the shredded meat or serve on the side. Keep the bowl covered as you're working on each section. This will help keep the meat warm. Serve by itself or with your favorite sides or in sandwiches.

Porchetta with Lemony Sage Rub

Prep time: 15 minutes | Cook time: 3½ hours | Serves 6

1 slab pork belly, skin on, 5 to 6 pounds (2.3 to 2.7 kg)
1 boneless pork loin roast, about 3 pounds (1.4 kg)
Rub:
2 tablespoons fennel seeds
1 tablespoon finely chopped fresh sage
Zest of 1 lemon
4 or 5 cloves garlic
2 teaspoons coarse salt
2 teaspoons freshly ground black pepper
1 teaspoon chopped fresh rosemary
1 teaspoon red pepper flakes
1½ teaspoons coarse salt
1 teaspoon freshly ground black pepper

1. Lay the pork belly, skin-side down, on a large cutting board. Place the pork loin on top and roll the pork belly together so that the ends meet. Trim any excess pork belly and loin so that it is a uniform cylinder. Do not tie yet.
2. To make the rub: Using a mortar and pestle or spice grinder, crush the fennel seeds to a medium grind. Combine with the remaining rub ingredients in a small bowl and apply all over the pork loin.
3. Roll the pork loin inside the pork belly and tie with kitchen twine every inch into a secure, round bundle. Season the outside of the pork belly with the coarse salt and pepper. Set onto a baking sheet and place in the refrigerator, uncovered, for 24 hours.
4. Run a long sword skewer through the center of the roast lengthwise to create a pilot hole. Run the rotisserie spit through the hole and secure with the forks. Balance as necessary.
5. Select Roast, set temperature to 400°F (205°C), Rotate, and set time to 3½ hours. Select Start to begin preheating.
6. Once preheated, place the prepared porchetta with rotisserie spit into the oven. Set a drip tray underneath. Watch for burning or excessive browning and adjust the heat as necessary. Once the porchetta has reached an internal temperature of 145°F (63°C), the roast is done. If the skin is not a deep brown and crispy in texture, increase the temperature to 450°F (235°C) and roast for an additional 10 minutes.
7. When cooking is complete, remove the porchetta using the rotisserie lift. Carefully remove the rotisserie forks and slide the spit out, and then set the meat on a large cutting board. Tent the roast with aluminum foil and let the meat rest for 15 minutes. Slice the meat ½ inch thick and serve.

Orange Honey Glazed Ham

Prep time: 10 minutes | Cook time: 45 minutes | Serves 12 to 14

1 ham, bone in and unsliced, 7 to 8 pounds (3.2 to 3.6 kg)
1 cup packed brown sugar
Glaze:
1½ cups orange juice
½ cup honey
2 tablespoons packed brown sugar
¼ teaspoon ground cinnamon
⅛ teaspoon ground nutmeg
⅛ teaspoon ground allspice
⅛ teaspoon ground cloves
⅛ teaspoon white pepper
2 tablespoons unsalted butter

1. To make the glaze: Combine the orange juice, honey, brown sugar, and spices in a saucepan and bring almost to a boil over medium-high heat. Decrease the heat to medium and simmer for 10 minutes, stirring often. The mixture should be a little runnier than real maple syrup. Remove from the heat and add the butter, stirring until melted. Let the mixture cool.
2. Run a long sword skewer through the center of the ham lengthwise to create a pilot hole. There is a bone in the middle of this ham, but generally it is just to one side. The skewer should easily go through, but feel for the bone before you start so you will know how to navigate around it. Run the rotisserie spit through the hole and secure with the forks. Balance the ham on the spit as well as possible.
3. Select Roast, set temperature to 375°F (190°C), Rotate, and set time to 45 minutes. Select Start to begin preheating.
4. Once preheated, place the prepared ham with rotisserie spit into the oven. Set a drip tray underneath. The ham should not take too long to heat up. Look for an internal temperature around 130°F (54°C). The surface should be hot.
5. Baste the ham with the glaze after 20 minutes on the air fryer oven. Repeat the process every 5 minutes and about 3 more times.
6. During the last 5 to 10 minutes of cooking time, the ham should be hot as well as sticky from the glaze. Increase the temperature to 400°F (205°C) and sprinkle the brown sugar evenly on the surface of the ham in small amounts until it is completely coated. Continue to cook until the sugar starts to bubble. Move quickly, as sugar tends to burn.
7. Once the sugar is bubbling rapidly, remove the ham using the rotisserie lift and place on a large cutting board. Remove the rotisserie forks and slide the spit out, loosely cover the ham with aluminum foil, and let it rest for 5 minutes. Carve into thin slices and serve warm.

Ham with Dijon Bourbon Baste

Prep time: 5 minutes | Cook time: 50 minutes | Serves 10 to 12

1 ham, unsliced, 5 to 6 pounds (2.3 to 2.7 kg)

Baste:
⅓ cup apple butter
¼ cup packed brown sugar
2 tablespoons bourbon
1½ teaspoons Dijon mustard
¼ teaspoon ground ginger
¼ teaspoon white pepper

1. Run a long sword skewer through the center of the ham lengthwise to create a pilot hole. Run the rotisserie spit through the hole and secure with the forks. Balance as necessary and secure tightly. Place the ham on the preheated air fryer oven and cook for 50 to 60 minutes. If there is room, set a drip tray underneath.
2. To make the baste: Combine all the baste ingredients in a small saucepan and simmer over medium heat for 2 minutes, stirring often. Remove from the heat and let sit for 5 to 10 minutes before using.
3. Select Roast, set temperature to 400°F (205°C), Rotate, and set time to 45 minutes. Select Start to begin preheating.
4. Once preheated, place the prepared ham with rotisserie spit into the oven. Set a drip tray underneath. During the last 20 minutes of the cooking time, begin basting the ham with the apple butter-bourbon mixture. Make at least 4 or 5 passes with the baste to coat evenly. Focus the coating on the outside of the ham and not on the cut side. The ham should not take too long to heat up. Look for an internal temperature around 130°F (54°C). The surface should be hot.
5. When cooking is complete, remove the ham using the rotisserie lift. Carefully remove the rotisserie forks and slide the spit out, and then set the ham on a large cutting board. Tent the ham with aluminum foil and let the meat rest for 10 minutes. Carve and serve immediately.

Spareribs with Paprika Rub

Prep time: 15 minutes | Cook time: 3½ hours | Serves 4 to 6

2 racks spareribs
Sauce:
1 tablespoon olive oil
2 cloves garlic, minced
1 cup ketchup
¾ cup water
⅓ cup packed brown sugar
1 tablespoon paprika
2 teaspoons mild chili powder
¼ teaspoon cayenne
Rub:
⅓ cup packed brown sugar
2 tablespoons paprika
2 teaspoons salt
2 teaspoons mild chili powder
1 teaspoon onion powder
½ teaspoon garlic powder
¼ teaspoon cayenne

1. To make the sauce: Heat the oil in a medium-size saucepan over medium heat and sauté the garlic for 15 seconds, until aromatic. Add the remaining sauce ingredients and simmer for 5 minutes, stirring often. Remove from the heat and let cool to room temperature before using.
2. To make the rub: Combine the rub ingredients in a small bowl and set aside.
3. Place the ribs on a cutting board and pat dry with paper towels. Cut away any excess fat from the ribs. Remove the membrane from the back of the ribs by using a blunt knife to work the membrane away from the bone in one corner. Grab hold of the membrane with a paper towel for a good grip and gently peel away. With a little practice, this becomes an easy process.
4. Lay the rib racks meat-side down. Apply a small portion of the rub, just enough to season, to the bone side of the racks. Lay one rack on top of the other, bone side to bone side, to form an even shape. Tie the two racks together with kitchen twine between every other bone. The ribs should be held tightly together. Run the rotisserie spit between the racks and secure with the forks. The fork tines should run through the meat as best as possible. The ribs will move a little as the rotisserie turns. They should not flop around, however. Secure to prevent this. Apply the remaining rub evenly over the outer surface of the ribs. A general rule with rubs is that what sticks is the amount needed.
5. Select Roast, set temperature to 375°F (190°C), Rotate, and set time to 3½ hours. Select Start to begin preheating.
6. Once preheated, place the prepared ribs with rotisserie spit into the oven. Set a drip tray underneath. Roast until the ribs reach an internal temperature of 185°F (85°C). Test the temperature in several locations. Baste the ribs several times with the sauce during the last hour of cooking to build up a sticky surface.
7. When cooking is complete, remove the ribs using the rotisserie lift. Carefully remove the rotisserie forks and slide the spit out, and then set the ribs on a large cutting board. Tent the ribs with aluminum foil and let the meat rest for 5 to 10 minutes. Cut away the twine and cut the racks into individual ribs. Serve.

Smoked Paprika Lamb Leg

Prep time: 10 minutes | Cook time: 1 hour 20 minutes | Serves 6 to 8

1 boneless leg of lamb (partial bone-in is fine), 4 to 5 pounds (1.8 to 2.3 kg)

Rub:
¼ cup packed brown sugar
1 tablespoon coarse salt
2 teaspoons smoked paprika
1½ to 2 teaspoons spicy chili powder or cayenne
2 teaspoons onion powder
1 teaspoon garlic powder
1 teaspoon freshly ground black pepper
½ teaspoon ground cloves
⅛ teaspoon ground cinnamon

1. Trim off the excess fat and any loose hanging pieces from the lamb. With kitchen twine, tie the roast into a uniform and solid roast. It will take four to five ties to hold it together properly. Run a long sword skewer through the center of the roast lengthwise to create a pilot hole. Run the rotisserie spit through the hole and secure with the forks. Balance as necessary.
2. To make the rub: Combine the rub ingredients in a small bowl and apply evenly to the lamb. Make sure you get as much of the rub on the meat as possible.
3. Select Roast, set temperature to 375°F (190°C), Rotate, and set time to 80 minutes. Select Start to begin preheating.
4. Once preheated, place the prepared lamb with rotisserie spit into the oven. Set a drip tray underneath. Roast until the lamb reaches an internal temperature of 140°F (60°C) for medium or 150°F (66°C) for medium well. The lamb will shrink during cooking, so adjust the forks when appropriate.
5. When cooking is complete, remove the lamb using the rotisserie lift. Carefully remove the rotisserie forks and slide the spit out, and then set the lamb on a large cutting board. Tent the roast with aluminum foil and let the meat rest for 10 to 12 minutes. Cut off the twine and carve. Serve.

BBQ Chicken with Mustard Rub

Prep time: 15 minutes | Cook time: 1 hour 10 minutes | Serves 4 to 6

1 whole chicken, 3 to 4 pounds (1.4 to 1.8 kg)
1 medium-size onion, peeled but whole (for cavity)

Barbecue Sauce:
¾ cup ketchup
⅔ cup cherry cola
¼ cup apple cider vinegar
2 tablespoons packed brown sugar
1 tablespoon molasses
¼ teaspoon salt
¼ teaspoon freshly ground black pepper

Rub:
2 teaspoons salt
2 teaspoons onion powder
1 teaspoon mustard powder
½ teaspoon freshly ground black pepper
½ teaspoon garlic powder

1. To make the barbecue sauce: Combine all the ingredients in a medium-size saucepan over medium heat and simmer for 5 to 6 minutes, until the mixture is smooth and well blended. Stir often and watch for burning. Remove from the heat and let the sauce cool at least 10 minutes before using.
2. To make the rub: Combine all the rub ingredients in a small bowl.
3. Pat the chicken dry inside and out with paper towels. Apply the rub all over the bird, under the breast skin, and inside the body cavity.
4. Truss the chicken with kitchen twine. Run the rotisserie spit through the onion and insert it into the chicken cavity. Use a paring knife to cut a pilot hole in the onion to make this easier. Continue to run the spit through the chicken and secure with the rotisserie forks.
5. Select Roast, set temperature to 400°F (205°C), Rotate, and set time to 70 minutes. Select Start to begin preheating.
6. Once preheated, place the prepared chicken with rotisserie spit into the oven. Set a drip tray underneath. Roast until the meat in the thighs and legs reaches 175°F (79°C). The breasts should be 165°F (74°C). Baste the chicken with the barbecue sauce during the last half of the cooking time. Do so every 7 to 10 minutes, until the bird is nearly done and well coated with the sauce.
7. When cooking is complete, remove the chicken using the rotisserie lift. Carefully remove the rotisserie forks and slide the spit out, and then set the chicken on a large cutting board. Tent the chicken with aluminum foil and let it rest for 10 to 15 minutes before cutting off the twine and carving.

Sirloin Roast with Porcini-Wine Baste

Prep time: 20 minutes | Cook time: 2 hours | Serves 8

1 top sirloin roast, 4 to 4½ pounds (1.8 to 2.0 kg)

Wet Rub:
½ cup dried porcini mushrooms
¼ cup olive oil
4 teaspoons salt
1 tablespoon chopped fresh thyme
2 cloves garlic, minced
1 teaspoon onion powder
1 teaspoon chili powder
1 teaspoon coarsely ground black pepper

Baste:
½ cup dried porcini mushrooms
1 or 2 cups boiling water
½ cup red wine (Cabernet Sauvignon recommended)
1 tablespoon wet rub mixture
1 teaspoon Worcestershire sauce

1. For the wet rub: Chop the mushrooms into small pieces. Place in a clean spice or coffee grinder and grind to a fine powder. Transfer to a bowl and add the remaining rub ingredients. Remove 1 tablespoon (6 g) of the mixture and set aside.
2. If the sirloin roast is loose or uneven, tie it with kitchen twine to hold it to a consistent and even shape. Run a long sword skewer through the center of the roast lengthwise to create a pilot hole. Run the rotisserie spit through the hole and secure with the forks. Balance as necessary. Apply the wet rub evenly to the meat.
3. Select Roast, set temperature to 400°F (205°C), Rotate, and set time to 2 hours. Select Start to begin preheating.
4. Once preheated, place the prepared roast with rotisserie spit into the oven. Set a drip tray underneath, and add 1 to 2 cups hot water to the tray. Roast until it reaches the desired doneness: 125°F (52°C) for rare, 135°F (57°C) for medium rare, 145°F (63°C) for medium, 155°F (68°C) for medium well, or 165°F (74°C) for well done. Adjust the forks when appropriate.
5. While the roast cooks, make the baste: Add the dried porcini mushrooms to 1 cup boiling water, or 2 cups boiling water if you would like to use the porcini broth for the gravy. Steep the mushrooms for 30 minutes, covered. Strain the broth and reserve the porcinis (for the gravy) and broth separately. Divide the broth into two equal portions, one for the baste and one for the gravy. Combine 1 cup broth with remaining baste ingredients. Let sit for 15 to 30 minutes to come to room temperature before using. Begin basting the roast during the last half of the cooking time and repeat every 10 to 12 minutes until the roast is ready.
6. When cooking is complete, remove the roast using the rotisserie lift. Carefully remove the rotisserie forks and slide the spit out. Tent the roast with aluminum foil and let the meat rest for 20 minutes. Cut into ¼-inch slices and serve.

Balsamic Chuck Roast

Prep time: 15 minutes | Cook time: 1 hour | Serves 8

1 chuck roast, 4 to 4½ pounds (1.8 to 2.0 kg)
1¼ teaspoons salt
½ teaspoon freshly ground black pepper

Marinade:
1 tablespoon olive oil
1 shallot, finely chopped
2 or 3 cloves garlic, minced
1½ cups tawny port
¼ cup beef broth
1½ tablespoons balsamic vinegar
1 teaspoon Worcestershire sauce
1 teaspoon chopped fresh thyme
¼ teaspoon salt
¼ teaspoon freshly ground black pepper

1. To make the marinade: Heat the olive oil in a saucepan over medium-low heat and cook the shallot for 3 minutes until translucent. Add the garlic and cook for 30 seconds. Increase the heat to medium-high and add the port. Stir thoroughly and cook for 1 minute. Add the remaining ingredients and simmer the sauce for 5 minutes, stirring occasionally. Remove from the heat and let cool for 10 to 15 minutes. Divide the mixture into two even portions, reserving one half for the baste and one for the marinade. Store in the refrigerator until ready to cook, then bring to room temperature before using.
2. Trim away excess fat from the outer edges of the chuck roast. Place the roast in a resealable plastic bag. Add half of the port mixture to the bag, making sure that all of the meat is well covered. Seal the bag and place in the refrigerator for 6 to 8 hours.
3. Remove the roast from the bag, discarding the marinade, and place on a large cutting board or platter. With kitchen twine, tie the roast into a round and uniform shape, pulling tightly. Start in the center and work toward the ends until it is tied into a solid round roast. This will take four or five ties. Run a long sword skewer through the center of the roast lengthwise to create a pilot hole. Run the rotisserie spit through the hole and secure with the forks. Balance as necessary. Season the roast with the salt and pepper.
4. Select Roast, set temperature to 400°F (205°C), Rotate, and set time to 1 hour. Select Start to begin preheating.
5. Once preheated, place the prepared roast with rotisserie spit into the oven. Set a drip tray underneath. Roast until it reaches the desired doneness: 125°F (52°C) for rare, 135°F (57°C) for medium rare, 145°F (63°C) for medium, 155°F (68°C) for medium well, or 165°F (74°C) for well done. Baste halfway through the cooking time, and repeat the process at least 3 times until the roast is done.
6. When cooking is complete, remove the roast using the rotisserie lift. Carefully remove the rotisserie forks and slide the spit out, and then set the roast on a large cutting board. Tent the roast with aluminum foil and let the meat rest for 15 to 20 minutes. Cut off the twine. Slice into ¼-inch slices and serve.

Chapter 12 Staples

Polenta with Butter

Prep time: 3 minutes | Cook time: 1 hour 5 minutes | Makes about 4 cups

1 cup grits or polenta (not instant or quick cook)

2 cups chicken or vegetable stock

2 cups milk

2 tablespoons unsalted butter, cut into 4 pieces

1 teaspoon kosher salt or ½ teaspoon fine salt

1. Add the grits to the baking pan. Stir in the stock, milk, butter, and salt.
2. Select Bake, Super Convection, set the temperature to 325°F (163°C), and set the time for 1 hour and 5 minutes. Select Start/Stop to begin preheating.
3. Once the unit has preheated, place the pan on the bake position.
4. After 15 minutes, remove the pan from the oven and stir the polenta. Return the pan to the oven and continue cooking.
5. After 30 minutes, remove the pan again and stir the polenta again. Return the pan to the oven and continue cooking for 15 to 20 minutes, or until the polenta is soft and creamy and the liquid is absorbed.
6. When done, remove the pan from the oven.
7. Serve immediately.

Enchilada Sauce

Prep time: 15 minutes | Cook time: 0 minutes | Makes 2 cups

3 large ancho chiles, stems and seeds removed, torn into pieces

1½ cups very hot water

2 garlic cloves, peeled and lightly smashed

2 tablespoons wine vinegar

1½ teaspoons sugar

½ teaspoon dried oregano

½ teaspoon ground cumin

2 teaspoons kosher salt or 1 teaspoon fine salt

1. Mix together the chile pieces and hot water in a bowl and let stand for 10 to 15 minutes.
2. Pour the chiles and water into a blender jar. Fold in the garlic, vinegar, sugar, oregano, cumin, and salt and blend until smooth.
3. Use immediately.

Spice Mix with Cumin

Prep time: 5 minutes | Cook time: 0 minutes | Makes about 1 tablespoon

1 teaspoon smoked paprika

1 teaspoon cumin

¼ teaspoon turmeric

¼ teaspoon kosher salt or ⅛ teaspoon fine salt

¼ teaspoon cinnamon

¼ teaspoon allspice

¼ teaspoon red pepper flakes

¼ teaspoon freshly ground black pepper

1. Stir together all the ingredients in a small bowl.
2. Use immediately or place in an airtight container in the pantry.

Baked Rice

Prep time: 3 minutes | Cook time: 35 minutes | Makes about 4 cups

1 cup long-grain white rice, rinsed
  and drained
1 tablespoon unsalted butter, melted,
  or 1 tablespoon extra-virgin olive
  oil
2 cups water
1 teaspoon kosher salt or ½
  teaspoon fine salt

1. Add the butter and rice to the baking pan and stir to coat. Pour in the water and sprinkle with the salt. Stir until the salt is dissolved.
2. Select Bake, Super Convection, set the temperature to 325ºF (163ºC), and set the time for 35 minutes. Select Start/Stop to begin preheating.
3. Once the unit has preheated, place the pan on the bake position.
4. After 20 minutes, remove the pan from the oven. Stir the rice. Transfer the pan back to the oven and continue cooking for 10 to 15 minutes, or until the rice is mostly cooked through and the water is absorbed.
5. When done, remove the pan from the oven and cover with aluminum foil. Let stand for 10 minutes. Using a fork, gently fluff the rice.
6. Serve immediately.

Roasted Mushrooms

Prep time: 8 minutes | Cook time: 30 minutes | Makes about 1 ½ cups

1 pound (454 g) button or cremini
  mushrooms, washed, stems
  trimmed, and cut into quarters or
  thick slices
¼ cup water
1 teaspoon kosher salt or ½
  teaspoon fine salt
3 tablespoons unsalted butter, cut
  into pieces, or extra-virgin olive
  oil

1. Place a large piece of aluminum foil on the sheet pan. Place the mushroom pieces in the middle of the foil. Spread them out into an even layer. Pour the water over them, season with the salt, and add the butter. Wrap the mushrooms in the foil.
2. Select Roast, Super Convection, set the temperature to 325ºF (163ºC), and set the time for 15 minutes. Select Start/Stop to begin preheating.
3. Once the unit has preheated, place the pan on the roast position.
4. After 15 minutes, remove the pan from the oven. Transfer the foil packet to a cutting board and carefully unwrap it. Pour the mushrooms and cooking liquid from the foil onto the sheet pan.
5. Select Roast, Super Convection, set the temperature to 350ºF (180ºC), and set the time for 15 minutes. Place the basket on the roast position. Select Start/Stop to begin.
6. After about 10 minutes, remove the pan from the oven and stir the mushrooms. Return the pan to the oven and continue cooking for anywhere from 5 to 15 more minutes, or until the liquid is mostly gone and the mushrooms start to brown.
7. Serve immediately.

Chile Seasoning

Prep time: 5 minutes | Cook time: 0 minutes | Makes about ¾ cups

3 tablespoons ancho chile powder
3 tablespoons paprika
2 tablespoons dried oregano
2 tablespoons freshly ground black
  pepper
2 teaspoons cayenne
2 teaspoons cumin
1 tablespoon granulated onion
1 tablespoon granulated garlic

1. Stir together all the ingredients in a small bowl.
2. Use immediately or place in an airtight container in the pantry.

Asian Dipping Sauce

Prep time: 15 minutes | Cook time: 0 minutes | Makes about 1 cup

¼ cup rice vinegar
¼ cup hoisin sauce
¼ cup low-sodium chicken or
    vegetable stock
3 tablespoons soy sauce
1 tablespoon minced or grated ginger
1 tablespoon minced or pressed garlic
1 teaspoon chili-garlic sauce or sriracha (or more to taste)

1. Stir together all the ingredients in a small bowl, or place in a jar with a tight-fitting lid and shake until well mixed.
2. Use immediately.

Simple Teriyaki Sauce

Prep time: 5 minutes | Cook time: 0 minutes | Makes ¾ cup

½ cup soy sauce
3 tablespoons honey
1 tablespoon rice wine or dry sherry
1 tablespoon rice vinegar
2 teaspoons minced fresh ginger
2 garlic cloves, smashed

1. Beat together all the ingredients in a small bowl.
2. Use immediately.

Appendix I: Measurement Conversion Chart

MEASUREMENT CONVERSION CHART

VOLUME EQUIVALENTS(DRY)

US STANDARD	METRIC (APPROXIMATE)
1/8 teaspoon	0.5 mL
1/4 teaspoon	1 mL
1/2 teaspoon	2 mL
3/4 teaspoon	4 mL
1 teaspoon	5 mL
1 tablespoon	15 mL
1/4 cup	59 mL
1/2 cup	118 mL
3/4 cup	177 mL
1 cup	235 mL
2 cups	475 mL
3 cups	700 mL
4 cups	1 L

VOLUME EQUIVALENTS(LIQUID)

US STANDARD	US STANDARD (OUNCES)	METRIC (APPROXIMATE)
2 tablespoons	1 fl.oz.	30 mL
1/4 cup	2 fl.oz.	60 mL
1/2 cup	4 fl.oz.	120 mL
1 cup	8 fl.oz.	240 mL
1 1/2 cup	12 fl.oz.	355 mL
2 cups or 1 pint	16 fl.oz.	475 mL
4 cups or 1 quart	32 fl.oz.	1 L
1 gallon	128 fl.oz.	4 L

TEMPERATURES EQUIVALENTS

FAHRENHEIT(F)	CELSIUS(C) (APPROXIMATE)
225 °F	107 °C
250 °F	120 °C
275 °F	135 °C
300 °F	150 °C
325 °F	160 °C
350 °F	180 °C
375 °F	190 °C
400 °F	205 °C
425 °F	220 °C
450 °F	235 °C
475 °F	245 °C
500 °F	260 °C

WEIGHT EQUIVALENTS

US STANDARD	METRIC (APPROXIMATE)
1 ounce	28 g
2 ounces	57 g
5 ounces	142 g
10 ounces	284 g
15 ounces	425 g
16 ounces (1 pound)	455 g
1.5 pounds	680 g
2 pounds	907 g

Appendix 2: Air Fryer Cooking Timetable

Air Fryer Cooking Chart

Beef

Item	Temp (°F)	Time (mins)	Item	Temp (°F)	Time (mins)
Beef Eye Round Roast (4 lbs.)	400 °F	45 to 55	Meatballs (1-inch)	370 °F	7
Burger Patty (4 oz.)	370 °F	16 to 20	Meatballs (3-inch)	380 °F	10
Filet Mignon (8 oz.)	400 °F	18	Ribeye, bone-in (1-inch, 8 oz)	400 °F	10 to 15
Flank Steak (1.5 lbs.)	400 °F	12	Sirloin steaks (1-inch, 12 oz)	400 °F	9 to 14
Flank Steak (2 lbs.)	400 °F	20 to 28			

Chicken

Item	Temp (°F)	Time (mins)	Item	Temp (°F)	Time (mins)
Breasts, bone in (1 ¼ lb.)	370 °F	25	Legs, bone-in (1 ¾ lb.)	380 °F	30
Breasts, boneless (4 oz)	380 °F	12	Thighs, boneless (1 ½ lb.)	380 °F	18 to 20
Drumsticks (2 ½ lb.)	370 °F	20	Wings (2 lb.)	400 °F	12
Game Hen (halved 2 lb.)	390 °F	20	Whole Chicken	360 °F	75
Thighs, bone-in (2 lb.)	380 °F	22	Tenders	360 °F	8 to 10

Pork & Lamb

Item	Temp (°F)	Time (mins)	Item	Temp (°F)	Time (mins)
Bacon (regular)	400 °F	5 to 7	Pork Tenderloin	370 °F	15
Bacon (thick cut)	400 °F	6 to 10	Sausages	380 °F	15
Pork Loin (2 lb.)	360 °F	55	Lamb Loin Chops (1-inch thick)	400 °F	8 to 12
Pork Chops, bone in (1 inch, 6.5 oz)	400 °F	12	Rack of Lamb (1.5 – 2 lb.)	380 °F	22

Fish & Seafood

Item	Temp (°F)	Time (mins)	Item	Temp (°F)	Time (mins)
Calamari (8 oz)	400 °F	4	Tuna Steak	400 °F	7 to 10
Fish Fillet (1-inch, 8 oz)	400 °F	10	Scallops	400 °F	5 to 7
Salmon, fillet (6 oz)	380 °F	12	Shrimp	400 °F	5
Swordfish steak	400 °F	10			

Air Fryer Cooking Chart

Vegetables					
INGREDIENT	AMOUNT	PREPARATION	OIL	TEMP	COOK TIME
Asparagus	2 bunches	Cut in half, trim stems	2 Tbsp	420°F	12-15 mins
Beets	1½ lbs	Peel, cut in ½-inch cubes	1Tbsp	390°F	28-30 mins
Bell peppers (for roasting)	4 peppers	Cut in quarters, remove seeds	1Tbsp	400°F	15-20 mins
Broccoli	1 large head	Cut in 1-2-inch florets	1Tbsp	400°F	15-20 mins
Brussels sprouts	1lb	Cut in half, remove stems	1Tbsp	425°F	15-20 mins
Carrots	1lb	Peel, cut in ¼-inch rounds	1 Tbsp	425°F	10-15 mins
Cauliflower	1 head	Cut in 1-2-inch florets	2 Tbsp	400°F	20-22 mins
Corn on the cob	7 ears	Whole ears, remove husks	1 Tbps	400°F	14-17 mins
Green beans	1 bag (12 oz)	Trim	1 Tbps	420°F	18-20 mins
Kale (for chips)	4 oz	Tear into pieces,remove stems	None	325°F	5-8 mins
Mushrooms	16 oz	Rinse, slice thinly	1 Tbps	390°F	25-30 mins
Potatoes, russet	1½ lbs	Cut in 1-inch wedges	1 Tbps	390°F	25-30 mins
Potatoes, russet	1lb	Hand-cut fries, soak 30 mins in cold water, then pat dry	½ -3 Tbps	400°F	25-28 mins
Potatoes, sweet	1lb	Hand-cut fries, soak 30 mins in cold water, then pat dry	1 Tbps	400°F	25-28 mins
Zucchini	1lb	Cut in eighths lengthwise, then cut in half	1 Tbps	400°F	15-20 mins

Appendix 2: Index

Made in the USA
Las Vegas, NV
22 November 2023